DATE DUE

GAYLORD			PRINTED IN U.S.A.

D1021916

CENSORED

"[*Censored*] should be affixed to the bulletin boards in every newsroom in America. And, perhaps read aloud to a few publishers and television executives."—Ralph Nader

"[*Censored*] offers devastating evidence of the dumbing-down of mainstream news in America....Required reading for broadcasters, journalists and well-informed citizens."—*Los Angeles Times*

"A distant early warning system for society's problems."
—*American Journalism Review*

"One of the most significant media research projects in the country."
—I.F. Stone

"A terrific resource, especially for its directory of alternative media and organizations....Recommended for media collections."—*Library Journal*

"Project Censored shines a spotlight on news that an informed public must have...a vital contribution to our democratic process."
—Rhoda H. Karpatkin, President, Consumer's Union

"Buy it, read it, act on it. Our future depends on the knowledge this collection of suppressed stories allows us."—*San Diego Review*

"This volume chronicles 25 news stories about events that could affect all of us, but which we most likely did not hear or read about in the popular news media."—*Bloomsbury Review*

"Censored serves as a reminder that there is certainly more to the news than is easily available or willingly disclosed. To those of us who work in the newsrooms, it's an inspiration, an indictment, and an admonition to look deeper, ask more questions, then search for the truth in the answers we get."—*Creative Loafings*

"This invaluable resource deserves to be more widely known."
—*Wilson Library Bulletin*

"Once again Project Censored has produced an invaluable guide to the sociopolitical landscape of the United States and the world.... A vital yearly addition to your library."—*Outposts*

CENSORED 1999

The News
That Didn't Make
the News —

The Year's Top 25 Censored Stories

PETER PHILLIPS & PROJECT CENSORED

INTRODUCTION BY GARY WEBB
CARTOONS BY TOM TOMORROW

SEVEN STORIES PRESS
New York / Toronto / London

Censored 1999: The News that Didn't Make the News—
The Year's Top 25 Censored Stories
ISSN 1074-5998

10 9 8 7 6 5 4 3 2 1

Seven Stories Press
140 Watts Street
New York, NY 10013

In U.K.:
Turnaround Publisher Services Ltd.
Unit 3, Olympia Trading Estate
Coburg Road, Wood Green
London N22 6TZ U.K.

In Canada:
Hushion House
36 Northline Road
Toronto, Ontario M4B 3E2
Canada

Designed by Cindy LaBreacht

Dedication

To my parents
DON AND JEAN PHILLIPS

lives joined from mountain cabins

lovingly shared

rope-tow skiing

summer trout

extended family

and

tomatoes

Table of Contents

Preface 11

Acknowledgments...15

Introduction by Gary Webb...27

CHAPTER 1 The Top 25 *Censored* News Stories of 1998............................31

1 Secret International Trade Agreement Undermines
  the Sovereignty of Nations 32

2 Chemical Corporations Profit Off Breast Cancer....................34

3 Monsanto's Genetically Modified Seeds Threaten
  World Production 37

4 Recycled Radioactive Metals May Be In Your Home 41

5 U.S. Weapons of Mass Destruction Linked to the Deaths
  of a Half-Million Children 43

6 U.S. Nuclear Program Subverts U.N.'s Comprehensive
  Test Ban Treaty 47

7 Gene Transfers Linked to Dangerous New Diseases 49

8 Catholic Hospital Mergers Threaten Reproductive Rights
  for Women..51

9 U.S. Tax Dollars Support Death Squads in Chiapas........................54

10 Environmental Student Activists Gunned Down on Chevron
   Oil Facility in Nigeria..56

11 Private Prison Expansion Becomes Big Business 58

12 Millions of Americans Received Contaminated Polio Vaccine Between 1955 and 1963 60

13 China Violates Human Rights in Tibet 63

14 Political Contributions Compromise American Judicial System 65

15 SWAT Teams Replace Civilian Police: Target Minority Communities 66

16 Mercenary Armies in Service to Global Corporations 69

17 U.S. Media Promotes Biased Coverage of Bosnia............................72

18 Manhattan Project Covered Up Effects of Fluoride Toxicity 74

19 Clinton Administration Lobbied for Retention of Toxic Chemicals in Children's Toys...77

20 Developers Build on Flood Plains at Taxpayers' Expense..............79

21 Global Oil Reserves Alarmingly Overestimated 81

22 Academia at Risk as Tenured Professors Vanish 83

23 Bureau of Land Management Charged with Human Rights Violations Against the Shoshone Nation 85

24 Coca-Cola Fails to Meet Recycling Pledge 87

25 ABC Broadcasts Slanted Report on Mumia Abu-Jamal 90

Project Censored Honorable Mentions for 1998....................................92

CHAPTER 2 *Censored* Déjà Vu: What Happened to Last Year's Most Censored Stories by Victoria Calkins, Corrie Robb, Craig Chapman, and Project Censored......................................99

CHAPTER 3 Building Media Democracy by Peter Phillips 129

CHAPTER 4 Missing News by Robert A. Hackett 137

CHAPTER 5 Voices of Censored Journalists...153

HOW FOX TV CENSORED THEIR OWN REPORTERS by Jane Akre and Steve Wilson 153

THE CENSORED SIDE OF THE CNN FIRINGS OVER TAILWIND by April Oliver...158

CHAPTER 6 Microradio Broadcasting...165

AGUASCALIENTES OF THE AIRWAVES by Greg Ruggiero 165

THE STRUGGLE FOR AMERICA'S AIRWAVES by Louis N. Hiken 182

CHAPTER 7 Voices of International Journalists and Scholars 189

ON THE FIFTIETH ANNIVERSARY OF THE UNIVERSAL
DECLARATION OF HUMAN RIGHTS by Ramsey Clark 189

THE TELLTALE SILENCE OF THE POST-OSLO
PALESTINIAN PRESS by Roni Ben Efrat 192

THE ATTEMPTED CHARACTER ASSASSINATION
OF ARISTIDE by Ben Dupuy 197

THE ROLE OF AMERICARES: A WOLF IN SHEEP'S CLOTHING
by Sara Flounders 207

CHAPTER 8 Fear in the News by David Altheide 215

APPENDIX A The Junk Food News Stories of 1998 227

APPENDIX B The Year's Most Under-reported Humanitarian Stories
by Doctors Without Borders/*Médecins Sans Frontières* 233

APPENDIX C Less Access to Less Information By and About the
U.S. Government by the American Library Association
(ALA), Washington Office 239

APPENDIX D Project Censored's Alternative Media/Activist
Resource Guide 271

NATIONAL ALTERNATIVE PUBLICATIONS 272

MEDIA ACTIVIST ORGANIZATIONS AND NEWS SERVICES 309

APPENDIX E Top 5 *Censored* Reprints 325

Index 389

About the Author 397

Project Censored Mission Statement 399

Postscript: How to Nominate a *Censored* Story 400

THIS MODERN WORLD by TOM TOMORROW

Panel 1: CONSERVATIVE MEDIA CRITICS SEEM TO VIEW MAINSTREAM JOURNALISM AS A SEETHING NEST OF *RADICALISM* AND *SUBVERSION*--

LATER, IN A SPECIAL "EYE ON AMERICA," WE'LL LOOK AT HOW CAPITALIST OPPRESSORS RUTHLESSLY EXPLOIT THE PROLETARIAT!

FIRST, PLEASE JOIN ME IN A ROUSING CHORUS OF "THE INTERNATIONALE"!

Panel 2: --A PLACE WHERE HARDCORE *LEFTISTS* HIDE BEHIND THE *PRETENSE* OF OBJECTIVITY-- WHILE SHAMELESSLY SLANTING THE NEWS TO SERVE THEIR OWN *NEFARIOUS AGENDA!*

YOU KNOW, BETTY, I DON'T THINK ANYTHING THESE KNUCKLEHEADED REPUBLICANS SAY IS EVEN WORTH *REPORTING!*

I QUITE AGREE! LET'S MOVE ON TO OUR GLORIOUS PRESIDENT'S LATEST BRILLIANT *POLICY PROPOSAL!*

ACTION McNEWS   ACTION McNEWS   ACTI McNE

Panel 3: RUPERT MURDOCH HAS RESPONDED BY BRINGING US THE *FOX NEWS CHANNEL*--RUN BY RUSH LIMBAUGH'S PAL *ROGER AILES* AND FEATURING CONSERVATIVES SUCH AS *BRIT HUME, MATT DRUDGE,* AND FREQUENT LIMBAUGH GUEST HOST *TONY SNOW,* FOX PROCLAIMS ITSELF TO BE THE FIRST TRULY *UNBIASED* NEWS CHANNEL...

WE REPORT-- YOU DECIDE!

OUR TOP STORY TONIGHT--ARE LIBERALS MORONS OR WHAT?

Panel 4: IN OTHER WORDS, *BLATANT* RIGHTWARD BIAS INTENDED TO COUNTER A *PERCEIVED* LEFTWARD BIAS IS BEING DEFINED AS A *LACK OF BIAS*...WHICH STRIKES *US* AS A BIT--WELL-- ORWELLIAN...

TONY SNOW SAYS THE MAINSTREAM MEDIA ARE *DOUBLEPLUS UNGOOD!*

AND IGNORANCE IS *STRENGTH,* EH BOB?

Preface

This is Project Censored's 23rd listing of the most important under-covered stories in the United States. *Censored 1999: The News that Didn't Make the News* is stronger and more extensive than ever before. Hundreds of authors, journalists, contributors, students, faculty, and community volunteers had a hand in this year's volume. The Project Censored network has now spread throughout the world. We receive daily tips and clippings on important under-covered news stories from our supporters worldwide. Over 200 alternative press organizations send us complementary copies of their publications for review, and alternative e-mail information services offer important news stories and updates. Our research capabilities expanded significantly last year as well, as the new Web-based full-text databases Nexis-Lexis, Dow Jones, and Proquest make it much easier to research news story coverage levels in mainstream media.

Our national media systems offer a cornucopia of channels and print. Yet this seemingly unlimited supply of news and entertainment provides little diversity or varied interpretation. The corporate media covered Bill Clinton's escapades in great detail and ignored hundreds of important news stories only available from alternative sources. The mainstream media's coverage of Bill Clinton's sex life is directly related to the increased significance of *Censored 1999*. What a list! From secret government-sponsored trade deals, terminator seeds, radioactive spoons, and death squads to militarized police, and government/media propaganda, this year's list is shocking. The 42 Sonoma State University students who worked on the 1998 stories are saying their lives will never be the same.

New to *Censored 1999* are "Voices of International Journalists and Scholars" (Chapter 7) and "Voices of Censored Journalists" (Chapter 5). Chapter 7 includes the words or writings of four journalists/scholars; former U.S. Attorney General Ramsey Clark, speaking on human rights; Roni Ben Efrat, editor of *Challenge* magazine in Jerusalem, writing on the Palestinian peace process; former Haitian ambassador Ben Dupuy, on the U.S. media's coverage of Jean-Bertrand Aristide; and Sara Flounders from the New York International Action Center, on CIA misinformation tactics on Iraq. Each gives us a distinctly informative new understanding of the mainstream media information process in the United States. What we know can hurt us or at least significantly misinform us.

Chapter 5 brings forth the voices of censored U.S. journalists. Each journalist has been fired in the recent past for producing news stories that offended the powerful. Steve Wilson and Jane Akre are involved in a legal and moral crusade to challenge their firings by Fox Television in Tampa for trying to tell the truth on the air about the dangers to our nations' milk supply. April Oliver and Jack Smith were terminated by CNN for producing a news story on the U.S. use of sarin gas in Laos during the Vietnam War. Their side of the story, and the assertion that the truth was retracted, reveals a corrupt media system too scared of profit reductions and the Pentagon to stand behind objective, substantiated news.

Bob Hackett from News Watch Canada (Formerly Project Censored Canada) tells us about the current media censorship in Canada (Chapter 4), and gives us a stronger sense of the nature and process of systemic-structural censorship.

Our original research (Chapter 8) this year comes from Arizona State University, where David Altheide and his students have been investigating the increased use of fear in the news. Mainstream media apparently believes that fear grips audiences and keeps them coming back for more. Included is a good discussion of how increased fear in the news may be transforming us into a frightened society.

Chapter 6 is about a new Free Speech Movement in the United States. Microradio stations are popping up faster than the Federal Communications Commission (FCC) can shut them down. Luke Hiken with the National Lawyers Guild is challenging the FCC in the courts on the First Amendment rights of microradio operators, while at the same time microradio activist Greg Ruggiero is advocating the establishment of hundreds of neighborhood radio stations. All it takes is a few hundred dollars of equipment and you can be on the air.

We spent six months updating and expanding the alternative press and media activist organizations resource guide. It is the most comprehensive up-to-date guide available. Please subscribe to a dozen alternative press publications, read them, and then share them with your lover, children, friends, and associates. Building a stronger alternative press system in the United States is our only protection against corporate-owned media and government spindoctors. Better yet, start your own alternative publication or microradio station in your home town. My chapter three, "Building Media Democracy," will get you headed in the right direction.

Peter Phillips
Director, Project Censored
Sonoma State University

Acknowledgments

BY PETER PHILLIPS

Sonoma State University in Rohnert Park, California, is the site for Project Censored. The Project is managed through the Department of Sociology in the School of Social Sciences. We are an applied sociological/media studies research project dedicated to freedom of information thoughout the United States.

Over 150 people were directly involved in the production of this year's *Censored 1999: The News that Didn't Make the News.* University and program staff, students, faculty and community evaluators, research interns, funders, and our distinguished national judges, all contributed time, energy, and money to make this year's book an important resource for the media and democracy movement in the United States.

I want to personally thank those close friends and intimates who have counseled and supported me through another year of Project Censored. The men in the Green Oaks breakfast group (Noel Byrne, Bob Butler, Rick Williams, and Bill Simon) are my weekly advisors and confidants who provide the ongoing personal support necessary for staying heart-centered in my work. A special thanks goes to my friends Tim Ogburn, Mary Lia, Doug Martin, Scott Suneson, Gail Johnson, and Stan Martin for their abilities to ask the hard, challenging questions only friends can ask. Thanks also to Carl Jensen, founder of Project Censored, and director for 20 years. His continued advice and support are very important to me and to our work.

A tremendous thanks needs to go to the people at Seven Stories Press, who, year after year, publish this book in record time. Specifically, this includes publisher Dan Simon, associate publisher Jon Gilbert, editors Paul

Abruzzo, Greg Ruggiero, Kera Bolonik, Michael Manekin, proofreader, indexer (and past editor) Mikola De Roo, and book designer Cindy LaBreacht. We really appreciate Elise Cannon and the great sales staff at Publishers Group West, who see to it every year that independent bookstores, chain stores, and wholesalers in the U.S. are aware of *Censored*. Thanks also to our international distributors Hushion House in Canada and Turnaround Publisher Services Ltd. in London.

Thanks also to the authors of the *Censored* stories for 1998, for without their often-unsupported efforts as investigative news reporters and writers, the stories presented in *Censored 1999* would not be possible.

We are especially grateful to Gary Webb for taking the time from his busy schedule to write the introduction to *Censored 1999*. Gary, more than most, understands the meaning of censorship in the American media and we are pleased that his work on the CIA-Crack-Contra connection is now being proven true through the CIA's own admission.

We have a long list of guest writers and presenters this year including: Ramsey Clark, Greg Ruggiero, Sara Flounders, Ben Dupuy, Roni Ben Efrat, Steve Wilson, Jane Akre, April Oliver, David Altheide, Luke Hiken, and Robert Hackett. Their continuing work for freedom of information in the world deserves acclamation and praise.

Once again, this year's book features the cartoons of Tom Tomorrow. "This Modern World" appears in over 90 newspapers across the country. We are extremely pleased to be able to use Tom Tomorrow's wit and humor throughout the book.

Our national judges, some of whom have been involved with the Project for 22 years, are among the most respected people in the country concerned with First Amendment freedoms and major social issues. We are honored to have them as the final voice in ranking the top 25 *Censored* Stories.

An important thanks goes to our major donors and funders, including: Anita Roddick and The Body Shop International, the Office of the President at Sonoma State University (SSU), the School of Social Sciences at Sonoma State University, Sonoma State University Associated Students, and the Sociology and Communication Studies Departments at SSU. The Playboy Foundation, and hundreds of people from throughout the United States, provide the financial support necessary for the continuing research activities of our students and faculty.

The Organization of News Ombudsmen deserves a thank you for their continuing assistance in identifying the most superfluous stories published in our Junk Food News chapter.

We are also indebted to the American Library Association Associate Director, Anne Heanue, for her assistance in coordinating the inclusion of the document "Less Access To Less Information By and About The U.S. Government" in Appendix C.

Thanks also to Anishinabe Native American activist Kathleen Kesterke for her participation in the Media in the Dark Ages conference in Athens, Greece and her continuing support for the Project.

This year we had 78 faculty/community evaluators assisting with our story assessment process. These expert volunteers read and rated the nominated stories for national importance, accuracy, and credibility. In November, they participated with the students in selecting the final top 25 stories for 1999.

Most of all we need to recognize the Sonoma State University students in the Media Censorship class, Sociology 435, who worked long hours in the library conducting coverage reports on over 160 under-published stories. Each has become an expert in library research and information retrieval. Student education is one of the most important aspects of the Project, and we could not do this work without their dedication and effort.

Many thanks to Trish Boreta who coordinated the work of over 30 student interns and is our major in-house editor, and manages the daily administrative tasks for the Project.

Scot Frazier served as our technical support this year, assisting with our World Wide Web site development and electronic outreach.

Community volunteer Cathleen Coleman wrote and researched the Junk Food News chapter. SSU graduate student Victoria Calkins edited and coordinated the development of the *Censored* Déjà Vu chapter.

Cartoonist and SSU student Jaime Crespo did the artwork for the cover of *Censored 1999*.

Lastly, I want to thank our readers, and supporters from all over the United States and the world. Hundreds of you nominated stories for consideration as the *Censored* news story of the year. Thank you very much!

PROJECT CENSORED STAFF AND STUDENT INTERNS 1998

Peter Phillips, Ph.D.	Director
Carl Jensen, Ph.D.	Director Emeritus and Project Advisor
Trish Boreta	Intern Coordinator
Kimberly Lyman	Fiscal Planning
Suzanne Z. Murphy, R.N.	Editor
Catherine Hickinbotham	Administrative Assistant

Yvette Tannenbaum	Administrative Assistant
Scot Frazier	Web Site Manager
Julieta Mancilla	Administrative Assistant
Mary Zimmerman	Administrative Assistant
Jaime Crespo	Artist

COMMUNITY VOLUNTEERS: Cathleen Coleman, Alix Jestrow, Rick Wallstrum, Mercedes Warren-Rivendell

WRITING AND EDITORIAL GROUP: Victoria Calkins, Craig Chapman, Corrie Robb, Chantille Hickman, Chuck Mosley, Suzanne Z. Murphy, RN, Amber Manfree, Cathleen Coleman

TEACHING ASSISTANTS: Deb Udall, Corey Hale

NEWS STORY MANAGEMENT: Katie Sims, Briana Pullen, Mercedes Warren-Rivendell, Molly Mosier, Mary Zimmerman, Chantille Hickman, Suzanne Z. Murphy, RN, Jaime Black

RADIO ANNOUNCERS: Linda McCabe, Carolyn Williams, Erich Schulte, Jonna Scherer, David Van Nuys

PUBLIC RELATIONS: Marci Pyle, Craig Chapman, Diane Blakney, Jonna Scherer, Erich Schulte, Carolyn Williams, Jenny Glennon

WEB SITE DEVELOPMENT: Scot Frazier, Michael Smith, Jeff Fillmore, Jay Barillaro

OFFICE SUPPORT/RESEARCH: Janice Garcia, Jenny Glennon, Briana Pullen, Pam Bigham, Ken Downing, Sam Rogers, Molly Mosier, Mary Zimmerman, Yvette Tannenbaum, Amber Manfree, Julieta Mancilla

1998 STUDENT RESEARCHERS IN MEDIA CENSORSHIP CLASS

Dan Bluthard	ITDS
Jason Bothwell	Sociology
Ryan Bruner	Undeclared
Craig Chapman	Sociology
Kelly Dahlstrom	Liberal Studies
Dayna DelSimone	Business Administration
Travis Duncan	Sociology
Scott Gross	Sociology
Jason Gunnarson	Sociology
Brooke Herron	Communication Studies

Yuki Ishizaki	Sociology
Richard Krigstein	Communication Studies
Tom Ladegaard	Philosophy
Amy Loucks	Communication Studies
Michael McMurtrey	Art
Jennifer Mintz	Communication Studies
Diana Nouveaux	Psychology
Aimee Polacci	Sociology
Corrie Robb	Biology
Patrick Ryan	Sociology
Jason Sanders	Sociology

PROJECT CENSORED 1998 NATIONAL JUDGES

DR. DONNA ALLEN, president of the Women's Institute for Freedom of the Press; founding editor of *Media Report to Women*; co-editor: *Women Transforming Communications: Global Perspectives* (1996)

BEN BAGDIKIAN,* professor emeritus and former dean, Graduate School of Journalism, University of California, Berkeley; former editor at the *Washington Post*; author of *Media Monopoly*, and five other books and numerous articles

RICHARD BARNET, author of 15 books, and numerous articles for *The New York Times Magazine*, *The Nation*, and *Progressive*

SUSAN FALUDI, Pulitzer Prize-winning journalist; author of *Backlash: The Undeclared War Against American Women*

DR. GEORGE GERBNER, dean emeritus, Annenberg School of Communications, University of Pennsylvania; founder of the Cultural Environment Movement; author of *Invisible Crises: What Conglomerate Media Control Means for America and the World*, and *Triumph and the Image: The Media's War in the Persian Gulf*

JUAN GONZALEZ, award-winning journalist and columnist for the New York *Daily News*

AILEEN C. HERNANDEZ, president of Urban Consulting in San Francisco; former commissioner on the U.S. Equal Employment Opportunity Commission

DR. CARL JENSEN, founder and former director of Project Censored; author, *Censored: The News that Didn't Make the News and Why, 1990 to 1996*, and *20 Years of Censored News* (1997)

SUT JHALLY, professor of communications, and executive director of The Media Education Foundation, University of Massachusetts

NICHOLAS JOHNSON,* professor, College of Law, University of Iowa; former FCC Commissioner (1966-1973); author of *How To Talk Back To Your Television Set*

RHODA H. KARPATKIN, president, Consumers Union, non-profit publisher of *Consumer Reports*

CHARLES L. KLOTZER, editor and publisher emeritus, *St. Louis Journalism Review*

NANCY KRANICH, associate dean of the New York University Libraries, and member of the board of directors of the American Library Association

JUDITH KRUG, director, Office for Intellectual Freedom, American Library Association; editor, *Newsletter on Intellectual Freedom; Freedom to Read Foundation News;* and the *Intellectual Freedom Action News*

FRANCES MOORE LAPPÉ, co-founder and co-director, Center for Living Democracy

WILLIAM LUTZ, professor of English, Rutgers University; former editor of *The Quarterly Review of Doublespeak;* author of *The New Doublespeak: Why No One Knows What Anyone's Saying Anymore* (1966)

JULIANNE MALVEAUX, PH.D., economist and columnist, King Features and Pacifica radio talk show host

JACK L. NELSON,* professor, Graduate School of Education, Rutgers University; author of 16 books and over 150 articles including *Critical Issues in Education* (1996)

MICHAEL PARENTI, political analyst, lecturer, and author of several books including: *Inventing Reality; The Politics of News Media; Make Believe Media; The Politics of Entertainment;* and numerous other works

HERBERT I. SCHILLER, professor emeritus of communication, University of California, San Diego; lecturer; author of several books including *Culture, Inc.* and *Information Inequality* (1996)

BARBARA SEAMAN, lecturer; author of *The Doctors' Case Against the Pill, Free and Female, Women and the Crisis in Sex Hormones,* and others; co-founder of the National Women's Health Network.

ERNA SMITH, chair of the journalism department at San Francisco State University, author of several studies on mainstream news coverage on people of color

SHEILA RABB WEIDENFELD,* president, D.C. Productions, Ltd.; former press secretary for Betty Ford

HOWARD ZINN, professor emeritus of political science at Boston University, author of *A People's History of the United States, You Can't be Neutral on a Moving Train: A Personal History of Our Times* and, most recently, *The Zinn Reader: Writings on Disobedience and Democracy.*

* Indicates having been a Project Censored Judge since its founding in 1976

IN MEMORIAM
Project Censored Evaluators:

PAUL V. BENKO
Biology
1929 to 1998
and
VANCE L. OSBURN
Forestry
1929 to 1998

PROJECT CENSORED 1998 FACULTY, STAFF, AND COMMUNITY EVALUATORS

Les Adler, Ph.D.	Provost, Hutchins School
	Sonoma State University (SSU) History
Julia Allen, Ph.D.	SSU English
Ruben Armiñana, Ph.D.	President, Sonoma State University
	SSU Political Science
Bryan Baker, Ph.D.	SSU Geography
Melinda Barnard, Ph.D.	SSU Communication Studies
Philip Beard, Ph.D.	SSU German Studies
Marty Bennett	Santa Rosa Community College
	History, Labor Studies
Elisabeth Burch, Ph.D.	SSU Communication Studies
Jim Burkland	Community Expert, Geology
Noel Byrne, Ph.D.	SSU Sociology

Barbara Butler, MLIS, MBA	SSU Library, Information Research
James Carr, Ph.D.	University of Nevada, Geology
Ray Castro, Ph.D.	SSU, Chicano and Latino Studies, Social Policy
T.K. Clarke, Ph.D.	SSU Business
Lynn Cominsky, Ph.D.	SSU Physics, Astronomy
Bill Crowley, Ph.D.	SSU Geography
Randy Dodgen, Ph.D.	SSU History, Asia
Fred Fletcher	Community Expert, Labor Unions, Peace and Justice
Dorothy (Dolly) Friedel, Ph.D.	SSU Geography
Richard Gale, Ph.D.	SSU Hutchins, Science & Technology
Susan Garfin, Ph.D.	SSU Sociology
Patricia Leigh Gibbs, Ph.D.	University of Hawaii, Sociology, Media Studies
Robert Girling, Ph.D.	SSU Business, Economics
Anne Goldman, Ph.D.	SSU English
Mary Gomes, Ph.D.	SSU Psychology
Myrna Goodman, Ph.D.	Candidate, SSU Sociology/ Gender Studies
Scott Gordon, Ph.D.	SSU Computer Science
Paula Hammett, MLIS	SSU Library, Information Resources in Social Sciences
Debra Hammond, Ph.D.	SSU Hutchins, History of Science
Dan Haytin, Ph.D.	SSU Sociology
Laurel Holmstrom, M.A.	SSU Sociology
Sally Hurtado, M.S.	SSU Education
Pat Jackson, Ph.D.	SSU Criminal Justice Administration
Thomas Jacobson, J.D.	SSU Environmental Studies and Planning
Mary King, M.D.	Community Volunteer
Kathleen Kesterke	Community Expert, Native American Studies
Jeanette Koshar, Ph.D.	SSU Nursing
John Kramer, Ph.D.	SSU Political Science
Virginia Lea, Ph.D.	SSU, Multicultural Education
Wingham Liddell, Ph.D.	SSU Business/Economics
Linda Lopez, Ph.D.	SSU Criminal Justice
Tom Lough, Ph.D.	SSU Sociology

John Lund	Community Expert, Politics, Stock Market
Rick Luttmann, Ph.D./CFP	SSU Economics
Kenneth Marcus, Ph.D.	SSU Criminal Justice
Perry Marker, Ph.D.	SSU Education
Dan Markwyn, Ph.D.	SSU History
Doug Martin, Ph.D.	SSU Chemistry
Elizabeth Coonrod Martinez, Ph.D.	SSU Foreign Languages
Eric McGuckin, Ph.D.	SSU Anthropology
Jeffrey McIllwain, Ph.D.	SSU Criminal Justice Administration
Robert McNamara, Ph.D.	SSU Political Science
Andy Merrifield, Ph.D.	SSU Public Administration
Catherine Nelson, Ph.D.	SSU Political Science
Robert Lee Nichols	Lt. General U.S. Army (Ret.) Community Expert, Military
Linda Novak, Ph.D.	SSU Business/Marketing
Tim Ogburn	Community Expert, Business and International Trade
Tom Ormond, Ph.D.	SSU Kinesiology
Jorge E. Porras, Ph.D.	SSU Spanish, Sociolinguistics
Arthur Ramirez, Ph.D.	SSU Chicano and Latino Studies
Rabbi Michael Robinson	Community Expert, Peace and Justice
R. Thomas Rosin, Ph.D.	SSU Anthropology
Richard Senghas, Ph.D.	SSU Anthropology/Linguistics
Cindy Stearns, Ph.D.	SSU Women's and Gender Studies
Elaine Sundberg, M.A.	SSU Academic Programs
Velma M.G. Taylor, Ph.D.	SSU Sociology/Women's and Gender Studies
Bob Tellander, M.A.	SSU Sociology
Laxmi G. Tewari, Ph.D.	SSU Music, Ethnomusicology
Suzanne Toczyski, Ph.D.	SSU Foreign Languages, French
Carol Tremmel	SSU Extended Education
David Van Nuys, Ph.D.	SSU Psychology
Francisco H. Vazquez, Ph.D.	SSU Hutchins, Cross-cultural Studies
Albert Wahrhaftig, Ph.D.	SSU Anthropology
Sandra Walton, MLIS	SSU Library, Archival Management
D. Anthony White, Ph.D.	SSU History
R. Richard Williams, J.D.	Community Expert, Legal Justice System

| Homero Yearwood, Ph.D. | SSU Criminal Justice |
| Richard Zimmer, Ph.D. | SSU Hutchins, History |

SONOMA STATE UNIVERSITY SUPPORTING STAFF AND OFFICES

Ruben Armiñana: President and Staff in the Office of the President
Bernie Goldstein: Vice President/Provost of Academic Affairs and Staff
Robert Karlsrud: Dean of School of Social Sciences and Staff
William Babula: Dean of School of Arts and Humanities
David Walls: Dean of Extended Education and Staff
Jim Myers: Vice President for Development and Staff
Larry Furukawa-Schlereth: Vice President Administration and Finance

THE PROJECT CENSORED CREW (SSU FACULTY, STUDENTS, AND PC STAFF), FALL 1997.

Susan Harris and the SSU Library Staff
Tony Apolloni and the staff at the California Institute on Human services
Carol Cinquini: Manager of School of Social Sciences
Paula Hammett: Social Sciences Library Resources
Steve Wilson and the Staff at the SSU Academic Foundation
Katie Pierce and Staff in Sponsored Programs
Alan Murray and Staff at SSU Bookstore
Jonah Raskin and Faculty in Communications Studies
Susan Kashack and Staff in SSU Public Relations Office
Laurel Holmstrom Sociology Department Secretary and Staff
Colleagues in the Sociology Department: Noel Byrne, Kathy Charmaz,
    Susan Garfin, Dan Haytin, and Robert Tellander

THIS MODERN WORLD

by TOM TOMORROW

Panel 1:

MORE JOURNALISTIC MEA CULPAS: THE RELEASE OF GARY WEBB'S NEW BOOK, *DARK ALLIANCE*, PROMPTS *THE NEW YORK TIMES* TO APOLOGIZE FOR ITS CLUMSY ATTEMPTS TO DISCREDIT HIS WORK ON THE CONNECTIONS BETWEEN THE CONTRAS, CRACK DEALERS, AND THE *CIA*...

WE IGNORED WEBB'S EXHAUSTIVE DOCUMENTATION--WHILE REPORTING THAT THE CIA HAD EXONERATED *ITSELF!*

IT'S A WONDER WE HAVE ANY CREDIBILITY LEFT AT ALL!

Panel 2:

THE *WASHINGTON POST* IS SIMILARLY MOVED TO APOLOGIZE FOR *ITS* ATTACK ON WEBB, WRITTEN BY A MAN NAMED WALTER PINCUS-- WHO, THE POST FAILED TO DISCLOSE, ACTUALLY *WORKED FOR THE CIA* AS A YOUNG MAN...

WE COMPLETELY VIOLATED THE TRUST OF OUR READERS -- AND MADE A *MOCKERY* OF JOURNALISTIC OBJECTIVITY!

OUR ENTIRE EDITORIAL STAFF HAS DECIDED TO RESIGN IN *SHAME!*

Panel 3:

MEANWHILE, THE *CINCINNATI ENQUIRER* APOLOGIZES PROFUSELY FOR RETRACTING THEIR ENTIRE SERIES OF ARTICLES ON *CHIQUITA'S* UNSAVORY BUSINESS PRACTICES, AFTER A REPORTER WAS FOUND TO HAVE ILLEGALLY ACCESSED CHIQUITA'S VOICEMAIL SYSTEM...

--EVEN THOUGH MANY OF THE ARTICLES WERE BASED ON FIRSTHAND REPORTING AND HAD *NOTHING TO DO WITH* THE VOICEMAIL MESSAGES!

LET'S FACE IT -- WE CAVED LIKE *MISERABLE, SPINELESS WORMS!*

Panel 4:

FINALLY, *CNN* AND *TIME* ISSUE A *JOINT APOLOGY*--FOR SERVING AS UNCRITICAL PENTAGON MOUTHPIECES DURING THE *GULF WAR*, THAT IS...

THEY TOLD US TO JUMP--AND WE ASKED HOW *HIGH!*

'LIBERAL MEDIA' MY *ASS!* ALL WE *DID* DURING THAT WAR WAS PARROT ADMINISTRATION PROPAGANDA!

WE ONLY HOPE YOU CAN FIND IT IN YOUR HEART TO *FORGIVE* US!

HEY, A FELLA CAN *DREAM*...

TOM TOMORROW © 8-12-98   tomorrow@well.com

Introduction

BY GARY WEBB

When the newspaper I worked for in Kentucky in the 1970s, *The Kentucky Post*, took the plunge and hiked its street price from 20 cents to a quarter, the executive editor, Vance Trimble, instructed our political cartoonist to design a series of full-page house ads justifying the price increase. One of those ads still hangs on my wall. It depicts an outraged tycoon, replete with vest and felt hat, brandishing a copy of our newspaper and shouting at a harried editor: "Kill that story, Mr. Editor...or else!"

Well worth a quarter, the ad argued, because we weren't some "soft, flabby, spineless" newspaper. We'd tell that fat cat to take a long walk off a short pier.

"Our readers would be shocked if any kind of threat swayed the editor," the ad declared. "If it happens, we print it. Kill a story? *Never!* There are no fetters on our reporters. Nor must they bow to sacred cows. On every story, the editor says: 'Get the facts. And let the fur fly!' Our reporters appreciate that. They are proud they can be square-shooters."

The newspaper for the most part held to that creed. When the executive editor was arrested for drunk driving, a photographer was dispatched to the city jail and the next day the paper carried a picture of our disheveled boss sitting forlornly in a holding cell. The newspaper had done the same thing to many other prominent citizens, he reminded the stunned staff after his release. Why should he be treated any differently?

How quaint that all sounds 20 years later. And how distant that post-Watergate era seems. Today, we see corporate news executives boasting not of the hardness of their asses, but of the value of their assets. We witness them groveling for public forgiveness because something their reporters wrote offended powerful interests, or raised uncomfortable questions about the past. Stories that meet every traditional standard of objective journalism are retracted or renounced, not because they are false—but because they are true.

The depth of this depravity (so far) was reached the day New York attorney Floyd Abrams decided CNN/Time Warner should retract its explosive report on a covert CIA operation known as Tailwind, which was alleged to have involved the use of nerve gas against American deserters in Southeast Asia in the 1970s. I saw Abrams on a talk show afterwards arguing that the ultimate truth of the Tailwind story was irrelevant to CNN's retraction of it.

"It doesn't necessarily mean that the story isn't true," Abrams insisted. "Who knows? Someday we might find other information. And, you know, maybe someday I'll be back here again, having done another report saying that, 'You know what? It was all true.'"

Stop and savor that for a moment. Let its logic worm its way through your brain, because it is the pure, unadulterated essence of what's wrong with corporate journalism today. Could anyone honestly have dreamed that one day a major news organization would retract and apologize for a story that even it acknowledges could well be true?

For that matter, who could have envisioned the day when a veteran investigative reporter would be convicted of a felony for printing the voice mail messages of executives of a corporation that was allegedly looting, pillaging, and bribing its way through Central America? Yet, like CNN producers April Oliver and Jack Smith, *Cincinnati Enquirer* reporter Mike Gallagher was fired, his work "renounced" as his editors ludicrously wrote in this front-page apology, and he has been uniformly reviled in the mass media as a fabricator for his devastating exposé of Chiquita Brands International. So far, however, no one has shown that his stories contain a single, solitary inaccuracy. Again, the truth seems irrelevant, a sideshow not worthy of serious discussion.

Astute readers may well wonder what the hell is going on, and the answer is this: the rules are being changed, and they are being changed in such a way as to ensure that our government and our major corporations won't be bothered by nettlesome investigative journalists in the next millennium.

When I started in the newspaper business the rules were simple: Get as close to the truth as you possibly can. There were no hard and fast requirements about levels of proof necessary to print a story—and there still aren't, contrary to all the current huffing and puffing about "journalistic standards" being abused. I worked as a reporter for nearly 20 years, wrote for dozens of different editors, and each had his or her own set of standards. Generally, if you diligently investigated the issue, used named sources, found supporting documentation, and you honestly believed it was true, you went with it. Period. That was the standard that gutsy editors used, at any rate. Some—like Ben Bradlee during Watergate, for example—occasionally went with less because instinct and common sense told them the story was right even if everything wasn't completely nailed down.

Nervous editors, on the other hand, used different standards. "Raising the bar" was the usual trick they used to avoid printing troublesome news. The squeamish demanded an admission of wrongdoing (preferably written) or an official government report confirming up the story's charge. What that meant, of course, was that stories about serious, unacknowledged abuses never got printed and eventually the reporters learned that it was useless to turn rocks over on their own if no one would officially confirm that something hideous had slithered out. And at that point they ceased being journalists and became like ancient scribes, doing little more than faithfully reproducing the pharaohs' words in clay.

It is this latter standard that was championed by Abrams in the Tailwind case and to some extent by *San Jose Mercury News* editor Jerry Ceppos in the case of my "Dark Alliance" series in 1996. Under these new rules, it isn't enough anymore for a reporter to have on-the-record sources and supporting documentation. Now they must have something called "proof." Investigative stories must be "proven" in order to reach the public; having "insufficient evidence" is now cause for retraction and dismissal.

"Having read all your stuff, as much as I can about this...I can't see where you prove it," CNN commentator Bill Press whined to former CNN producer April Oliver. "None of your sources add up to that."

"What is the standard of proof in a black operation where everyone's supposed to deny, or information is tightly compartmentalized?" Oliver demanded.

Her question, which cuts to the heart of the debate, went unanswered. But judging from Abrams' report, "proof" apparently is a statement no one disagrees with, or something that can be demonstrated, as Ted Turner phrased it, "beyond a reasonable doubt"—the courtroom standard of proof.

Some, including Turner, say this is good for journalism, that it will keep unsubstantiated stories out of public circulation, and there's no doubt about that. But it will also have the same muffling effect on a lot of important stories that happen to be true. Such a standard would have kept Watergate out of the papers. Love Canal, the CIA's mining of Nicaragua's harbors, the El

Mozote massacre in El Salvador—all would have been suppressed. Don't believe it? Consider the Iran-Contra scandal. It was only after Ronald Reagan and Edwin Meese held their famous press conference and confessed that something funny had been going on in the White House basement that the Washington press corps felt emboldened enough to start covering the scandal seriously. Until then, the idea of a secret parallel government had been sneeringly dismissed as some left-wing conspiracy theory.

What is devious about these standards of proof is that they sound so eminently responsible. They are doubly handy because they can be applied *after* publication, when the heat comes down. Then, as CNN/Time Warner did, lawyers and former government operatives can be called in to produce palliative reports bemoaning the lack of "proof" and the bothersome story can interred without further adieu. (Few will question the validity of these reports because, after all, they come straight from the top.)

But somewhere along the way it's been forgotten that journalism was never meant to be held to courtroom standards of proof. As investigative reporter Pete Brewton once put it: "I'm not in the proof business. I'm in the information business." Unlike police and prosecutors, reporters don't have the power to subpoena records or wiretap phone conversations. We can't conduct 24-hour surveillances, or pay informants for information. We write what we can find on the public record (which becomes less public all the time). Or at least we used to.

Fortunately, as the book you are holding proves, there are still some reporters and editors out there who consider an official denial to be a starting point, rather than the end, of a promising story. It is these men and women who are the true journalists, the ones who will carry on where the giants of yesterday—George Seldes, I.F. Stone, and the late Jonathan Kwitny—left off. Though many of them toil in relative obscurity, for little money and even less appreciation, their work contributes more to our lives than the million-dollar celebrity correspondents that we see on the nightly news.

Back in 1938, as fascism was sweeping across Europe, George Seldes presciently observed: "It *is* possible to fool all the people all the time—when government and press cooperate."

Today, such mass deception is possible on a scale that Seldes never could have imagined. That is why it is more important than ever to support the journalists represented between these covers. If these few bits of illumination flares should ever sputter and disappear, out of neglect or frustration or censorship, we will be enveloped by a darkness the likes of which we've never seen.

CHAPTER 1

The Top 25 Censored Stories of 1998

BY PETER PHILLIPS & PROJECT CENSORED

Selection of the "most censored" stories of the year is a complex task involving hundreds of people nationwide. This year thousands of news stories were screened by Sonoma State University (SSU) student reading teams. Seven hundred of these stories were selected for a detailed review by our 78 evaluators from every academic department at SSU and community experts from the surrounding area, including doctors, lawyers, a retired military general, a stockbroker, and a rabbi. These expert evaluators, using a standardized grading sheet, rate the stories for importance and credibility. The highest rated stories are researched during the fall semester by SSU students for their levels of coverage in the national media. The top 60 stories with the highest rating and the lowest levels of coverage are then reviewed by all the evaluators and students and voted on in November. The 25 stories with the highest votes are then forwarded to our national judges for final ranking.

While this process is evaluative and subjective it reflects the judgments of over 150 people who have studied each story and shared their collective opinions. We are proud of this 1998 most censored story list and are sure you will find them both shocking and informative.

We specifically want to thank and honor the authors and publishers for their brave work in keeping freedom of the press alive in the United States. We have asked the authors, in their update sections, to address how readers can find out more, or become involved in specific issues brought to light by each story. We think you will find their comments instructive and action oriented.

1 CENSORED

Secret International Trade Agreement Undermines the Sovereignty of Nations

Sources:
IN THESE TIMES
Title: "Building the Global Economy"
Date: January 11, 1998
Author: Joel Bleifuss

DEMOCRATIC LEFT
Title: "MAI Ties"
Date: Spring 1998
Author: Bill Dixon

TRIBUNE DES DROITS HUMAINS
Title: "Human Rights or Corporate Rights?"
Date: April 1998, Vol., Nos. 1-2
Authors: Miloon Kothari and Tara Krause

SSU Censored Researcher:
Corrie Robb
SSU Faculty Evaluators:
Tony White and Richard Gale

Mainstream media coverage:
Denver Post, August 2, 1998, page A33;
Charleston Gazette, September 7, 1998,
page A5; *San Francisco Chronicle*,
April 10, 1998, page A22; *Washington
Times*, March 21, 1998, page A1

The apparent goal of the latest international trade negotiations is to safeguard multinational corporate investments by eliminating democratic regulatory control by nation-states and local governments. The Multilateral Agreement on Investment (MAI) plans to set in place a vast series of protections for foreign investment. It would threaten national sovereignty by giving corporations nearly equal rights to those of nations. MAI delegates from 29 of the world's richest nations have been meeting secretly in France since 1995. A draft of their work was leaked in January of 1997. More wide-reaching and one-sided than NAFTA or GATT, MAI would thrust the world economy much closer to a transnational *laissez-faire* system where international corporate capital would hold free reign over the democratic wishes and socioeconomic needs of people.

Pushed by the International Chamber of Commerce and U.S. Council on International Business, the major goal of the MAI is to safeguard direct foreign investment, defined broadly as encompassing any assets—factories, products, services, currency, stocks, etc.—which may be located in one country, but owned by a company, corporation, or individual in another country. U.S. direct foreign investment alone has more than doubled in the last ten years.

Traditionally, foreign investment has involved enormous risk, most notably in developing nations where the social, political, and economic climate is not always as conducive to foreign investment as corporations would like. Governments have commonly also put into place tariffs and subsidies favoring their home economies. These provisions shrink foreign profit margins and reduce the dollar amount multinational corporations can take out of a host country.

The new and controversial MAI agreement requires "national treatment" for all foreign investors. Governments will no longer be able to treat domestic firms more favorably than foreign firms. It will be illegal to implement restrictions on what foreign firms can own. Subsidy programs focused on assisting and developing domestic industries will be eliminated. Host nations will also be liable and can be sued by corporations for lost competitiveness and profits. There are no provisions for localized citizen and community legal recourse.

The MAI will also have devastating effects on a nation's legal, environmental, and cultural sovereignty. It will force countries to relax or nullify human, environmental, and labor protection in order to attract investment and trade. Necessary measures such as food subsidies, control of land speculation, agrarian reform, and the implementation of health and environmental standards can be challenged as "illegal" under the MAI. This same illegality is extended to community control of forests, local bans on use of pesticides and hormone-induced foods, clean air standards, limits on mineral, gas and oil extraction, and bans on toxic dumping.

A telling example involves the U.S.-based Ethyl Corporation's suit against the Canadian government. A Canadian law bans the use of MMT, a gasoline additive and known toxin which Ethyl produces. Under the NAFTA protocols which serve as a "model for the MAI," Ethyl is suing Canada for $251 million, arguing that the regulation is unnecessary and violates their rights as a firm under NAFTA. While still pending, the case is an excellent example, and will test what corporations can claim as their rights under transnational policies like NAFTA and GATT. MAI would go a step further and allow corporations to directly sue any level of government—state, municipal, or federal—for what they perceive as losses based on legislative action, strikes, or boycotts.

Most at risk are developing nations and the natural resource and common property resource base. MAI would seriously exacerbate the pressure on undeveloped nations to deplete their own agricultural, mining, fishing, and forestry assets. The conditions of the agreement would undermine the capacity of local communities and municipalities to govern sustainably and democratically.

First proposed by the World Trade Organization just after the passage of GATT in 1995, MAI negotiations continue among the member countries of the Organization of Economic Cooperation and Development (OECD). The 29-member OECD, an association composed of 29 of the world's richest countries, originated in the aftermath of World War II to administer U.S. aid to Europe.

UPDATE BY AUTHOR JOEL BLEIFUSS: "The Multilateral Agreement on Investment

(MAI) has been described by Renato Ruggerio, the director general of the World Trade Organization as 'the constitution for a new global economy.' Yet this is a constitution that has been written outside of the public gaze by anonymous trade bureaucrats. And while there has been almost no citizen participation in the process, the United States Council for International Business, representing 600 corporations as the U.S. affiliate of the International Chamber of Commerce, has been integrally involved in the MAI negotiations. In fact the group has reported, that it has 'helped shape the U.S. negotiating positions by providing business views and technical advice on specific policy issues at regular meetings with U.S. negotiators immediately before and after each MAI negotiating session.'

"By late 1998, the negotiations at the Organization for Economic Cooperation and Development (OECD) had reached an impasse. Some countries thought that the World Trade Organization should oversee implementation of the agreement, while others, principally the United States, wanted MAI kept within the confines of the much more exclusive OECD.

"The mainstream press has almost completely ignored the MAI negotiations. MAI will likely only become a 'story' when the negotiations are finalized and the treaty is submitted to the Senate for ratification. And at that point there will be no room for public or legislative discussion over what such a treaty should entail. Public Citizen's Global Trade Watch [Tel: (202)546-4996; http://

www.citizen.org] and the Preamble Center [Tel: (202) 265-3263; http:// www.preamble.org] are the two organizations doing the most to monitor the MAI negotiations and to raise public awareness of how the treaty will affect the U.S. and world economics."

2 CENSORED

Chemical Corporations Profit Off Breast Cancer

Sources:
RACHEL'S ENVIRONMENT AND HEALTH WEEKLY
Title: "The Truth About Breast Cancer"
Date: December 4, 1997
Author: Peter Montague

THE GREEN GUIDE
Title: "Profiting Off Breast Cancer"
Date: October 1998
Authors: Allison Sloan and Tracy Baxter

SSU Censored Researchers:
Dan Bluthardt and Patrick Ryan
SSU Faculty Evaluator: Mary Gomes

Leaders in cancer treatment and information are the same chemical companies that also produce carcinogenic products.

Breast Cancer Awareness Month, initiated in 1985 by the chemical conglomerate Imperial Chemical Industries, currently called Zeneca Pharmaceuticals, reveals an uncomfortably close connection between the chemical industry and the cancer research establishment. As the controlling sponsor of Breast Cancer Awareness Month (BCAM), Zeneca is able to approve—or veto—any promotional or informational materials, posters, advertisements, etc. that BCAM uses. The focus is strictly limited to information regarding early detection and treatment, avoiding the topic of prevention. Critics have begun to question why.

With revenues of $14 billion, Zeneca is among the world's largest manufacturers of pesticides, plastics, and pharmaceuticals. Forty-nine percent of Zeneca's 1997 profits came from pesticides and other industrial chemicals, another 49 percent came from pharmaceutical sales, and the remaining 2 percent came from health care services including 11 cancer treatment centers. Zeneca's herbicide acetochlor, considered a probable carcinogen by the EPA, accounted for around $300 million in sales in 1997. Their product tamoxifen citrate (Nolvadex) is the most commonly prescribed breast cancer treatment drug on the market, and accounted for $500 million in 1997 sales. Cancer prevention would clearly conflict with Zeneca's business plan.

In response to criticism that BCAM is not promoting the prevention of breast cancer, Zeneca was instrumental in convincing the FDA to approve tamoxifen as a "prevention" measure to reduce the incidence of breast cancer in healthy women at risk. However, the World Health Organization's International Agency for Research on Cancer considers tamoxifen itself a "probable human carcinogen." While tamoxifen reduces the incidence of breast cancer in healthy women at risk, it doubles the incidence of uterine cancer as well as posing other significant, and often fatal, health risks, including embolisms and deep vein thrombosis.

Other large corporations have a vested interest in breast cancer as well. General Electric sells upwards of $100 million annually in mammography machines; Du Pont supplies much of the film used in those machines. These companies aggressively promote mammography screening of women in their 40s, despite the risk of its contributing to breast cancer in that age group. And while biotech giant Monsanto sponsors Breast Cancer Awareness Month's high profile event, the Race for the Cure, it continues to profit from the production of many known carcinogens.

The incidence of breast cancer has been increasing about 1 percent a year since 1940. In the past 20 years, more American women have died from breast cancer than all Americans killed in World Wars I and II, the Korean War, and Vietnam. Breast cancer has both lifestyle and environmental causes, but research into the environmental links has received little funding or attention by corporate and governmental entities.

Hormones have been at the center of breast cancer research for the past two decades. Five years ago, however, researchers began to consider the possibility that chlorinated chemicals might contribute to the rising occurrences of breast cancer. Researchers Devra Lee Davis and Leon Bradlow hypothesized that environmental and pharmaceutical estrogens are likely culprits. "The research world began to buzz with interesting new work," quotes *Rachel's Environment & Health Weekly*, "asking whether chemicals that mimic or block estrogen might contribute to breast cancer." Seen as a threat by chemical interests, the Chemical Manufacturers Association and the Chlorine Chemistry Council banded together to develop a strategy to discount Davis and Bradlow's hypothesis, including hiring a public relations firm to discredit Davis personally.

Although early detection does save some lives, 7 of 11 recent studies found elevated organochlorine levels in breast cancer victims. As Tracy Baxter says, "Let's face it: We're no dummies, and it's time to expose companies that, by producing environmental poisons and providing breast cancer services, get us coming and going."

UPDATE BY AUTHOR PETER MONTAGUE: "In the year since we published our series on breast cancer, evidence has continued to accumulate showing that a significant portion of breast cancer is preventable because it is caused by exposure to carcinogens. This is still not a message that the 'cancer establishment' wants to embrace because it means that the modern chemical industry is dangerous to women's health. The chemical industry introduces between 1,000 and 2,000 new chemicals into use each year, almost none of them tested for their effects on human health.

"The federal government is feeling great pressure to adopt a 'preventive' approach to breast cancer. Accordingly, the National Cancer Institute announced in April 1998 that breast cancer could be 'prevented' by treating women continuously with a powerful drug called tamoxifen. *The New York Times* editorialized on April 8th that treating women with tamoxifen is a 'breast cancer breakthrough.' However, *The Times* acknowledged that treating 1,000 women with tamoxifen for five years would prevent 17 breast cancers but would cause an additional 12 cases of endometrial cancer and 20 cases of serious blood clots in the same 1,000 women. Blood clots can cause strokes and heart attacks. This is hardly an unalloyed success story and certainly not a 'breast cancer breakthrough.' Indeed, treating women with a potent drug to counter the effects of lifelong exposure to industrial carcinogens hardly seems like a success at all. To me, it seems more like an admission of defeat in the battle to control murderous discharges from the chemical industry."

UPDATE BY AUTHORS ALLISON SLOAN AND TRACY BAXTER: "In spite of its dangerous side effects, tamoxifen (Nolvadex) was approved by the FDA on October 29, 1998 for use in reducing the risk of breast cancer in healthy women at high risk of the disease. Using the FDA's criteria, this includes virtually all females possessing breasts. Women considered at risk are those who are over 50 years old, have direct-line relatives with breast cancer, have had atypical breast biopsies, bore their first child after age 30, or began menstruating before age 12. Disturbing, however, is the fact that only 30 percent of women with breast cancer match any of these risk factors other than age. Nevertheless, a Zeneca spokeswoman claimed in *The New York Times* that 29 million women are at increased risk for breast cancer. If only 10 percent of them took tamoxifen sales would amount to $14.5 billion! Zeneca announced that they would immediately begin promoting tamoxifen to doctors and women—a sure sign they've done their math.

"The pharmaceutical industry spent $74.4 million on lobbying efforts in the U.S. in 1997—more than any other lobby group. At the same time, a growing number of pharmaceutical companies are doubling as pesticide manufactures. Zeneca, however, has the distinction of spending millions to convince women, through its sponsorship of Breast Cancer Awareness Month, that toxic treatment and mammography are our *only* weapons in fighting this scourge.

"Monte Paulsen first revealed the BCAM-Zeneca sponsorship link in a May 1993 article in the *Detroit Metro Times*. We are not aware whether it was reported in the mainstream media, but women's health activist organizations pounced on the story, and some stage their own 'Cancer Industry Awareness Month' each October to expose the deceptive nature of the Zeneca-sponsored event. For more information, contact Breast Cancer Action, Tel: (877) 2STOPBC; the Toxic Links Coalition (at Communities for a Better Environment), Tel: (415) 243-8373, ext. 305; or the Women's Community Cancer Project, Tel: (617) 354-9888.

3 CENSORED

Monsanto's Genetically Modified Seeds Threaten World Production

Sources:
MOJO WIRE
Title: "A Seedy Business"
http://www.motherjones.com/news_wire/broydo.html
http://www.motherjones.com/news_wire/usda-inc.html
Date: April 27, 1998
Author: Leora Broydo

THIRD WORLD RESURGENCE #92
Title: "New Patent Aims to Prevent Farmers From Saving Seed"
Author: Chakravarthi Raghavan

GLOBAL PESTICIDE CAMPAIGNER and EARTH ISLAND JOURNAL
Title: "Terminator Seeds Threaten an End to Farming"
Date: June 1998, Fall 1998
Authors: Hope Shand and Pat Mooney

THE ECOLOGIST
Title: "Monsanto: A Checkered
History" and "Revolving Doors:
Monsanto and the Regulators"
Date: September/October 1998,
Vol. 28, No. 5
Author: Brian Tokar

SSU Censored Researchers:
Tom Ladegaard, Amber Manfree,
and Amy Loucks
SSU Faculty Evaluators:
Paul Benko and Tom Lough

Over the 12,000 years that humans have been farming, a rich tradition of seed saving has developed. Men and women choose seeds from the plants that are best adapted to their own locale and trade them within the community, enhancing crop diversity and success rates. All this may change in the next four to five years. Monsanto Corporation has been working to consolidate the world seed market and is now poised to introduce new genetically engineered seeds that will produce only infertile seeds at the end of the farming cycle. Farmers will no longer be able to save seeds from year to year and will be forced to purchase new seeds from Monsanto each year.

On March 3, 1998, Delta Land and Pine Company, a large American cotton seed company, and the U.S. Department of Agriculture (USDA) announced that they had been awarded a patent on a technique that genetically disables a seed's ability to germinate when planted a second season. This patent covers not only the cotton and tobacco varieties, but, potentially, all cultivated crops. Scarcely two months after the patent was awarded, Monsanto, the world's third largest seed corporation and second largest agrochemical corporation, began the process of acquiring Delta Land and Pine and with it the rights to this new technology.

It is noteworthy that the USDA stands to earn 5 percent royalties of net sales if this technology is commercialized. Historically the USDA has received government money for research aimed at benefiting farmers, but recently the USDA has been turning more and more often to private companies for funding. As a result, for the first time in history, research is being done for the benefit of corporations, sometimes in direct opposition to farmers' interests.

In an interview with Leora Broydo, Melvin Oliver, USDA researcher on the patent-producing technique, stated that the research is a way to put "billions of dollars spent on research back into the system." When Broydo called back to ask exactly whose billions would be recouped by USDA's patent, Oliver said he had been instructed not to speak to the press any further.

Dubbed "Terminator technology" by Hope Shand of the Rural Advancement Foundation International (RAFI), Monsanto's new seeds have diverse implications, including the disruption of traditional farming practices around the world, the altering of the earth's biodiversity, and possible impacts on human health.

Monsanto has euphemistically called the process by which seeds are disabled the "technology protection system." A primary objective of Terminator technology is to grant and protect corporate rights to charge fees for patents on products that are genetically modified. Terminator technology offers no advantage by itself, but when coupled with the production of the strongest, highest yielding seeds, farmers may be compelled to buy single-season plants. Due to the nature of modern farming, many farmers will have little choice. Up to this point the boldest attempt at policing crops has been made by Monsanto, who hires Pinkerton agents to ferret out wayward American farmers who save patented soybean seeds for reuse or trade. However, this method is minimally effective in foreign markets.

Genetic engineering is still in its early stages and the effects of flooding the environment with extensive transgenic monocrops are unpredictable. Traits from genetically engineered plants can sometimes be passed on to wild relatives in the area, causing genetic pollution, which has the potential to alter ecosystems in unknown ways for an indefinite period of time.

Terminator plants, if introduced on a wide scale, will effectively constrict worldwide crop diversity by preventing farmers from engaging in the seed selection and cross breeding that has, for thousands of years, given them the ability to adapt crops to local conditions. Crop uniformity increases vulnerability to pests and disease and heightens the potential for mass famine.

UPDATE BY AUTHORS HOPE SHAND AND PAT MOONEY: "RAFI's story on Terminator seed technology alerted the world to a dangerous new genetic technology that threatens to eliminate the right of farmers to save seeds from their harvest. This technology offers no agronomic benefit to farmers—it is designed simply to increase seed industry profits by forcing farmers to return to the commercial seed market every year.

"Terminator technology is a threat to global food security because it is aimed for use in Africa, Asia, and Latin America, where over 1.4 billion people—primarily poor farmers—depend on farm-saved seed.

"There is an avalanche of public opposition to this technology. When we learned that Monsanto had entered into negotiations with the USDA to obtain an exclusive license on the Terminator patent, we launched an international e-mail protest campaign on our Web site. In recent months over 3,500 people have written to U.S. Secretary of Agriculture Dan Glickman from 60 countries, urging him to cease negotiations with Monsanto, abandon research on Terminator, and withdraw patent claims that are pending in over 87 countries.

"The specter of genetic seed sterilization is so serious that the world's largest network of agricultural researchers adopted a policy in October 1998 prohibiting the use of the technology in its Third World plant-breeding programs. India's agriculture minister says he will ban the import of Terminator seeds because of the potential harm to Indian agriculture. Terminator technology is on the 1999 agenda of two United Nations agencies. Civil society organizations and national governments aim to reject the Terminator patent on the basis of public morality."

For more information: http://www.rafi.org.

UPDATE BY AUTHOR BRIAN TOKAR: "*The Ecologist* magazine's special issue on Monsanto has helped crystallize a growing, worldwide opposition to the company's aggressive promotion of its genetically engineered crop varieties. When *The Ecologist*'s printer of 26 years refused to release the magazine and discarded 14,000 copies, citing fears of a libel suit, the ensuing controversy helped contribute to Monsanto's rapidly deteriorating image all across Europe and worldwide. Public controversies over genetically engineered foods have escalated throughout Europe, as well as in Latin America, East Asia, and elsewhere. A farmers' movement in southern India burned test plots of Monsanto's pesticide-secreting cotton in November of 1998, calling for a worldwide campaign to 'Cremate Monsanto.'

"*The Ecologist* story has received little play in the United States, outside of alternative outlets such as *Z Magazine*, the *Multinational Monitor*, and various electronic mailing lists for opponents of biotechnology. Still, opposition is growing here as well, and Monsanto has faced declining stock values and the collapse of its planned merger with the pharmaceutical giant American Home Products.

Farmers report persistent problems with Monsanto's genetically engineered corn and cotton varieties, and there is growing evidence that biotech crops contaminate neighboring fields with their pollen. A new coalition of biotech opponents and environmental activists in the Northeast has called for a nationwide campaign against the sale of genetically engineered seeds."

CONTACTS:

New England Resistance Against
Genetic Engineering
c/o Institute for Social Ecology
P.O. Box 89, Plainfield, VT 05667
(802) 454-8493
briant@earth.goddard.edu

Biodevastation Network
c/o Edmonds Institute
20319-92nd Avenue West
Edmonds, WA 98020
(425) 775-5383
beb@igc.org

Gateway Green Alliance
P.O. Box 8094
St. Louis, MO 63156
(314) 727-8554
fitzdon@aol.com

London-based genetics e-mail list:
genetics@gn.apc.org
http://www.dmac.co.uk/gen/genup.html

Campaign for Food Safety
http://www.purefood.org

Rural Advancement
Foundation International
http://www.rafi.ca

4 CENSORED

Recycled Radioactive Metals May Be in Your Home

Source:
THE PROGRESSIVE
Title: "Nuclear Spoons"
Date: October 1998
Author: Anne-Marie Cusac

SSU Censored Researchers:
Jennie Glennon, Dayna Del Simone,
and Jason Sanders
SSU Faculty Evaluator: Peter Phillips

Under special government permits, "decontaminated" radioactive metal is being sold to manufacture everything from knives, forks, and belt buckles to zippers, eyeglasses, dental fillings, and IUDs. The Department of Energy (DOE), the Nuclear Regulatory Commission (NRC); and the radioactive metal processing industry are pushing for new regulations that would relax current standards and dispense with the need for special radioactive recycling licensing. By one estimate, the DOE disposed of 7,500 tons of these troublesome metals in 1996 alone. The new standard being sought would allow companies to recycle *millions* of tons of low-level radioactive metal a year while raising the acceptable levels of millirems (mrems), a unit of measure that estimates the damage radiation does to human tissue. By the NRC's own estimate, the proposed standards could cause 100,000 cancer fatalities in the United States alone.

Metal companies want to raise the standard from an almost unmeasurable amount to something more in the vicinity of 10 mrems per year. The NRC studied the health effects of that exact standard back in 1990 and found that this dosage would lead to about 92,755 additional cancer deaths in the United States alone. According to *Progressive* reporter Cusac, some scientists argue that exposure to continual low-dose radiation is potentially more dangerous than a one-time, high-level dose. She cites Steve Wing, epidemiologist at the University of North Carolina, Chapel Hill: "The cancer curve rises more steeply at low doses than high doses." Richard Clapp, associate professor in the department of environmental health at the Boston University School of Public Health, says that the greatest threat comes from those household products with which you have the most contact, where "you're sitting on it or if it's part of your desk, or in the frame of your bed—where you have constant exposure and for several hours."

While the DOE waits for new standards to be released, says Cusac, "hot metal" is being marketed to other countries. Three major U.S. oil companies—Texaco, Mobil, and Phillips—shipped 5.5 million pounds of radioactive scrap metal to China in 1993. In June 1996, Chinese officials stopped a U.S. shipment of 78 tons of radioactive scrap metal that exceeded China's safety limit, some of it by 30-fold. As of January 1998, 178 buildings in Taiwan, containing 1,573 residential apartments, had been identified as radioactive.

Radioactive recycled metal has shown up in domestic markets as well. When a Buffalo, New York television station offered to survey suspect gold jewelry in the 1980s, it turned up three radioactive pieces in the first two days, which prompted the New York State Health Department to begin a comprehensive campaign to find radioactive, contaminated jewelry. According to the journal *Health Physics* in 1986, out of more than 160,000 pieces surveyed, 170 pieces were radioactive. News accounts reported that at least 14 people had developed finger cancer and several more had fingers and even parts of their hands amputated because of "hot" jewelry.

"This is not a glamorous industry," says Tom Gilman, government accounts manager for U.S. Ecology, which buys, cleans, and resells low-level radioactive scrap metal. Most of it comes from commercial sites, but some comes from DOE. U.S. Ecology "scrubs" and sells it as clean scrap. From there, the metal travels to a steel mill and enters the general consumer market. Gilman claims that U.S. Ecology is "turning waste into assets." He is careful to add, however, that the metal his company is recycling into the metal stream isn't completely clean. "'Acceptable' levels is the word to use," he explains, "There's always going to be some level of radioactivity."

UPDATE BY AUTHOR ANNE-MARIE CUSAC: "The recycling of radioactive metal into household products could pose a serious public-health threat in the coming century. The radioactive metal recycled from decommissioned nuclear reactors in the United States alone could number in the millions of tons. But by the NRC's own estimate, even an exposure standard of 10 millirems a year (the standard favored by the radioactive metal industry) would lead to 92,755 cancer deaths in the United States alone.

"Since my story was published, the commerce in hot metals has been proceeding briskly. In mid-September, *Nuclear Waste News* reported: 'Western authorities are growing increasingly concerned about illegal trafficking in radioactive scrap metal from Russia and other former Communist states.' According to the article, the contaminated metal, 'most of which comes from decommissioned nuclear power stations, radiation monitoring equipment, and waste containers, is finding its way into metal products, including household items in Europe.' The International Atomic Energy Agency says that the problem is growing, partly as a result of the recent fall in the value of the ruble, and that some of the metal is 'going even further afield.'

"One new development suggests that radioactive metal recyclers in the United States are looking toward hot metal imports as a big moneymaker. In September, the Nuclear Regulatory Commission issued a license to Allied Technology Group of Richland, Washington. The license gives that company permission to import approximately 1.5 million pounds of 'radioactive scrap tubing and tube plate' from the Taiwan Power Company's Chinshan Nuclear Power Station for the purposes of 'decontamination and recovery of the metal for recycling,' says James Kennedy, senior project manager in the Division of Waste Management at the NRC. Shipments should begin in February 1998.

"Meanwhile, the NRC is working on the development of a new standard that could allow for a huge increase in the amount of radioactive metal allowed into consumer goods. The Commission plans to solicit public comment on the issue beginning next August.

"But the public has little idea that radioactive metal could be turning up in frying pans and belt buckles. The mainstream media has not covered this issue. Such a lapse of this important health issue effectively blocks public monitoring of the Nuclear Regulatory Commission."

5 CENSORED

U. S. Weapons of Mass Destruction Linked to the Deaths of a Half-Million Children

Sources:
SAN FRANCISCO BAY GUARDIAN
Title: "Made in America"
Date: February 25, 1998
Author: Dennis Bernstein

I.F. MAGAZINE
Title: "Punishing Saddam or the Iraqis"
Date: March/April 1998
Author: Bill Blum

SPACE AND SECURITY NEWS
Title: "Our Continuing War Against Iraq"
Date: May 1998
Author: Most Rev. Dr. Robert M. Bowman, Lt. Col., USAF (Ret.)

SSU Censored Researcher:
Diana Nouveaux
SSU Faculty Evaluator: John Steiner

For the past seven years, the United States has supported sanctions against Iraq that have taken the lives of more Iraqi citizens than did the war itself. The Iraqi people are being punished for their leader's reticence to comply fully with U.S.-supported U.N. demands "to search every structure in Iraq for weapons of mass destruction." Ironically, 1994 U.S. Senate findings uncovered evidence that U.S. firms supplied at least some of the very biological material that the U.N. inspection teams are now seeking. Although the United States defames the Iraqi government for damaging the environment and ignoring U.N. Security Council resolutions, it has itself engaged in covert wars in defiance of the World Court, and left behind a swath of ecological disasters in its continuing geopolitical crusade. Blum considers the U.S. demands both excessive and hypocritical.

A 1994 U.S. Senate panel report indicated that between 1985 and 1989, U.S. firms supplied microorganisms needed for the production of Iraq's chemical and biological warfare. The Senate panel wrote: "It was later learned that these microorganisms exported by the United States were identical to those the United Nations inspectors found and removed from the Iraqi biological warfare program." Blum writes that shipments included biological agents for anthrax, botulism, and e-coli. The shipments were cleared even though it was known

at the time that Iraq had already been using chemical and possibly biological warfare since the early 1980s. The Simon Wiesenthal Center in Los Angeles reported in 1990 that more than 207 companies from 21 western countries, including at least 18 from the United States, were contributing to the buildup of Saddam Hussein's arsenal.

In one stunning incident in September 1989, according to Bernstein, U.S. military officials invited several Iraqi technicians, along with some 400 other participants from 20 countries, to attend a crash course on how to detonate a nuclear weapon. The course was held at the Red Lion Inn in Portland, Oregon. Sponsors included several military agencies, Lawrence Livermore Laboratory, Honeywell, Hewlett-Packard, and Sperry/Unisys, among others.

The sanctions imposed on Iraq are causing shortages of food, medical supplies, and medicines. Since the war ended, more than half a million children under the age of five have died. UNICEF reports that 150 children are dying every day. Moreover, countless Iraqi deaths

have been caused by exposure to depleted uranium (DU) weapons left behind at the end of Desert Storm. According to *Space and Security News*, DU can be linked to birth defects known to be caused by radiation exposure. In the last seven years the rate of cancer among Iraqi children has increased dramatically. DU has a half-life of millions of years. Attempts at cleanup will be largely futile and are a low priority for a people faced with finding the basic necessities of food and medicine. Iraqi children wade daily through this poisoned "playground."

The United States holds the position that sanctions against Iraq must continue until it can be proven that the country is unable to build biological and chemical weapons. Noam Chomsky observed in a 1990 PBS appearance that, since the 1940s, U.S. foreign policy has been one of maintaining control over the abundant energy resources in the Gulf region. Blum contends that the true purpose of the sanctions is to ultimately oust Hussein from power and lessen any threat to U.S. control of the region's oil resources.

UPDATE BY AUTHOR DENNIS BERNSTEIN:
"As of this writing, the United States and Great Britain have just concluded Operation Desert Fox, a massive four-day bombing of Iraq, unleashing more explosives on the country in 96 hours than during the entirety of the 1991 Gulf War. The timing of the high-tech missile attack was curious, to say the least. It began the day before impeachment hearings were due to commence in Washington, DC and ended on Ramadan, the Muslim high holy day.

"U.S. officials denied the assault was timed to distract attention from Clinton's impending impeachment or to push the process into a new congress with a slimmer republican majority. Instead, they claimed the bombings were a result of a brand-new UNSCOM report compiled by chief inspector Richard Butler, which stated that Iraq failed to fully cooperate with U.N. inspectors. But the bottom line of the Butler Report was that the overwhelming majority of inspections were going forward with Iraqi cooperation and that officials of the International Atomic Energy Agency received 'sufficient

cooperation to carry out all the inspections they want.'

"So then, beyond the obvious impeachment distractions and the long-standing U.S. policy of dominating and controlling Middle Eastern oil resources, why the desperate need to bomb now? Critics and supporters of the bombing seem to agree that it was an attempt to destabilize Iraq, so America's former good friend and ally, Saddam Hussein, could be overthrown by CIA-supported opposition forces. Defense Secretary William Cohen denied that was the U.S. objective, but stated it would certainly be a welcome outcome. The real significance of 'Made in America' is not only that the U.S. and its allies played a significant role in arming Iraq with weapons of mass destruction, but that those companies and politicians that were responsible for this lucrative but deadly policy were never held accountable. And there has been no attempt to take them to task.

"'We know that, throughout the 1970s and 1980s, companies in the U.S., France, Germany, Russia, Britain, and elsewhere were providing technology and advice to the Iraqis,' said Middle East expert, Phyliss Bennis. 'We don't know if that's still going on. We don't know the sources because UNSCOM has been forbidden from making that public. That has to change. If they were serious about disarmament, rather than serious about providing justifications for bombing, they would take up the disarmament issue in a regional context and go after the suppliers,' said Dennis."

UPDATE BY AUTHOR MOST REV. DR. ROBERT M. BOWMAN, LT. COL., USAF, RET.: "Few Americans are aware of the enormous human toll of our continuing war against Iraq. Five months after the publication of our article, the mainstream press reported Iraq's 'claims' of dying children and soaring cancer rates. But one TV 'expert' after another denied that depleted uranium could have caused these effects. One said, 'After all, it's just what the name says—depleted.' Another described it as just 'the scrap metal left when you take out radioactive uranium.'

"The truth is, depleted uranium is just as radioactive as 'natural' uranium. All that's gone is the U-235 isotope which gives off excess neutrons required for a fission chain reaction. The U-238 left gives off alpha particles, creating Thorium-234. This, in turn, gives off beta and gamma radiation, creating Protactinium. The chain continues through a dozen radioactive isotopes, finally producing the stable element lead. Every hunk of depleted uranium contains all these other radiation by-products, with half-lives ranging from a few millionths of a second to a quarter of a million years. The stuff gives off every type of natural radiation, both the beta and gamma rays—which attack the body from without, even through clothing—and the alpha, which is deadly if ingested and becomes trapped inside the body. What's more, it's water-soluble and (unlike the plutonium in RTGs) capable of getting into the food chain. And *this* Chernobyl was no accident!"

To learn more, see http://www.ramausa.org.ccnr.org, or http://www.rmbowman.com.

6 CENSORED

U.S. Nuclear Program Subverts U.N.'s Comprehensive Test Ban Treaty

Source:
THE NATION
Title: "Virtual Nukes—When is a Test Not a Test?"
Date: June 15, 1998
Author: Bill Mesler

SSU Censored Researchers: Kelly Dahlstrom and Tom Ladegaard
SSU Faculty Evaluator: Sue Garfin

When scientists in India conducted a deep underground test on May 11, it was seen as a violation of the United Nation's Comprehensive Test Ban Treaty (CTBT). However, two months before, the United States carried out a test that went largely unnoticed by the American media. Code-named "Stagecoach," the U.S. experiment called for the detonation of a 227-pound nuclear bomb at the Department of Energy's (DOE) Nevada Test Site, which is co-managed by Bechtel Corporation, Lockheed Martin, and Johnson Controls. While perceived as a hostile act by many nations of the world, government officials claim that since it was a "subcritical" test, meaning no nuclear chain reaction was maintained, it was "fully consistent with the spirit and letter of the CTBT." Furthermore they claim it was necessary to ensure the "safety and reliability" of America's aging nuclear arsenal.

Disputing this "safety and reliability" claim, foreign leaders believe that "Stagecoach" was in fact designed to test the effectiveness of America's weapons if, and when, they are ever used again. Though India refused to sign the Treaty because it wasn't comprehensive enough, the countries that did felt the CTBT would halt new weapons development and promote the move toward disarmament. The European Parliament issued an official warning to the United States declaring that further experiments might open the door for other nations to progress to full-scale testing. Leaders from China and Japan also harshly criticized the United States, calling for America to stop "skirting its responsibility for arms reduction."

Underground experiments aren't the U.S. government's only method of subverting the treaty, says *The Nation*. In July 1993, Clinton introduced the Stockpile Stewardship Program (SSP) which allots $45 billion over the next 10 years to finance new research facilities. Even when adjusted for inflation, this amount is larger than the per-year budget during the Cold War when much of the cost went to actually producing the nuclear arsenal. While the CTBT prohibits the "qualitative improvement of nuclear weapons," this program will fund the building of nuclear accelerators, giant x-ray machines, and the largest glass laser in the world.

One of the most controversial elements of the SSP is the Accelerated Strategic Computing Initiative (ASCI), which is intended to develop a "full-system, full-physics predictive code to support weapons designs, production analysis, accident analysis, and certification"—in other words, a *virtual* nuclear testing program. The ASCI will create a $910 million network of powerful supercomputers that will allow scientists to continue developing and testing new weapons without attracting the wrath of actual experimentation. Despite this, DOE officials still insist the SSP was born only to maintain the safety of the current stockpile.

Other government officials claim the U.S. nuclear policy is heavily influenced by non-scientific factors. Referring to the powerful nuclear lobby, one anonymous Clinton Administration official explained that, "In order to get the treaty through Congress, we had to buy off the labs." While the SSP may be viewed as the U.S. "cost" of the Test Ban, further testing, real or virtual, could have untold consequences for the world.

UPDATE BY AUTHOR BILL MESLER: "On December 9, the United States Department of Energy (DOE) conducted its fifth subcritical nuclear weapons test at the Nevada test site. A DOE press release claimed that the test was carried out to 'ensure the safety and reliability of the stockpile without nuclear testing.' On the same day as the U.S. test, Russia conducted a subcritical test at its site at Novaya Zemlya. In defending the exper-

iment to the press, Russian officials pointed to the U.S. test as proof that subcritical tests of nuclear weapons are permissible under the Comprehensive Test Ban Treaty (CTBT).

"There are no signs that either country will change its policy on subcritical nuclear testing. Nor does the DOE appear ready to end other activities in the Stockpile Stewardship Program (SSP) that violate the principals and goals of the CTBT. Many American anti-nuclear groups remain reluctant to raise these issues because they fear it will hamper already difficult efforts to get the Republican Congress to ratify the treaty itself. Despite overwhelming opposition to nuclear testing, the vast majority of Americans remain ignorant of the controversy surrounding the SSP."

In August of 1999, on the anniversaries of the nuclear bombing of Hiroshima and Nagasaki, Peace Action Network will hold a demonstration at Los Alamos, the birthplace of the atomic bomb, to demand an end to subcritical nuclear testing and the SSP.

To learn more about this issue and what you can do to help stop continued nuclear weapons testing, contact:

The Nuclear Program of the Natural Resources Defense Council, Tel: (202) 289-6868; e-mail: cpaine@nrdc.org.

Peace Action Network, contact Bruce Hall, Tel: (202) 862-9740.

7 CENSORED

Gene Transfers Linked to Dangerous New Diseases

Sources:

THIRD WORLD RESURGENCE, #92
Title: "Sowing Diseases, New and Old"
Authors: Mae-Wan Ho and Terje Traavik

THE ECOLOGIST
Title: "The Biotechnology Bubble"
Date: May/June 1998, Vol. 28, No. 3
Authors: Mae-Wan Ho, Hartmut Meyer, and Joe Cummins

SSU Censored Researchers:
Jennifer Mintz and Amber Manfree
SSU Faculty Evaluator: Tom Lough

The world is heading for a major crisis in public health as both emergent and recurring diseases reach new heights of antibiotic resistance. At least 30 new diseases have emerged over the past 20 years, and familiar infectious diseases such as tuberculosis, cholera, and malaria are returning with vigor. By 1990 nearly every common bacterial species had developed some degree of resistance to drug treatment, many to multiple antibiotics. A major contributing factor, in addition to antibiotic overuse, just might be the transfer of genes between unrelated species of animals and plants which takes place with genetic engi-

neering, according to *Third World Resurgence*. Despite the fact that the evidence is quite compelling, there is currently no independent investigation of the relationship between genetic engineering and the etiology (cause, or origin) of infectious diseases. What's worse is that regulators are considering a further relaxation of the already lax safety rules regarding this unpredictable and inherently hazardous field.

The technology of genetic engineering, also called biotechnology, uses manipulation, replication, and transference techniques to insert genes "horizontally" to connect species which otherwise cannot interbreed. Normal genetic barriers and defense mechanisms, which degrade or deactivate foreign genes that they recognize as dangerous to the self, are in this way broken down. Used to facilitate horizontal gene transfer, genetic engineering can also result in antibiotic-resistant genes, which can inadvertently spread and recombine to generate new drug and antibiotic-resistant pathogens.

This, say the authors, has occurred. Horizontal gene transfer and subsequent genetic recombination may have been responsible for bacterial strains which caused a 1992 cholera outbreak in India, and for a streptococcus epidemic in Tayside in 1993. Antibiotic-resistant genes spread readily between human beings, as well as from bacteria inhabiting the gut of farm animals to human beings. Antibiotics can create the very conditions that facilitate the spread of antibiotic resistance because they can increase the frequency of horizontal gene transfer 10 to 10,000-fold.

Biotechnology firms have billions of dollars invested in these new technologies, and are concerned that their speculation bubble may burst, due to public outrage, before they can recoup their investments. In Europe, where the public support for such programs is dismal at best, EuropaBio, the non-government organization representing the interests of the biotech industry, hired public relations firm Burson Marsteller to initiate a public relations campaign to promote the benefits of biotechnology. In a document leaked to *The Ecologist*, it was reported that Burson Marsteller recommended that the industry stay quiet on the risks of genetically engineered foods, as they could never win on that argument, and instead focus on "symbols that elicit hope, satisfaction, and caring."

Biotechnology is presented to the public as a highly precise science. Implications are that genes are linear causal chains, seldom influenced by the environment. We assume that genes are stable, and tend to remain in the organisms in which they've been created. Nothing could be further from the truth. Genes never work in isolation, but rather in extremely complicated networks with other genes. The network is always subject to layers of feedback from the physiology of the organism. This feedback can cause genes to replicate, reorganize, or even travel outside the organism. The danger is enhanced by the fact that microorganisms genetically engineered for "contained use" may not be effectively contained. DNA released from cells is not readily broken down in the environment, so it retains the ability to transform other organisms. Many varieties of dangerous rDNA, which contain cancer-causing viruses and antibiotic-resistant genes, can almost certainly transform bacteria in the environment, and further recombine, say the authors.

The need to reassess the safety regulations pertaining to genetic engineering is urgent. Effects of both deliberate release and contained use are in desperate need of further study. A greater understanding of the general mechanisms behind horizontal gene transfer must be reached. Research results should be used to strengthen the barriers against the transfer of rDNA and to provide a basis for scientific risk assessment. It is vital that this research be conducted by independent groups, and not left in the hands of those laboratories which are involved in the commercial exploitation of biotechnology.

UPDATE BY AUTHOR MAE-WAN HO: "A sound technology is underpinned by good, reliable science; but that's not the case in gene biotechnology. Our story exposes the discredited science of genetic determination at the heart of the biotechnology bubble. It is misguiding a hit-or-miss technology and promoting projects that are not only dangerous and unrealistic, but socially and morally irresponsible.[1]

"The mainstream press, not surprisingly, has ignored our story. There is a general reluctance to question the sci-

ence by all concerned, which is not helping the debate.

"Since our paper was published,
many more problems with transgenic
crops have come to light. For example,
three transgenic potato lines planted in
Georgia (of the former Soviet Union)[2]
yielded one-third to one-half of the
expected harvest, two lines yielding ugly
deformed tubers that could not be sold.

"Further evidence of controllable
horizontal gene transfer has emerged. A
genetic parasite belonging to yeast is
found to have jumped into many unrelated species of higher plants very
recently.[3] And the genes transferred into
transgenic plants can be up to 30 times
more likely to spread than the plant's own
genes.[4]

"Opposition to gene biotechnology
has 'skyrocketed.' France, Greece, the
United Kingdom, and Denmark have
joined Austria, Luxembourg, and Norway
in imposing a moratorium or specific
bans."

1. See M.W. Ho, *Genetic Engineering
Dream or Nightmare? The Brave New
World of Bad Science and Big Business*,
(Bath: Gateway Books, 1998).
2. *Greenpeace Report*, August 1998.
3. Y. Cho, et. al., *Proc. Natl. Acad.
Sci.* USA 95, 1998: 14244-9.
4. J. Bergelson, et. al., *Nature* 395,
1998: 25.

8 CENSORED

Catholic Hospital Mergers Threaten Reproductive Rights for Women

Source:
Ms.
Title: "Women's Health: A Casualty
of Hospital Merger Mania"
Date: July/August 1998
Author: Christine Dinsmore

SSU Censored Researchers:
Jennifer Mintz and Yuki Ishizaki
SSU Faculty Evaluators:
Cindy Stearns and Jeanette Koshar

Nationwide hospital mergers with Roman
Catholic Church medical facilities are
threatening women's access to abortions, sterilization, birth control, *in vitro*
fertilization, fetal tissue experimentation,
and assisted suicide. In 1996, over 600
hospitals merged with Catholic institutions in 19 states. The merged partnerships extend from Portland, Maine to
Oakland, California, and these mergers
and partnerships with hospitals and
health maintenance organizations
(HMOs) are resulting in the impairment
of reproductive health care rights across
the nation.

Ms. gives the example of Kingston
Hospital in Rhinebeck, New York.

Kingston once performed about 100 abortions a year, but if merged with Benedictine Hospital, a Roman Catholic facility, it will provide the service for medical reasons only. No hospital in the community would provide birth control counseling or family planning services.

Collaborations between secular and Roman Catholic hospitals have made the Roman Catholic Church the largest private health care provider in the nation. Why would they want to join forces with secular hospitals? "The big money in the hospital comes when you have a closed system of doctors, HMOs, and hospitals all feeding each other in a closed loop," writes Dinsmore.

Though activists object to partnerships between religious and secular hospitals that result in the ban of reproductive services, they are sometimes willing to accept lesser collaborations, such as joint ventures or affiliations, in which it's more likely religious directives won't be imposed. In response to community pressure, some health care agreements have resulted in independently-run women's health clinics. Some activists, however, say it's a lousy solution because separate women's health clinics are often easier targets for anti-abortion extremists. There are other drawbacks, says Frances Kissling, president of Catholics for a Free Choice: "Establishing a free-standing clinic as part of the elimination of services from an existing hospital is not a good compromise. Women should not have to go to more than one provider for their reproductive health services. They should be able to choose between a hospital and a clinic—the decision should not be made for them. In addition, most women deliver their babies in hospitals; it is important for those seeking tubal ligation to be able to have them immediately postpartum."

"Another problem with separate clinics planned by hospitals," says Kissling, "is that they often experience financial difficulties because women's health care is not as profitable as a lot of other specialties." Lastly, hospitals often say they'll set up a separate women's health clinic as part of a partnership agreement, and then simply don't follow through on that part of the agreement, says *Ms.*

Besides the decrease in women's health care services, other changes have occurred because of the mergers. According to Susan Fogel, legal director of the California Women's Law Center, Sierra Nevada Hospital in Grass Valley, California, had been part of a sexual assault response team in which medical staff, domestic violence specialists, and members of the sheriff's office worked together to make certain that the needs of both the sexual assault victim and law enforcement were met. Since the takeover, writes Dinsmore, Catholic Health Care West no longer participates in the program. It claims that it takes care of the victims in-house without coordination with its former team members.

Men are also affected by the mergers; when a hospital moves to free-standing clinics for women only, men seeking vasectomies will need to find that service elsewhere.

Health care workers, clergy, women's groups, and HIV/AIDS advocates are creating coalitions to inform the public about possible future mergers. Currently there are few laws requiring community notification of impending non-profit partnerships, but activists are pressuring state lawmakers to pass protective legislation. California and New York are two states which have introduced bills for legislators to review. In response, a lobbying group called the New York Catholic Conference has made defeat of these bills "a priority." Seeing them as "pressure to force Catholic entities to abandon their moral and ethical principles." The stopping of these bills has become "second only to banning late-term abortions," says *Ms*.

UPDATE BY AUTHOR CHRISTINE DINSMORE:
"While abortion clinic violence grabs the headlines, the biggest threat to comprehensive reproductive services and a woman's right to choose remains underreported. Nationwide, Catholic hospitals are merging with secular hospitals in record numbers, resulting in communities losing access to abortion, birth control, tubal ligations, emergency contraception, and comprehensive HIV counseling.

"Although the entire community loses, poor woman are most affected. They depend on hospitals for reproductive health care when local physicians do not accept Medicaid. And if the community hospital doesn't provide comprehensive services, like adequate transportation, many poor women struggle to get to hospitals miles away from where they live.

"Merger madness is not only wreaking havoc on communities' medical services; it's also producing the largest health care conglomerate. The Roman Catholic Church is now the largest private health care provider in the nation. With over $16 billion in assets, the Roman Catholic health care system wields tremendous power.

"But despite their Goliath foe, activists have succeeded in stopping some mergers. In New York's Hudson Valley, activists and a Federal Trade Commission's investigation into monopoly charges stopped a three-way hospital merger. In Baltimore, facing community protests, the secular hospital's board of directors defeated its planned merger by one vote. In Batavia, New York, activists each paid $25 to become voting members of the hospital board. They created a majority voting block to control a proposed merger.

"In spite of successes, the Catholic's 'merger mania' continues, according to Lois Uttley, director of Merger Watch. Her organization's Web site (http://www.mergerwatch.org) provides updates on the threats to reproductive health care."

9 CENSORED

U.S. Tax Dollars Support Death Squads in Chiapas

Sources:
SLINGSHOT
Title: "Mexico's Military:
Made in the USA"
Date: Summer 1998
Authors: Slingshot collective

DARK NIGHT FIELD NOTES
Title: "Bury My Heart At Acteal"
Author: Darrin Wood

SSU Censored Researchers:
Travis Duncan and Jason Gunnarson
SSU Faculty Evaluators:
Carol Tremmel and Francisco Vasquez

On December 22, 1997, in the village of Acteal, in the highlands of the Mexican state of Chiapas, 45 indigenous men, women and children were shot as they were praying, their bodies dumped into a ravine. Elsewhere throughout the state of Chiapas, unarmed indigenous women face down armies "with fists held high in rebellion and babies slung from their shoulder." In Jalisco, more than a dozen young men were kidnapped and tortured. One of them, Salvador Jiménez López, died, drowning in his own blood when his tongue was cut out. The group responsible for these and other atrocities are allegedly members of the Mexican Army

Airborne Special Forces Groups (GAFE)—a paramilitary unit trained by U.S. Army Special Forces.

Mexican soldiers are being trained with U.S. tax dollars to fight an "alleged" War on Drugs. The real motive driving the U.S.-supported war, say peasant activists, is the protection of foreign investment rights in Mexico. "In Chiapas, U.S. tax money pays for weapons and military…to destroy a movement for social justice…because it stands in direct opposition to the right of international economic interests to maintain control of our lives. Any such movement for greater economic justice and political democracy means cutting into Wall Street's profits. The call for democracy, liberty, and justice isn't good for business," says the *Zapatismo*.

The United States transfers aid to the Mexican military in cash, weapons, and counterinsurgency training. The 1998 Clinton Administration budget earmarked more than $21 million dollars for the Mexican Drug War, including $12 million for Pentagon training in "procedures for fighting drug traffic." Anti-drug effort seems to continue to focus on the Chiapas region where 80 percent of the communities are in conflict zones.

According to the *Zapatismo Papers* (Wood), acts of inhumanity by GAFE were led by Lt. Col. Julian Guerrero Barrios, a 1981 graduate of the U.S.-sponsored School of Americas (SOA). Although it remains unknown how many of the 15 soldiers charged in the Acteal incident were trained at U.S. bases, the Pentagon has admitted that some of the soldiers arrested were U.S. trained.

The number of Mexican military officers and personnel receiving U.S. specialized training has been increasing significantly since 1996. According to a February 26 *Washington Post* report, the United States is now training Mexican officers at a rate of 1,067 a year at 17 bases. An estimated 3,200 Mexican soldiers will have received training at Fort Bragg, North Carolina from the U.S. Army 7th Special Forces (aka Green Berets) from 1996 through 1999. In the past 18 months, 252 Mexican officers have taken a 12-week course at Fort Bragg, also known as the "School of Assassins." The U.S. Central Intelligence Agency is now training an elite 90-member intelligence unit, says Wood.

According to an article published by *Slingshot* in the summer of 1998, Mexico's military purchases from the United States have increased sharply since 1997. The Mexican government also wants the people of Chiapas to become accustomed to, and even dependent on, having the armed soldiers in their midst. The government has been providing and withholding health care based on political affiliation, and even resorting to involuntary sterilization. Armed soldiers have blockaded clinics, preventing residents of Zapatista communities from getting care. Harassment of foreign visitors has increased, forcing human rights observers to keep a low profile to avoid deportation. The war in Chiapas is not an ethnic or religious conflict, says the *Zapatismo Papers* (Wood), but rather "a conflict over the control of resources."

UPDATE BY AUTHORS, SLINGSHOT COLLECTIVE: "Since the article 'Mexico's Military: Made in the USA' appeared in *Slingshot* #61 during the summer of 1998, the U.S. military has trained hundreds of thousands more Mexican officers in counterinsurgency tactics, which these officers then use against Mexicans struggling for self-determination, all under the guise of U.S. efforts against drugs.

"The U.S. government is so anxious to fight the War on Drugs that they have waived any right to oversee how U.S. military training is used back in Mexico. As a result, training that these officers receive, supposedly to conduct anti-drug activities, is being used to fight democracy advocates in Mexico. U.S. officials admit that the 'counter-narco' training offered on U.S. bases, like the School of the Americas in Georgia, and at Fort Bragg, North Carolina in the 1990s, is highly similar to training in 'counterinsurgency' tactics, used in El Salvador, Guatemala, and Nicaragua in the 1980s to fight communism during the Cold War.

"In testimony before the House International Relations Committee Subcommittee on the Western Hemisphere on July 29, Joel Solomon of Human Rights Watch recounted the results of this reckless policy. The Mexican army, fighting the Zapatista resistance (EZLN) in Chiapas, as well as the Popular Revolutionary Army (EPR) in Guerrero and Oaxaca, is increasingly guilty of gross human rights violations. According to Solomon, there have been hundreds of arbitrary arrests, forced confessions, temporary disappearances, torture, and even extrajudicial executions as the Mexican military has increased efforts against the EZLN and the EPR. Officers trained by the U.S. military have been implicated in these violations, including three senior officers listed in a letter by Rep. Joseph Kennedy II (D-MA).

"Reports from Americans living in Chiapas and observing the conflict zones describe how Mexican counter-drug agents accompany patrols engaged in counter Zapatista raids against pro-rebel communities.

"Resistance to U.S. military training of Mexican officers is increasing. On November 22 of this year, 2,319 non-violent protesters trespassed at Fort Benning, Georgia, to protest the School of the Americas (SOA), which is located there. Although the SOA is now primarily training Mexicans, in the past the SOA has trained military officers from all over the Americas, including the officers who killed six Jesuit priests and two women in El Salvador in 1989, Panamanian dictator Manuel Noriega, Nicaraguan General Anastasio Somoza, and El Salvadoran death squad leader Robert D'Aubuisson.

"Most Americans don't support the use of U.S. tax dollars for the kind of training found at the School of the Americas. Only increased publicity about this issue, together with citizen action, can stop U.S. training programs for Mexican armies."

Slingshot is an independent, quarterly, radical newspaper published in the East Bay (California) since 1988. Sample copies are $2 from 3124 Shattuck Avenue, Berkeley, CA 94705.

Because of *Slingshot's* unique collective structure, *Slingshot* was not able to determine the author of the article "Mexico's Military: Made in the USA." It may have been compiled from information off the Internet, from a flyer, or even reprinted from some other source.

10 CENSORED

Environmental Student Activists Gunned Down on Chevron Oil Facility in Nigeria

Sources:
AINFO NEWS SERVICE
Title: "Chevron in Nigeria—
ERA Environmental Testimonies"
Date: July 10, 1998
Authors: Environmental Rights
Action/Friends of the Earth Nigeria

PACIFICA RADIO—
DEMOCRACY NOW
Title: "Drilling and Killing: Chevron and Nigeria's Oil Dictatorship"
Date: Summer 1998
Authors: Amy Goodman and Jeremy Scahill

SSU Censored Researchers: Michael McMurtrey and Craig Chapman
SSU Faculty Evaluator: Les Adler

Mainstream media coverage: *San Francisco Chronicle*, November 19, 1998, page A1

On May 28, 1998, Nigerian soldiers were helicoptered by Chevron employees to the Chevron owned oil facility off the coast of Nigeria in order to attack student demonstrators who had occupied a barge anchored to the facility. After multiple attacks, two students lay dead, and several others were wounded. The students had been peacefully protesting at the site since May 25. One hundred and twenty-one youths from 42 different communities had gathered to oppose the environmental destruction brought on by Chevron's oil extraction practices.

For decades, the people of the Niger Delta have been protesting the destruction of their wetlands. Discharges into the creeks and waterways have left the region a dead land, resulting in the Niger Delta becoming one of the most heavily polluted regions in the world.

The students claim they had voiced their concerns many times and had scheduled a number of meetings with the company, but the meetings had been repeatedly canceled by Chevron. As a next step, the students organized the protest around the Chevron barge in order to draw Chevron's attention to the goal of environmental justice.

According to student leader Bola Oyinbo, approximately 20 of the 121 students surrounding the barge in small boats went on board to meet with a Nigerian Naval officer who was working for Chevron. Oyinbo stated that the students wanted to speak to a Mr. Kirkland, Chevron's managing director. Although the director never came, other Chevron officials did arrive the next day and promised to set up a meeting with the students at the end of May. The students agreed to leave the barge on May 28 in order to attend the proposed meeting.

As the students were getting ready to leave the barge, three helicopters piloted by Chevron employees attacked the student protesters. Oyinbo remembers the moment, "they came like eagles swooping on chickens. We never expected what came next." Soldiers in the choppers fired on students while in the air and after landing. "They shot everywhere," he says. "Arulika and Jolly fell. They died instantly. Larry, who was near them rushed to their aid, wanting to pick them up, but he was also shot." Eleven students were detained by the military group and taken to Akure for prosecution. Chevron filed a complaint against the group, saying they were pirates and should be interrogated.

During his imprisonment, one activist said he was handcuffed and hung from a ceiling fan hook for hours for refusing to sign a statement written by Nigerian federal authorities.

11 CENSORED

Private Prison Expansion Becomes Big Business

Source:
TURNING THE TIDE
Title: "The Prison Industry and
The Global Complex"
Date: Summer 1998
Authors: Eve Goldberg and
Linda Evans

SSU Censored Researcher:
Travis Duncan
SSU Faculty Evaluator: Linda Lopez

Private prisons are one of the fastest growing sectors of the prison industrial complex. Under contract by the government to run jails and prisons, and paid a fixed sum per prisoner, corporate firms operate as cheaply and efficiently as possible to insure a profit. This means lower wages for staff, no unions, and fewer services for prisoners. Substandard diets, extreme overcrowding, and abuses by poorly trained personnel have all been documented as practices of this private business approach to incarceration.

The "need" for more prisons was created in the 1980s, say the authors, when many businesses in the United States decided to take their factories out of the country, seeking higher profits and lower wages. Most seriously hurt by these plant

closures and layoffs were African-Americans and semi-skilled workers in urban centers. Both a drug economy and the international prison industrial complex have filled the gaping economic hole left by the exodus of jobs from the U.S. cities. Currently 1.8 million people are behind bars in the U.S. Many who once made a living wage are now making only 22 cents per hour from behind prison walls.

For those who have invested in private prisons, say the authors, prison labor is like a pot of gold. There are no strikes, no unions, no unemployment insurance, or worker's compensation. Prisoners can now be found doing data entry for Chevron, telephone reservations for TWA, raising hogs, shoveling manure, and sometimes making lingerie for Victoria's Secret.

Investment houses, construction companies, architects, and support services such as those which provide food, medical supplies, transportation, and furniture, all profit by prison expansion, say Goldberg and Evans. Investment firm Smith Barney is partial owner of a prison in Florida. American Express and General Electric have invested in private prison construction in Oklahoma and Tennessee. Communication giants such as AT&T, Sprint, and MCI are getting into the act as well; gouging prisoners with exorbitant rates for phone calls, often six times the normal long distance charge.

Small businesses are now competing with the prison industry. Many small furniture businesses are closing due to the cheap labor provided by UNICOR, the federal prison industry corporation. UNI-COR pays 23 cents per hour, and also has the inside track on all governments contracts. In another case, U.S. Technologies sold its electronics plant in Texas, leaving 150 workers unemployed, and opened in a nearby prison six weeks later.

With the transformations in the global economy that have occurred over the past two decades, the authors say, wage decreases and standards for workers have suffered. Privatization of prisons contributes to this cycle as the prison industrial complex rapidly becomes a primary component of the U.S. economy.

UPDATE BY AUTHORS EVE GOLDBERG AND LINDA EVANS: "1.8 million and counting. While the corporate media was looking the other way, mass incarceration became a reality in the U.S. About one in every 150 citizens is now behind bars. The Prison Industrial Complex is becoming the defining institution of our era.

"One prison story did make headlines: At California's Corcoran State Prison, guards organized 'gladiator' fights between rival gang members—then shot the fighting inmates dead. Luckily, courageous guards blew the whistle; the father of a slain inmate sued; and for now the Corcoran killings have ceased.

"Most prison stories, however, never make the news. Pennsylvania and California have passed laws denying prisoners the right to speak with the media. Already muzzled by this gag rule, journalist Mumia Abu-Jamal, now on death row, will be silenced forever by execution unless popular support can stop it. Thousands more are locked away in 'control units'—tiny isolation cells commonly used to punish inmates who file law suits against prison officials, participate in work stoppages, or generally 'speak up.'

"But the other half of the story, also being ignored by the mainstream media, is the rapid growth of a movement to confront prison issues. Grassroots groups are springing up everywhere. A 1998 national conference called 'Critical Resistance: Beyond the Prison Industrial Complex' drew over 3,000 participants to University of California Berkeley."

A good place to find out what's happening and how to get involved is the Prison Activist Resource Center Web site: http://www.prisonactivist.org/.

Some other organizations are:

The Prison Moratorium Project,
Tel: (212) 427-4545 and (510) 594-4060

California Prison Focus
(human rights watch group),
Tel: (415) 821-6545

Families Against Mandatory
Minimums, Tel: (202) 457-5790

Jericho Amnesty Campaign
(freedom for political prisoners),
Tel: (323) 294-3836

CURE (prison reform),
Tel: (202) 789-2126."

12 CENSORED

Millions of Americans Received Contaminated Polio Vaccine Between 1955 and 1963

Sources:

CHICAGO LIFE
Title: "Ticking Time Bomb"
Date: October 1997
Author: Vicky Angelos

http://www.sightings.com/
health/salk.htm
Title: "The Forty Year Legacy
of Tainted Polio Vaccine"
Date: May 14, 1998
Author: Harold Stearley

SSU Censored Researcher:
Jennifer Mintz
SSU Faculty Evaluator: Mary King, M.D.

The polio vaccine that was given to millions of children during the late 1950s and early 1960s may be causing rare cancerous tumors in adults today.

The once hailed "miracle" vaccine was contaminated by a virus called Simian Virus 40 (SV40) between the years of 1955 and 1963. The virus hid in the renal cells of the monkeys which were used to make the vaccine. SV40 has been linked to rare, incurable cancers such as ependymomas (brain tumors), mesotheliomas (pleural tumors, usually of the lung), and osteosarcomas (bone malignancies).

The author quotes from the December 1996 issue of *Money* magazine: "Federal regulators have stymied many efforts to investigate the impact of those monkey viruses but are now paying attention to particularly disturbing research by a Chicago molecular pathologist linking one to human cancer. This is the same monkey virus that a new Italian study suggests is being passed on sexually by people throughout the world, and from mothers to babies in the womb." One study estimates that 25 percent of the population today is carrying the SV40 virus.

A 1960 study (the only one previously existing) on SV40 and its possible cancer connection noted that it tested all victims of common cancers, not rare cancers. Rare cancers such as those listed above remain latent for 10-40 years and could not be detected in the 1960 study.

The National Cancer Institute (NCI) claims that the agency is not ignoring public concern over SV40. A spokeswoman for the NCI says that no batches of the Salk Vaccine produced after 1961 contained SV40, but that previously existing batches may have circulated until 1963. When asked if there was a recall of the contaminated batches in 1961, she had no comment.

SV40 genes and proteins were discovered in 60 percent of patients with cancer, writes author Vicky Angelos.

"Unless one was an animal handler or a lab technician, or had worked in the jungles of India or the Philippines, there was only one logical way to be exposed to SV40: the polio vaccine handed out by our government."

The National Institutes of Health, the Food and Drug Administration, and the Centers for Disease Control and Prevention are "all aware of the possible link between cancer and the polio vaccine." It has been suggested that SV40 may be responsible for the 30 percent increase in brain tumors in the United States over the last 20 years.

Because of recent legal actions, attention is now being focused on the correlation between rare cancers and SV40. Two attorneys who once represented businesses that were being sued by cancer patients with pleural mesotheliomas, now represent the patients. By examining maps of the states which received high levels of SV40 tainted vaccines, the pair found links between the SV40 and these rare cancers. What they have discovered is that the NCI tested stored batches of the vaccine and that shipments made between May and June of 1955 were "heavily contaminated," says Angelos.

The link between SV40 and polio may be the next "asbestos" for attorneys. There is now evidence of high levels of disease in people born before 1940 and after 1965 who received SV40 during vaccination.

Mainstream media has mentioned this story over the years, but never fully developed it. In January of 1998, Associated Press and several newspapers in the United States carried a press release by the National Cancer Institute claiming that a 30-year study found that children exposed to SV40 did not have higher cancer rates as adults. The headline read "No Cancers Tied to 50s Polio Vaccine" (Chicago Tribune January 28, 1998). A story carried by PR newswire on January 27, 1998, released by the National Vaccine Information Center, which criticized the National Cancer Institute's study as a biased, premature dismissal of the polio vaccine issue, failed to receive coverage in the mainstream media.

UPDATE BY AUTHOR VICKY ANGELOS AND PUBLISHER PAM BERNS: "It is known that Simian Virus 40 (SV40) has tumor-causing effects in hamsters. A scientific study conducted in 1959 by Ben Sweet proved the virus had jumped the species barrier from monkeys to hamsters. The question remains: Does it have the same effect on humans? The answer is crucial to the 80-90 percent of U.S. children that were injected at least once with variable amounts of SV40 in contaminated batches of the Salk polio vaccine in the 1950s.

"Today, a multi-institutional study supported by the International Mesothelioma Interest Group confirms the presence of SV40 in humans with rare forms of cancer, such as malignant mesotheliomas. The study printed in *Cancer Research* on October 15, 1998 suggests a 'co-carcinogenic interaction between SV40 and asbestos in humans should be carefully tested in future investigations.' The study goes on to state, 'If SV40 and asbestos are co-carcinogens, people who are SV40-positive may be at a higher risk of developing mesothelioma when exposed to asbestos. Identifying individuals at higher risk may offer opportunities for prevention.'

"The *Journal of the American Medical Association* (JAMA) released 'Contamination of Poliovirus Vaccines with Simian Virus 40 (1955-1963) and Subsequent Cancer Rates' in January 1998. NIH official Howard D. Strickler, M.D. and others announced in JAMA that exposure to a polio virus vaccine contaminated with live SV40 did not increase the risk of cancer in ependymomas and other brain cancers, osteosarcomas, and mesotheliomas.

"Michele Carbone, M.D., Ph.D., of Loyola Medical Center and one of the pioneers in SV40 detection in rare tumors, questioned the JAMA Strickler study, citing new methodologies soon to be published and his research concerning the co-carcinogenic interaction between SV40 and asbestos.

"The National Vaccine Information Center (NVIC) also criticized the JAMA Strickler study for the 'inherent conflict of interest in having government officials lead investigations of health problems associated with vaccines which the government researches, regulates, and promotes for universal use,' and because the study depended heavily on cancer statistics provided by the National Cancer Institute, which began collecting data in 1973. (Thus, children who received contaminated polio vaccines and died of cancer before 1973 were excluded from the data included in the analysis.) NVIC questioned the government's analysis because it reflected less than one-tenth of the nation. It was therefore not a complete reflection of cancer rates in the entire U.S. population. Moreover, NVIC claimed that their study ignored the fact that 'the SV40 virus DNA has been detected in cancers of children born during the past five years'—which suggests that government scientists do not actually know how SV40 is transmitted from person-to-person or parent-to-child. Finally, NVIC criticized the government study because it also dismissed the evidence that 'SV40 and asbestos could be co-factors in the development of mesothelioma' and cited the rising cases of mesothelioma despite the fact that the population studied has not reached the peak age when these tumors tend to occur.

"Epidemiologist Susan Gross Fisher, Ph.D., of Loyola Medical Center also disagreed with JAMA's conclusions, stating that '[t]he analysis by Strickler et al. provides no reliable evidence regarding the presence or absence of an increased cancer risk relative to SV40 exposure.' Dr. Fisher explained that because of the unavailability of specific data regarding the actual population exposed and the amount of the virus in the vaccines, data will remain incomplete. She said also that because of the small case numbers of these rare cancers, research funding will probably remain limited. However, she said, 'molecular study is warranted for SV40 and other viruses to understand the exact role these viruses play in cancer development.'"

For more information, contact the cancer centers for the following universities: Loyola University Cardinal Bernadin Cancer Center, Maywood, Illinois; Finnish Institute of Occupational Health, Helsinki, Finland; Allegheny University of the Health Sciences, Philadelphia, Pennsylvania, and the Memorial Sloan-Kettering Cancer. Also contact the NVIC at (703) 938-0342.

13 CENSORED

China Violates Human Rights in Tibet

Source:
TOWARD FREEDOM
Title: "China's War on Women"
Date: March/April 1998
Author: Natasha Ma

SSU Censored Researchers:
Dan Bluthardt and Corrie Robb
SSU Faculty Evaluator: Laxmi Tewari

Since China's invasion of Tibet in 1959, women have been at the forefront of the nonviolent struggle for independence—nearly half of the protests staged over the last decade have been led by nuns. During that time, however, thousands of Tibetan women have been arrested, incarcerated, sexually abused, tortured, and publicly executed.

Ma's story reveals that the Chinese "Strike-Hard" anti-crime campaign, which began in April 1996, has been directed particularly against monks and nuns in Tibet. According to the International Committee of Lawyers for Tibet, at least 1,295 had been expelled from their monasteries by January 1997. The expulsions reportedly occurred after they refused to denounce either the Dalai Lama, specific religious vows, or the Panchen Lama, the occupied nation's second most important figure.

In direct opposition to the U.N.-recognized rights to freedom of religion and education, these expulsions are carried out by "work teams" sent even to remote areas of Tibet to conduct political and religious re-education. Human Rights Watch/Asia recently noted reports that it is now official Chinese policy to prevent the admission of new monks and nuns to monasteries.

According to Amnesty International, nuns, once they are incarcerated, are treated more sadistically than monks—raped, sexually abused, and subjected to attacks by dogs. Forms of torture reserved especially for women include electric batons applied to the pudendum and lighted cigarettes to the torso and face. There have also been numerous reports of rape with electric cattle prods. New methods of torture have been added in the last few years including exposure to extreme temperatures and special "physical training" sessions in which nuns, on the pretext that they are "soldiers," are brutally beaten. When released, the victims are forbidden to return to their nunneries or participate in public religious activities.

Women in Tibet's general population are also being mistreated. In October 1994, China's National People's Congress adopted the Mother and Child Health Law, which can prevent marriages and births based on the mental and physical health of the parents. As a result, the illnesses and family histories of political prisoners who have been interred in psychiatric hospitals are being used as an excuse to subject children to sterilization.

Mistreatment of Tibetan women also exists outside of the medical and prison environment, says Ma. Young girls often face coerced sterilizations, and abortions are performed on married women. Between September and October 1996, for example, over 300 Tibetan women were involuntarily sterilized in the Chushar district of Lhasa alone. The author reports that one of these, 27-year-old Nyima Dolma, died as a result.

Another area of abuse is the methods of birth control which China employs. These include surgical abortion, sterilization (conducted without consent and often performed when women enter the hospital for other surgery), and infanticide. In China, it is legal to inject women nine months pregnant in order to induce abortion, and to kill infants still in the birth canal with a lethal injection.

International laws and conventions such as the U.N.'s 1979 Convention on the Elimination of All Forms of Discrimination Against Women (CEDAW)—which China ratified—have specified that reproductive choice is a basic human right, and that population policies must consider not only economic interest but other political, social, and cultural impacts. Officially, China's "one family, one child" policy covers only nationalities in China with populations over 10 million. Thus, Tibet, with a population of six million, should be exempt.

UPDATE BY AUTHOR NATASHA MA: "We as Americans can do much to protest and work toward a change for women whose culture within Tibet is close to extinction. First, we can boycott products made in China (many of which are made by prisoners to fund military operations in Tibet). Second, we can lobby the U.N. Special Rapporteur on Violence Against Women to investigate the plight of Tibetan women in Tibet. Third, we can urge all appropriate local, regional, national, and international bodies to address the issue of violence against Tibetan women.

"The International Committee of Lawyers for Tibet has just completed a year-long project focusing on the plight of Tibetan women. A summary of findings is available on their Web site, as well as in their recent newsletter. Four young Tibetan nuns died in Drapchi Prison on June 7, 1998. All had been under solitary confinement. Two others reportedly died around the same time. On June 18, 1998, Gyaltsen Wongmo, a Tibetan nun, testified before the House Subcommittee on International Operations and Human Rights about religious persecution in Tibet. Now living in retreat in the mountains of Dharamsala, in northern India, she welcomes new female arrivals from

Tibet, many of whom are victims of severe punishment and torture."

For more information on this issue, contact International Committee of Lawyers for Tibet at 2288 Fulton Street, Berkeley, CA 94704, Tel: (510) 488-0588; http://www.tibeticlt.org., and International Campaign for Tibet at 1825 K Street, NW, Suite 520, Washington, DC 20006, Tel: (202) 785-1515; http://www.savetibet.org.

14 CENSORED

Political Contributions Compromise American Judicial System

Source:
THE NATION
Title: "The Buying of the Bench"
Date: January 26, 1998
Author: Sheila Kaplan

SSU Censored Researchers:
Corrie Robb and Tom Ladegaard
SSU Faculty Evaluator: Ken Marcus

America's justice system is being compromised by campaign contributions to judges from special interest groups and Corporate Political Action Committees (PACs).

The campaign fundraising scandals have drawn new attention to the way moneyed interests buy political favors in Washington. Far from the nation's capital, however, many of these same donors operate unchecked in a different venue: the state courts.

In 39 states that elect judges at some level, the cost of judicial races is rising at least as fast as that of either Congressional races or presidential campaigns—as candidates for the bench pay for sophisticated ads, polls, and consultants. A recent study by the California Commission on the Courts found that the cost of the average superior court race in the Los Angeles area has more than doubled every year, increasing 22-fold from 1976 to 1994. In Washington state, winners in 1980 spent between $30,000 and $50,000; by 1995, winners spent at least $150,000. In North Carolina, the American Judicature Society reported that the biggest spender for the Supreme Court in 1988 paid $90,330; by 1994, it was $241,709.

Fueling these campaigns is an influx of money from the tobacco industry, casinos, insurance companies, doctors, and businesses. Other contributors include defense lawyers and trial lawyers, unions, and recently, the religious right. It adds up to a system of justice in which judges are compromised by the time they take the bench, and those who are perceived as unsympathetic to well-funded interest groups often end up simply kicked out of office.

The Nation analyzed campaign contributions in 1996 state Supreme Court races, finding several cases of donations that were notable conflicts of interest. For example, in Nevada, Justice William

Maupin received more than $80,000 from casinos and gambling interests, much of it while ruling favorably on a landmark casino case. In West Virginia, Justice Elliot Maynard's largest contributors were coal companies and their employees, among them A.T. Massey Coal Company, Golden Chance Coal Company, and the lawyers that represent them.

The pleas from the legal community to regulate these contributions are being ignored. The American Bar Association, the American Judicature Society, and the Fund for Modern Courts have all recommended setting spending caps for candidates, putting limits on donations, and providing free advertising. But effecting real change is up to the states. Likewise, changes from election to merit selection, backed by groups such as the American Judicature Society, can also only be accomplished through state action. In merit selection, judges are appointed by a chief executive, who has been chosen from a list compiled by a nonpartisan panel. The judges then run for retention rather than reelection.

In 1996, the National Voting Rights Institute filed suit in Los Angeles on behalf of a coalition of civil rights groups, challenging private financing of judicial elections there. The group says that under the current system, money determines the outcome of judicial races, effectively shutting out those without sufficient means. *The Nation's* coverage of this case illustrates the threat posed to our nation's judicial system by a campaign process gone amuck.

15 CENSORED

SWAT Teams Replace Civilian Police: Target Minority Communities

Source:
COVERTACTION QUARTERLY (CAQ)
Title: "Operation Ghetto Storm: The Rise In Paramilitary Policing"

THIS MODERN WORLD
by TOM TOMORROW

Date: Fall 1997
Author: Peter Cassidy

SSU Censored Researchers: Michael McMurtrey and Jason L. Sanders
SSU Faculty Evaluator: Robert Lee Nichols

In the 25 years since the creation of the first Special Weapons and Tactics (SWAT) teams in Los Angeles, police forces across the United States have become increasingly militarized. Paramilitary police teams originally only operated in urban areas, but in recent years the number of special task forces throughout the country, including rural police departments, has dramatically increased. A study by Eastern Kentucky University's School of Police Studies shows that these forces are now responding to many call-outs that could have been handled by regular police officers, and some 20 percent of departments have reported that their special forces are used for community patrols.

The first SWAT teams were begun in the mid-1960s by the then-Los Angeles Police Chief Daryl Gates and were used during civil disturbances in the 1960s and 1970s. As the war on drugs escalated in the 1980s, paramilitary forces were used against drug dealers in many cities. Police agencies around the country organized SWAT or Special Response Teams (SRT) that operate in battle dress uniform with automatic assault rifles, percussion flash-band grenades, CS gas, and armored personnel carriers.

Experts partially blame the militarization of police forces on the proliferation of military-style weapons in the general public. As gangs and drug dealers became much more heavily armed, the police became increasingly militarized. Cheap war-surplus material was made available as a result of the military spending cuts at the end of the Cold War, and the abundance of military hardware facilitated the trend towards high-tech weaponry on both sides of the drug war.

Professor Peter Kraska, of Eastern Kentucky University's School of Police Studies, believes that the increasing amount of police violence against citizens

will be answered by greater force from armed lawbreakers. This may result in a Cold War-style escalation of arms in the streets of United States. As a result of this increased armament, paramilitary forces have begun maintaining a semi-permanent presence in "dangerous" neighborhoods in order to keep control.

According to the author, paramilitary forces now specifically target minority groups and communities. Joseph McNamara, of the Hoover Institution at Stanford University, points to the racism evident in many of the incidents occurring where paramilitary forces are used. Most of the paramilitary operations occur in inner-city neighborhoods. During an "Operation Readi-Rock" raid in North Carolina, an entire block of an African-American neighborhood was isolated. Nearly 100 black individuals were detained, while all whites were allowed to leave the area.

A 1990 raid in Albuquerque started with a commando-style attack on an apartment building and resulted in the death of a suspect who had two marijuana joints on the premises. In 1994, a wrong address raid resulted in the heart failure of a 75-year-old minister in Boston who was chased to his death, and died handcuffed in his own apartment.

On the Mexican border, law enforcement is being reinforced by the U.S. military. In May 1997, U.S. Marines killed a teenage shepherd tending his flock near the Texas-Mexican border. Police are required by law to announce their presence and fire only if their lives were in danger. Yet in this case, the Marines remained hidden and unannounced as they stalked the high school student for several hours.

The link between community-based civilian police departments and military/paramilitary operations raises serious questions regarding civil liberties in the United States.

UPDATE BY AUTHOR PETER CASSIDY: "The state's monopoly on force is a privileged commission discharged every day by local law enforcement, an institution which is being increasingly militarized by misdirected government programs and, of course, the highly cultivated perception that crime, civil unrest, and terrorism are out of control, requiring extraordinary measures—even those that resemble artifacts of martial law.

"Few media outlets noticed the story. It resulted in an interview with a *Boston Globe* reporter who needed a national perspective for a report on a SWAT raid that destroyed a home in Central Massachusetts, and a radio interview in Philadelphia with a talk show host who feared the racist aspect of police paramilitarism. I shared his alarm.

"Drug War-funded training programs that expose local police to military culture continues to expand, acculturating the police to thinking like soldiers. (Also, the President's budget includes $52.1 million in Fiscal Year 1999 for the Department of Defense [DOD] to continue to provide emergency preparedness training to local police and service agencies in U.S. cities.) Material transfer programs continue to flood police armories with war-surplus weapons that have little law enforcement utility—everything from bayonets to grenade launchers.

"The DOD, meanwhile, is feeling ever more comfortable discussing its new role in providing what one DOD called 'homeland' defense (against civil disturbances, biological attack, and terrorist incidents) in a Congressional hearing last summer, and in waging information warfare, enterprises that bring it directly into civil affairs and into plain confrontation with our American traditions.

"The militarization of local law enforcement is but one part of an overall fusion of the law enforcement and defense institutions in the United States that is the greatest threat of the Cold War. Tolerate it much longer and the people will forget that there is a difference between being governed and being garrisoned."

Here are some links that might provide further perspective on the subject:

http://intellectualcapital.com/issues/97/0612/iccon.asp—Essay on SWAT from veteran cop and police commissioner.

http://emergency.com/swat0797.htm—Profile and analysis of Fresno's full-time, patrolling SWAT team.

http://www.sfbg.com/News/33/07/Features/cops.html—News story on recent—November 1998—SWAT operation in San Francisco.

http://www.injusticeline.com/victims.html—Drug war discussion with a number of items about SWAT victims.

http://www.ntoa.org—SWAT Team association. Check out titles of study papers—including case studies on offshore military operations.

http://www.policeguide.com/swat.htm—Abridged index of state and local SWAT teams. Check out the machine gun graphic.

http://www.netxn.com/7Ejayebird/Russ/swat.html—On-line pictorial SWAT fanzine.

http://i2i.org/SuptDocs/Waco/CanSoldiersBePeaceOfficers.htm#h6—Essay on the military's induction into law enforcement with a segment on the military's training role in training local cops.

16 CENSORED

Mercenary Armies in Service to Global Corporations

Sources:
CAQ
Title: "Mercenary Armies & Mineral Wealth"
Date: Fall 1997, No. 62
Author: Pratap Chatterjee

MULTINATIONAL MONITOR
Title: "Guarding the Multinationals"
Date: March 1998
Author: Pratap Chatterjee

SSU Censored Researchers:
Jason Bothwell and Kelly Dahlstrom
SSU Faculty Evaluators: Linda Lopez
and John Steiner

In many countries, multinational corporations have paid directly for private policing services from the local army; or have hired outside security companies to harass nationals who protest against the environmental impact of their operations. The firms involved represent a growing number of new corporate security operations around the world, linking former intelligence officers, standing armies, and local death squads.

One of these security companies is Defense Systems Limited (DSL). DSL is run by two ex-Special Air Service commandos out of London offices, across the street from Buckingham Palace. Their clients include petrochemical companies, multinational banks, embassies, non-governmental organizations, and national and international organizations. One of DSL's biggest contracts is with Mark Heathcote, a former MI6 (British equivalent of the CIA) officer who ran operations in Argentina during the Falklands War. Heathcote is now the chief of security for British Petroleum (BP). In 1996, DSL sent a group of British personnel to train Colombian Police on BP-owned rigs. Training included lethal-weapons handling, sniper fire, and close quarter combat.

Another firm, Executive Outcomes, also offers mercenary armies to multinationals. Executive Outcomes fielded a private mercenary army in Angola in 1993, and offers high-tech security forces to corporations all over the world.

In Nigeria, the Anglo-Dutch multinational Shell corporation has been accused of causing major pollution in the Niger Delta for the last 38 years. Shell directly employs an elite detachment of Nigerian police to protect its own interests. Numerous demonstrators have been beaten and executed because of Shell operations in Nigeria.

In Indonesia, a U.S. company, Freeport McMoram, has been accused of dumping more than 110,000 tons of mining waste into local rivers every day. When the Indonesian populace protested the devastation to its land, Indonesian troops, hired to protect Freeport McMoram, moved in and cracked down on the protesters. Human rights groups estimate that the army has killed nearly 2,000 people in the region in the two decades the company has been in residence.

In Burma, two oil companies, Unocal and Total, are combining to build a $1.2 billion, 40-mile long pipeline that will deliver natural gas to a power plant in Thailand. Officials from the government-in exile say the Burmese army has rounded up some 500,000 people to provide unpaid, forced labor on the pipeline.

In India, armies have recently become available to multinational corporations for a very cheap price. Enron, a gas producing multinational from Texas, reportedly paid soldiers about $3.50 per person, per day for a battalion to guard a power plant under construction. Since then, Amnesty International has recorded several incidents of violence towards protesters, says Chatterjee.

The Cold War kept national armies throughout the Third World well supplied with weapons as the superpowers vied for control of almost every country on the planet. Now, with the Cold War over, a new market has been created for these specially trained armies, and for privatized security businesses such as DSL. They can now be hired to protect multinational corporations from the wrath of the local people trying to protect their own communities.

UPDATE BY AUTHOR PRATAP CHATTERJEE:
"Multinational mineral extraction companies like British Petroleum and Shell finance some of the bloodiest conflict zones around the world today in countries from Algeria to Zaire. Although nonprofit organizations chronicle human rights and environmental abuses in these situations, and international organizations like the United Nations regularly attempt to negotiate peace between warring factions, none of these institutions point out that these operations are often financed by companies that sell products from gold rings to gasoline in every neighborhood. Nor is there any system in place to address the root causes of these day-to-day disasters.

"Many of the mercenaries mentioned in the story seem to have gone undercover. Alastair Morrison and Richard Bethell of Defense Systems Limited have apparently been laid off, while Tony Buckingham has resigned from the board of Diamond Works and Eeben Barlow of Executive Outcomes has mysteriously vanished. The conflicts, however, continue in every one of the countries described in the story, from Colombia to Sierra Leone, with assistance from well-financed mercenaries.

"Although the mainstream press, from *The New York Times* in this country to the *Financial Times* in Britain, often cover conflict and provide daily business coverage of multinational corporations, they only occasionally cover mercenaries. These reports typically refer to mercenaries as individual "soldiers-of-fortune" failing to point out that the companies in their business pages pay for daily murder and that these companies are often guilty of rampant environmental abuses that are the source of community protest and conflict.

"A Web version of winning stories (with clickable maps and links to both human rights groups, other media, and the mercenaries themselves) exists at the following URL: http://www.moles.org/ProjectUnderground/mil/milindex.html. To get regular updates on the subject of mercenaries and the mineral industries I recommend that readers subscribe to a twice-monthly electronic magazine named *Drillbits & Tailings* which I edit for Project Underground, a non-profit organization which supports communities affected by the mineral industries. The magazine is available electronically for free (financial support is encouraged) by e-mailing project_underground@moles. org. All back issues (57 by mid-December 1998) are archived and completely searchable on the World Wide Web at http://www.moles.org."

17 CENSORED

U. S. Media Promotes Biased Coverage of Bosnia

Sources:
CAQ
Title: "Misinformation: TV Coverage of a Bosnian Camp"
Date: Fall 1998, No. 65
Author: Thomas Deichmann

CAQ
Title: "Seeing Yugoslavia Through A Dark Glass"
Date: Fall 1998, No. 65
Author: Diana Johnstone

SSU Censored Researchers:
Victoria Calkins and Sam Rogers
SSU Faculty Evaluator: Phil Beard

In August 1992, media coverage of the civil war in Yugoslavia gained unprecedented influence on military decision-making processes in the West. Reports of horrifying conditions in camps run by the Bosnian Serbs galvanized world opinion. A visit to the camps of Omarska and Trnopolje by a British team from Independent Television (ITN) on August 5, 1992, gave rise to the image of the Serbs as the new Nazis of the Balkans. A widely published photo taken by ITN pictured an emaciated Muslim behind barbed wire with comrades imprisoned behind him. This famous photo became

the symbolic link between the Bosnian Serbs and the Nazi concentration camps of World War II. International politicians sent troops into Bosnia. A wave of sanctions against Bosnian Serbs were established. In the United States, presidential candidate Bill Clinton took the initiative in his campaign, making references to the ITN pictures as he requested military action against the Serbs. The world became convinced that Bosnia was full of "bad Serbs" persecuting "good Muslims."

ITN's photo was not, however, as accurate as it seemed. The men in the photo were not standing behind barbed wire. In fact the Hague Tribunal confirmed that there was no barbed wire surrounding the Belsen '92 at Trnopolje. ITN's photo was taken looking outward from a small fenced enclosure inside the camp, not from outside looking in as the photo implies. The emaciated Muslim shown with his shirt off was in fact a very ill man selected to be featured in the photo. The other men in the photo look healthier and are clothed. Trnopolje was not a concentration camp, it was a refugee and transit center. Many Muslims traveled there for protection and could leave whenever they wished.

While the coverage of this image was not directly responsible for international diplomacy and military planning, it was the trigger that brought on an avalanche of actions. This was aided by Croatian secessionists and Bosnian Muslims who hired Ruder Finn (an American public relations firm) to advance their cause by targeting key publics in the United States who would respond appropriately to their demonization of the Serbs. Ruder Finn focused their public relation releases to target women and the Jewish community in the United States. The Western press was soon filled with stories of rape camps, death camps, and horrendous attacks by Bosnian Serbs with little or no verification of particular events, and little coverage of the Bosnian Serb side of the war. As the war in Bosnia-Herzegovina got underway in mid-1992, American journalists who repeated unconfirmed stories of Serbian atrocities could count on getting published. On the other hand, there was no market for stories by a journalist who discovered that Serbian "rape camps" did not exist (German TV reporter Martin Lettmayer). Nor was there a market for reporters who wrote stories about Muslim or Croat crimes against Serbs (Belgian journalist Georges Berghezan). It became increasingly impossible to challenge the dominant interpretation in the major media. Western editors seemed to prefer to keep the story simple: one villain and as much blood as possible.

Foreign news has always been easier to distort. TV crews sent into strange places, about which they know nothing, send back images of violence that give millions of viewers the impression that "everyone knows what is happening," and an aggressor is easily identified as the evil villain in need of the discipline of outside moral authorities.

UPDATE BY AUTHOR DIANA JOHNSTONE: "The truth about Yugoslavia may well be the most important censored, self-cen-

sored, distorted, and misunderstood story, not only of 1998, but of the whole decade. A drastic critical reevaluation is urgently necessary to prevent even greater disasters in the foreseeable future—notably in Kosovo. There, the one-sided anti-Serb bias has given both Albanian and Serb residents the impression that NATO is ready to support armed ethnic Albanian secessionists.

"Not only mainstream media, but even alternative outlets have turned down stories that fail to fit established stereotypes. However, even when journalists produce balanced reports, the effect is often offset by extremely biased editorials, cartoons, and commentaries, not to mention statements by Western government officials deliberately exploiting a troubled situation in order to justify a new expanded mission for NATO.

"By the end of 1998, it was clear that the conflict in Kosovo was merging dangerously with the debate over NATO's new strategy, with both scheduled to dominate the news in the spring of 1999, when NATO's 50th anniversary meeting appeared destined to coincide with the spring offensive of the armed ethnic Albanian separatists in Kosovo.

"There is no quick fix for understanding this story. A vast amount of information is available, but it takes time, experience and above all judgment to sort out truth from falsehood, and to evaluate the meaning of events. An excellent current source of information about Kosovo is the Web site of the Decani monastery: http://www.decani.yunet.com."

"Since the publication of my article there have been few discussions in the media about it. Many editors ignored the story. Supportive comments often were overwhelmed by smear articles coming mostly from the *London Observer* and *Guardian* that questioned my professional and personal integrity. Despite the slurs, no evidence disputing my story has been presented.

"ITN chose to use the repressive British libel laws to keep my story under wraps in the U.K. The writ threatens the very existence of *LM* magazine which published my piece. This action is a serious threat to the freedom of the press. Since the writ was served, the plaintiffs have done little to get the case to court. The many delays suggest that ITN is reluctant to do so. *LM* has already spent around £50.000, and is anxious to start the proceedings so all matters can be up for public discussion.

"During the Bosnian war, some reporters started following a morally-driven agenda. My article invited a discussion about how this dangerous trend has started. From the response to my piece however, it is obvious that I questioned an established orthodoxy which is not allowed to be challenged.

"BBC world affairs editor John Simpson alluded to this in his recently published book *Strange Places, Questionable People*. With reference to my story and the anti-Serb media coverage of intolerant liberals and right-wingers, he recalled Salman Rushdie's remark that religious people have 'a God-shaped hole in their lives.' Simpson concluded that 'one of the strangest coalitions of modern times seems to have a crusade-shaped hole in their lives, and Bosnia was cut and shaped to fit it.'

"You can find all information about my story and the libel case, and about ways to support *LM* at: http://www.informinc.co.uk/ITN-vs-LM/. You can contact *LM* at: lm@informinc.co.uk, Tel: (44) 171 269-9231, Fax: (44) 171-269-9235. A German website with the article can be found at: http://www.novo-magazin.de/. If you want to get further involved in the issue you can reach me at: Thomas. Deichmann@t-online.de."

18 CENSORED

Manhattan Project Covered Up Effects of Fluoride Toxicity

Source:
WASTE NOT
Title: "Fluoride, Teeth and the Atomic Bomb"
Date: September 1997
Authors: Joel Griffiths and Chris Bryson

SSU Censored Researcher: Corrie Robb
SSU Faculty Evaluator:
Daniel Markwyn

Recently declassified government documents have shed new light on the decades-old debate over the fluoridation of drinking water, and have added to a growing body of scientific evidence concerning the health effects of fluoride. Much of the original evidence about fluoride, which suggested it was safe for human consumption in low doses, was actually generated by "Manhattan Project" scientists in the 1940s. As it turns out, these officials were ordered by government powers to provide information that would be "useful in litigation" and that would obfuscate its improper handling and disposal. The once top-secret documents, say the authors, reveal that vast quantities of fluoride, one of the most toxic substances known, were required for the production of weapons-grade plutonium and uranium. As a result, fluoride soon became the leading health hazard to bomb program workers and surrounding communities.

Studies commissioned after chemical mishaps by the medical division of the "Manhattan Project" document highly controversial findings. For instance, toxic accidents in the vicinity of fluoride-producing facilities like the one near Lower Penns Neck, New Jersey, left crops poisoned or blighted, and humans and livestock sick. Symptoms noted in the findings included extreme joint stiffness, uncontrollable vomiting and diarrhea, severe headaches, and death. These and other facts from the secret documents directly contradict the findings concurrently published in scientific journals which praised the positive effects of fluoride.

Regional environmental fluoride releases in the northeast United States also resulted in several legal suits against the government by farmers after the end of World War II, according to Griffiths and Bryson. Military and public health officials feared legal victories would snowball, opening the door to further suits which might have kept the bomb program from continuing to use fluoride. With the Cold War underway, the New Jersey lawsuits proved to be a roadblock to America's already full-scale production of atomic weapons. Officials were subsequently ordered to protect the interests of the government.

After the war, experimentation and the dissemination of misinformation continued. Most notably, the authors state, bomb program scientists embarked on a campaign to calm the social panic about fluoride in the early 1950s, through lectures on fluoride toxicology and by promoting its usefulness in preventing tooth decay. Bomb program scientists played a leading role in the design and implementation of a fluoride study conducted in Newburgh, New York, from 1945 to 1956 in which fluoride was secretly added to public drinking water. In a classified follow-up operation referred to as "Program F," blood and tissue samples were covertly collected from Newburgh citizens with the assistance of the State Health Department. The government eagerly studied the effects of fluoride in Newburgh, as a community-level fluoride exposure experiment.

The formerly top-secret papers—including letters, memos, and health reports—raise important questions about the U.S. government's possible conflict of interest regarding fluoride use and promotion. If lower dose ranges were found hazardous by the Manhattan Project studies, these findings "might have opened the bomb program and its contractors up to lawsuits for injury to human health, as well as public outcry," say the authors. The documents also state that "clinical evidence suggests that uranium hexafluoride may have a rather marked central nervous system effect.... It seems most likely that the F [code for fluoride] component rather than the T [code for the uranium] is the causative factor."

It is feared that the Manhattan Project agenda directed researchers away from objectively evaluating the effects of fluoride well into the Cold War. "Information was buried," concludes Dr. Phyllis Mullenix, the former head of toxicology at Forsyth Dental Center in Boston who was interviewed by Griffiths and Bryson. "There is so much fluoride exposure now, and we simply do not know what it is doing."

UPDATE BY AUTHORS JOEL GRIFFITHS AND CHRIS BRYSON: "It's an old story, fluoride. The early U.S. industrial polluters and their victims knew it best. It was just another day for them when the government announced fluoride would reduce children's cavities. They would have been much better at enlightening the public about fluoride than the dentists of today, but they're gone now.

"The fluoride story is a hangover from the Cold War, when the U.S. media would not abrogate 'national security.' They publicized the official line about fluoride,

and that was that. The critical role of fluoride in the production of the atomic bomb and in many of the new industrial processes (rocket propellants, fluorocarbons, plastics, etc.) that made America the world's leader after World War II was never mentioned. The nationwide damage wreaked by industrial fluoride pollution, and the role and motives of the bomb program and U.S. industry in establishing fluoride's safety, was not mentioned either.

"At least a dozen mainstream media outlets here and in the U.K. expressed strong interest in our story, but all later declined. The facts were never in question. The 155 pages of supporting documentation are available for the cost of mailing from *Waste Not*, Tel: (315) 379-9200. For further information, contact Dr. William Hirzy, Senior vice-president, National Treasury Employees Union, EPA Headquarters chapter, Tel: (202) 260-4683; or e-mail: hirzy.john@epa. gov. Also Mike Ewall, Pennsylvania Environmental Network, Tel: (215) 743-4884; or e-mail: pen@envirolink.org."

19 CENSORED

Clinton Administration Lobbied for Retention of Toxic Chemicals in Children's Toys

Source:
MULTINATIONAL MONITOR
Title: "Out of the Mouths of Babes"
Date: June 1998
Author: Charlie Gray

SSU Censored Researchers:
Scott Gross and Brooke Herron
SSU Faculty Evaluator: Richard Gale

Mainstream media coverage:
Associated Press, *Press Democrat*,
November 14, 1998, page A1

The Clinton Administration and the Commerce Department have lobbied on behalf of U.S. toy and chemical manufacturers against proposed new European Union (EU) restrictions which would prevent children's exposure to toxic chemicals released by polyvinyl chloride (PVC) toys such as teething rings. Documents obtained under the Freedom of Information Act (FOIA), suggesting that the U.S. government lobbied at the behest of toymaker Mattel and chemical manufacturer Exxon, may help explain the European Commission's rejection of the proposed emergency ban. A cable from Vernon Weaver, the U.S. Representative to the EU in Brussels, sent "heartfelt thanks" to Washington and U.S. missions in Europe for "making contact" with member state representatives of the EU Product Safety Emergencies Committee. "We are told by Exxon Chemical Europe Inc. that the input was very effective and the weigh-in was invaluable."

Health authorities in several European countries, including Austria, Belgium, Denmark, Germany, and the Netherlands, have recommended a ban on PVC toys, such as teething rings and bath toys. The Spanish government requested action by the EU in March 1998. PVC, or polyvinyl chloride (also known as vinyl), is a common plastic that frequently contains toxic additives. *The Front* reports that no major U.S. retailers have taken precautionary action, chiefly because the U.S. Consumer Product Safety Commission (CPSC), which is responsible for toy safety regulations, has yet to take action.

At issue, writes Mr. Gray, are a family of chemicals called phthalates (phthalic esters or benzenedicarboxylic acid esters). Phthalates are used primarily as plasticizer additives to give vinyl products softness and elasticity. Plasticizers comprise over half the weight of some flexible vinyl products. Ninety-five percent of phthalates are used in the production of vinyl products. Although phthalates vary in toxicity, the most widely-used phthalates, DEHP [di(2-ethylhexyl)phthalate], have been linked in animal studies to a variety of illnesses including reproductive damage and damage to the kidneys and liver. Several agencies, including the U.S. Environmental Protection Agency (EPA), have labeled DEHP a probable human carcinogen. Other studies suggest that phthalates or their metabolites can interact synergistically with other common chemical contaminants, may be slightly estrogenic, can affect blood pressure and heart rate, and may cause asthma when absorbed on airborne particles.

The simple truth about phthalates toxicity is revealed by the warning label on a bottle of DINP, the phthalate most commonly found in toys. The label on a bottle of DINP, sold to an experimental laboratory, says, "May cause cancer; harmful by inhalation, in contact with skin, and if swallowed; possible risk of irreversible effects; avoid exposure; and wear suitable protective clothing, gloves, and eye/face protection." Although no standard method exists for the investigation of release of phthalates from toys, a group of Danish scientists found significant migration of phthalates used in toys. Some of Denmark's biggest retailers then took precautionary action by pulling a number of chewable PVC toys off their shelves. Since then, a number of retailers in Spain, Italy, Germany, the Netherlands, and Belgium have stopped selling PVC teething toys. Several European retailers, including Foetex and FDB in Denmark, and Brio and KF in Sweden, have already recalled PVC toys. The makers of Lego are eliminating soft PVC toys from their product line entirely. U.S. toymakers did voluntarily substitute another phthalate for DEHP in the mid 1980s, after the CPSC looked into the leaching of DEHP from teethers.

The Associated Press story dated November 14, 1998, while listing the deleterious effects of the plasticizers, states that "the process that caused the liver damage in animals does not occur in humans." No mention is made about the strong lobbying efforts made by the United States on behalf of U.S. toy manufacturers and chemical manufacturers, after which the European Commission rejected the proposed emergency ban.

UPDATE BY AUTHOR CHARLIE GRAY: "Since our story about PVC in toys came out in the *Multinational Monitor*, media interest has grown tremendously. ABC's *20/20* ran a major story in November. Many network affiliates and major newspapers, including *The New York Times*, the *Washington Post*, the *Los Angeles Times* [and *The San Francisco Chronicle*] picked up the story.

"Toy companies have begun to respond. Toys R Us and other retailers pulled vinyl teething rings off their shelves. Mattel announced in September that it would soon stop selling vinyl toys containing phthalate additives for kids under three. Little Tikes said it would go entirely PVC-free. Most manufacturers followed Mattel, pledging only to take the phthalates out of their toys. This fails to address other important problems posed by PVC, including dioxins produced when it is made or burned, and the many other toxic additives (including some phthalate replacements) used to make it flexible and stable. Safer, naturally flexible plastics are available for toys and other products.

"There has been a considerable backlash coming mostly from the chemical and vinyl industries. That's because there's a lot more at stake than toys—'the industry will go the way toys go,' one industry official told the *Wall Street Journal* (November 12). Numerous corporate front groups have blitzed the media with op-eds characterizing the issue as one based on emotion rather than science. Look for future stories about PVC medical products, construction materials, etc."

For more information on PVC and other toxic chemical issues contact Greenpeace, Tel: (800) 326-0959 or (202) 462-1177; http://www.greenpeace.org/~campaigns/toxics

20 CENSORED

Developers Build on Flood Plains at Taxpayers' Expense

Source:
MOTHER JONES
Title: "Rain Check"
Date: March/April 1998, Vol. 23, issue 2
Author: Marc Herman

SSU Censored Researcher:
Brooke Herron
SSU Faculty Evaluator: Bryan Baker

According to the Federal Emergency Management Agency (FEMA), some 10 million people in the U.S. currently live on flood plains. Of these households at risk of flooding, only one-fourth actually carries insurance; the rest will rely on federal disaster relief funds if their homes are flooded. Many of these people face repeated flooding, and the American taxpayer is paying the tab.

Flood plains are nice flat places to build homes and businesses. Developers get a sweet deal from the government at the expense of U.S. taxpayers. As long as there is proof of economic benefit for developing in flood plains, developers can obtain: (1) a government-built levee to protect their investment, (2) the government's near total subsidy of repairs should flood damage occur, and (3) the right to offer property buyers guaranteed, federally underwritten flood insurance policies through the National Flood Insurance Program.

The government's levee-building program, started 100 years ago, was based on the logic of financial viability. Lowlands along rivers were desirably productive areas sought for agricultural purposes. The U.S. Army Corps of Engineers would build the levees to protect the land for agricultural use. In recent times, as cities and towns expanded into traditional farming areas, the extension of levee building and maintenance for suburban developments has increased. Damages from a suburban flood can have a significantly higher loss value than flooding of farm land.

Herman writes that the National Association of Home Builders and the National Association of Realtors are two leaders paying lobbyists to actively campaign for continuation of the levee subsidies. Both are big contributors to congressional candidates who support continued levee building and maintenance.

In the Mississippi floods of 1993, taxpayers paid between $12 and $16 billion to cover damages. The Federal Emergency Management Agency created a buyout plan to relocate families living within the boundaries of flood plains. A lot of press attention was given to the relocation of some 900 people who lived in Valmeyer, Illinois, as they moved the entire town to nearby limestone bluffs. The much publicized move was designed to show the public that Congress was doing something in the wake of the 1993 Mississippi floods. The program, however, has only succeeded in relocating 12,000 people, leaving millions still in harm's way.

"Those who extract the most profit from building on the flood plain, experience none of the risk," says Jeffrey Mount, a professor of geology at the University of California, Davis. Mount points out that areas such as Arboga, a town in nearby Yuba County, are being newly zoned for subdivisions on the very same land inundated by floods in 1997. Currently some 58,000 structures are being planned by developers in California Central Valley flood plains. "As long as you can build a house, sell it, and walk away, you will," said Mount.

The Clinton Administration's Council on Environmental Quality opposed the rebuilding of levees following the 1993 floods. Then came the 1994 elections: The Democrats were swept from congressional control and the proposed changes have been lost amid bipartisan bickering.

UPDATE BY AUTHOR MARC HERMAN: "In 1998 the federal government's National Flood Insurance Program wrote an additional $60 billion in policies, and now covers $482.5 billion worth of homes, businesses, and property located in severely flood-prone areas. At the same time, the Federal Emergency Management Agency reported $268 million in damages from floods in 1998, which it called a relatively light year following $687 million in damages in 1997, and $1.1 billion in 1996.

"Meanwhile, flood risks have not changed in the past year, and the failure of policies to address these largely avoidable tragedies has gotten little attention. It is still the case that flood-control levees are maintained by the government if there is an economic incentive to do so, with little thought to the area's history of flood damage. Free repair of those multi-million dollar levees, subsidized flood insurance for people who private insurers won't touch, and the safety net of disaster relief are still considered a dubious sort of protection, but in practice have acted as incentives to stay in flood zones, keeping people in harm's way. And levees continue to fail.

"The year since publication of 'Rain Check' has, fortunately, been a lucky one. Though there was $268 million in flood damage, there was no Grand Forks Flood, Yosemite Flood, Great Mississippi Flood, Texas Flood, Arkansas Flood, or Louisiana Flood, to name just a few disasters of the past decade. On the other hand, when floods aren't on the front page, neither is flood policy; it's hard to write about causes without a show of the effects.

"If flood policy was absent from national newspapers, though, it was not only because of Mother Nature's momentary mercy, but also because some of those involved with the issue have simply given up on the press.

"'I've stopped feeding stories to the newspapers,' said one lobbyist, who asked to remain anonymous. 'Honestly, I really don't need you. I can get things done without it [press coverage],' he said."

21 CENSORED

Global Oil Reserves Alarmingly Over-Estimated

Source:
SCIENTIFIC AMERICAN
Title: "The End of Cheap Oil"
Date: March 1998
Authors: Colin J. Campbell and
Jean H. Laherrere

SSU Censored Researcher:
Rick Krigstein and Diana Nouveaux
SSU Faculty Evaluator: Jim Burkland

Colin J. Campbell and Jean H. Laherrere, two independent oil-industry consultants, predict that global production of conventional oil will start to decline within the next 10 years, and be unable to keep up with demand. Their analysis contradicts oil-industry reports which suggest we have another 50 years worth of cheap oil to sustain us. As the independent report points out, economic and political motives cause oil-producing companies and countries to publish the inflated figure, and this affects all of us.

An estimate of existing oil reserves is one of the factors used to predict the ultimate recovery of oil, that is, all the cheap oil there is to be had. Even with modern technology, says *Scientific American*, estimating reserves is an inexact science. Petroleum engineers express reserves in terms of probability. Geologists may calculate that an oil field has a 90 percent chance of containing 700 million barrels of recoverable oil, but only a 10 percent chance of containing 2,000 million barrels of oil. Many companies and countries, however, freely report their reserves using any figure between 10 and 90 percent depending on which figures serve them best. For example, exaggerated estimates can raise the price of an oil company's stock. Also, a government may use inflated reserve estimates in order to enhance their political clout and their ability to obtain loans.

Member-nations of the Organization of Petroleum Exporting Countries (OPEC) have an even more tangible reason to inflate their reported reserve estimates: the higher their reserves, the more oil they are allowed to export. This represents immediate income for those countries. During the 1980s, 6 of the 11 OPEC nations reported huge increases in their reserve amounts, ranging from 42 to 197 percent. There is good reason to suspect that this was done to increase their export quotas.

Many people believe that improved technology will get more oil out of the ground. It will, but oil companies routinely take improved technology into account when calculating reserve estimates. Current calculations already include improvements in recovery. Campbell and Laherrere's analysis takes other factors into account. For instance, the rate of oil consumption has been rising at over 2 percent per year. The rate of discovery of new oil has been declining. Large reserves of unconventional oil such as heavy oil, tar sands, and shale oil exist, but it is not economically feasible to extract them. Also, to do so might cause extreme environmental damage. Tar-sand oil has to be strip-mined, and heavy oils contain sulfur and heavy metals which must be removed.

Perhaps the biggest reason oil companies grossly inflate cheap oil estimates is that it removes a major motivation to develop alternative energy sources which would directly compete with oil as an energy source. The longer the oil companies (and countries) lull us into thinking there is plenty of cheap oil available, the longer we delay developing solar power, fuel cells and other technologies that could replace oil.

UPDATE BY THE AUTHOR C.J. CAMPBELL: "'The End of Cheap Oil' covered a subject of the utmost importance to our subspecies. Hydrocarbon Man is today virtually the sole surviving human subspecies. He was born 150 years ago and will have become extinct by the end of the next century. The peak of oil production within the next decade will be a turning point with immense political and economic consequences. With about half of the remaining conventional oil lying in five Middle East countries, world tensions are likely to erupt as the industrial countries vie with each other for access. Failure to understand that depletion is a natural phenomenon may lead to misguided military intervention.

"'The End of Cheap Oil' emphasized the atrocious state of public data on production and reserves, which have been corrupted by vested interests. Accordingly, the study evolves all the time as new information on the status of depletion in different countries comes in. The interpretation of the data is, however, simply a case of solving the equation: Peak Discovery + Time = Peak Production.

"The article has been subject to comment in a wide range of serious journals in many countries, including the *Observer* newspaper of London, *Barron's Science*, *Science News*, *Geopolitique*, and *Die Stern*. It has also led to lectures, seminars, and broadcasts. Even aircraft manufacturers and Walt Disney have reacted, seeing the impact on their businesses. But perhaps the most important response is the position of the International Energy Agency, the world's premier authority on energy supply, which has advised the G8 of the impending peak."

Further information and updates may be obtained from Campbell (etanjou@ perigord.com); Laherrere (j.h.laherrere @infonie.fr); and http://www.oil.crisis. com/laherrere

22 CENSORED

Academia at Risk as Tenured Professors Vanish

Sources:
ON CAMPUS
Title: "The Vanishing Professor"
Date: September 1998
Author: Barbara McKenna

SSU Censored Researchers:
Jason L. Sanders, Yuki Ishizaki,
and Aimee Polacci
SSU Faculty Evaluator: Perry Marker

AFT HIGHER EDUCATION
DEPARTMENT REPORT
Title: "The Vanishing Professor"
http//www.aft.org

The bedrock of higher education, tenured full-time faculty, have become an endangered species. According to the American Federation of Teachers (AFT), the number of tenured full-time faculty is rapidly decreasing on college campuses. Full-time faculty are being replaced by part-time faculty who are paid two-thirds what tenured professors earn, and receive substandard benefits. At least 43 percent of college instructors nationwide are now part-time faculty. The hiring of part-time lecturers increased by 266 percent between 1979 and 1995.

In 1995, 51 percent of the new full-time faculty were appointed to short term, year-to- year positions, which were ineligible for tenure. From 1975 to 1995, the number of full-time instructors on the tenure track actually decreased nationally by 12 percent.

At the University of California, the budget has been cut dramatically since the beginning of the 1990s and the university encouraged over 2,000 early retirements. Today, the teaching staff at the University of California is comprised of only 20 percent tenured or tenure-track faculty; the remainder is made up of 58.2 percent graduate students, 11.6 percent part-timers, and 8.9 percent non-tenure-track instructors.

The City University of New York system, the premier urban higher education system in the United States, suffered a 21 percent decline of full-time faculty between 1987 and 1997.

Nationally, over two-thirds of all faculty at Community Colleges are part-time. On the 106-campus California Community College system, the number of full-time faculty decreased by 8 percent in the last decade while the actual number of students increased by 8 percent. Part-time lecturers have taken up the slack, along with increasing class sizes and speed-ups for the remaining faculty. Today 30,000 part-time faculty, representing twice as many instructors as the full-time tenure faculty, teach 40 percent of the courses in the California Community Colleges.

Part-time faculty are not paid to serve on university committees, seldom participate in shared governance, and are treated as hired hands with lower pay and benefits within university communities. This diminished involvement on campuses can have a demoralizing effect on classroom performance, student access, and the university community as a whole. Tenured faculty have the advantage of being able to maintain high academic standards for students, while temporary part-time faculty may try to please students by giving higher grades and lowering requirements in order to insure higher student evaluations on their performance.

Higher education research in the United States leads the world. Research requires sustained periods of study and experimentation. The increased use of temporary faculty will eventually undermine this important function in the United States.

UPDATE BY AUTHOR BARBARA McKENNA:
"The declining number of full-time tenured faculty is a story that tends to get lost within the larger story of the forces transforming higher education in the 1990s. At the beginning of the decade, cash-strapped states cut funding of the public universities and two-year colleges. When the state economies bounced back, higher education funding did not. Thus, institutions set a course of 'doing more with less' that has brought a progression of lean, mean accommodations. These include corporatizing and downsizing operations and service, relying on a less expensive labor force (part-time and adjunct faculty, full-time, temporary instructors, graduate teaching assistants), and embracing technology and distance learning as an alternative to providing face-to-face instruction. If the effect of these accommodations would be a decline in the quality of education provided, it would be the full-time tenured faculty who, in a proprietary way, would note it and oppose it. Quietly allowing these faculty to retire and not be replaced makes it easier for institutions to put cost efficiency, rather than educational quality and serving students, as their first priority.

"This story has generated great interest among college faculty, some of whom have contacted our union for information on how they might fight the trend. Many readers have shared the story with their college administrations, to remind them that the vanishing professor trend will have an effect on quality down the road. We know they've also sent copies to state legislators. We are not aware of any mainstream press response.

The story was based on a longer report by the same name released by the American Federation of Teachers in July 1998. The report is available at http://www.aft.org/higheduc/professor."

23 CENSORED

Bureau of Land Management Charged with Human Rights Violations Agaist the Shoshone Nation

Source:
NEWS FROM INDIAN COUNTRY:
THE NATION'S NATIVE JOURNAL
Title: "BLM fines Western Shoshone
$564,000 Despite OAS Request"
Date: May 1998, Vol. 12, No. 9
Author: Pat Calliotte

SSU Censored Researchers:
Amy Loucks and Corrie Robb
SSU Evaluator: Kathleen Kesterke

Mainstream media coverage:
The Salt Lake Tribune, April 29, 1998,
page A12
Dallas Morning News, May 11, 1997,
page A1

A decades-old dispute with the Bureau of Land Management (BLM) has led the Western Shoshone tribe to take the conflict to an international level. What the BLM is calling a grazing issue, the Western Shoshone, a 10,000 member tribe, is calling a systematic and historical discrimination against American Indians. In early April 1998, the BLM fined a Shoshone family who have for decades been tending livestock on their ancestral land. The BLM not only issued an order to the Shosone to remove the livestock from "public land," but also levied fines totaling $564,000 against the Western Shoshone National Council (WSNC) and Mary and Carrie Dann, two sisters of the Shoshone tribe. The Shoshone consider this action to be a denial of their sovereignty and an attempt to interfere with their livelihood. After unsuccessful attempts to negotiate with the BLM and the Department of the Interior, and despite an unfavorable Supreme Court ruling, the Danns have sought the help of an international agency, the Organization of American States (OAS), charging human rights violations. The OAS' Inter-American Commission on Human Rights has asked the United States to "stay" all actions pending further investigations; but, according to *News From Indian Country* (NFIC), the BLM has "not responded" to documents supporting Western Shoshone land rights.

Although a reservation was never created, in 1863, the Western Shoshone signed a pact with the U.S. government to receive food, clothing, and land, in exchange for stopping wagon train raids. A dozen Shoshone warriors signed with "x's" on the pact, dubbed the "Treaty of Peace and Friendship at Ruby Valley." Though in 1979 the Indian Claims Commission ordered the United States to pay the Shoshone $26 million for the land, the money has never been distributed to tribal members and is still, according to *The Salt Lake Tribune*, held "in trust."

Also in that ruling, the *Dallas Morning News* reports, the title was deemed to have been "lost to white encroachment." Although the Shoshone have never accepted payment for the land, in 1985 the Supreme Court upheld that the title of the land had "passed to the federal government," according to *The Tribune*. In that article, the Danns say that the ruling was about whether there was payment, not about whether the Shoshone title is "intact."

While the BLM claims that issues of overgrazing are the main reason for their fines and attempts to remove livestock and other equipment, the *Dallas News* reports that the millions of acres of desolate ranchland is "on the edge of one of the largest gold rushes in recent years, with mining companies scrambling to find gold."

The mining companies are also paying meager penalties for environmental damage, says *News From Indian Country*. The Shoshone assert that the fines aimed at them are unfair compared to the meager penalties imposed upon mining companies for environmental damage on the same land. In 1992, Cortez Gold, which operates in the Crescent Valley near the Dann's land, was initially charged $4,000 for violating their water pollution control permit. According to NFIC, Cortez later struck a deal with the BLM which waived their fine in return for an agreement to build a cattle guard and maintain a fence. In fact, this practice is not unusual and mining companies are rarely, if ever, punished in the first place.

The Western Shoshone do not enjoy the same treatment. The BLM has been unrelenting in their policy enforcement. It has not responded to documents supporting the Shoshone's ancestral claim of the land and has refused repeated requests by WSNC to negotiate. According to the BLM, the $494,000 fine against the WSNC and the $70,000 fine against the Dann family will stand. "Fines are the newest way that the BLM is using to bring an end to traditional Western Shoshone peoples, and our spiritual and cultural ways," said Carrie Dann. "We are tied to this land and we are not leaving."

The fight for what they consider to be sovereignty and human rights has won the Shoshone an international human-rights award in 1993 from the Right Livelihood Foundation in Sweden. The $200,000 award, presented at the Swedish Parliament, was shared with three women from other countries. The Danns used their share to continue their fight on behalf of the Western Shoshone. They and other indigenous-rights activists have also caught the attention of the United Nations.

The Western Shoshone have made several attempts to negotiate the conflict with the Department of Interior and the BLM. The BLM has rejected the offers and continues to insist that the Western Shoshone be in full compliance with BLM regulations.

UPDATE BY AUTHOR PAT CALLIOTTE: "Mary and Carrie Dann are still actively pursuing their complaint before the Organization of American States' (OAS)

Inter-American Commission on Human Rights. This complaint was filed in 1993 by the Indian Law Resource Center on behalf of the Danns and other Western Shoshone to secure their aboriginal rights to their land. Over the past year, tribal resolutions have been passed by Te-Moak, Yomba, Ely, South Fork, Winnemucca, and Timbisha in support of the OAS complaint.

"The Bureau of Land Management is respecting the stay, issued in August 1998 by the Interior Board of Land Appeals (ILBA), for any BLM actions against a sacred hot spring, a cultural and spiritual encampment, and sections of the Dann Ranch that are on traditional Western Shoshone lands in Crescent Valley. The stay, which curbs any fines and other penalties against the Danns or the Western Shoshone National Council, and prohibits the BLM from razing any structures or confiscating any property, is binding until the ILBA rules on the appeal of Trespass Decisions issued on May 26, 1998.

"Other Western Shoshone not covered in the appeal, who continue to graze their traditional lands, are currently still subjected to BLM issuance of orders, fines and notices of impoundment. The Indian Law Resource Center hired a DC-based firm, the Hauser Group, to promote mainstream media coverage on the Western Shoshone/OAS issue. Tracy Zimmerman of the Hauser Group said that there was some media interest, but in midsummer there was nothing fresh occurring to encourage mainstream media to run the story."

For more information:

Indian Law Resource Center, 602 North Ewing Street, Nelena, MT 59601, Tel: (406) 449-2006; or Fax: (406) 449-2031.

Western Shoshone Defense Project, PO Box 211308, Crescent Valley, NV 89821, Tel: (775) 468-0230; or http://www.alphacdc.com/wsdp.

24 CENSORED

Coca-Cola Fails to Meet Recycling Pledge

Source:
EARTH ISLAND JOURNAL
Title: "Coca-Cola: Recycling Outlaw"
Date: Winter 1998
Author: Marti Matsch

SSU Censored Researchers:
Jason Bothwell and Aimee Polacci
SSU Faculty Evaluator: Mary Gomes

In the next 24 hours U.S. consumers will use 50 million #1 polethyene therephthalate (PET) plastic soda bottles. As quickly as we throw them away, the plastic bottle industry extracts more nonrenewable resources from the earth to make 50 million new soda bottles for us to toss away again. Some soda bottles will be recycled and converted into carpeting, bleaches, or jacket-fill—but not into new bottles.

In 1990 Coca-Cola made a promise to

use its recycled plastic bottles in new production as it has successfully done in Europe and numerous other countries. Eight years later they have yet to follow through with that promise. This failure to act has kept the price of recycled PET bottles low in the marketplace and discouraged expanded PET recycling programs nationwide.

One organization that has tried to change the way the industry is doing things is the Grass Roots Recycling Network (GRRN). GRRN wrote to Coca-Cola in 1997, asking that it live up to its promises. GRRN asked Coca-Cola, as the leader in the soda industry, to begin immediately noting on their labels the percentage of recycled materials being used, begin using refillable bottles, and establish a voluntary deposit on Coca-Cola containers. Coca-Cola refused to even respond to the letter and has made no comment to date on the request.

GRRN is keeping the pressure on. They have initiated a petition asking Coca-Cola to "Do The Real Thing" and support recycling. When GRRN posted

information on the Internet, 25 independent voluntary actions against Coke were staged across the country. Boycotts are being planned on university and college campuses in many different states.

Fourteen percent of airborne toxic emissions come from plastics production. The average plastics plant can discharge as much as 500 gallons of contaminated wastewater per minute. If Coca-Cola were to immediately move into even a 25 percent recycled content for their bottles, says Matsch, significant progress could be made on recycling in the United States. The price for PET bulk recycled product would increase and financial incentives would make recycling far more attractive to cities and recyclers throughout the United States.

The cost of using recycled bottles is actually quite low. Soda companies are making an average of 21 cents on each new bottle. The cost of using recycled bottles would only cost .01 cent more per bottle. So Coca-Cola which now makes an average 21 cents per bottle profit would still make 20.9 cents on each bottle with

THIS MODERN WORLD by TOM TOMORROW

THIS IS TRUE: A HIGH SCHOOL IN EVANS, GA., RECENTLY HELD A SPECIAL "COKE IN EDUCATION" DAY-- AS PART OF AN EFFORT TO WIN A $500 PRIZE FROM THE COCA COLA COMPANY...*

$500!? WHY, THEIR GENEROSITY IS SURPASSED ONLY BY THEIR EXPERTISE IN PRODUCING *DELICIOUS CARBONATED BEVERAGES!*

YES--THAT'S *ALMOST ENOUGH* TO BUY EACH OF OUR STUDENTS A REFRESHING, ICE COLD CAN OF *COCA COLA--* AMERICA'S *FAVORITE* SOFT DRINK!

ACCORDING TO A.P., THE SCHOOL "INVITED A COKE MARKETING EXECUTIVE TO ADDRESS ECONOMICS STUDENTS, HAD CHEMISTRY STUDENTS ANALYZE THE SUGAR CONTENT OF COKE, AND USED A COCA-COLA CAKE RECIPE IN HOME ECONOMICS..."

SO WHAT HAVE WE LEARNED TODAY, CHILDREN?

UM--COKE HAS A *LOT* OF SUGAR...

...AND CAN BE USED AS AN INGREDIENT IN SICKLY SWEET BAKED GOODS!

VERY GOOD!

*AND, TO BE FAIR, A SHOT AT A $10,000 NATIONAL PRIZE. BUT *STILL*....

a full recycling program in place. Coca-Cola used to use returnable glass bottles but they now produce all their store-shelf products in plastic. There is no apparent reason why Cola-Cola can not use recycled bottles. Eight years is long enough for Coca-Cola to "do the real thing."

UPDATE BY AUTHOR MARTI MATSCH: "More than a year after the campaign against Coca-Cola was launched, Coca-Cola still has not answered consumer demands to use recycled plastic bottles. They are shifting their packaging from recycled aluminum and glass to non-recycled plastic. Every second, 200 plastic bottles made of virgin, non-renewable resources are landfilled, while hazardous emissions poison our environment. Meanwhile, their increased demand for virgin plastic drove prices down which added $150 million to their bottom line in one year.

"The Grass Roots Recycling Network (GRRN) has responded with a new, 'Take it Back!' campaign. Consumers are encouraged to mail empty plastic Coke bottles to the company's CEO, demand-

ing the company take responsibility for its packaging and use recycled plastic.

"Interest has sparked nationwide. Dozens of protest events have been held, and 81 organizations in 26 states have endorsed the campaign. The issue has not, however, received extensive coverage in the mainstream press. Small town newspapers, alternative publications, and the Internet have been the primary source of information."

WHAT YOU CAN DO:

1. Mail rinsed, flattened plastic Coke bottles (with the cap) back to Coca-Cola addressed to Chairman and CEO M. Douglas Investor, One Coca-Cola Plaza, Atlanta, GA 30313. Put a mailing label on the bottle with a 55 cent stamp. No envelope or package is needed.

2. Call Coke at (800) 571-2653 and tell them you won't buy Coke until they use recycled plastic.

3. Contact GRRN for more info or to organize a protest in your community. Tel: (706) 613-7121; e-mail: zerowaste @grrn.org; http://www.grrn.org.

25 CENSORED

ABC Broadcasts Slanted Report on Mumia Abu-Jamal

Sources:
REFUSE AND RESIST
Title: "A Case Study in Irresponsible Journalism"

www.walrus.con/~reist/
mumia/061881kgov.html
Authors: C. Clark Kissinger and Leonard Weinglass

REVOLUTIONARY WORKER
Title: "KGO-TV Report: A Case Study in Irresponsible Journalism"
Date: June 28, 1998
Authors: C. Clark Kissinger and Leonard Weinglass

SSU Censored Researchers:
Tom Ladegaard, Jason Sanders, and Corrie Robb
SSU Faculty Evaluator:
Elizabeth Martinez

On May 7 and 8, 1998, KGO-TV, an ABC affiliate in San Francisco, broadcast a two-part series attacking the international movement to prevent the execution of Mumia Abu-Jamal. Mumia, a black activist, has been on death row in the state of Pennsylvania for 16 years for the killing of a Philadelphia police officer in 1981. A large international movement has been active in demanding a retrial of his case that would include evidence not covered in his first trial.

KGO claimed to do an objective review of the case. KGO staff interviewed supporters of Mumia and many people from the other side. The final broadcast presented a very one-sided story, however, claiming that the evidence indeed showed that Mumia was guilty, and that four eyewitnesses saw the shooting. Only four eyewitnesses originally testified in the trial and their stories were not in complete agreement, but an additional six witnesses were added in the 1995-96-97 hearings for a new trial. Four of the new witnesses claimed that they saw another man running away from the scene at the time of the shooting (Mumia was shot by the police officer and was arrested on the scene). Additionally, the slain officer was found with a driver's license of another person in his possession. KGO did not report about the third person running away, nor about the driver's license.

KGO also asserted that, "In fact, there was extensive ballistics testimony, and although the bullets were mangled, tests showed them to be .38 caliber, with marking consistent with Jamal's gun." Weinglass and Kissinger report, however, that the medical examiner who removed the bullet from the officer's body reported it to be a .44 caliber slug. Furthermore, Mumia was never tested for nitrate residues to prove that he had recently fired a gun, nor was his gun tested to see if it had been recently fired. None of these challenging facts were presented by KGO in their broadcast.

KGO included an interview with the widow of the slain police officer. She told an emotional story about how, during the trial, when her husband's uniform was shown as evidence, Mumia turned around to her and smiled. The problem with this story is that, according to the [official] transcript, Mumia was absent from the courtroom on the day the shirt was displayed, say the authors.

The authors also claim that all of the above evidence and much more was given to KGO and that they have a tape of the KGO interview. KGO had every reason to know that much of the material they were presenting as fact was contested by knowledgeable parties to the case. Yet they failed to present the counter-arguments, thereby making Mumia look guilty and discrediting activists worldwide who have been calling for a retrial of the case.

UPDATE BY AUTHOR CLARK KISSINGER:
"We chose to expose the KGO-TV series on Mumia Abu-Jamal because we suspected that it was a pilot for an attack by the national network. In June the Fraternal Order of Police raised the money to place a full-page ad in *The New York Times* calling for Jamal's execution. On December 9, ABC's news magazine program *20/20* ran a half-hour segment on Jamal, which repeated most of the outrageous claims in the KGO report. Once again fresh interviews were done with the prosecutor and the widow of the slain

police officer, but Jamal was not allowed to speak.

"ABC's excuse for not interviewing Jamal was a new state prison regulation prohibiting recorded interviews with any prisoners. When Jamal's challenge to this regulation was accepted by the Federal District Court in Pittsburgh on December 7, ABC rushed to air the material they had on December 9 before a federal court could make Jamal available. The segment was hosted by White House correspondent Sam Donaldson.

"ABC's attitude was expressed well in a letter to prison authorities suggesting that they should be allowed to interview Jamal because they were going to set the record straight and counteract an alleged excess of pro-Jamal material in the media. The letter went on to state: 'We are currently working in conjunction with Maureen Faulkner and the Philadelphia Fraternal Order of the Police.' For further information on the case and the media controversy, see http://www.calyx.com/~refuse."

Project Censored Honorable Mentions for 1998

PUBLIC CITIZEN'S HEALTH RESEARCH

Title: "International Comparison of Drug Prices: Antidepressants and Antipsychotics"
Date: November 17, 1998
Authors: Larry D. Sassich, Pharm. D., M.P.H., FASHP, E. Fuller Torrey, M.D. and Sidney Wolfe, M.D.

Pharmaceutical prescription prices in the United States are, on the average, twice as high as those in other countries for the same drugs.

CAQ

Title: "U.S. Intervention in Cambodia: From Bombs to Ballots"
Date: Fall 1997
Author: David Roberts

The United States has worked against the democratic process in Cambodia by interfering with free elections and promoting specific pro-U.S. candidates.

COUNTERPUNCH

Title: "How GM (with Jesse Jacksons's Help) Screws Its Black Dealers"
Date: November 1-15, 1997, Vol. 4, No. 19
Authors: Ken Silverstein and Alexander Cockburn

General Motors has been undermining African-American car dealers. When one dealer turned to Jesse Jackson for help, Jackson instead cut a deal with GM.

THE TEXAS OBSERVER

Title: "Death in the Desert"
Date September 25, 1998
Author: Debbie Nathan

Deaths of illegal immigrants along the U.S./Mexico border have skyrocketed in recent years.

AFRICA NEWS

Title: "Sudan: U.S. Bombing"
Will Worsen
Date: August 27, 1998
Author: Nhial Bol

The U.S. bombing of a pharmaceutical factory in Sudan accomplished nothing except to worsen the health and economic problems faced by the Sudanese people, halting their ability to produce antibiotics and other life-saving drugs.

SAN FRANCISCO BAY GUARDIAN

Title: "Slow Motion Execution: AIDS"
Date: December 17, 1997
Authors: Dennis Bernstein and Leslie Kean

In Burma, the threat of exposure to the AIDS virus, along with medical reuse of needles, is being used to intimidate and infect outspoken political prisoners in the pro-democracy movement.

SAN FRANCISCO BAY GUARDIAN

Title: "The Fisher King"
Date: August 12, 1998
Author: Daniel Zoll

Don Fisher, founder and CEO of the Gap empire has become a major, unelected political power in the San Francisco Bay area and beyond. He helped to shape NAFTA and GATT, advocated for the commercialization of KQED; and helps to fund and lobby for privatization of a national park (the Presidio) and public schools (Thomas Edison and UCSF Mission Bay). This Republican apparel magnate is a growing force.

COLOMBIA BULLETIN

Title: "Caught in the Crossfire"
Date: Spring 1998
Author: Robin Lloyd

Rural Colombian families are caught in a crossfire of harmful chemical herbicides sprayed on their land, water, and food crops, by low flying planes, in the name of "the war on drugs."

EXTRA

Title: "Out of Sight, Out of Mind"
Date: November/December 1997, Vol. 10, No. 6
Author: Neil Demause

Since the passage of welfare reform, 1.4 million people have been dropped from the welfare rolls—but where have they gone? Neither the government nor the press seem to know or care.

MULTINATIONAL MONITOR

Title: "The Oil Royalty"
Date: March 1998
Author: Jennifer Schecter

U.S. oil companies are seeking legislation to allow them to pay royalties on federal oil and gas taken from federal lands, with a share of the oil and gas removed.

THE NATION

Title: "Tortured Logic from Langley's Spies"
Date: November 10, 1997
Author: David Corn

The CIA's history in Honduras includes the training and protection of torturers.

RACHEL'S ENVIRONMENT & HEALTH WEEKLY

Title: Landfills are Dangerous
Date: September 24, 1998
Author: Peter Montague

New studies show higher cancer rates for people living near landfills.

BUNDESTAG PRESS

Title: "Screwworm"
Date: September 7, 1998
Author: George Pumphrey

The CIA may have deliberately spread screwworms in Iraq to destroy their livestock populations and undermine Saddam Hussein.

EXTRA

Title: "The Global Media Giants"
Date: November/December 1997,
Vol. 10, No. 6
Author: Robert W. McChesney
Free press is facing extinction. Control of global media and information is now down to nine multinational corporations.

MOTHER JONES

Title: "Iceland's Blond Ambition"
Date: May/June 1998
Author: Eliot Marshall

Private companies in Switzerland and Iceland are hoping to cash in on and own the unique genetic heritage of the Icelandic people.

CAQ

Title: "The Battle for the Airwaves:
Free Radio vs. The Feds"
Date: Fall 1997, No. 62
Author: Lawrence Soley

Microradio stations are the free speech movement of the '90s, using the First Amendment to challenge the Federal Communications Commission.

THE PROGRESSIVE

Title: "The Pentagon's New Toy"
Date: July 1998
Author: Michael Klare

The new Objective Individual Combat Weapon, developed by the U.S. Army can kill hidden targets by exploding a grenade behind or above them, taking military horror to a new high.

CAQ

Title: "Apartheid's Poison Legacy:
South Africa's Chemical and Biological Warfare Program"
Date: Winter 1998, No. 63
Author: De Wet Potgieter

New information is coming to light on South Africa's chemical and biological warfare (CWB) program. The alleged crimes include the combat use of chemical weapons, the intent to spread cholera and yellow fever in neighboring countries, the distribution of drugs in the South African ghettos, the establishment of illicit drug factories in neighboring countries to fund covert projects, and a seemingly endless list of political poisonings and assassinations.

COMMENTS BY PROJECT CENSORED NATIONAL JUDGES

DONNA ALLEN, president of the Women's Institute for Freedom of the Press; founding editor of Media Report to Women: "It is startling to note that nearly all of these stories are at least partially about damage to our environment, a battle we thought we had won back in the 1960s and 1970s, when we brought the problem to public attention for the first time in history. Obviously that battle is won only as long as we are able to keep before the public the continuing corporate and government/military pollution of our air, water, food, earth, and sky. But can we do that?

"The real lesson is in what this tells us about our corporate media. They claim it is their job to keep the public informed. Yet, we can see the vital information in these many stories that they almost totally ignored, though it comes from and affects a significant proportion of the public. And, even as they claim to be a 'watchdog' on government, we see here their near total lack of coverage of the U.S. military's pollution and other damage to the environment. And again there is the non-coverage of a significant proportion of citizens who are trying to inform the public.

"Isn't it time we assembled a class action suit to reverse the 1886 Santa Clara Supreme Court decision that held corporations to be 'persons' under the First Amendment? We need to return the media to the people, so it serves the citizens it was intended to serve—and not corporate wealth. Only greater equality of communication outreach is going to enable us to get these important facts to the public for corrective action."

SUSAN FALUDI, Pulitzer Prize-winning journalist: "For anybody who wondered if the media's 'All-Monica-All-the-Time' fixation would have a deleterious effect on the coverage of the news, all you have to do is glance at this past year's *Censored* list. It's brimming over with uncovered crucial stories which have devastating implications for the world's future health and well-being. I had a very difficult time this year narrowing the list down to the 10 most important. They were all important. Many of them shared an underlying story: the disturbing consequences of the rise of a global economy. It's distressing that at the very time the world is going global, the media have narrowed their sights to an Oval Office broom closet."

CARL JENSEN, Project Censored founder and director emeritus: "The censored news stories of 1988 confirm, once again, the continued and increasing need for Project Censored.

"Despite increased criticism and outrage by some media groups and members of the general public, the mainstream media couldn't control themselves in 1998 when it came to junk food news coverage. The near-pornographic coverage of every aspect of President Clinton's relationship with Monica Lewinsky embarrassed real journalists. There was a time when you could not tell the difference between *The New York Times* and *The National Inquirer.* Unfortunately, the headlines covering the Clinton affair were often interchangeable between the two publications.

"The continuing failure of the media to cover critical issues, such as those cited by Project Censored, is highlighted by the reappearance of censored stories over the years. Stories reported in 1998 that had previously been cited by the Project as overlooked issues included pesticides and cancer (1976 and 1980), the fluoridation issue (1991), genetically altered seeds (1987), and the downgrading of radioactive waste levels (1989). It's troubling that we have to continue reminding the national press of the same critical issues that should have been covered much earlier."

NANCY KRANICH, associate dean of the New York University Libraries: "Reading this year's Project Censored nominations was a pleasant diversion from reading the news—no hint of Monica Lewinsky, impeachment, partisan politics or international monetary crimes. Instead, the stories focused on threats to human life, corporate control, and U.S. domination of world developments. On the one hand, reading these stories was a relief from the daily barrage of political manipulation and sensationalized crime stories. On the other hand, the reality that the grave dangers facing our world are so grossly underreported reminds me that our freedoms and future are threatened by a media caught up in promoting the will of multinational conglomerates whose interests lie more in co-modifying information and maximizing profits than informing the public.

"As a librarian, I fear the effects of a narrowly-cast published base of information. It is the mission of libraries to provide a broad diversity of sources on all topics from many points of view. Conglomeration in the publishing arena has resulted in fewer and fewer marginal ideas emerging in print. Unfortunately, ideas outside the mainstream rarely appeal to the 'infotainment' industry, which reaps rich returns on stories embraced by the marketplace. Libraries mirror society's thinking and culture. They collect what is produced, from commercial and non-profit publishers. If the output of our publishing industry does not include the breadth of ideas and points of view expressed by a highly diverse public, then the institutions collecting the record of our achievements cannot fully reflect the entire array of knowledge so essential to advancing society as well as nourishing individual growth."

WILLIAM LUTZ, professor of English, Rutgers University: "It is always difficult to spot the really important news when it happens—Sir Alexander Fleming's discovery of penicillin wasn't big news the year it occurred. Yet, over time, Project Censored has demonstrated a remarkable ability to find the really important stories buried beneath the flotsam that passes for news these days. With increasing regularity, we find that a story cited by Project Censored years ago is now recognized as important. So, too, with this year's nominees. I think that a number of stories this year will prove to be among the most significant of the year. Here are the stories that the mainstream news media don't find interesting or entertaining enough, stories that don't lend themselves to sound bites, stories that well-coiffured talking heads don't find 'sexy.' Instead, Project Censored finds the stories about the people and events that really affect our lives, stories about the corruption of the judicial system, the spread of breast cancer, the control of the world economy by a select few, and much more. Project Censored continues to do the job of the mainstream press, the job that is the essential function of the press in a democracy."

JULIANNE MALVEAUX, economist, columnist, president and CEO of Last Word Productions, Inc.: "How does one speak truth to power? In the United States, a free press helps articulate the truth. Unfortunately, the majority of the press does not often embrace a description of police brutality, an assault on women's health, or the exploitation and unfair fining of Native American people. The beauty of the Internet, of the alternative press, of the Project Censored process, is that there are ways to lift these truths up and to use them as a stinging indictment of both the ossification of power and the myopia of the mainstream press.

"Because the United States continues to experience economic expansion, I am especially interested in the question of 'expansion for whom?' If this is as good as it gets, why the police brutality, the growth of the prison industrial complex, the abuse of children through the development of toxic toys? There is another set of untold stories that we've ignored here—stories of poverty, the failure of welfare reform, the status of subminimum wage workers, the hostility toward immigrants, and the demonization of the poor. In any case, those economic forces that dictate the difference between Wall Street and Main Street are our nation's greatest untold story. I'd like to see far more focus on the economic trends that represent the ugly underbelly of economic 'expansion' as part of the Project Censored report.

"This year's set of most censored stories touches on some of those economic themes, but more broadly on the issue of speaking truth to power, of shedding light on dark, dirty secrets, some generations old. This year's set of censored stories reminds us to seek out alternative sources of information, and to remember the issue of social, political, and economic bias as we consume mainstream news."

JACK NELSON, professor emeritus: "If there is such a thing as a depressing pleasure, it is illustrated in selecting the '10 Best *Censored* Stories' each year: 'Depressing,' in that so many important stories are so widely under-reported in the mass media, and seem to recur in the packets sent to judges; and 'pleasure,' in helping to bring visibility to these stories. This year, I selected several stories related to health problems and potential large-scale international public health crises. If information is power, we need to further empower the public to insist on more complete knowledge and monitoring of possible health predicaments. Bring back Upton Sinclair and other Muckrakers!"

HERBERT I. SCHILLER, professor emeritus of Communications at the University of California, San Diego: "Individual cases are important, but in my judgment, more important are the processes which produce consequences. These are far more difficult to get at but crucial if popular understanding is to be widened. Several of Project Censored's stories, thankfully, are in this category. The extent of corporate takeover of the present informational/cultural environment is beyond most people's imaginations. This has to be the target of your efforts. Actually, it is exciting to document and analyze the current scene at this starting point. The many pieces of the puzzle come together."

SHEILA RABB WEIDENFELD, president of D.C. Productions: "Once again, Project Censored shines a spotlight on stories that are too complex, too intellectually demanding, or too uncomfortable for an affluent country to face. American mainstream journalism's preoccupation with Monica Lewinsky this year has diverted our attention from stories like China's abuse of women, major producers of carcinogenic products who profit from cancer treatment, and the ticking time bomb of the polio vaccine. 'Junk food journalism,' as Carl Jensen calls it, still rules.

"Network executives wonder why they continue to lose viewers. It is not the overabundance of news reporting, though between cable and the Internet, news/information is available 24 hours a day. It is because people are not getting the news that touches their daily lives."

HOWARD ZINN, historian: "I think the censored stories on events abroad, like the massacre at Acteal and Chevron's activities in Nigeria, are especially important because what happens overseas is especially easy to conceal.

"The selections represent a good balance between issues of foreign policy and domestic matters.

"What I find particularly flagrant is the absence in the media of historical background to current events. Without that, the public has no way of evaluating what is happening today."

CHAPTER 2

Censored Déjà Vu: What Happened to Last Year's Most Censored Stories

BY VICTORIA CALKINS, CORRIE ROBB, CRAIG CHAPMAN, & PROJECT CENSORED

Chapter 2 is designed to give readers a 1998 update on the top stories from previous years. This year's focus is on 1998 coverage of stories from 1997 and 1996. For follow-ups on previously under-covered news stories in the United States, an excellent reference is *20 Years of Censored News* by Carl Jensen & Project Censored (Seven Stories Press, 1997). *20 Years* gives updates on the *Censored* stories for the years 1976 to 1995 and is available direct from the publisher (Tel: (800) 596-7437) and in bookstores nationwide.

CLINTON ADMINISTRATION AGGRESSIVELY PROMOTES U.S. ARMS SALES WORLDWIDE

Over the course of the Clinton Administration the United States has risen to become the world's leading arms merchant. U.S. weapons are used in almost every global conflict, taking a devastating toll on civilians, U.S. military personnel, and the socioeconomic status of many developing nations.

In June 1997, the House of Representatives overwhelmingly passed the Arms Transfer Code of Conduct. These important pieces of legislation prohibited U.S. commercial arms sales, or military assistance and training, to foreign governments that are undemocratic, abuse human rights, or engage in aggression against neighboring states. Still, the Clinton Administration, in conjunction with the Defense, Commerce, and State Departments, has continued to aggressively promote U.S. arms industry sales on all levels. The U.S. percentage of global arms sales jumped from 16 percent in 1988 to 63 percent today, while U.S. foreign military aid amounted to $36 billion in Clinton's first year in office.

The majority of U.S. weaponry is sold to strife-torn regions such as the Middle East. The sales and accumulation of such weapons fan the flames of war rather than promote peace, and, ironically, place U.S. soldiers based around the world at mounting risk. The last five times U.S. troops were sent into conflict, they found themselves battling forces who had previously received U.S. weapons, military technology, or training. At the same time, the Pentagon, backed by the arms industry, uses the presence of advanced U.S. weapons in foreign arsenals to argue for increased weapons spending to preserve U.S. military superiority.

SOURCES: Lora Lumpe, "Costly Giveaways," *The Bulletin of Atomic Scientists*, October 1996; Martha Honey, "Guns 'R' Us," *In These Times*, August 11, 1997.

COVERAGE 1998: During 1998, the mainstream U.S. media continued to pay little attention to America's leading position in global arms sales and giveaways. A flurry of coverage followed the August 1997 lifting by the Clinton Administration of the imposed moratorium on arms sales to Latin America initially set in place by the Carter Administration. Reports began surfacing mid-October 1997 during Clinton's week-long visit to South America to bring Chilean officials and U.S. arms dealers together. At the same time, Clinton declared Argentina—Chile's rival—a major "non-NATO ally."

Costa Rican President Oscar Arias, winner of the 1987 Nobel Peace Prize, visited several corporate defense industry conferences and U.S. universities where he spoke out against lifting the ban. There was little media coverage as he implored Clinton to allow Latin America the chance to recover from decades of civil war and violence. "In some cases these democracies are still fragile," Arias told the *Christian Science Monitor*. Clinton Administration spokesmen replied that the newly sold weapons "will be good for U.S. jobs and [will] improve the peace in the region." Clinton argued that the region's militaries have a "right and obligation to modernize." Sales of weapons will be selective throughout the area, raising the probability of sales to non-U.S. recipients by other arms-barons like Russia and China. Protests against the lifting by 50 Congressional members went completely unreported. By December 1998, fears of wide-scale arms sales to Latin America had diminished as the global economic downturn decimated the Latin American coffers. Chile, the first country scheduled to make a large purchase after the ban-lift, reneged earlier this year on purchasing 24 fighters.

According to the *Boston Globe*, Congress passed the Pentagon's $248 billion budget by huge margins, "funding a hefty defense program even though there isn't a formidable enemy in sight." The 1998 military budget, on par with the 1980 budget, "is higher than the next eight military spenders in the world combined." A central issue is the power of the defense industry and the fear of lost defense-industry jobs. These are the same corporations (including Lockheed Martin and Boeing) that aggressively lobbied for Clinton to lift the Latin American embargo.

An April *New York Times* report stated that the Senate had "overwhelmingly rejected a measure to limit the cost to American taxpayers of the weapons to three Eastern European countries nominated to join NATO." Concerns were voiced by certain media over the level of U.S. involvement in expanding NATO to include Poland, Hungary, and the Czech Republic. Critics feared the expansion could cost American taxpayers billions of dollars in arms subsidies in addition to the $1.2 billion spent by the United States in the last three years alone. Newly inducted NATO nations are also major recipients of "surplus" arms and weapons systems giveaways.

Finally, in July 1998, Lora Lumpe, one of the original *Censored* authors, was noted in *The New York Times* for her ongoing arms-monitoring at the Association of Atomic Scientists. The piece also revealed that the United States has been the number one seller of arms for the last seven years, and that U.S. sales exceeded $15.2 billion in 1997. This was picked up by a considerable number of regional newspapers around the country. In another *New York Times* story, the Clinton Administration's reported reluctance to upset the gun lobby fueled their hesitation to host a multinational conference on the control of small arms proliferation. While Clinton was anxious to curb the legal sales of light weaponry, an American arms official acknowledged that a significant percentage of legal sales are later re-sold illegally. The action was likened to the U.S. refusal to sign the international ban on land mines.

Still, the close political relationship between the U.S. defense industry and the Clinton Administration went largely unreported. Arms markets in Taiwan, Saudi Arabia, and the United Arab Emirates continue to remain strong. Arms export subsidies are still among the largest categories of corporate welfare, second only to agricultural subsidies. The United States continues to use weapons sales and giveaways even after the conclusion of the Cold War as a means of international diplomacy and to insure trade partnerships. After repeated violations and contradictions, the House's "Policy on Conventional Arms Transfer" has become a non-policy.

At the same time, the mainstream U.S. media is quick to condemn certain countries who sell arms, most notably Russia, China, and North Korea, while it ignores sales by Britain, France, and Israel. The relationship of international arms sales to Saddam Hussein or, most recently, the defunct dictator of Chile, Augusto Pinochet, remains unreported; both were supplied with the weapons necessary to strengthen their dictatorships by the United States while their countries were "U.S. allies." Reports on the U.S. policy of giving weapons to favored leaders and regimes of African nations began to surface by the end of the year. In this time of constantly emerging and dissolving leaders, regimes, and governments, a large percentage of these weapons often fall into the wrong hands or make it into the illegal global trade.

For more information on U.S. military sales, exports, and giveaways, see:

Lora Lumpe and Jeff Donarski, *The Arms Trade Revealed: A Guide for Investigators and Activists* (Federation of American Scientists, 1998).

The Arms Sales Monitoring Project, Federation of American Scientists, 307 Massachusetts Avenue, NE, Washington, DC 20002, Tel: 202/675-1018, e-mail: fas@fas.org; http://www.fas.org/ asmp.

SOURCES: *CNN Worldview*, October 15, 1997; *Dallas Morning News*, October 15 & 17, 1997; *Christian Science Monitor*, October 16, 1997; *Boston Globe*, January 1, 1998; *Jane's Defense Weekly*, January 28, 1998; *Aviation Week and Space Technology*, March 16, 1998; *The New York Times*, April 29, July 13, & August 4, 1998; *Time*, May 11, 1998; *The Progressive*, May 1998.

1997 #2 CENSORED STORY

PERSONAL CARE AND COS-METIC PRODUCTS MAY BE CARCINOGENIC

Unbeknownst to many consumers, seemingly safe personal care and cosmetic products such as Clairol's "Nice and Easy" hair color, Crest toothpaste, Cover Girl makeup, and Vidal Sassoon shampoo contain potential carcinogens. Of particular concern to consumer advocates are those products which include nitrosamines, once readily found in bacon and preserved meat before strict regulation curtailed their indiscriminate use. Although the Food and Drug Administration (FDA) has known of the risk posed to the public by nitrosamines in cosmetics since 1979, they have done little to monitor their presence.

Much of the American public mistakenly believes that the FDA regulates and monitors the cosmetics industry. In reality they do little beyond prohibiting the inclusion of seven known toxins in beauty aids. Although the FDA has the power to pull products it considers unsafe from store shelves, it rarely does.

Individual FDA scientists are finally beginning to speak out, calling for a reduction in the levels of all possible carcinogens in cosmetics and personal care products.

SOURCES: "To Die For"; "Take a Powder," *In These Times,* February 17, 1997 and March 3, 1997, both by Joel Bleifuss; *Chicago Tribune,* July 29, 1997, page 3, zone C.

COVERAGE 1998: With few exceptions—most notably *CBS This Morning*—the mainstream press has remained silent about the possible carcinogenic nature of the personal care products the public uses on a regular basis. A preliminary study by the National Toxicology Program (NTP), headquartered at the National Institute of Environmental Sciences (NIEHS), detailed the inclusion of several suspected carcinogens in commonly used products in December 1997 after *Censored 1998* had gone to press. In February 1998, CBS reported on the questionable inclusion of diethanolamine (DEA) and/or cocamide-DEA in most shampoos, lotions, and creams, and children's bubble bath products. The FDA released a statement following the CBS report which urged consumers not to be alarmed. However, the director of its own Office of Cosmetics & Colors, John Bailey, found the NTP findings "very relevant," and urged the office to look into other potential carcinogenic substances as well, such as triethanolamine (TEA).

Already recognizing the potential risks of these ingredients, much of the European community has restricted the use of DEA in cosmetic products.

FDA sources reported that the NTP was doing a "fast-track review" which was due to be released in early summer 1998. The testing must be repeated, however, as it was "'compromised" by the presence of bacteria. According to a chief proponent for further research, Dr. Samuel S. Epstein, M.D., professor of environmental medicine at the University of Illinois School of Public Health and chairman of the Cancer Prevention Coalition, the cosmetics industry has effectively squelched the release of this information to the public.

Within the cosmetic and toiletries industry, an open dialogue continues on the pros and cons of including DEA and other potential carcinogens in personal care products. The industry itself either disputes the accuracy of testing, or maintains that current guidelines are sufficient. Dr. Epstein disagrees, citing that previously held safe levels are no longer justified. Additionally, other studies are bringing previously-considered safe ingredients into question, including the cosmetic fragrances musk xylol and methyleugenol (a known carcinogen), a plasticizer polyethylene glycol (PEG), and a variety of hair dye chemicals. Information, especially regarding the use of DEA, has been regularly reported on news wire services, giving the media opportunities to follow the debate and bring the American consumer into the ensuing dialogue.

SOURCES: *CBS This Morning*, February 23, 1998; *Women's Wear Daily*, February 27, 1998; *The Rose Sheet*, March 30 and November 9, 1998; *Indianapolis Star*, May 24, 1998; *Vegetarian Times*, September 1, 1998; *Boston Globe*, September 17, 1998.

1997 #3 CENSORED STORY

BIG BUSINESS SEEKS TO CONTROL AND INFLUENCE U.S. UNIVERSITIES

Academia is being auctioned off to the highest bidder. Corporations avoid incurring research costs by endowing professorships, funding think tanks and research centers, sponsoring grants, and contracting for university services. Federal tax dollars fund about $7 billion worth of research to which corporations can now buy access for a fraction of the actual cost. This is largely the result of two 1980s federal laws that encourage "rent-a-researcher" programs. The consequence has been a covert transfer of resources from the public to the private sector and the changing of universities from centers of instruction to centers for corporate R & D (research and development).

MIT's Industrial Liaison Program, for example, sells the university's expertise, resources, laboratories, and professors to 300 corporations for an annual fee ($10,000 to $50,000 per year). The British pharmaceutical corporation, Boots, paid the University of California, San Francisco, to research its hypothyroid drug, Synthroid. When the results showed

that there were other, less expensive bioequivalents on the market, the information was subsequently suppressed.

University presidents often sit on the boards of directors of major corporations, and university boards of trustees are dominated by captains of industry who hire chancellors and presidents with pro-industry biases.

SOURCES: Lawrence Soley, "Phi Beta Capitalism," *CovertAction Quarterly*, Spring 1997; Lawrence Soley, "Big Money on Campus," *Dollars and Sense*, March/April 1997.

COVERAGE 1998: There has been little in the way of mainstream coverage of the corporatization of the country's universities during the past year. Still, corporate intervention continues to compromise the integrity and quality of the American educational experience.

In Jefferson County, Colorado, Pepsi donated $2 million for a new college football stadium. In return, the soft drink company received exclusive rights to sell their product in the district's 140 schools for a projected return of $7.3 million. At the University of California (UC) Berkeley, the Swiss biotechnology firm, Novartis gave $25 million for agricultural research in return for access to Berkeley's researchers and first rights to any potentially lucrative discoveries.

The presidents of over half of the *U.S. News and World Report's* leading universities sit on corporate boards. Judith Rodin, president of the University of Pennsylvania, is a director of Aetna Life and Casualty, Electronic Data Systems, and American Airlines. UC Berkeley's former Chancellor, Chang-Lin Tien, is a director of Wells Fargo Bank which handles the university system's estimated $1.5 billion payroll account. Carnegie Mellon's past president, Robert Mehrabian, received compensation from four publicly traded corporations in 1996.

Corporate control of education is also being felt at the elementary and secondary levels. The under-20 demographic is well-known as a hot consumer group for advertisers. *The Bay Guardian* reports that San Francisco is privatizing two of its elementary schools, turning them over to a for-profit corporation funded by Gap, Inc. *Channel One*, a 12-minute news program with two minutes of commercials for students, is beamed into 40 percent of the nation's high schools. According to *CyberBrook*, one Texas school even rented its roof as advertising space.

Since the 1980s, when federal funding for higher education plummeted from 14.9 to 12.4 percent, and state contributions from 30.7 to 27.5 percent, universities and colleges have been scrambling for funds to meet basic research needs. As they look to make up the deficit, many have turned to the private sector for help. The "education industry" is fast becoming a multi-billion dollar investment opportunity for corporations worldwide.

SOURCES: *San Francisco Bay Guardian,* April 29, 1998; *CyberBrook,* July 8, 1998; *San Francisco Examiner,* November 23-24, 1998.

1997 #4 CENSORED STORY
EXPOSING THE GLOBAL SURVEILLANCE SYSTEM

Unknown to its citizens and most government officials, New Zealand's largest intelligence agency, the Government Communications Security Bureau (GCSB), has been helping its Western allies (the United States, Great Britain, Australia, New Zealand, and Canada, known collectively as UKUSA) spy on countries throughout the Pacific region for the last 40 years. In the late 1980s, the United States convinced New Zealand to join a new and highly secret post-Cold War global intelligence system. One of the world's largest, most closemouthed projects, it allows spy agencies to monitor most of the telephone, e-mail, and telex communications that are carried over the world's telecommunication networks.

The ECHELON system, designed and coordinated by the U.S. National Security Agency (NSA), is used primarily for the harvesting of electronic transmissions from nonmilitary targets throughout the world: governments, organizations, businesses, and individuals. The system works by indiscriminately intercepting very large quantities of communications, searching them for preprogrammed key words, and then cataloging them for future reference. Although such computer systems have been in existence since at least the 1970s, the ECHELON system was designed by NSA to interconnect systems and coordinate their data.

More than 50 people experienced in

intelligence and its related fields and concerned about UKUSA activities agreed to be interviewed by Nicky Hager, author of *Secret Power*, prompting other intelligence workers to come forward. When Hager's book was released, the intelligence bureaucrats met to decide if they could prevent its distribution, but soon realized that the political costs were too high.

SOURCE: Nicky Hager, "Secret Power: Exposing the Global Surveillance System," *CovertAction Quarterly* (CAQ), Winter 1996/1997.

COVERAGE 1998: Hager's book sparked a debate in the European Parliament about global surveillance systems. A report commissioned in 1996 by its Civil Liberties Committee and released this past year, provides details about an "American-controlled" spy network, ECHELON, which "'routinely and indiscriminately monitors' countless phone, fax, and e-mail messages." It fills in what had previously been a "sketchy" history of the spy network's existence. Although it caused quite a stir in the United Kingdom, it received little if any attention stateside or on the continent until mid-1998 when it became front-page news in France, Italy, Belgium, and Russia—and in the *Village Voice* (Jason Vest).

The British report "confirms that the citizens of Europe are subject to an intensity of surveillance" which will have an impact on "the future of European civil rights." Activities of the NSA—"more secretive than the CIA" according to Vest—also came under fire. Said a former NSA official: "Consider that anyone can type a key word into a Net search engine and get back tens of thousands of hits in a few seconds . . . . Assume that people working on the outer edges have capabilities far in excess of what you do." Although some experts argue that the spy network is not "omniscient" and gathers more information than can ever be digested, others raise its potential misuse and abuse of privacy. According to *Reuters/Wired*, the European Union is readying legislation to allow police eavesdropping of "Internet conversations and Iridium satellite telephone calls without obtaining court authorization," part of a wider "understanding between the EU, the United States, Canada, New Zealand, and Norway."

Accounts of abuse are beginning to surface. There are reports that commercial information is given to U.S. companies bidding for international contracts and that the activities of organizations like Amnesty International, Greenpeace, and Christian Aid are regularly monitored. According to Vest, there are even hints of U.S. involvement in the death of Chechnyen rebel leader Dzokhar Dudayev: NSA satellites could have been used to help Russian missiles locate Dudayev's position through his cell phone signal.

Requests for information about ECHELON activities are regularly deflected, even those petitioned for under the Freedom of Information Act. Recently, however, news of ECHELON, other SIGINT (Signals Intelligence) operations, and NSA activities has begun to surface in mainstream American newspapers. Some have reprinted an article by retired Canadian electronic eavesdropper, Mike Frost, exposing NSA and SIGINT activities. Not only did Frost describe the logistics of signal interception and how it could infringe upon the individual's right to privacy, but he provided specific examples of possible misuse.

In 1995, for example, "the Clinton Administration used NSA intercepts during trade negotiations with Japan over luxury car imports." In 1996, the e-mail system that links 5,000 European Union officials was tapped. Such activities are not new. Already by 1975, the U.S. government had requested Canadian eavesdroppers to spy against an American citizen suspected of KGB involvement, and, under a directive from the Royal Canadian Mounted Police, listened in on the car-phone conversations of Margaret Trudeau. As Frost noted, "One can't help wondering if the wife of a prime minister is not safe from the prying ears of Signals Intelligence, where does that leave you and me?" Interestingly, in December, the *Washington Post* revealed that the NSA had 1,056 pages of information about Princess Diana, gleaned from electronic eavesdropping, that it would not release.

SOURCES: "Brits Weary of U.S. Eavesdropping," *Spotlight*, February 16, 1998; Jason Vest, "Listening In," *Village Voice*, August 18, 1998; Neal Thompson, "NSA Listening Practices Called European Threat," *The Baltimore Sun*, September 19, 1998; "Spy Agency Helped U.S.

Companies by Listening In On Competitors," *AP Worldstream*, September 19, 1998; Mike Frost, "Big Brother is Listening," *The Sacramento Bee*, November 8, 1998; Niall McKay, "Europe Readies Police Techno-Surveillance Law," *Reuters/Wired*, December 8, 1998; "NSA Admits to Holding Secret Information on Princess Diana," *Washington Post*, December 12, 1998.

1997 #5 CENSORED STORY

UNITED STATES COMPANIES ARE WORLD LEADERS IN THE MANUFACTURE OF TORTURE DEVICES FOR INTERNAL USE AND EXPORT

A March 1997 Amnesty International report listed 100 companies which produced and sold instruments of torture. Forty-two of these are U.S. firms, giving the country the dubious distinction of leading the world in the manufacture of stun guns, stun belts, cattle probe-like devices, and other equipment which can cause devastating pain in the hands of torturers.

The U.S. government is a large purchaser of stun devices, especially stun guns, electroshock batons, and electric shields. Both the American Civil Liberties Union (ACLU) and Amnesty claim the devices are unsafe and may encourage acts of sadism, especially the stun belt which leaves little physical evidence. In June 1996, Amnesty asked the Bureau of Prisons to suspend the use of the electroshock belt, citing the possibility of physical danger to inmates and its potential for misuse. In 1991, Terence Allen, a specialist in forensic pathology, linked the taser (a product which shoots two wires attached to electrified darts with metal hooks which deliver a debilitating shock when they hook into a victim's skin or clothes) to fatalities. Manufacturers continue to denounce allegations that the use of electroshock devices is dangerous and may constitute a gross violation of human rights.

In her update in *Censored 1998,* Cusac noted that citizens often do not realize that the abuse of prisoners is epidemic in the United States. Prison guards have been reported mistreating inmates with stun guns. Stun belts had by then appeared in South Africa, the first documented export of the device.

SOURCES: Anne-Marie Cusac, "Shock Value: U.S. Stun Devices Pose Human Rights Risk," *The Progressive,* September 1997; Mainstream media coverage: *Chicago Tribune,* March 4, 1997; *Washington Times,* March 4, 1997.

COVERAGE 1998: Although the international press widely covered the export of electroshock torture devices from both the United States and Great Britain to countries around the world, little coverage on the subject could be found in the U.S. media until *Time* did a 1300-word exposé called "Weapons of Torture," by Douglas Waller on the export of U.S.-manufactured stun guns throughout the world. From the Democratic Republic of Congo's use of stun batons to shock a prisoner unconscious, to Tibetan monks reported to have had shock batons

rammed down their throats, leaving them "crumpled on the floor in a pool of blood and excrement and in extreme pain," the use of these devices is becoming more common internationally.

Even though a license is required to restrict the exportation of shock weapons, Washington often approves their shipment to countries with a history of human rights abuses. Other manufacturers avoid the restrictions by shipping to NATO countries which do not require licenses and from there the devices can be distributed around the world. According to the *Times* article, Mexico is now a production and "transshipment" site for American- and Asian-made stun devices.

Several companies have established manufacturing facilities in other countries as well, getting around restrictions by paying countries with looser export rules to manufacture the devices and then ship them with a U.S. label.

In the United States, shock devices are becoming an increasing part of the judicial system's arsenal. In Long Beach, California, Judge Joan Comparet-Cassani's courtroom use of a stun device drew critical headlines. While in her courtroom, Ronnie Hawkins, a defendant with a reputation for courtroom outbursts, was belted with an electronic security belt manufactured by Cleveland's Stun-Tech. Whenever Hawkins interrupted the judge, she ordered the bailiff to administer a 50,000-volt jolt. Public Defenders were outraged, but the judge reportedly felt "threatened" by the interruptions. Hawkins has since been granted a new trial. In October, Amnesty International launched a campaign against conditions in United States prisons, and the use of electroshock and other devices against prisoners.

The private sector has discovered stun guns. Specialty stores have begun to stock them along with home surveillance systems and pepper spray for personal defense. One family was recently arrested for using a stun gun to discipline an unruly child.

The use of electroshock devices to control foreign civil demonstrations has been noted by the press, but little attention has been paid to the source of manufacture of those weapons.

SOURCES: Douglas Waller, "Weapons of Torture," *Time,* April 6, 1998; Jack Leonard and Miles Corwin, "Stun Belt Used for First Time on Defendant in L.A. Court," *Los Angeles Times,* July 8, 1998; "Abuses in America Put Under Scrutiny," *Chicago Tribune,* October 5, 1998.

1997 #6 CENSORED STORY
RUSSIAN PLUTONIUM LOST OVER CHILE AND BOLIVIA

On November 16, 1996, Russia's Mars 96 space probe broke up and burned while descending over Chile and Bolivia, scattering its remains across a 10,000-square-mile area. The probe carried about a half pound of plutonium divided into four battery canisters. Most alarming, no one seemed to know where the canisters went.

Gordon Bendick, Director of Legislative Affairs for the National Security Council, postulated two possibilities: Either the canisters were destroyed "coming through the atmosphere [and the plutonium dispersed]," or the canisters survived re-entry, "impacted the earth, penetrated the surface...or could have hit a rock and bounced off like an agate marble."

The amount of plutonium that was "lost" has devastating potential. According to Dr. Helen Caldicott, president emeritus of Physicians for Social Responsibility, "Plutonium is so toxic that less that one-millionth of a gram is a carcinogenic dose. One pound, if uniformly distributed, could hypothetically induce lung cancer in every person on earth." Dr. John Gofman, professor emeritus of radiological physics at the University of California, Berkeley, confirms her report.

On November 17, 1996, when the U.S. Space Command initially announced that the probe would re-enter the earth's atmosphere with a predicted impact point in East Central Australia, President Clinton telephoned Australian Prime Minister John Howard and offered assistance to deal with any radioactive contamination. Howard placed the Australian military and government on full alert and warned the public to use "extreme caution" if they came into contact with the remnants of the Russian space probe. The day after the probe fell on South America, the Space Command remained focused on Australia. Together with a Russian news source, they later reported that the probe had fallen into the Pacific. Major media in the United States reported the probe as having crashed "harmlessly" into the ocean.

On November 29, the U.S. Space Command's final report placed the crash site directly on Chile and Bolivia. The date of the crash was also revised backward one day to November 16. The United States did nothing to help South Americans to locate and recover the radioactive canisters.

SOURCE: Karl Grossman, "Space Probe Explodes, Plutonium Missing," *Covert-Action Quarterly* (CAQ) Spring 1997.

COVERAGE 1998: There has been virtually no establishment news coverage regarding the Mars probe since *Censored 1998* was released, except for a chilling 390-word report in the December 30, 1997 *Boston Globe* by reporter David L. Chandler. In an interview with aerospace engineer James Osberg who writes extensively about the Russian space program, Osberg stated that he had heard nothing about the satellite from Bolivia. He also found nothing unusual in this since a satellite which had crashed previously in Ghana had been found by villagers and not reported. "It could be sitting in a cradle, keeping the baby warm," Osberg told Chandler.

Special author update: See 1996, #1 *Censored* story.

SOURCES: David L. Chandler, "Mystery Persists Over Plutonium-Carrying Probe That Fell To Earth," *Boston Globe*, December 28, 1997.

NORPLANT AND HUMAN LAB EXPERIMENTS IN THIRD WORLD LEAD TO FORCED USE IN THE UNITED STATES

Low-income women in the United States and the Third World have been the unwitting targets of a U.S. policy to control birth rates. Despite continuous reports of the debilitating effects of the surgically implanted contraceptive, Norplant, women with the implant had difficulty making their complaints heard, and in some instances had been deceived about its effects.

Medicaid often covers the cost of Norplant insertion. The contraceptive is considered to be effective for a period of five years. Writer Jennifer Washburn revealed the agencies' rejection of removals for low-income women prior to the standard five-year period, even when side effects are chronic. Journalist Rebecca Kavoussi reported on Washington Senate Bill 5278 that would have required women who give birth to a drug-addicted baby to have two chances to undergo drug treatment and counseling before requiring their use of "long-term pharmaceutical birth control" (Norplant).

When Norplant hit the market in 1990, a flurry of state legislation provided AFDC recipients monetary incentives to use the implant. At the same time, state Medicaid agencies were crafting policies that denied coverage for early Norplant removal. Laws that deny additional benefits to children born to mothers on welfare have spread to at least 21 states. Meanwhile, legislation encourages competition among states for "illegitimacy bonuses." In the United States, over 400 lawsuits have been filed against the maker of Norplant, Wyeth-Ayerst, because of side effects of the drug.

Internationally, Joseph D'Agostino reported on the British Broadcasting Corporation (BBC) documentary, *The Human Laboratory*, that the U.S. Agency for International Development (USAID) had acted in conjunction with the Population Council of New York City to test Norplant on uninformed women in Bangladesh, Haiti, and the Philippines. Women in those places who complained of debilitating side effects were also rebuffed when they asked to have the implants removed. They, too, had been told that the drug was safe and not experimental. Now, says the BBC, many women who were used in the trials are suffering debilitating side effects. The documentary also claimed that the U.S. government considers global population control a "national security issue" and has increased U.S. population control efforts around the world.

SOURCES: Jennifer Washburn, "The Misuses of Norplant: Who Gets Stuck?" *Ms.*, November/December 1996; Rebecca Kavoussi, "Norplant and the Dark Side of the Law," *Washington Free Press,* March/April 1997; Joseph D'Agostino, "BBC Documentary Claims That U.S. Foreign Aid Funded Norplant Testing On Uninformed Third World Women," *Human Events,* May 16, 1997.

1998 COVERAGE: Although litigation has virtually halted Norplant's use domesti-

cally, it continues to be exported to Third World countries. A *Ms.* article (to which Jennifer Washburn was the main contributor) shows that Norplant exports to Bangladesh have increased while abuses continue. In a recent update to her story, Rebecca Kavoussi reports that although Washington State Senate Bill 5278 was passed, those sections mandating Norplant implantation were vetoed by Democratic Governor Gary Locke.

Perhaps the hottest debate over the reproductive rights of women in the news media was that of the export of the non-FDA-approved drug quinacrine to Third World countries. Originally use to treat malaria, quinacrine is inserted into the uterus where it dissolves, burning the tissue, and scarring the Fallopian tubes closed. Also known as the Q-Method, it is a cheap procedure (as little as $2) which can be performed in a doctor's office without anesthesia, making it especially appealing to Third World countries. "Quinacrine smacks of eugenics, racism, and contraceptive imperialism," said Stephen Mosher, president of the Population Research Institute. The drug has been banned for use in Chile and India.

Because of continued liability fears, pharmaceutical manufacturers have pulled back on the release of implantable contraceptives and contraceptive research in general. According to an *Los Angeles Times* report, the number of U.S. companies doing contraceptive research has dropped from "several dozen in the 1960s to just two today," compromising the chances for further development of safe and sane contraception.

For more information on quinacrine use abroad contact: Committee on Women, Population, and the Environment, c/o Population and Development Program/SS Hampshire College, Amherst, MA, 01002; Tel: (413) 559-5506.

Special update by Jennifer Washburn: "Norplant shipments to Bangladesh have risen dramatically in recent years. The United Nations Fund for Population Activities (UNFPA) is the agency most responsible for this increase. Whereas in 1994 Bangladesh received just 500 units of Norplant, by 1996 deliveries from UNFPA shot up to 80,600 sets, and the U.S. Agency for International Development (USAID) threw in another 2,000. This year, according to a U.N. source, deliveries will jump to 100,000 units. Although these quantities are still small relative to Bangladesh's population of 120 million, the Bangladeshi government is launching a massive promotion campaign to popularize Norplant. According to a UNFPA source, the government plans to distribute Norplant nationwide at 181 clinics 'in all districts of the country.'

"Given its prior history of abuse, Bangladesh's decision to launch a massive promotion campaign to popularize Norplant—with financial backing from international family planning agencies—has received surprisingly little attention in the West. In fact, when U.S.-based women's health activists were first contacted for this story, few had any knowledge of this dramatic policy shift. Adrienne Germaine, a widely respected expert on Bangladesh at the International Women's Health Coalition in New York, and other prominent health advocates, expressed concern about the potential for coercion.

"From its inception, when Norplant was first introduced in Bangladesh in a series of clinical trials that ran from 1985-1990, there were problems. During those years, Bangladeshi activists Nasreen Huq and Farida Akhter, uncovered evidence that hundreds of women participants in the trials were being denied removal services. The abuses were later confirmed in a 1990 study by Family Health International (FHI), one of the principal U.S. donor groups financing the early Norplant trials, together with USAID and the Population Council, the original developer of Norplant. FHF's study revealed that less than half of the early trial participants obtained removal services on the first request; 37 percent had to make two and three requests; while 16 percent made more than three requests or sought removal elsewhere (where surgery, without proper training, would likely have been quite gruesome).

"In the spring of 1998, Nasreen Huq, and other members of Naripokkho, a Bangladeshi women's health group, were at work on a film documenting ongoing Norplant removal problems among women who live in the slums of Dhaka and other poor sections of Bangladesh. The last time I spoke to Huq, she was trying to complete the film by July 1998, so that it could be shown during the government launch of Bangladesh's newest population plan, valued at $2.9 billion, when Dhaka would be filled with representatives from the world's largest international donor agencies. She said she hoped her film would help call them to account."

SOURCES: "Chile: Quinacrine Banned," "Quinacrine: Not Enough Research," *Women's Health Journal,* March 1998; Shari Roan, "The Chill in Birth Control Research," *Los Angeles Times,* March 23, 1998; Alix M. Freedman, "Population Bomb: Two Americans Export Chemical Sterilization To the Third World," *Wall Street Journal,* June 18, 1998; Bobbie Battista, "The Controversy Over Quinacrine: A Sterilization Drug," *CNN Talkback Live,* June 19, 1998; "Norplant is Back in Bangladesh," *Ms.,* July/August 1998; Sydney Freedberg, "A New Chemical Sterilization Technique Sparks Global Debate," *The Houston Chronicle,* November 18, 1998; "FDA Warning Won't Deter Birth-Control Crusader," Associated Press, October 22, 1998.

1997 #8 CENSORED STORY

LITTLE KNOWN FEDERAL LAW PAVES THE WAY FOR NATIONAL IDENTIFICATION CARD

In September 1996, President Clinton signed the Illegal Immigration Reform and Responsibility Act of 1996. Buried on approximately page 650 was a section that created a framework for establishing a national ID card for the American public. This piece of legislation was slipped through without fanfare or publicity.

A major section of the law provides for the establishment of a "Machine Readable Document Pilot Program" requiring employers to swipe a prospective employee's driver's license through a special reader linked to the federal government's Social Security Administration. This gives the federal government the discretion of whether or not to approve the applicant for employment, in effect making the driver's license a "national ID card."

Another provision provides $5 million-per-year grants to any state that wants to participate in any one of three pilot ID programs. One such program is the "Criminal Alien Identification Program" in which federal, state, and local law enforcement agencies record the fingerprints of previously arrested aliens. A third part of the law states that federal agencies may only accept driver's licenses with digital fingerprints.

The state of Georgia passed its own legislation shortly before the federal bill was signed into law, creating something similar to the federal ID program. The Georgia law requires residents to give digital fingerprints before obtaining a driver's license or state ID. Again, like its federal counterpart, the Georgia bill was signed into law in April of 1996 and received no public or media attention at the time. Georgian lawmakers have since made several unsuccessful attempts to repeal the law.

SOURCES: Cyndee Parker, "National ID Card is Now Federal Law and Georgia Wants to Help Lead the Way," WITWIGO, May/June 1997.

MAINSTREAM MEDIA COVERAGE: *The New York Times,* September 8, 1996, Section 6; page 58, column 1; related article in the *San Francisco Chronicle,* September 19, 1996, page A1.

1998 COVERAGE: The existence of an already established National Identity Card program hidden within the Illegal Immigration Reform and Responsibility Act of 1996 (IIRRA) went largely unreported by the mainstream media in 1998 along with plans for several other national and international "ID" or "smart" cards.

In 1996, Congress approved a national patient identifier number to link citizens to their medical records which are archived on a government-run database. The debate surrounding the Patient Identifier, part of the 1996 Health Insurance Portability and Accountability Act, also known as the Kennedy-Kassebaum health care bill, has gone largely unreported in the U.S. media. The U.S. Department of Health and Human Services has been charged with implementing the program, and has promised stringent security. Opponents argue, however, that privacy concerns need to be addressed before such a nationwide system is put into place. According to *Insight Magazine,* the Kennedy-Kassebaum bill was written by a "coalition of private interests ranging from the American Health Information Management Association to IBM." The American Medical Association does not see a need for the identifier.

According to Harvard Law School research fellow, Richard Sobel, five government databanks related to identification documents have already been created in recent legislation or by executive action. These include the IIRRA, the Welfare and the Welfare Reform acts, and the Computer Assisted Passenger Screening System (CAPS). All focus on centralized identification systems. The two welfare-related policies require Social Security numbers prior to the issuance of driver, professional and occupational, and marriage licenses; welfare benefits; divorce proceedings;

THIS MODERN WORLD by TOM TOMORROW

and child support determinations.

The controversy continues at the state level as Social Security numbers increasingly become part of the driver's license process. The National Highway Safety Traffic Administration is a chief advocate for this system; the U.S. Department of Transportation has plans for other, similar ID card proposals. The Conference of State Legislatures signed a regulation that would implement IIRRA and force all states to imprint licenses with the numbers. This issue received very little media attention and little is known about its status. The fight against a national identity card has brought together a diverse coalition of political and social organizations. Regular newswire accounts of coalition efforts to repeal the IIRRA mandate which compels the inclusion of Social Security numbers on state driver's licenses has gone unreported.

Identity cards are becoming increasingly important on college campuses as well. The University of Central Florida and Huntington National Bank plan to distribute thousands of "smart cards" for students to use both as a photo ID and an electronic wallet. The card will store students' financial information as well as academic status, Social Security number, and any other administratively pertinent information. Most importantly, the cards will be used to pay loans and other fees as well as exchange funds on campus.

Plans to implement global Biometric Card Identification systems are still in place, although this also is not a matter of public record. The corporate world continues to press forward with new technology that holds increasing amounts of information. The international business of creating, reading, and storing identity data generates over $1 billion in global sales annually. Thailand, China, South Korea, the Philippines, Egypt, Argentina, and many European nations have, or plan to implement national ID card programs in the near future. Argentina is in the beginning stages of implementing one of the biggest biometric card systems in the world with a goal of converting every one of its 28 million

citizens to the system. In July 1998, the Philippine Supreme Court declared the use of a computerized identification system unconstitutional and a violation of individual rights.

SOURCES: *Los Angeles Times*, November 27, 1998; *National Journal*, October 24, 1998; *Baltimore Sun*, September 16, 1998; *PR Newswire*, September 15, 1998; *Chicago Tribune*, September 1 & July 21, 1998; *American Medical News*, August 8, 1998; *Insight Magazine*, August 24, 1998; *Orlando Sentinel*, August 25, 1998; *U.S. Newswire*, August 6, 1998.

1997 #9 CENSORED STORY
MATTEL CUTS U.S. JOBS TO OPEN SWEATSHOPS IN OTHER COUNTRIES

America's toy industry wholeheartedly embraced both the North American Free Trade Agreement (NAFTA) and the General Agreement on Tariffs and Trade (GATT), citing them as a boon to its workers. In reality, since the inauguration of the agreements, the toy industry's American labor force has been reduced by over half. Moreover, many of those lost jobs have reappeared in other countries—countries notorious for their sweatshop practices.

Mattel, the largest toy manufacturer in the world (Barbie, Hot Wheels, Fisher-Price toys) lobbied heavily for NAFTA. Although it now employs over 25,000 people worldwide, only 6,000 of them live in the United States and those numbers are dwindling. Furthermore,

workers at Mattel factories abroad report abuses including environmentally-induced illness, sub-standard wages and work conditions, intimidation of and physical force against workers who promote workers' rights, and child labor.

The toy industry's response has been primarily one of self-monitoring.

SOURCES: Eyal Press, "Barbie's Betrayal: The Toy Industry's Broken Workers," *The Nation*, December 30, 1996; Anton Foek, "Sweatshop Barbie: Exploitation of Third World Labor," *The Humanist*, January/February 1997.

COVERAGE 1998: Media giants have reported on the sweatshop abuses of high-profile corporations like Disney, Wal-mart, K-Mart, Ann Taylor, Liz Claiborne, and Ralph Lauren who continue to patronize foreign operations and inflate the market with inexpensive products. However, it has, for the most part, failed to inform the public about the lost jobs and trail of dollars trickling out of the United States to foreign soils, leaving that coverage up to the regional media.

Gannet News Service reported on the wage-drain from Western New York state to Mexico in October 1997, a fact not picked up by the mainstream media. Job exports to Mexico by Kodak alone is estimated at $250 million annually. Swingline Staplers moved its entire operation south of the border, while New York–based Pal Plastics was forced into bankruptcy from lost revenues when Has-bro shifted its manufacturing operation to Mexico.

While company profits continue to

soar, American workers continue to lose jobs. A *Buffalo News* report revealed that Mattel cut over 700 jobs in Medina and shut down its last union plant in June in Indiana. Kodak cut 6,300 jobs in Rochester last fall. Hasbro closed its plant in El Paso, cutting 850 jobs from its American payroll in a bid to compete with international toy companies. U.S. Department of Labor figures show that as of April 1998, 170,395 jobs have been lost because of NAFTA (that figure reflects only those unemployed who have sought assistance). Moreover, the Economic Policy Institute reported that U.S. employers use foreign contractors as threats in domestic wage and benefits disputes.

The toy industry is especially suspect in sweatshop abuses. More than half the toys made in America come from China, the latest country being monitored for sweatshop abuse. Mattel announced in November 1997 that it would self-monitor its relationships with foreign contractors by instituting bans on the employment of under-age workers (according to local standards) and a "same wage" pay scale (again, relative to local standards). In May 1998, however, shareholders voted down a proposition that would have tied executive salary and "perks" to the implementation of such a program.

SOURCES: *Dallas Morning News,* December 21, 1997; *Sun Sentinel,* March 22, 1998; *Multinational Monitor,* April 1998; *Buffalo News,* April 3, 1998; *The Ecologist,* May 15; *Extra!* June 1998; *Los Angeles Times,* June 26, 1998.

1997 #10 CENSORED STORY

ARMY'S PLAN TO BURN NERVE GAS AND TOXINS IN OREGON THREATENS COLUMBIA RIVER BASIN

Ignoring evidence that incineration is the worst means of chemical weapons disposal, the Oregon Environmental Quality Commission (EQC) has approved Raytheon Corporation's bid to spend $1.3 billion U.S. tax dollars and build five incinerators at the Umatilla facility in Eastern Oregon. The EQC made its final decision in February 1997 to approve the United States Army's plan to build a chemical weapons incineration facility near Hermiston, Oregon, scheduled to be operational in 2001.

A list of the chemicals to be incinerated includes nerve gas, mustard agents, bioaccumulative organochlines such as found in dioxin, furans, chloromethane, vinyl chloride, PCBs, and arsenic, as well as metals like lead, mercury, copper, and nickel. These represent only a small portion of the complete list of thousands of toxic substances that will be potentially emitted as toxic ash and effluents. All pose a health threat to the Columbia River watershed.

Problems that continue to arise in other incineration facilities across the country foreshadow the future. The Umatilla incinerators will be modeled after the Tooele Utah facility which has had problems with agent detection in heating, ventilation, and air conditioning vestibules as well as other issues compromising safety since Tooele began operations in 1996.

SOURCE: Mark Brown and Karyn Jones, "Army Plans to Burn Surplus Nerve Gas Stockpile," *Earth First!*, March 1997.

1998 COVERAGE: What to do with America's massive stockpile of chemical, biological, and nerve warfare agents has been a major media focus in 1998. Two separate, but related, issues were raised in the original *Censored* article: storage versus incineration of chemical and biological weapons, and what the presence of a storage and/or incineration facility means to the surrounding community and environment.

The activities in and around the Umatilla Chemical Depot continue to serve as an example of the issues faced by approximately nine such depot sites around the country and off the Pacific Coast. All either have or are slated to have incinerators. Incineration advocates in the military and government maintain that long-term storage and containment is becoming increasingly more dangerous as weapons begin to age and de-stabilize. Incineration opponents fear the potential malfunction of the facilities and subsequent disaster as well as long-term trace exposure to harsh agents.

Before incineration can begin at the Hermiston site, the nearby town must meet strict state and environmental conditions including disaster preparedness. Although Congress initially allocated $25 million for an emergency system, local officials say they've received little of the promised funds and equipment. It is disquieting that the Umatilla depot has been a storage facility for decades and never had *any* disaster program in place. A *60 Minutes* report revealed that $900 million has been spent on the storage facilities since 1989; another $25 million is earmarked for community education and safety. At this time, medical, safety, and administrative professionals have little or no training for treating potential victims, protecting themselves from exposure, or simply recognizing the symptoms of chemical poisoning. There is no known study on the effects of the various nerve gases on the human body of either sudden large-dose exposure or prolonged long-term exposure. According to the *Desert News*, the military is still unsure of how toxic exposure to extremely minute levels of the chemical arms may be over time and that "there are no plans to address the question."

The Umatilla incinerator is modeled after that at Tooele, Utah, home to 42 percent of the chemical and biological weapons in the United States. The Tooele incinerator has shut down four times in the last year alone due to reported leaks and technical difficulties and is still not operating at capacity. The former plant manager was fired after he called attention to what he perceived as "unsafe conditions." Ironically, a *New York Times* article praised the facility while ignoring its questionable safety record, prompting one local official to suggest that other weapon stocks be transported to Tooele for disposal.

Critics claim that the Umatilla Depot and others like it are operated strictly for corporate profit by private companies such as Raytheon Corporation. At last count, the total estimated cost for incinerating all of America's stockpiled chemical weapons had risen to $15.7 billion although the complete destruction of the Army's chemical weapons stockpile could take up to 34 months longer at some sites and cost as much as $2.89 billion more than estimated.

SOURCES: *AP Online,* October 27, 1998; *Desert News* (Salt Lake City, UT) *Associated Press,* July 19, October 8, August 8, & September 30, 1998; *The Economist,* September 5, 1998; *Oregonian,* August 8, July 29, & April 10, 1998; *Chicago Sun-Times,* June 7, 1998; *San Diego Union-Tribune,* May 7, 1998; *New York Times,* April 13, 1998; *Boston Globe,* March 30, 1998; *CBS 60 Minutes,* March 8, 1998.

Other Project Censored Stories in the News in 1996 and 1997

1997 #13 CENSORED STORY
AMERICAN DRUG INDUSTRY USES THE POOR AS HUMAN GUINEA PIGS

Over 40,000 human guinea pigs participate annually in drug testing experiments run by the huge pharmaceutical companies in the United States. Most of these people are poor and "down-and-outers" who need the money that drug testing provides.

Ever since the mid-1970s, when the Federal Drug Administration (FDA) issued stricter rules on informed consent, high compensation has been necessary to attract research subjects for pharmaceutical tests. In Fall 1997, the *Wall Street Journal* reported that Eli Lilly, the maker of Prozac, uses homeless people to test drugs for FDA approval. The Eli Lilly program, which pays $85 per day, is reportedly famous "through soup kitchens, prisons, and shelters from coast-to-coast."

Participation in drug and medical studies is a serious gamble; no one knows the long-term side effects of the drugs that volunteers take. Animal drug testing, however, which is supposed to minimize the danger of drugs that have never been tested on humans, is unreliable. For example, in the early 1990s, the FDA approved fialuridine for healthy human volunteers after it proved non-toxic to dogs. Dogs, however, have an enzyme which humans apparently do not, which neutralizes the drug. Five "Phase II" patients died after taking fialuridine.

SOURCE: Scott Handelman, "A Reserve Army of Guinea Pigs," *CounterPunch,* September 1997.

1998 COVERAGE: The ethics of medical research received substantial coverage in 1998. Biomedical advancements in drug treatment and therapy continue to extend beyond the laboratory into everyday life, and the media coverage reflects that significance.

The ethics of such so-called advancements are being questioned by health agencies. A Department of Health and Human Services (DHHS) report noted that people who participate in medical research are "at undue risk of being harmed, and in some cases may not even know they are research subjects, because the federal system for protecting these people is failing." Many medical institutions, it continued, "increasingly in need of research funds, may be tempted to approve financially lucrative but ethically marginal study proposals." The report did not allege widespread abuses, but rather emphasized the imbalance caused by the nonexistence of a functional system with which to keep medical research in check. In October 1998, the Clinton-appointed National Bioethics Advisory Council called for greater protection for research subjects, especially in the area of mental disorders. The members recommended a series of research protocols aimed at clarifying the required ethical framework.

President Clinton's formal apology to the subjects and families involved in the 1930s Tuskegee Syphilis Trials was a major step towards a more ethical and consensual human research system, but reports continue to surface of past atrocities. A 1961 Canadian LSD experiment conducted on unknowing prison inmates received considerable media coverage in the United States, drawing critical attention to the global and ethical issues involved.

Concern has also been raised over medical research conducted in Veteran's Administration (VA) hospitals throughout the country. Six VA doctors were offered a "ready supply" of subjects with psychiatric diseases. Hospital employees were paid bonuses based on how many patients they could enroll in drug experiments. Many pharmaceutical companies pay according to how long a subject is involved in the research project so patients were tricked and/or talked into staying on for unnecessary periods of time. Physicians have even been reported offering Toys R Us gift certificates to 36 healthy black and Hispanic elementary school students to participate in a medical drug study.

The Centers for Disease Control (CDC) has acknowledged conducting foreign medical research projects, often relating to the AIDS virus, without the required agreements to avoid human rights abuses. Patients were given drugs, blood samples were taken, and research was conducted without the full informed consent of those involved. Other global tests have been conducted in Africa and Asia on pregnant women infected with the AIDS virus. These U.S. government-sponsored studies are trying to determine if a short regimen of the anti-AIDS drug AZT can reduce the chances of the mother infecting her unborn child. The testing involved the use of placebos for some of the participants, which resulted in an international public outcry. Critics have also argued that the participants are poor minorities who do not fully understand the premises of the testing.

SOURCES: *Milwaukee Journal Sentinel,* November 9, 1998; *Los Angeles Times,* October 20 and March 30, 1998; *Wash-*

ington Post, June 12, 1998; *Newsday,* June 23, 1998; *The New York Times,* May 19, 1998; *Washington Post,* March 3, May 13, 1997, and August 1, 1998; *Atlanta Journal Constitution,* June 7, 1998.

1997 #17 CENSORED STORY
TOXINS AND ENVIRONMENTAL POLLUTION CONTRIBUTE TO HUMAN AGGRESSION IN SOCIETY

Two studies have linked exposure to toxins and pollutants with violent behavior in society. A 1996 study conducted by Herbert Needleman and published in the *Journal of the American Medical Association* (JAMA) found that boys with high amounts of lead in their bones had more reports of aggressive and delinquent behavior, and that their behavior got worse over a period of time regardless of social factors. Newer research by Roger D. Masters and colleagues at Dartmouth College suggested that exposure to toxic pollutants, specifically lead and manganese, may contribute to violent crimes. Masters developed the "neurotoxicity hypothesis of violent crime" to try and explain why these rates have such a geographic variance. He found that U.S. counties with measures of neurotoxicity—lead, manganese, and alcohol—have violent crime three times the national average.

Despite government attempts to regulate the potential dangers of environmental exposure to toxins, an estimated 1.7 million American children ages one through five had lead levels of 10 micro-grams per deciliter of blood (ug/dl) or more in 1994; 36.7 percent of African-American children had levels exceeding that. Levels of 7 ug/dl produces reduced IQ. Brain damage persists for years; the IQ reduction is permanent.

The majority of toxic poisoning in children derives from soil and dust released by lead-based paint in older buildings. The Centers for Disease Control estimates taxpayers could realize a net profit of $28 billion by removing all lead-based paint from old buildings. In an author update in *Censored 1998,* Montague stated that scientists are "coming to learn that certain pollutants can affect our behavior" and that there is "a growing body of evidence suggesting that pollutants can affect our sexual behavior."

SOURCES: Peter Montague, Ph.D., "Toxins Affect Behavior," January 16, 1997, #529; "Toxins and Violent Crime," June 19, 1997, #551; both in *Rachel's Environment & Health Weekly.*

COVERAGE 1998: Research on the link between pollutants and toxins with criminal and delinquent behavior has continued in earnest through 1998. With few exceptions, the mainstream media has failed to pick up the story. Both Needleman and Masters have continued their research, piquing the interest of the Environmental Protection Agency (EPA) Office of Criminal Enforcement, Forensics and Training enough to award Masters $50,000 for research into the impact of chemicals used in water treatment on the nervous system. Needleman's study has been instrumental in the inauguration of stricter legislation in 1997 and 1998 regarding lead.

Interestingly, it was *Popular Mechanics* that reiterated the 1984 findings of autopsies performed on criminals who died while committing violent crimes. In tests of their scalp hair ("a log of the chemicals to which an individual has been exposed"), much higher-than-normal levels of metals were typically found. William J. Walsh, "an expert on the link between metal poisoning and violence," claims that at an outpatient center he manages in Naperville, Illinois, he and his staff have managed to reduce violent behavior in children by adjusting their diets. "We're talking about kids who are terrors at age one and torturing the cat when they are two," he is reported as saying. Foreign papers have reported on American research which suggests a link between dietary mineral deficiencies, especially zinc, and violent behavior. It is known that high levels of cadmium (from smoking) and lead affect the absorption of zinc.

Children are especially sensitive to toxic exposure. Researchers are uncovering a whole host of symptoms in newborns whose cause is best explained by environmental exposure to toxins. Lead, manganese, and PCBs are particularly harmful in the early stages of fetal development. The rate of increase in incidents of Attention Deficit Hyperactivity Disorder (ADHD), often linked to problems in behavior and aggression); abnormal fetal development; and childhood cancers is startling. *Mother Jones*, in an interview with Theo Colborn, author of *Our Stolen Future*, notes that "even low-dose exposures to many of the man-made chemicals found in common plastics, cleaning compounds, and cosmetics can affect newborn babies and developing fetuses, and can cause a range of problems, including low IQs, genital malformations, low sperm counts, and infertility."

Industry magazines and newsletters such as *Asbestos and Lead Abatement Report, Occupational Health & Safety Letter*, and *Public Health Reports* have vigorously addressed this issue. In an argument against the Centers for Disease Control's 1997 retreat from recommending universal lead screening for children (*Public Health Reports*, January 1, 1998), Eric W. Manheimer and Ellen K. Silbergeld point out that the analysis "failed to include the benefit of reduced crime."

SOURCES: Alison Jones, "Small Doses of Lead Come Under Scrutiny," *Washington Post*, March 3, 1998; Jim Wilson, "The Chemistry of Violence," *Popular Mechanics*, April, 1998; Marilyn Berlin Snell, "Theo Colborn: A Controversial Scientist Speaks On Plastics, IQ, and the Womb," *Mother Jones*, March/April 1998; Claude Morgan, "Fill 'Em With Lead," *E*, September 1, 1998.

1996 Stories

1996 #1 CENSORED STORY

RISKING THE WORLD: NUCLEAR PROLIFERATION IN SPACE

In October 1997, NASA launched the Cassini space probe. Its destination: Saturn and its rings. On board the probe was 72.3 pounds of plutonium used to run electrical equipment—never before has so much plutonium been used in any space mission.

Using plutonium in space missions is risky business. The Cassini probe, for instance, was propelled by a Titan IV rocket which has a history of launch accidents. In 1993, a Titan rocket exploded shortly after launch destroying a $1 billion spy satellite system. Also, Cassini will not have enough momentum to reach Saturn directly, and will have to circle Venus twice and then fly back toward Earth using Earth's gravity to reach its final destination. During the flyby in August 1999, the probe will reach a speed of 42,300 mph at an altitude of just 500 miles above Earth. If the probe comes too close and enters the Earth's atmosphere, it will burn up and discharge plutonium into the atmosphere.

In an environmental impact statement, NASA estimated that if plutonium from the probe were released into the Earth's atmosphere, approximately 5 billion of earth's population would receive 99 percent or more of the radiation exposure. NASA projects that over the next 50 years, an estimated 2,300 people would die and many others would fall victim to latent cancer fatalities and nuclear fallout. Other scientists estimate the death total as nearer hundreds of thousands.

The energy generated by the plutonium is not substantial (745 watts). Some agencies believe that this could be generated with solar panels. Reports by the European Space Agency and others insist that the Department of Energy's national nuclear laboratories and the corporations that manufacture the nuclear hardware for NASA insisted on using plutonium.

SOURCES: "Risking the World: Nuclear Proliferation in Space," *CovertAction Quarterly*, Summer 1996; "Don't Send Plutonium Into Space," *Progressive Media Project*, May 1996, both by Karl Grossman.

SPECIAL 1998 UPDATE BY KARL GROSSMAN: "The push to 'nuclearize' and 'weaponize' space has been repeatedly cited by Project Censored through the years and continues to be an extremely under-reported *Censored* story.

"As protests mounted, there was a flurry of media interest before the October 1997 launch of the Cassini space probe. But little attention was given to the most dangerous part of the mission—NASA's plan to send the Cassini probe hurtling back towards Earth at 42,300 mph and have it buzz Earth just 500 miles above the surface in August 1999 in a 'gravity assist' or 'slingshot' maneuver aimed at giving the probe additional velocity so it can reach its final destination. Indeed, a September 1997 *60 Minutes* report on Cassini didn't mention the

Earth flyby at all and instead framed the story as one involving a catastrophic problem for Florida should there have been an accident on launch.

"No mention was made by mainstream U.S. media of the declaration in NASA's 'Final Environmental Impact Statement for the Cassini Mission' which stated that if, in the flyby of Earth, the probe dips down into the Earth's 75-mile high atmosphere and makes an 'inadvertent reentry,' it will break up, release plutonium, expose 'approximately 5 billion of the estimated 7 to 8 billion world population at the time…to 99 percent or more of the radiation exposure.' Quite an issue to ignore.

"Media, meanwhile, parroted NASA's claim that the likelihood of a launch accident involving the Titan IV rocket lifting Cassini was infinitesimal. The Titan IV launched in October 1997 did make it up safely with Cassini, but on August 12, 1998, another Titan IV—the 25th Titan IV to be launched—exploded on liftoff, blowing a $1.3 billion spy satellite to smithereens. This followed a similar 1993 Titan IV launch explosion. As it turned out, there had been a 1-in-25 chance of the Titan which lofted Cassini blowing up on launch, but mainstream media didn't make the connection.

"Also in 1998, Dr. Earl Budin, Radiology Professor at UCLA, obtained the government's 'Interagency Nuclear Safety Review Panel Safety Evaluation Report on the Cassini Mission.' It acknowledged the possibility of 'several tens of thousands' of cancer deaths in a Cassini Earth 'flyby' accident. As to NASA's public relations claims prior to launch that the plutonium canisters were built like 'bank vaults,' the pre-launch report to the White House of the Interagency Nuclear Safety Review Panel—a five-agency body including NASA—acknowledged that the plutonium canisters 'have not been designed for the high speed reentry.' Therefore, in an Earth 'flyby' accident, 'much of the plutonium is vaporized' and provides 'a collective dose to the world's population.' Again, there was no media mention of such important specifics. Also, the report lists some 18 ways that Cassini can undergo an 'Earth impact' on its planned 'flyby'— from rocket-engine failure to ground-control error.

"Moreover, even if the Cassini Earth 'flyby' goes ahead and is successful, NASA is planning eight more plutonium space probe shots in coming years according to a report issued in May 1998 by the U.S. General Accounting Office (GAO). An April 1998 NASA statement spoke of up to 13 such missions. With a 12-percent failure rate already in both the U.S. and Soviet/Russian space nuclear programs, accidents—and disasters—would seem inevitable. Again, no media mention.

"A key question: why is the United States insisting on using nuclear power in space even though solar power would suffice? The European Space Agency is readying its Rosetta space probe to go beyond the orbit of Jupiter to rendezvous with a comet using new, high-efficiency solar cells to substitute for plutonium as a source of on-board electric power.

NASA insists on plutonium over solar power because of pressure from the manufacturer of the plutonium systems, formerly General Electric, now Lockheed Martin, the national nuclear laboratories, and the U.S. Department of Energy—and there is a military connection.

"The 1996 U.S. Air Force report, *New World Vistas*, states that 'in the next two decades, new technologies will allow the fielding of space-based weapons of devastating effectiveness to be used to deliver energy and mass as force projection in tactical and strategic conflict.... These advances will enable lasers with reasonable mass and cost to effect very many kills.' But, notes the report, 'power limitations impose restrictions' on such-based weapon systems 'making them relatively unfeasible.... A natural technology to enable high power,' it goes on, 'is nuclear power in space.'

"In 1998, there were many follow-ups to this, including the U.S. signing of a $10 million contract with TRW and Boeing to build a space-based 'laser demonstrator' and to develop a 'National Missile Defense Program,' and the issuance of such documents as the United States Space Command's 'Vision for 2020' plan which states: 'U.S. Space Command—dominating the space dimension of military operations to protect U.S. interests and investment.'

"In the wake of the Cassini launch, mainstream media returned to simply cheerleading for the U.S. space program. Indeed, Walter Cronkite, who set the media lead in the 1960s and 1970s as NASA's chief cheerleader, was back in 1998 with an encore performance for the shuttle shot with John Glenn aboard. Meanwhile, the 'nuclearization' and weaponization of space moves ahead aggressively. And mainstream media sleep."

Censored update: Many scientists and experts, as well as many concerned citizens, have voiced strong opinions on the debate over the "nuclearization" of space vehicles past, present and future. Project Censored's goal remains that of fostering a national dialogue in the media on the merits and demerits of the Cassini program and nuclear powered missions in space.

For more information, contact the Stop Cassini Earth Flyby Action Site on the World Wide Web at http://www.non-violence.org./noflyby/

1996 STORY #6:

NEW MEGA-MERGED BANK-ING BEHEMOTHS = BIG RISK

Bank mergers were at an all-time high in 1995. Chase Manhattan and Chemical Bank combined to create the nation's largest bank with $300 billion in assets, while the merger of First Interstate and Wells Fargo created a new West Coast giant with over $100 billion in assets. The massive consolidation of the nation's banking resources resulted in 71.5 percent of U.S. banking assets being controlled by the 100 largest banking organizations which represent *less than 1 percent of the total banks* in the nation.

Under the Bank Merger and Bank Holdings Company Act, the Federal Reserve is required before approving any application of a merger to test how well the convenience and needs of the public will be met by the merger. Critics charge that the Federal Reserve Board is doing a disservice to the American public by not applying this "public convenience and needs" test to the wave of banking mergers. Analysts are concerned that the growing giants of the banking industry will "shift insurance risks to taxpayers, cost jobs, lead to increased rates for bank customer service, make it harder to get loans and lessen community access to bank branches."

The trend toward bigger banks is creating a system where giant banking institutions are taking on "too big to fail" status. Indeed, a failure of any one of these new giants would have a devastating effect on the nation's financial health. And with the Federal Reserve capping the amount at $25 billion that financial institutions have to pay into the governments' bank insurance fund, just 1.25 percent of deposits are now insured. Consequently, any bailout of one of these new megabanks would come directly from the pockets of taxpayers.

Studies have also found that banks in concentrated markets tend to charge higher rates for certain types of loans, and tend to offer lower interest rates on certain types of deposits than do banks in less concentrated markets. A 1995 study by the U.S. Public Interest Research Group and the Center for Study of Responsive Law showed that fees on checking and savings accounts increased at twice the rate of inflation from 1993 to 1995 as bank mergers moved forward. The trend toward megabanks is also closing out community access and making it harder to get loans.

SOURCE: Jake Lewis, "The Making of the Banking Behemoths," *Multinational Monitor,* June 1996.

1998 COVERAGE: Corporate megamergers made history in 1998 in all areas—banking, commerce, and industry. One writer checked his newspaper's electronic library to see how many times the paper had reported on mergers since 1985: 5,385 times. Some of this past year's proposed and completed mergers include: 1) the $70.4 billion union of banking giant Citicorp and brokerage-insurer Traveler's Group to form the world's biggest financial-services firm; 2) Daimler-Benz's acquisition of Chrysler Corporation for $34.8 billion, the largest industrial merger in history; 3) the $56.6 billion merger between SBC Communications Inc. and Ameritech Corp., combining two "baby bells" into a local telephone giant controlling one-third of U.S. phone lines; and 4) the merger of Exxon with Mobil to create the largest oil company in the world. Other mergers are the $60 billion joining of NationsBank and BankAmerica to upset Chase and create the largest bank in the United States worth $570 billion; America Online's buy-out of Netscape; and Tyco industries purchase of electrical connector maker AMP.

The mainstream media coverage of these mergers follows a simplistic, business-centric model. Sometimes, significant antitrust speculations are raised, but they are rarely pursued. The bulk of the coverage usually lasts for a week or less depending on the logistics of the merger. Most importantly, there is very little follow-up regarding a merger's impact on people and regions.

Of the 10 major mergers in 1998, all but one involved the loss of more than 10,000 jobs. According to a corporate monitoring organization, companies fired 523,000 employees between January and October of 1998. Despite the positive economic outlook we continue to hear about, 1998 could be the worst year this decade for workers. While the chances of those laid off finding new work is good, no one mentions that these jobs commonly involve a decrease in pay, working conditions, and lifestyle. Meanwhile, executives continue to receive enormous golden parachutes. For example, the CEO of Bank of America received $25.5 million in salary, bonuses, and stock options in 1997 alone, typical of megamerger executives around the country.

In the case of bank mergers, it is feared that loans to minority and women-owned businesses will significantly decline. The small business environment is also seriously threatened. Huge corporate mergers put small-town businesses at an even greater financial risk, forcing them to compete rather than cooperate with other local businesses. To the massive corporations, personal service has become a "cost analysis calculation."

A significant number of mergers do not produce the promised effects. Many critics believe that antitrust laws simply cannot keep up with the lightning changes of the global economy. Still, the media continues to miss the big picture. The concern is over the enormous and rapid concentration of economic and political power. The Fortune 500 is becoming the Fortune 100 with nothing else in sight. Finally, arguably the largest issue raised by megamergers that continues to go unmentioned is whether or not the government will have to bail out these companies if they fail.

SOURCES: *Orlando Sentinel,* December 13, 1998; *Washington Post,* December 8, 1998; *Fresno Bee,* December 3, 1998; *Austin American Statesman,* December 3, 1998; *The New York Times,* November 30, 1998; *Nation's Business,* November 1998; *San Diego Union-Tribune,* April 14, 1998; *San Francisco Chronicle,* April 17, 1998; *Newsday,* June 17, 1998.

CHAPTER 3

Building Media Democracy

BY PETER PHILLIPS

"A popular government without popular information, or the means of acquiring it, is a prologue to a farce or a tragedy, or perhaps both."—James Madison

The U.S. media has lost its diversity and its ability to present different points of view. Instead there is a homogeneity of news and a regurgitation of the same news stories on nearly all channels and in the headlines. Every corporate media outlet in the country spent hundreds of hours and yards of newsprint to cover Bill Clinton's sexual escapades and in the process ignored many important news stories.

Mainstream media tends to disregard news stories that affect the working people of our country, and instead seeks to entertain us. Corporate media ignores socioeconomic concerns of the 75 percent of us of who are blue-and white-collar workers surviving paycheck to paycheck. They fail to answer the relevant questions for working people about why the value of our labor has on average declined for 25 years, why health care costs are so high, why housing is so expensive, why we can't afford to send our kids to public colleges, and why our taxes keep increasing.

Corporate media no longer seeks to inform the public on important relevant issues. Instead, major media markets entertainment to people so they can sell advertising. Advertisers purchase the ads to encourage the public to buy their products. The more viewers/readers media can attract the more they earn from advertisers. They do this by studying the demographic indicators of target markets and designing titillating, exciting, and provocative entertainment to capture as large a market share of the potential audience as possible. Corporate media today includes news reporting as part of their marketing strategy, and news programming on television and news reporting in print is now expected to turn a profit on it's own within the corporate structure. Independent journalists have never had a totally free hand since their stories always have to pass by editors and newspaper management. But in the past it has seemed that these latter felt an obligation to respect the integrity of certain journalistic principles of independence and the citizens' right to know. Whereas today, the corporate bottom line seems to have displaced such principles as never before. Gone are the days when journalists were semi-free to write the stories they chose to expose the corruption of the powerful and the abuses of the business corporate elite.

A new media era has emerged. In 1997, the new CEO of the *Los Angeles Times* assigned a business manager to each section of the newspaper in order to insure that a proper profit-oriented product was developed that would insure readership of their upper-middle class target market. News story selection is now made with audience appeal as an essential element. What do upper-middle class people (whites) want to read in the paper and what will keep them returning for more? Stories about crime and fear emerge as attention grabbers, as well an celebrity stories, gossip news, sexual titillation, vacations, gourmet foods, entertainment, and consumer goods.

As media corporations join the ranks of the corporate 1,000, questions arise such as: How can we trust the objectivity of *The New York Times* book reviewers now that book reviews are linked to profit sharing with a Barnes and Noble Web site, or how can we believe the objectivity of General Electric-owned NBC's reporting on defense contracts or nuclear energy?

Project Censored's research on the corporate media in *Censored 1998* showed that the 11 largest most influential media corporations are directly connected through shared boards of directors to 144 of the Corporate 1,000 companies in the United States.

Little wonder that the U.S. news is so biased against democratic liberation struggles all over the world and so favorable to multi-national capital flow, International Monetary Fund policies, GATT, MAI, NAFTA, and all the other neoliberal economic policies that favor the free flow of international capital and wealth acquisition.

Might the failure of the media to cover the carcinogens in cosmetics story (*Censored* #2 1998) have to do with cosmetics companies being one of the largest advertisers in the country, and could it also be related to the fact that some of our major media outlets have direct links with cosmetic companies and large retail outlets through shared boards of directors? The *Washington Post* shares a board director with Gillette as does CBS. CBS also shares board members with Wal-Mart, Pharmacia & Upjohn. The *Los Angeles Times* shares board directors with Procter & Gamble and Nordstrom. *The New York Times* shares a board member with Bristol-Meyers Squibb, as does NBC. Gannett shares a board member with Du Pont Chemical company, and Time Warner shares board members with Colgate-Palmolive, K-Mart, and Sears.

It seems clear that the media have no interest in awakening the socio-political consciousness of the working people in the United States. So what hope have we? What direction can resistance and change take? I believe that we are not going to reform the media system in the United States anytime in the near future. Media wealth is too concentrated, too solidified, and too integrated into the corporate-government elite to make social change within the existing system possible.

We can, however, look to ourselves for the direction we must go. In the past three years there have been two Media and Democracy Conventions in the United States. One was in San Francisco three years ago, and the other in New York in October of 1997. They each brought together 1,500 to 2,000 independent/alternative writers, editors, film producers, and broadcasters, who share many of the same concerns about corporate media and agreed that a new alternative media system is needed. With no plans in the works for a Third Media and Democracy Congress, it seems time, not to reassemble nationally to discuss directions, but rather to begin the necessary grassroots organizing to build a national alternative media system based on democracy and the First Amendment. It is time to let working people find their own voices and tell each other the truth about the powerful and the corrupt.

A grassroots Media and Democracy movement exists based on a shared vision of building alternative news and information systems independent from corporate influence. Hundreds of pirate radio stations have sprung up all over the U.S. offering a diversity of programs. Project Censored's resource guide gives readers an up-to-date listing of over 200 media activist organizations currently operating in the United States. There are over 400 nationally distributed alternative press news publications and thousands of regional ones. Activists are finding local groups and getting involved and many are creating their own First Amendment rights groups, alternative publications, and micro-radio stations. Activists everywhere are starting to monitor the corporate bias in their own local media and are connecting to other alternative news outlets.

We need to start with a vision of a democratic citizen-based news and information future. There are a number of recommendations that Media and Democracy movement activists are suggesting for the transformation of the mainstream media into becoming more democratic and responsive. They include:

➤ Require all major media outlets to establish an Ombudsman office, responsible only to a publicly elected advisory board, that can write and discuss any issue they choose and require media organizations to provide fair coverage.

➤ Have each corporate media organization tenure, with budgets, a fixed percentage of their journalists and producers and allow them to investigate any story they choose.

➤ Restrict the libel laws to make it more difficult for corporations to use slap-suit tactics to suppress controversial news about their organizations.

➤ Increase public involvement in major media systems through time and space requirements for access by diverse community organizations and alternative opinions.

➤ Create diverse, culturally sensitive citizen advisory boards for local programming choices.

➤ Tax commercial advertisements to support publicly-owned ad-free media outlets including radio, TV, and print, in every city in the United States.

➤ Require high licensing fees for commercial use of the public airways and use the revenue from the fees to support training and development for community-based productions and investigative reporting.

➤ Create thousands of local microradio licenses and use Small Business Administration loans/training to support community-based neighborhood residents in developing 100-watt radio stations nationwide.

➤ Support alternative non-profit wire services that circulate news stories from alternative press sources for re-publication in local newsweeklies and community journals, or for broadcasting on public/microradio stations and cable access systems.

➤ Research worldwide contacts for alternative news sources and investigative reporters and use the Internet to build global links and Web sites for downloading international new stories for local publication.

➤ Build a progressive labor-activist national newspaper.

Alternative/independent media sources in the U.S. are still small and underfinanced. Yet they offer a hope for the future. An alternative/independent press can be a key element in a social movement that empowers working people in the U.S. to take control of their government-corporate power structures for their own betterment. "Free the Media" can become a real rallying cry that will allow the emergence of what the new democratized AFL-CIO calls "Common Sense Economics," an economics that unmasks corporate wealth exploitation for the betterment of working people.

How do we get to a new vision of democratic citizen-based news and information? It won't happen by itself. Mario Savio used to say that social movements take a lot of heartfullness, hard work, and grassroots organizing. He was very right. But the process has already begun. Fairness and Accuracy in Reporting (FAIR), the Institute of Alternative Journalism (IAJ), and numerous First Amendment groups, Internet newsletters, and news magazines are active all over the United States. Progressive media networks exist in L.A., Chicago, Denver, San Francisco, Houston, New York, and Seattle. TV producers from Free Speech TV, People's Video, Globalvision, Deep Dish, and Paper Tiger TV are being joined by small progressive shoe-string-budget cable show producers all over the country: People like school teacher John Moriarty in Stockton, California, who for six years has been doing a weekly hour long progressive TV show aired in his local community. Pacific Radio network has been joined by Hightower Radio and United Broadcasting, and hundreds of alternative newsweeklies are published in almost every major metropolitan area in the U.S.

But it is nowhere near enough, nor adequately filled with current up-to-date alternative news and information. We have to begin to reach the 200 million working people and work our way up from there. Microradio is a good start, but is under attack by the Federal Communications Commission. We are close, however, to local community activists being able to download or use as sources news stories from the Internet and have enough good solid news material to fill a weekly progressive local newspaper. Small teams of peace center activists, environmentalists, civil rights workers, political activists, school teachers, labor organizers, college students, and working people can, and I believe will, start the publication of thousands of newsprint publications for distribution in the cities, towns, and neighborhoods of our society. Some will sell advertising, some will work from their convictions. As Media and Democracy activists, we have to help them find each other, share materials, and literally make it easy for them to put out high quality interconnected news publications locally nationwide.

Unfortunately, some of our best liberal-leaning national weekly/monthly news magazines tend to see themselves as in competition for a small group of left-wing intellectuals and rarely follow-up and reinforce news stories that are printed in each other publications. While I think we can encourage students and working people to read *The Nation, Mother Jones, Z Magazine,* CAQ, and many other important high quality news sources, this will only be a small part of creating a new democratic news and information system in the U.S. What if national progressive news publications released their best articles after publication for free re-publication in alternative news locals? Given that local micropress editors will seek to include stories that are interesting to and important for their constituency, it would seem that this would encourage a broader section of working people to consider opting for *The Nation* instead of *Time* magazine.

We can mobilize the necessary resources to build and expand a Media and Democracy Movement, by sharing news stories and reinforcing and expanding national alternative press publications through selective re-publication at the local level. Additionally, we could easily facilitate Web sites that would allow thousands of writers, scholars, and activists to post their work and make it available for local progressive newspapers to download and publish. Journalists and activists who attended the international conference on Ownership and Control of the Media in Athens, Greece, in June 1998, have started a Progressive International Media Exchange (PRIME) list-serve to exchange news stories from around the world. These efforts are inexpensive and can offer extensive content choices for local progressive publishers. A populist army of diversified news and information gatherers and publishers is ready to emerge. Not all in agreement, not lockstep within a ideological framework, but working people finding access to their own voices.

Back in the late 1970s, the nation's beer supply was dominated by a half-dozen companies. In the early 1980s in Chico, California, two young entrepreneurs started a shoestring microbrewery called Sierra Nevada Brewing. They, along with other microbreweries in the U.S., transformed the quality and diversity of beer consumption in the United States. Now, brewpubs abound, and even the major breweries now have their own microbeer look-alikes.

If it can be done with beer, we can transform the news and information systems in the United States with micropresses, desktop publishing, microradio and alternative Internet connections, and modify the diversity and quality of the media forever. We don't need to capture more than 3 to 5 percent of the local market share of news consumers before the media will take notice and begin to reform itself. That is when we will need to be ready with suggestions and legislation that will make their willingness to accept change a permanent transformation.

Millions of people are turning away from mainstream media news, questioning the dogma of a corporate owned press, and trusting more in alternative news and information from sources like the Alternet, Project Censored, Noam Chomsky, Mike Davis, and Howard Zinn. Gary Webb's popularity in the country rose as *The New York Times*, and *Los Angeles Times* tried to dismiss the CIA-Crack-Contra connections. The Internet and alternative sources, heard by millions, mobilized the necessary political pressure that resulted in the CIA's admission to their knowledge of Contra drug dealings during the 1980s.

As media and democracy activists, we still need to work on making it easy for small-circulation editors to download news stories without having to obtain copyright permissions from hundreds of different sources. For progressive activists, all that is needed is an Internet-connected computer and you can being accessing important alternative news sources. You don't need to write and produce a full 16-page weekly newspaper on your first try. Build up to it. Find local sponsors and network with community groups anxious to have their stories told in the local press. Fill your pages with quality news stories and op-ed pieces from alternative sources all over the world. Expand your contacts by using the Project Censored alternative press resource guide. It is a good start and as you find other sources let us know so we can add them to our annual guide.

Here are a few Web sites to perk your interest.

Project Censored Alternative Press Links
www.sonoma.edu/projectcensored

Progressive News Wire
www.commondreams.org

People's News Agency
www.prout.org/pna/

Institute for Global Communications
www.igc.org

THIS MODERN WORLD

by TOM TOMORROW

IF YOU ASK ME, THE MEDIA HAVE REALLY GONE INTO A *FEEDING FRENZY* OVER CLINTON'S ALLEGED SEXUAL MISCONDUCT.

YES--WHILE A STORY WHICH COULD POTENTIALLY LEAD TO THE DOWNFALL OF A PRESIDENT IS CLEARLY *IMPORTANT*, IT ALSO MUST BE KEPT IN *PERSPECTIVE!*

FOR INSTANCE, WHILE JOURNALISTS RUSH TO REPORT THE LATEST SALACIOUS RUMORS, *CAMPAIGN FINANCE REFORM* HAS BEEN QUIETLY DEFEATED FOR ANOTHER YEAR.

AND WITHOUT MEDIA SCRUTINY, THE PUBLIC SIMPLY ISN'T GOING TO PRESSURE POLITICIANS TO RESTRICT THE FLOW OF CORPORATE MONEY!

AND CONGRESS KNOWS THAT NO ONE IS PAYING ANY ATTENTION... SEN. MITCH McCONNELL OPENLY GLOATS THAT "NO ONE IN THE HISTORY OF AMERICAN POLITICS HAS EVER WON OR LOST A CAMPAIGN ON THIS ISSUE..."

YET WHAT COULD BE MORE IMPORTANT THAN CONFRONTING THE FACT THAT OUR DEMOCRACY IS BEING AUCTIONED OFF TO THE *HIGHEST BIDDER?*

UNFORTUNATELY, THESE MEDIA ELITISTS SEEM TO BELIEVE THAT AMERICANS WON'T PAY ATTENTION TO *ANYTHING* UNLESS IT INVOLVES *SEX!*

IT'S TRULY *APPALLING!*

I WISH THEY'D SHOW A LITTLE *RESTRAINT!*

©TOM TOMORROW 4-8-98

CHAPTER 4

Missing News

BY ROBERT A. HACKETT

America's northern neighbor Canada avoided the excesses of Cold War militarism from the 1950s to the 1980s. During the Vietnam War, Canada provided refuge for many American draft evaders. And in the 1990s, American supporters of publicly funded Medicare cited Canada as a model. But, if America's news media are overlooking hugely significant stories, as Project Censored has admirably demonstrated for over 20 years, do Canada's media match the country's relatively progressive image, or are they as subject to censoring forces as their American counterparts? This is one of the questions which inspired the launch of a Canadian version of Project Censored in 1993, News Watch Canada.

A PROJECT IS BORN

Project Censored Canada (PCC)—now called News Watch Canada—owes its origins to Bill Doskoch, a journalist for the *Regina Leader-Post* in Saskatchewan. While browsing through the magazines at a Montreal newsstand in 1990, Doskoch came across an article on Project Censored in the *Utne Reader*. Several events over a period of three years convinced Doskoch that Canada needed a Project Censored of its own.

Canada's main public broadcaster, the Canadian Broadcasting Corporation (CBC) was recently hit with the first in a series of massive cutbacks. Since the 1940s, first in radio then in television, CBC has provided news services largely free of the commercial and corporate pressures affecting the private sector media.

During the economic recession of the early 1990s, reorganization and cutbacks threatened to erode the quality and independence of Canada's internationally recognized private sector news media. Conrad Black's Hollinger Inc. bought a minority stake in *Southam*, Canada's largest newspaper chain. At the time, *Southam* was struggling with the government's antitrust watchdogs, whom were on their case for the company's takeover of a significant portion of the community newspapers in metropolitan Vancouver, Canada's third largest city. (Since then, Hollinger has taken majority control of *Southam*, and other papers. Hollinger now owns over half of Canada's 105 dailies, as well as papers in the U.S. and overseas, making most American newspaper chains look like mom-and-pop operations by comparison.)

Doskoch wondered if all the cutbacks and ownership changes impacted the news. At CBC, in the face of cutbacks and the fear of being perceived as too liberal (especially after the election of a conservative federal government in 1984), management was apparently retreating. With an increasingly conservative political climate, press owners were less willing to invest in legally risky and time-consuming investigations. Exposés of culturally mythologized institutions, like the Royal Canadian Mounted Police, might benefit democratic accountability, but they weren't necessarily good for media profitability (Hackett & Zhao, 1998: 50, 152).

Led by the advice of Project Censored founder Carl Jensen and the permission of the Canadian Association of Journalists (CAJ), CAJ board member Doskoch contacted journalism and communications programs across Canada to find academic partners. Donald Gutstein and I answered his call from Vancouver's Simon Fraser University back in 1993, and we were joined the following year by Professor James Winter from the University of Windsor, Ontario. The project was an opportunity for us to teach research methods to students, while also offering an alternative to a steady stream of media research undertaken by free market fundamentalists, notably the Vancouver-based Fraser Institute, implementing a left-liberal bias in Canadian journalism. Although the conclusions they draw are often highly contestable (Hackett, Gilsdorf & Savage, 1992; Cross, 1997), the Institute's studies have demonstrated some impact, especially on CBC.

In its first few years, we used Carl Jensen's methodology as a model. Our students scanned Canada's best "alternative" magazines, supplemented for 1994 and 1995 by more establishmentarian and conservative periodicals to produce lists of under-reported stories. We invited the editors of these periodicals, as well as librarians, journalists, and members of the general public, to nominate stories they felt deserved wider coverage. One year, we even invited every Member of Parliament, representing five different political parties. They sent us a total of three nominations. We mailed surveys to 300 advocacy and professional groups representing a range of interests and collected between 100 to 200 potential stories per year. Ultimately, we winnowed the nominees down in the annual seminar to a short list, and sent them on to our national judging panel, including distinguished academics, journalists and politicians from both the left and the right.

In 1993, we presented our first annual under-reported story list. We immediately noticed parallels between the U.S. media, and that of Canada. Minimal coverage was given to important stories about tax breaks for the wealthy, government mismanagement of resource industries, Canada's heavy involvement in arms exports, Canada's cozy relationship with Indonesia's repressive regime, possible oil interests underlying the United Nations intervention in Somalia, and hidden corporate ties to political power. *Winnipeg Free Press* reporter Frances Russell wrote that our selection of her piece on the undemocratic implications of the North American Free Trade Agreement (NAFTA) for Canada "is worth more to me than any number of nominations for a National Newspaper Award." Russell revealed in her letter that for years, she had experienced "the pressure to become silent created by watching the topic be shunned and avoided by my fellow journalists," but finally, "other journalists have validated that what I see happening around me is, in fact, news."

The following year, we fine-tuned our methods and expanded our search. The top three under-covered stories for 1994 included: Canada's official watchdog on government spending criticized the federally-owned Atomic Energy Canada Ltd. for expecting a $200 million bailout to clean up potentially toxic hazards at old nuclear facilities; Canadian provinces negotiated the domestic equivalent of international free trade in 1994. Opponents of the Interprovincial Trade Agreement dismissed it as a "bill of rights for the private sector," because it reduced provincial governments' powers to set higher environmental standards or to encourage regional development and local employment; and, the General Agreement on Tariffs and Trade (GATT) extended multi-national corporate control over valuable food and medicinal crops, allowing genetically altered plants to be patented, and preventing farmers from saving seeds for replanting, forcing scientific researchers to pay potentially prohibitive royalties.

The top three stories of 1995 concerned the USA's growing influence on Canada. They pointed to the proposed weakening of American environmental protection laws, which would harm Canada's air and water in the Great Lakes region; the intrusion of American-style privatized health care to Canada under the rubric of NAFTA; and the environmental implications of the Pentagon's High Frequency Active Auroral Research Program in the northern ionosphere (Project Censored's #9 story, 1994).

During the same year, we included a story about how the federal government tried to bury a 1991 Statistics Canada report which challenged the conventional assumption that social spending was the major contributor to the government deficit. We also revealed the costs (crime, suicide, unemployment, poverty) of New Zealand's approach to public debt, an approach which had been trumpeted by free market fundamentalists in Canada; the senior governments' reluctance to intervene against lawlessness and unaccountability of local government at the Mohawk First Nations community of Kanehsatake near Montreal; widespread human rights violations in Mexico, now Canada's NAFTA partner; the smokescreening of an international arms bazaar behind an air show marketed as family entertainment; the exploitation of home-based garment workers, mainly Asian or other Third World immigrant women; and the federal government's waste of money through selling CF-5 training jets cheaply, shortly after spending millions on their upgrading.

To be fair, many of the stories were mentioned in the mainstream media, so investigative journalism is not entirely dead. However, none of the stories received the attention that our student researchers and national panelists felt they warranted.

In addition to the under-covered stories, James Winter's seminar produced Junk Food News lists. In his view, the "junk" news stories clustered into several types: an important story covered in a sensational manner with minimal exploration of the underlying issues (the O.J. Simpson murder trial); a trivial story that receives more coverage than it deserves (actor Hugh Grant nabbed with prostitute); a superficial approach to an important issue ignoring more complete information about the subject; or an advertisement dressed up as news (the release of Microsoft's Windows 95). Like some of our underreported stories, many of the junk food stories were American imports, but, unlike the former, the junk news had no particular relevance to Canada.

These lists were useful in generating a certain amount of public discussion. We presented them at CAJ conferences and published articles in *Media*, Canada's main English-language journalism review, as well as some of the alternative monthlies and urban weekly papers. *The Toronto Star*, a Canadian daily that boasts the largest circulation, ran several stories, including a feature by a supportive journalist. One of the annual lists was distributed by Canadian Press, Canada's main news agency, resulting in articles in papers across the country. We did occasional interviews and talks shows on local CBC and private radio, mainly in our home towns of Vancouver and Windsor.

This is not to say that Canada's press suddenly erupted with stories highlighting their own blind spots. Our coverage was at best sporadic and usually cursory. The business-oriented *Globe & Mail*, Canada's national newspaper ran two pieces by our critics before actually giving us a chance to state our case. In one such piece, journalism professor Chris Dornan (1994) argued that PCC's stories were not really censored, and if you haven't heard of them, you haven't been paying attention. (At least the *Globe* ran a rebuttal from Doskoch [1994].) News organizations were most inclined to publicize the list when it included a story they had originally broken. The junk news stories were considered more newsworthy than the under-reported story lists: familiarity, it seems, breeds repetition.

SHIFTING FOCUS

On the whole, Canada's under-covered story lists did not rival Project Censored's revelations of American corporate, governmental, and military violations of the public interest. We speculate that there are at least three possible reasons:

1. Canada's military-industrial complex does not rival the size of America's military, with the U.S.'s huge budgets and international connections.

2. Canada's alternative press, from which many of our under-covered stories derive, has fewer resources than its American counterpart. With smaller-scale circulation and fewer foundation grants, Canada's alternative magazines have difficulty financing time-consuming, ground-breaking journalism. Moreover, due to public broadcasting's cutbacks in the 1990s, the electoral setbacks suffered by Canada's main left-wing party (the New Democratic Party, or NDP), and Conrad Black's increasing right-wing influence in the press, Canada's progressive left has not established a press of its own.

3. Canada's news media system may be less constrained and monolithic than America's corporate-owned papers and TV networks. After all, Canada's Parliament has five political parties representing a much broader ideological range than America's Republican-Democrat duopoly. And in the CBC, Canada has a much stronger public broadcaster than America's PBS, adding balance and diversity to the system.

It seems we should be celebrating here in Canada. As far as we can tell, the press north of the U.S. border is not overlooking jaw-dropping infamy on the scale uncovered by Peter Phillips and Project Censored.

Does that mean that Canada's press is a bastion of independence, diversity, and democratic debate? Not necessarily. Our top 10 lists point towards more subtle blind spots than the blatant gaps in America's agenda-setting media. From 1996, our project shifted focus from individual stories to more significant, under-covered whole issues.

In order to search for such news blind spots, we turned to content analysis. This more "academic" approach kept with our major funding source for 1994-97, a research grant from the Social Sciences and Humanities Research Council of Canada. For the purpose of our work, content analysis has two advantages:

First, while never simply a value-neutral descriptive technique, an efficient content analysis has a certain rigor and reliability. Different analysts using the same coding rules should produce the same results.

Second, content analysis helps not only in identifying blind spots in news coverage, but also in testing hypotheses about the impact of various "filters" on the production of news coverage. Those filters may include such factors as journalists' notions of professionalism, institutionalized routines and ownership priorities within news organizations, and external influences like advertisers, commercial pressures, technology and legal considerations (like avoiding libel suits; Shoemaker and Reese, 1996).

Our project also implemented other traditional social science tools to supplement the top 10 lists with modest pilot studies. We interviewed and surveyed over 30 Canadian journalists, and conducted a mail-out survey to 300 Canadian interest groups of both progressive and "establishment" orientations.

Here's what our respondents told us:

Most journalists agreed that important news was missed due to insufficient resources, complexity, traditional news values, and aspects of their own work routines (too narrow a range of sources, and "pack journalism"). They were more ambivalent about external pressures (ownership, advertiser, interest group, or audience influence); and less willing to concede the influence of internalized pressures (e.g., self-censorship for fear of offending sources or owners) or their own biases. In open-ended interviews, close to one-third of the journalists identified power-related filters, such as the dominance of older, white males in newsrooms, journalists' reluctance to burn sources, and the background influence of ownership (Lowes et al., 1996: 24-29).

As for blind spots in news coverage, journalists identified the lack of investigative reporting as the most important, followed by critical coverage of business, and the social implications of government's social policies. Sports and right-wing perspectives were the only 2 of 26 topics considered to be over-covered (Green, 1998; Hackett, 1998).

Journalists are prepared to be critical of their trade and of the media system, but they seem relatively unwilling to concede to the presence of the structural factors that call into question their own occupational self-image as independent truth-seekers.

By contrast, interest groups were more critical of the media. A large majority expressed unqualified dissatisfaction with coverage of their own particular issues, as well as general media performance. While there were areas of agreement, their perceptions of blind spots and filters differed somewhat from those of journalists. Interest groups were more likely to see journalists' ignorance or laziness, entertainment values, and catering to audiences as filters, and the absence of "positive news" as a blind spot.

Our survey of interest groups also suggested that contrary to conventional wisdom, media critics on both the left and the right do not necessarily cancel each other out. In many respects, left- and right-wing critiques overlap, or differ without being contradictory. Even when they contradict one another (as when both labor and business perceive a hostile media bias against them), it is quite possible that one side has a more valid case. In this regard, it is noteworthy to mention that compared to establishment organizations, progressive groups were measurably more dissatisfied with the media than the more conservative groups (Karlberg and Hackett, 1996).

In the interest of being consistent with our switch from the top 10 lists to more conventional social science, and to distinguish ourselves from the original Project Censored, we officially changed our name to News Watch Canada in January 1997. While Carl Jensen, Peter Phillips, and former associate director Mark Lowenthal have provided us with indispensable advice and support, the two projects are quite distinct. Moreover, we also wanted to avoid premature debates about "censorship" in Canada's media.

BLIND SPOTS IN THE NEWS

What do our top 10 lists and content analyses indicate about the blind spots themselves? While our research is still ongoing, here are some topics which have been under-covered in Canada's English-language press:

➤ The extent of Canada's involvement in militarism, and its negative consequences.
➤ Environmental degradation as a systemic and ongoing problem.

➤ The perspective of French-language minorities in Canada's language and constitutional debates. (A similar blind spot probably applies with Quebec's French-language press's lack of attention to the perspective of Quebec's anglophone minority. Our research, however, has been confined to Canada's English-language press.)

➤ Religion and traditional social values.

➤ Human rights abuses by Canada's trading partners.

➤ White-collar and domestic crime.

➤ The power of the public relations industry.

➤ Exploitation and resistance in Canada's labor force.

➤ Poverty and class inequality.

➤ The "free market" neoliberal agenda: absent alternatives and hidden consequences.

➤ The power of corporate media: How self-interest skews the news.

Do these blind spots share a common thread? It would be easy to conclude that they generally reflect the power of "the establishment," a power which includes deflecting the adversarial and watchdog instincts of journalists away from systemic problems to relatively safe targets like illegal immigrants or the indiscretions of individual politicians.

The reality of news-making is a little more complicated. There are a variety of filters in the news, and they interact with each other. One of the defining characteristics of news is its focus on events, rather than long-term conditions or trends. News is about what went wrong today, not what goes wrong every day. Moreover, news beats are routinely oriented towards bureaucratic institutions like police, courts, government agencies, and legislatures. Through their everyday routines for handling cases and producing knowledge, these institutions help to shape the media's sense of newsworthy events and legitimate expertise (Fishman, 1980).

Acting together, these two filters—the reliance on events and on institutional sources—combined with the decline of investigative journalism, result in news that tends to legitimize established institutions. Particular scandals may get headlines, but unless institutions are internally divided or blatantly incompetent, the press generally does not scrutinize their day-to-day functions, or give voice to perspectives which challenge their core agendas.

There's more to it than that, however. Not all institutions are equal. Some have much more money, power, credibility, or "cultural capital" than others. Our research suggests that the business community consistently receive better coverage—or less critical attention—than other major institutions. By contrast, organized labor only receives attention for the confrontational and disruptive aspects of strikes, while government receives frequent negative attention, with the news illuminating political self-interest and bureaucratic red tape.

Why might there be little in the way of media scrutiny of the business system?

Perhaps the free enterprise system runs so smoothly that it doesn't qualify as news. When a plane crashes, it is newsworthy. When thousands of planes land safely, there is nothing to report. So why, then, are issues such as the "Asian flu" and subsequent global financial crises, widespread unemployment, the growing gap between the world's richest and poorest people, the monopolistic implications of huge corporate mergers, and large-scale frauds like the Bre-X "gold fine" in Indonesia subject to less critical coverage? Each of these render perfection an unlikely explanation for the relatively less critical coverage of business as an institution.

While business is as subject to human shortcomings as any other institution, it's less newsworthy than political scandals because its problems are considered to be "private" rather than public matters. There is something to this explanation. In the libertarian tradition, government has been perceived as the main potential threat to press freedom and civil liberties. Governments spend public money, which taxpayers are legally compelled to provide. By contrast, business has supposedly earned its money in the marketplace, through the voluntary purchases of consumers.

Given these libertarian assumptions, still influential in journalism's culture, it is understandable that media watchdogs have barked much louder at government than at private capital. But there are many good reasons for rethinking the traditional boundaries between public and private. In banking, communications, and other economic sectors, mergers and takeovers are producing national and global monopolies which dwarf most national governments. Fifty-one of the world's largest 100 economies are corporations, only 49 are countries. The world's largest 200 corporations, with a combined revenue of $7.1 trillion, carry far more economic clout than the poorest four-fifths of humanity ($3.9 trillion; Barlow and Winter, 1997: 209-10). Moreover, deregulation and international trade agreements like NAFTA have given the corporate sector more political leverage over national governments. Corporate practices significantly affect labor, the environment, politics, and society at large. For these reasons, it would be appropriate to expand journalism's scrutiny of institutional accountability to the private sector.

Another explanation may focus on the media themselves, calling attention to power imbalances—from the relatively direct influence of advertising and corporate ownership, to the more subtle ways in which free market fundamentalism has come to dominate public discourse. This interpretation is consistent with a good deal of media theory which suggests that the dominant media are so highly integrated into the economic system that, crudely put, they do not want to bite the hands that feed them.

James Winter offered a similar interpretation. In his view, our under-reported story lists appear to support the political-economic or instrumentalist perspectives in the academic literature, which regard ownership and corporate concentration as primary explanations for news media content. As might be expected from a review of the literature, or indeed the simple fact that without exception the news media are owned by large corporations, we seem to be seeing evidence of the systematic exclusion of material which presents "free market economics" and "private enterprise" in a negative light. In the words of American sociologist Gaye Tuchman, this could be evidence of the news media's "support of corporate capitalism."

At the same time, however, the project's more recent research on religion and abortion news suggests that traditional or conservative social values may also be under-represented in Canada's urban press. If so, as two Canadian political scientists proposed in the 1970s, there may be an "implicit understanding" between journalists and media owners, in which newsworkers are permitted "greater radicalism on social matters than on economic or party-related issues." Journalists' sympathy may help explain "the enormous media exposure" given to the pro-choice movement, and by contrast, the media's silence and conservatism "on such economic questions as the capital gains

THIS MODERN WORLD

by TOM TOMORROW

THE SUMMER OF '98 DRAWS TO A CLOSE--AND NOT A MOMENT TOO SOON FOR SOME OF US...

I'M SICK OF EVERYTHING!

I'M SICK OF STEPHEN GLASS, SARIN GAS, THE Y2K GLITCH, AND THE DOW JONES AVERAGE! I'M SICK OF MAUREEN DOWD, I'M SICK OF BILL GATES, AND I'M SICK OF FAWNING ARTICLES ABOUT THE TRUE MEANING OF SAVING PRIVATE RYAN!

I'M SICK OF KEN STARR'S PUDGY LITTLE FACE AND I'M SICK OF THE PRESIDENT AND HIS PENIS! I'M SICK OF LINDA TRIPP'S HAIR, LUCIANNE GOLDBERG'S RASP, AND MATT DRUDGE'S SMIRK--

--AND I'M REALLY SICK OF THE SEMEN-STAINED DRESS!

tax, corporation taxes, and the price-fixing powers of the legal and medical professions" (Winn and McMenemy, 1976: 132).

Generally, if journalists are "permitted" to express liberal views on social or moral questions, they are discouraged from challenging the core political and economic interests of the corporate elite. Most of News Watch Canada's research supports this conclusion. For instance, our most recent seminar in 1998 examined several aspects of political diversity in western Canada's largest newspaper, the *Vancouver Sun*, before and after its takeover by Conrad Black's Hollinger, Inc. in 1996. We found that the *Sun* tended to favor business over labor and right-wing over left-wing policy institutes. Labor and left-wing sources were more likely than their more conservative, business-oriented counterparts to find counter-balancing quotes in news articles about them. Coverage of poverty between 1987 and 1997 declined, and while most news still portrayed the poor sympathetically, there was a detectable increase in the proportion of stories depicting them as threatening or undeserving. News coverage of the 1986 and 1996 provincial elections in British Columbia was not noticeably partisan; the general tendency is for more attention, and more critical attention, to the governing party, be they left-wing or right-wing. However, the opinion/editorial pages were more supportive of the main "free enterprise" party and its policy options than of the Social Democratic NDP.

Similar patterns can be found at many other Canadian dailies, and they probably reflect the political climate and the relative resources of different interest groups rather than Conrad Black's influence as such. Still, one of our studies found a double standard, almost certainly tied to ownership. The *Vancouver Sun* was more cautious and less critical in covering its own par-

ent corporation, Hollinger, than the coverage of independent paper *Toronto Star*. The *Sun*'s current coverage of Hollinger is also less critical than its coverage of other media corporations, and its previous coverage of Hollinger prior to the 1996 takeover. Few people will be terribly surprised by such a conclusion—but it does show that corporate ownership can directly influence news judgment.

Needless to say, in contrast to our top ten lists, content analysis received almost no mention in the *Sun* or other daily papers. Instead, we turned to selected broadcasting programs, the alternative press, and our own *News Watch Monitor*, a thrice-yearly summary of our research distributed with the help of the Canadian Centre for Policy Alternatives (CCPA), a leading progressive, labor-funded think tank. We are also working with the CCPA to co-publish a book summarizing our years of research—*The Missing News: Filters and Blind Spots in Canada's Press* (Hackett et al., forthcoming.)

IS CANADA'S PRESS "CENSORED"?

If there are significant blind spots, and if they are systemic rather than haphazard, perhaps it is time to revisit the question of censorship. Is it appropriate to call Canada's news omissions "censorship"?

We suggest expanding the traditional notion of censorship in several ways:

First, governments *and* private centers of power are capable of suppressing "taboo" topics.

Second, we don't need to accept an absolutist conception of censorship. That is, to be effective, censorship doesn't need to suppress all traces of a "forbidden" topic. It may be sufficient to marginalize it. Such counter-information might be formally reported somewhere, but it's buried so deeply in the back pages of the media system that it doesn't really matter. If that is the case, then censorship can arguably be offensive as well as defensive (Phillips and Harsløf, 1997: 139-141). Defensive censorship proceeds by snipping, banning or burning unwelcome information to prevent it from reaching the public. In contrast, offensive censorship involves flooding the media with a particular version of reality, preventing alternative perspectives from gaining a public hearing, or rendering their perspectives off the wall. A classic case of offensive censorship was the selective and irresistibly televisual images that the Pentagon fed the media during the 1991 Gulf War.

Third, censorship can be structural or latent, as well as deliberate or manifest. In a highly commercialized media system with few nonprofit or publicly funded media, the needs of advertisers largely determine which media will survive. Advertisers are interested in media which appeal to the sensibilities of upscale audiences, or which promote the value of privatized consumption (Bagdikian, 1996). Media that promote anti-consumerist social values (like ecology), or which serve the interests or needs of less well-heeled audiences, are likely to be marginalized as a by-product of the very structure of the media system. Thus, media theorists are starting to talk of "structural" or "market censorship" (Phillips and Harsløf, 1997: 141-143).

At the same time, it would hardly be fair or useful to label all forms of editorial decision-making as "censorship." When it is guided by public service criteria, or when the values shaping the process are made explicit (as in the partisan press of yesteryear), editorial gate-keeping serves a valuable function in an age of informational overload.

Mindful of these considerations, our project's working definition of censorship includes:

➤ the marginalization or suppression of publicly relevant information;
➤ a conscious decision or policy—for example, to avoid covering a particular topic, or to assign newsgathering resources in such a way that the exclusion of certain kinds of news is fairly predictable;
➤ an imbalance of power relations: that is, those whose actions or decisions result in the omission have the power to enforce their preferences;
➤ sanctions or penalties against those who dare to violate the censorship by placing the counter-information in the public domain.

Conscious exclusion backed by power and penalties—these are surely the hallmarks of censorship.

Of course, gray areas abound. Under what conditions does a successful advocacy or public relations campaign become offensive censorship? If a reporter herself decides not to pursue a newsworthy story that would likely be spiked because it treads on powerful toes, is that self-censorship? Perhaps, but what if the reporter genuinely believes that the story really isn't newsworthy after all? What counts as "publicly relevant" information, as a genuinely significant and newsworthy story, or as an idea that deserves to be in the public domain? If a letter to the editor is tossed into the wastebasket because it is poorly written or incites hatred against an ethnic group, is that censorship? Probably not, but what if all letters on an appropriately public topic are rejected? What if a newspaper doubles its business section and transfers its last remaining labor reporter so that the positive contributions of trade unions become even less publicly visible?

Food for thought. One could endlessly debate the concept of censorship and its boundaries. It is especially murky when there lacks a clear decision to exclude a particular story or topic, and yet the possibility exists that the very criteria that news media use to decide what is newsworthy rest upon shaky but unexamined assumptions. (Consider the traditional libertarian distinction between private and public, noted above.) We would need to address the complex question of ideology, the ways that power relations can influence media routines, and the very consciousness of news producers and consumers—a question much discussed by media scholars (Hackett and Zhao, 1998; Shoemaker and Reese, 1996: Chapter 9).

That discussion, however, takes us beyond the scope of this chapter on News Watch Canada, as a project which seeks primarily to call attention to the presence of blind spots in Canada's press. Our analysis certainly does not lead us to a blanket indictment of working journalists, whom, after all, initially covered some of our under-reported stories. The worrying question, in Canada as much as in the U.S., is whether they have enough encouragement and resources from the news organizations which employ them, to provide citizens with the full range of relevant information which a democracy needs.

Encouraging public interest-oriented journalism is one of the purposes of News Watch Canada. We also see ourselves as engaging in a long-term process of media education, one oriented towards showing trade unions and advocacy groups that the media need to be taken more seriously as a site of struggle. Encouragingly, in response to Conrad Black's expansion in 1996, the progressive Council of Canadians joined with several trade unions to create the Campaign for Press and Broadcasting Freedom. If Canadians and Americans concerned about the impact of media concentration and commercialism could work together around this kind of initiative, there may be hope for reviving media diversity and democratic debate.

ROBERT HACKETT, associate professor of communication at Simon Fraser University in Vancouver, is co-director of News Watch Canada. He has written a number of books and articles on news, politics, and the media, including (with Yuezhi Zhao) *Sustaining Democracy?: Journalism and the Politics of Objectivity*, and (with Tim Gibson, Richard Gruneau, Donald Gutstein and NewsWatch Canada) *The Missing News: Filters and Blind Spots in Canada's Press* (forthcoming).

BIBLIOGRAPHY

Bagdikian, Ben H. *The Media Monopoly*, 5th Edition. Boston: Beacon Press, 1996.

Barlow, Maude & James Winter, *The Big Black Book: The Essential Views of Conrad and Barbara Amiel Black*. Toronto: Stoddart, 1997.

Cross, Kathleen, "Off Balance: How the Fraser Institute Slants its News Monitoring Studies," *Canadian Forum*, October 1997: 10-11.

Dornan, Chris, "If It's News to You, You Haven't Been Paying Attention," *Globe & Mail*, April 22, 1994.

Fishman, Mark, *Manufacturing the News*. London and Austin: University of Texas Press, 1980.

Green, Michele, "Telling it Like it Isn't," *Media*, Summer 1998: 21.

Hackett, Bob. "Filters and Blind Spots," *Media*, Summer 1998: 22.

Hackett, Robert, William O. Gilsdorf & Philip Savage, "News Balance Rhetoric: The Fraser Institute's Political Appropriation of Content Analysis," *Canadian Journal of Communication*, Vol. 17, No. 1, Winter 1992: 15-36.

Hackett, Robert A. & Yuezhi Zhao, *Sustaining Democracy: Journalism and the Politics of Objectivity*. Toronto: Garamond, 1998.

Hackett, Robert, with Tim Gibson, Richard Gruneau, Donald Gutstein & NewsWatch Canada, *The Missing News: Filters and Blind Spots in Canada's Press* (forthcoming).

Karlberg, Michael and Robert A. Hackett, "Cancelling Each Other Out? Interest Group Perceptions of the News Media," *Canadian Journal of Communication*, Vol. 21, No. 4, Autumn 1996: 461-472.

Lowes, Mark, Robert Hackett, James Winter, Donald Gutstein & Richard Gruneau, eds., *Blindspots in the News Agenda: Project Censored Canada 1996 Yearbook*. Burnaby, Canada: Project Censored Canada, 1996.

Phillips, Peter & Ivan Harsløf, "Censorship Within Modern, Democratic Societies," in Peter Phillips & Project Censored, *Censored 1997: The News that Didn't Make the News*. New York: Seven Stories Press, 1997: 139-158.

Shoemaker, Pamela J. & Stephen D. Reese, *Mediating the Message: Theories of Influences on Mass Media Content, 2nd Edition*. White Plains, NY: Longman, 1996.

Winn, Conrad & John McMenemy, *Political Parties in Canada*. Toronto: McGraw-Hill Ryerson, 1976: 132.

Winter, James, *Democracy's Oxygen: How Corporations Control the News*. Montreal: Black Rose, 1997.

THIS MODERN WORLD

by TOM TOMORROW

IF YOU BELIEVE THAT A FREE-MARKET INSURANCE SYSTEM MAKES *SENSE*...

WELL OF *COURSE* A PARASITICAL MIDDLE-MAN HAS TO MAKE A PROFIT BEFORE I CAN BE ALLOWED ACCESS TO HEALTH CARE!

IT'S THE AMERICAN WAY!

IF YOU BELIEVE THAT HEALTH INSURANCE *SHOULD* BE INEXTRICABLY LINKED TO EMPLOYMENT STATUS...

IF THOSE SELF-EMPLOYED PEOPLE WANTED TO BE ABLE TO SEE *DOCTORS*--

--THEY SHOULD HAVE GOTTEN *NORMAL* JOBS-- LIKE THE *REST* OF US!

IF YOU BELIEVE THAT THE CANADIAN SINGLE-PAYER SYSTEM IS SOME SORT OF *COMMUNIST PLOT*...

YOU KNOW--IT ACTUALLY SOUNDS LIKE A PRETTY *SENSIBLE SOLUTION*...

HEY--YOU WATCH YOUR MOUTH, CANADA-LOVER! WE DON'T GO FOR THAT KIND OF TALK HERE IN THE *U.S. OF A!*

More Doctors Smoke CAMELS than any other cigarette!

Shot and a beer $1.50

...THEN I GUESS YOU GET THE HEALTH CARE SYSTEM YOU *DESERVE*.

SURE, I HAVE TO WAIT FIVE WEEKS FOR AN APPOINTMENT WITH MY OFFICIALLY-DESIGNATED *PRIMARY CARE PROVIDER*--WHO THEN REFERS ME TO A *SPECIALIST* WHO CAN'T SEE ME FOR *ANOTHER* FIVE WEEKS--

--BUT AT LEAST I DON'T HAVE TO DEAL WITH SOME *GOVERNMENT BUREAUCRACY!*

YES, WHAT A NIGHTMARE *THAT* WOULD BE...

TOM TOMORROW © 6-3-98

CHAPTER 5

Voices of Censored Journalists

Recently there have been two very important overt acts of censorship by mainstream media corporations. In both cases reporters were fired for trying to reveal the truth about important news stories that offended the powerful. Steve Wilson and Jane Akre were fired by Fox TV in Tampa Bay for attempting to tell the truth about the dangers of bovine growth hormones in the nation's milk supply (*Censored* story #12 1997). April Oliver and Jack Smith were fired by CNN for their story on the use of sarin nerve gas in Laos during the Vietnam War. Here are their words on corporate media censorship at its worst.

How FOX TV Censored Their Own Reporters

BY JANE AKRE AND STEVE WILSON

We are a former CNN anchor and reporter with 20 years of experience from Miami to San Francisco, teamed up with an investigative reporter with 26 years on local and national television and a reputation as a tenacious bulldog who loved to shine bright lights in dark places.

"The Dream Team of investigative reporting on local television," that's how the station described us to the TV writers at the Tampa Bay area newspapers. If you were a channel 13 viewer, it was hard to miss the commercial that aired repeatedly, showing us walking down a dark, smoke-filled alley while a baritone announcer introduced the intrepid new Investigators, a team on a mission. Find the Truth and tell it. Never take "No" for an answer. Those were our marching orders from station managers who promised their support no matter where a story led and no matter whose ox it gored.

But in the process of getting our very first story on the air, there came a very rude awakening and the dream was suddenly every reporter's biggest nightmare. Fox Television, which had bought Tampa's WTVT and a string of other big-market stations months before we were hired, was now in firm control. The marching orders had changed; the news on this station was not to include anything that had the potential of making trouble for a business whose chief aim now was making money, as much and as fast as it could.

The manager who hired us was fired and replaced by a career salesman named David Boylan, a micro-manager on a short leash to Rupert Murdoch's local television headquarters. Some of his first words to us still ring in our ears: "We paid $3 billion for these television stations, we'll tell you what the news is. The news is what we say it is."

This is the story of the year-long struggle to tell the truth, we found, a story that's been largely censored to this day. It's the story of how nature's most perfect food, milk, has quietly become the first genetically engineered food to be fed to all of us with virtually no human safety testing.

Five years ago, consumers across America were dumping milk into the streets in protest against the government's decision to allow the Monsanto Company to sell dairy farmers a synthetic bovine growth hormone. This BGH was shown to stimulate cows to produce 20 to 30 percent more milk, but there was concern about how those hormones might affect that milk and other dairy products we consume at the average rate of a pound-and-a-half per day. The biggest concern was the potential for promoting cancer in humans, a worry that has lingered, and strengthened, long after the controversial FDA approval and official pronouncements that it was safe for humans to consume.

At the time, we had just become the Fox 13 Investigators and were eager for our first story. Our child was two years old and just started loving ice cream. Whatever happened to that BGH issue that sent people on the march three years back, Jane wondered? Florida consumer groups had told us the BGH issue had pretty much died after the biggest grocers in the state promised, in the wake of the protests, never to buy milk from treated cows until it was widely accepted as safe.

When Jane picked seven Florida dairy farms at random, and found BGH use a pretty well-kept secret at each and every one of them, we figured we were on to something. Jane did much of the early digging and traveled to shoot interviews and videotape in five states. Two months later, the end result was an important story the station was very proud of. Thousands of dollars worth of radio commercials were bought to encourage viewers to learn what had been slipped into the milk supply despite promises that it would never happen until consumers approved.

It was after 5 o'clock on the Friday evening before the four-part series was to begin the following Monday. We'd had spent some of the past several days in the pre-broadcast review process with Fox lawyers and an assistant news director, common procedure wherever strong investigative reports are aired or printed. Those were the same kind of discussions both of us have had at stations and networks through the years, until someone brought a letter down to the newsroom from the general managers' office. Suddenly, everything changed.

The letter was addressed to Roger Ailes, the CEO of Fox News. Ailes is the former Republican operative who Murdoch had chosen to guide the development of a national news organization for a network that has hung its hat on the kind of low-brow fare routinely criticized as being the worst TV has to offer. The letter was from John J. Walsh, arguably one of the most feared libel lawyers in America.

There is a lot at stake in what is going on in Florida, not only for Monsanto but also for Fox News and its owner, Walsh wrote in his four-page attack on the journalists. Whether deliberately or through ignorance, he scattered enough scientific misrepresentations to scare any broadcaster. I ask that you and your Fox News colleagues consider thoroughly what is at stake and the enormous damage that can be done, Walsh warned.

Ailes supposedly has nothing to do with the operation of the Fox Television Stations divisions but the letter could not have hit a better target to have its desired effect. Minutes later, we were told the broadcasts would be postponed until they could be reviewed by the station man-ager. Jane was blunt with her question to the news director that night: Is the story being pulled because of that letter? We were both a little surprised at how quickly and directly he replied, "Yes."

Four days later the general manager who hired us, himself a former investigative reporter, reviewed the story and found no evidence of unfairness or inaccuracy. As he was about to set another air date, the lawyers reminded him of the recent Food Lion suit, a point Walsh made so bluntly in his first letter. That case, which ABC News lost, has caused many sleepless nights for publishers and broadcasters who now know a news organization can be sued and lose even when the story is true. We all agreed to contact Monsanto again and offer a second interview if there was anything new they wished to add. This only prompted a second, more-threatening letter from Walsh.

In our invitation for Monsanto to appear in a second interview, we listed areas that might be discussed in an interview. Some of the points clearly contain the elements of defamatory statements which, if repeated in a broadcast, could lead to serious damage to Monsanto and dire consequences for Fox News, Walsh threatened. He wrote off BGH critics worldwide as scientifically incompetent persons. He labeled both Fox journalists as: reporters more interested in sensational soundbites than establishing the facts.

What the first letter didn't accomplish, his second letter did. (The letters in their entirety, along with all other relevant documents, can be found on the

Internet at www.foxBGHsuit.com). We produced a three-inch binder filled with scientific support for our story. We doubt it was ever read. Within days of the new general manager's arrival, Fox lawyers were attacking us and simultaneously rewriting our story in a more Monsanto-friendly way. On the phone from her Atlanta office, a Fox Vice President for Legal Affairs lost her cool long enough to blurt out, "We don't think this story is worth a half-million dollars to go to court with Monsanto!"

By this time, we also discovered Monsanto was an advertiser on WTVT in Tampa and several other Fox-owned stations that ran commercials for NutraSweet, Roundup, and Ortho home and garden products. We learned Monsanto is also a good customer of another Murdoch-owned company which advertises on carts and shelves at supermarkets around the globe. And of course, exposing how big local supermarkets had broken their promises not to by BGH milk would not make them or the Florida dairy council too happy, either.

We wrote and rewrote the story at least 83 times, but not one of those versions was ever acceptable for broadcast. We made it clear that some of what we were ordered to write was demonstrably false. We reminded the lawyers and the managers alike, orally and in writing, that using the public airwaves to lie was not only ethically wrong, it was a violation of the Communications Act of 1934 and the stations' license.

The Fox folks didn't quite know what to do with us. When they invited us to leave, we reminded them how important we thought the story was and said we'd stay to tell it accurately, honestly, and fairly. When they offered us a large cash settlement, we refused to sign the legal document that also included a gag order which would have prevented us from ever revealing what we'd learned about BGH and how Fox tried to cover it up. When they threatened to fire us for not reporting what we knew to be a false and slanted story, we told them that would leave us with plenty of time to go to the FCC and ask for a full investigation. And, when they said they were suspending us without pay, we kept right on writing and turned in the final two versions they said they wanted.

In the end, they said they were firing us for no cause, during a window period in our contract. Later, in response to a letter from Steve, a Fox lawyer admitted that there were definite reasons for our dismissal and all of them directly related to our standing up for the truth. In the days that led up to our dismissal, they tried again to offer a deal that would have kept us on the payroll as consultants in exchange for our silence. When that story got out, the station manager insisted it could not in any way be considered hush money.

We were fired just before Christmas 1997 and filed suit April 2, 1998 in a Florida state court where we have claimed a violation of the state's whistle-blower law and violation of our employment contracts. We decided to post details of what happened to us and more importantly, the news we were never allowed to tell on television, to a site on the World Wide Web (www.foxBGH-suit.com). The station promptly replaced us both with a relatively inexperienced reporter from High Point, North Carolina, making good on their often-repeated promise, "If you don't tell it the way we want, we'll get someone who will." Six months after we left, their new investigative reporter went on the air with many of the same lies and distortions we refused to broadcast.

What were some of the details the audience in Tampa Bay never got to hear in that watered-down, censored version that finally did air?

➤ Many experts now agree there has been an appalling lack of human safety testing prior to FDA approval. Despite Monsanto's repeated claims to the contrary, the milk from cows injected with BGH is indeed different than milk from cows not injected and that important difference is at the heart of scientific concern that BGH milk may promote cancer in humans. The money trail of millions of Monsanto dollars sent to the University of Florida where agricultural extension agents were promoting BGH like a wonder drug for Florida farmers, always neglecting to mention the results of the university's own experiments which revealed potentially serious problems.

➤ Florida supermarkets knew they could never keep their promises to keep BGH milk off of the supermarket shelves, but have kept the news quiet for years. We were about to report how, far from gaining widespread acceptance,

there is a large and growing body of scientific evidence to suggest BGH milk poses a serious threat of breast, colon, and prostate cancer in those of us who drink milk and other dairy food products.

➤ BGH injections are known to make cows sicker, which in turn prompts farmers to use more antibiotics. We were going to reveal how that in turn increases the likelihood that those drug residues end up in the milk we pour on our family's cereal each morning.

➤ Canadian government health officials have reported that Monsanto attempted to bribe its way to approval in Canada where scientists remain unconvinced about its safety for humans. Monsanto has always denied those charges, claiming there was a misunderstanding over offers to support research unrelated to BGH.

➤ Consumers have been left in the dark on the BGH issue by state and federal officials who have worked with Monsanto to prevent the labeling of milk on the supermarket shelves.

On the up side, the 13,000-member Society of Professional Journalists has honored us with its award for Ethics and we've also received an Award for Civic Courage from the public service trust administered by Ralph Nader and his family.

But more importantly, there has been convincing new evidence that the complete story we wanted to tell was on the right track all along.

The study in which the FDA indicated proof of human safety was actually misreported by the FDA. It has now been revealed that rats which were supposedly not affected by the drug were adversely affected, indicating further studies are needed. A coalition of consumer groups has demanded the FDA take the drug off the market until those studies are done.

Details of the rat studies were revealed by government scientists in Canada who have risked their own careers by admitting they have been under incredible political pressure to approve Monsanto's BGH despite their concerns that it is not safe.

New studies from Harvard and another published in *The Lancet* have shown what appears to be a much stronger link between the risk of cancer and drinking BGH milk.

We've both been frequently told that our stand on this issue will mean neither of us can work in the television news business again. Some, including our former Fox managers, say it was unprofessional to stand up as we did. Frankly, had the story been about some petty crook turning back odometers at the local car dealership, I'm not sure we would have done what we have.

Censoring a story is bad enough, you will no doubt agree as you turn these pages, but when a reporter is asked to lie, to misreport, cover up the truth, twist and distort it into something that is known to be false, that reporter has a duty to draw a line, no matter what the personal cost.

(more details on the Akre/Wilson story are available at their Web site: http://www.foxBGHsuit.com)

The Censored Side of the CNN Firings over Tailwind

BY APRIL OLIVER

We as television producers are accustomed to being behind the scenes. The furor of the past few months has, however, shifted my co-producer Jack Smith and me to center stage. We are grateful for the opportunity to put our views forward, particularly at a time when so many powerful people—from the Pentagon to Time-Warner—are trying to kill the Tailwind story.

Last July, in what was perhaps a first for broadcast journalism, our story was retracted—not based on any known error or fabrication. CNN did not, and could not, say the story was wrong. The report, after all, featured the direct on-camera testimony of the officers and men who actually fought on the Tailwind mission.

The Tailwind report was retracted by CNN based on a new standard of proof—that for these volatile charges of nerve gas use and a hunt for defectors, according to Ted Turner, it was necessary to have enough airtight proof to *persuade a jury in a courtroom of law*. It was a demand for a smoking gun, three weeks after the fact. Such a smoking gun is, of course, completely counter to the intent of a so-called "black operation," the purpose of which is to cover up the truth so no one can ever *prove* what happened.

We stand by the story. We are not novices at news-gathering, who slapped this report together to garner headlines. The Tailwind story was carefully researched and reported over eight months, with our bosses' approval of each interview request and every line of the story's script. It was based on the accounts of multiple sources, from senior military officials to firsthand participants, some of whom paid high compliments to the Tailwind broadcast, even after the controversy ignited. A former chairman of the Joint-Chiefs-of-Staff, as well as two other confidential sources, read and approved the script prior to airing. All these men who stepped forward to talk about a black operation during President Nixon's secret war in Laos displayed great courage and should be commended.

In addition to the more than half-dozen on-camera sources that confirmed or supported the Tailwind story, more than a dozen pilots told us of the availability or use of a special "last resort" gas that they called "nerve gas," "killer gas," "drop-dead gas," "sleeping gas," "gb," (the military name for sarin), or cbu-15 (a sarin cluster bomb).

The veterans of the elite and covert world of black operations—the SOG— were pledged to secrecy. We told the CNN executives in charge that they should expect strident denials from the military establishment, even from some of the sources who had privately confirmed the story to us. We knew a paper trail proving the story was probably nonexistent. Documents were likely to have been sterilized in order to prove the military innocent of any wrongdoing: Ref-

erences to the gas would likely be changed to "tear gas," and the target, some nameless bridge. Please keep in mind that this unit was the most highly trained killing force that the United States had ever produced, some of them trained in delivering "backpack" nukes. Special weaponry, disinformation, and denial are tools of the trade for the secret elite special operations unit. "Plausible deniability" for the U.S. government is the golden rule for these commandos.

Almost immediately after broadcasting, CNN was bombarded with a chorus of denials from vets as well as such luminaries as Henry Kissinger and Richard Helms. Soon after, we were booted sky-high, out CNN's front door, with CNN top executives denying their part in approving the story.

Since the broadcast and our firing, however, we have received even more leads regarding similar missions. In addition, CNN's most experienced investigative reporter, John Camp, interviewed a veteran, on camera, who described killing four defectors by calling in nerve gas on a 1970 raid into Cambodia. In a memo to CNN management, Camp detailed his extensive background check of the veteran, and said that he seemed "extremely reliable." The videotapes detailing this entirely separate mission to kill defectors were in the hands of CNN's management at the time we were fired.

Two lawyers paid by CNN, CNN general counsel David Kohler and corporate attorney Floyd Abrams, wrote a hasty justification for the retraction. Calling that report "independent" is a fraud. Simply put, the Abrams/Kohler report is a vehicle for a corporate whitewash. CNN wanted to cut-and-run because they couldn't take the heat from the mobilized vets, Henry Kissinger and Colin Powell. Whatever happened 28 years ago in the rainforests of Laos wasn't nearly as important to CNN as what will happen in the next war. CNN's bread-and-butter is in the covering of conflict around the globe. Corporate calculus showed that they needed the Pentagon more than they needed us.

At the heart of this controversy I see the issue of freedom: Do Americans have the right to know—the freedom to pursue knowledge of—government secrets, 28 years after the fact? Or should knowledge of certain government activities be forever denied? In this brave new world of mega media mergers, is a free press alive and well? Or are corporate values dictating what news is?

At the time the controversy ignited, we the producers were gagged by CNN management, while they solicitously listened to complaints from the military establishment, such as those from Retired General Perry Smith. Allow me to say that General Smith did not participate on the Tailwind mission, and is not a veteran of special operations; he comes from the conventional side of the Air Force. He is precisely the sort of "fine-upstanding soldier" that the covert operatives desire to keep hidden, compartmentalizing information and to sterilize the paper trail to insure that the Pentagon establishment has complete and total "plausible deniability" of such activities. Representatives such as General Smith can make a convincing case that these actions simply did not happen. But a former SOG commander, Retired General John Singlaub bragged to us on camera, "We went to great lengths to conceal what we were doing." General Singlaub also said on TV recently that when SOG missions were compromised, there would be no way for anyone back at the Pentagon to tell what really happened. We made a good-faith effort to find out what really happened on "Tailwind," and we had sources well positioned to tell us what occurred.

In retrospect, I sincerely regret obeying CNN's order not to speak to the press, as we could have easily corrected the hearsay and military disinformation floating around as facts. These included such egregiously inaccurate assertions as, "Sarin kills by one droplet to the skin." Think back to the Tokyo subway attack where 6,000 people were exposed to a small amount of sarin gas in a confined space; only 12 people died. Sarin kills when inhaled. The U.S. servicemen had special chemical masks. Another charge is that I used discredited repressed-memory tactics to force the secrets out of a Special Forces veteran. I did no such thing, as the transcripts of each interview prove. A final charge is that I badgered these hardened combat veterans into saying things they really did not mean. Imagine a 36-year old pregnant lady bulldozing Rambo!

We expected the military disinformation campaign. What we did not predict were the attacks by colleagues in the press, or the lack of courage by our own company, CNN, to stand by us. CNN executives became Jello-kneed at the thought of congressional hearings with the establishment on one side of the room, and CNN teamed up with Special Force's vets on the other. CNN president Rick Kaplan told us flatly in a meeting that he did not want to proceed to congressional hearings with CNN on the opposite side of the room from Retired General Colin Powell. As Kaplan explained it to us, "This is not a journalism problem, it is a public relations problem."

Please note that the continuing controversy still centers mostly around the question of nerve gas. Very little outcry in the press has been about the issue of whether defectors were targeted or killed. Perhaps one reason is that a retired four-star army general has privately conceded to CNN management that defectors were indeed legitimate military targets during the Vietnam conflict. This flatly flies in the face of the Pentagon's continued assertion that there were only two known defectors during the Vietnam War. We are surprised that the public has not demanded more explicit accounting from the Pentagon on this topic.

In July, CNN's press officers publicly stated, "The story is dead!" This official view was reflected in statements by CNN management on the day of the retraction that "we're going to try and kill this thing, drive a stake through its heart and bury it, so it's gone." This is the speech of a corporate warrior defending the mother company; it is *not* the speech of a journalist, intent on fact-finding. It's as if CNN itself has adopted the military tactic of "plausible deniability."

Soon after CNN retracted the story, the Pentagon came out with its own report on the Tailwind investigation. At a press conference featuring members of that mission, Secretary Cohen declared that nerve gas had obviously not been used, because so many Americans had survived. Secretary Cohen's remarks are disingenuous. As Secretary of Defense, he must certainly know that there are different kinds of nerve gas, and that the nerve gas we report was used in Operation Tailwind was sarin gas. As mentioned earlier, sarin does not kill through skin contact, it kills when inhaled. The Pentagon's leading chemical authority, General Walter Busbee, admitted this to CNN on camera. So Cohen's opening remarks immediately signaled a whitewash designed to mislead the public about the nature of the gas which we report was employed.

Our many sources confirm that so many American servicemen survived precisely *because* nerve gas was used. The Americans had the right protective masks, the enemy didn't. After all, the Americans and their Montanyard team were completely surrounded, out of ammunition, 100 percent wounded, and out in the open with three enemy anti-aircraft guns bearing down on them from a ridge about 1,000 meters before them. The only tactical advantage the American SOG team had was possession of M-17 protective gas masks. Scores of enemy died that day, and every single American made it out alive from this dire, last-resort situation. The gas worked.

Ironically, the two gentlemen that the Pentagon and Secretary Cohen marched in front of the press corps last summer to represent the Tailwind heroes, were the same two veterans who had, over the course of our eight-month report, changed their stories so many times that we almost lost track. One of these vets, Captain of the mission, Eugene McCarley, declared to CNN (on-camera), "If being cross-border was considered unethical or deniable, I reckon I was never there." McCarley suggests he will deny anything and everything related to "Tailwind."

Then there was the other vet, medic "Doc" Rose. In contrast to nearly every other man on the mission, he swore to CNN, upfront early in our research, that *no* gas was used at all. The only reason he put on his gas mask, he said, was to protect himself from the "crap" kicked up by the helicopter. He later amended that statement to say that the gas used was "awful stuff." He doesn't know what it was, but he doesn't think it was cs tear gas. After the broadcast, his only complaint about the show was that we showed the wrong gas mask, one with external instead of internal filters. He also said that he was required to carry extra atropine, nerve gas antidote, on that mission. At the Soldier-of-Fortune press conference later in June, however, Rose arrived at his new and final position: It *was* merely cs tear gas that was used.

As Alexander Cockburn wrote last summer regarding the Pentagon's whitewash of Tailwind:

> Whatever the final word may be on this story, there was something absurd about the Pentagon being treated as a credible witness. Remember, the Pentagon and the CIA conducted a secret airwar on Laos, which involved dropping high explosives every eight minutes on average for many years. At the end of the war, one-third of the population had become refugees. By 1971 the CIA was practicing a scorched-earth policy in Hmong territory against the incoming *Pathet Lao*. The land was drenched with herbicides, which killed the rice and opium crops and also poisoned the Hmong . . . amid the attack on Smith and Oliver, the fact that the Pentagon had an inventory of 30 million pounds of sarin, some of it in Southeast Asia, was mentioned but never explored.

Cockburn's was one of the few pieces which placed the Operation Tailwind story in context, the time when Nixon was running secret wars with separate chains of command; when officers were getting fragged by their men; when the chemicals Agent Orange and Napalm were being used liberally by the U.S. military; and when it was not technically illegal for the U.S. to use nerve gas, as the Senate had not yet ratified the Geneva protocol. Yet most of the media coverage neglected such details, instead honing in on us, the messengers. "Amateurs," they called us, "left-leaning ideologues." For the record, my only political job was with Reagan's 1980 presidential campaign.

The name-calling, however, successfully shifted attention away from what the highly secret unit SOG was, what their rules of engagement were, and what weapons they had at their disposal. It's an age-old tactic of warfare—*kill the messenger, obliterate the message.*

Some of the veterans who ran the disinformation campaign came forward to crow about their kill. They boasted to *Forbes Magazine* and others about how they did indeed mount a pressure campaign on CNN, utilizing the power of the Internet to gather sources, and then bombarded the CNN executive suite with a letter-writing campaign and threats to boycott. There is a Website devoted to the disinformation campaign, at www.greenberet.com—one which sports pictures of a dozen body bags, one with our names and images on it with blood oozing out of our heads. Make no mistake about it. These guys regard this as warfare, and we were their target.

A family member who is a Texas A & M graduate, a veteran, and a former officer in the Chemical Weapons Corps, recently wrote me to say, "Your job as a journalist is to keep the public properly and accurately informed. The job of the military is to defend the country. The real clash comes in deciding where secrecy is justified, to what degree, and for how long. Even the most honest, well-intentioned leaders disagree on where the line should be between secrecy and complete disclosure. You have succeeded in doing what journalists are charged with doing—that is to move the line ever closer to openness and ever away from unnecessary or, even worse, self-serving cover-up."

Such insight helps to fight the bitterness of suddenly being unemployed. Unemployed even though CNN management had vetted the script carefully, knew the depth and breadth of our sources, and CNN lawyers had approved every word. After the broadcast, CNN president Rick Kaplan even sent me white orchids, along with high accolades. We believe CNN's treatment of us is transparent, and calls into question the integrity of that company, as well as its commitment to investigative journalism.

APRIL OLIVER is a former producer with CNN. She and co-producer Jack Smith were fired by CNN during the summer of 1998 for producing a story on the U.S. military's use of sarin nerve gas in Laos during the Vietnam War.

THIS MODERN WORLD

by TOM TOMORROW

SPECULATION ABOUT JERRY SEINFELD'S POST-TELEVISION CAREER ENDED ABRUPTLY--WITH THE STUNNING ANNOUNCEMENT THAT HE WOULD SOON BEGIN TRAINING FOR THE NEXT *SPACE SHUTTLE MISSION!*

IT'S ONE SMALL STEP FOR A COMEDIAN-- AND ONE GIANT LEAP FOR *PAY-PER-VIEW!*

SEINFELD

NASA ADMINISTRATORS INSISTED THAT THEIR DECISION TO *SEND* THE POPULAR COMEDIAN INTO SPACE HAD *NOTHING WHATSOEVER* TO DO WITH PUBLIC RELATIONS.

WE'VE BEEN WANTING TO STUDY THE EFFECTS OF SPACE TRAVEL ON *STANDUP COMEDY* FOR QUITE SOME TIME NOW! HONEST!

THE PUBLIC QUICKLY RALLIED BEHIND HIS SELECTION...

HE'S NOT *COMPLETELY* INEXPERIENCED! WE KNOW FROM HIS AMUSING COMEDY ROUTINES THAT HE HAS SPENT A GREAT DEAL OF TIME ON *AIRPLANES!*

ANYWAY, HE HAS BEEN MAKING AMERICA LAUGH FOR *NINE YEARS!* IT'S TIME WE GAVE SOMETHING BACK!

...THOUGH NOT EVERYONE IN THE *SCIENTIFIC COMMUNITY* WAS PLEASED.

DAMN THOSE GRANDSTANDING BUREAUCRATS! THEY'RE SIPHONING SCARCE RESOURCES AWAY FROM *MY* RESEARCH--

--INTO THE EFFECTS OF SPACE TRAVEL ON *ELDERLY POLITICIANS!*

DON'T THEY HAVE ANY SENSE OF *PRIORITIES?*

STROM THURM SIMULATION

CHAPTER 6

Microradio Broadcasting: The Struggle for America's Airwaves

BY GREG RUGGIERO & LOUIS N. HIKEN

Hundreds of media activists are defying the Federal Communications Commission (FCC) and the corporate-owned media by broadcasting from "illegal" microradio stations. These stations offer the American people an alternative to the homogenized corporate programming currently produced for national radio. Operating in basements and hidden rural mobile locations, these radio "pirates" are the free speech movement of the 1990s.

Microradio Broadcasting: Aguascalientes of the Airwaves

TEXT AND PHOTOS BY GREG RUGGIERO

Based on notes prepared for a presentation given at the "Festival of Resistance" organized by the NY Zapatistas, NYC, October 12, 1998. To be published in the Open Media Pamphlet Series in Spring 1999.

"Where there is even a pretense of democracy," writes Noam Chomsky, "communications are at its heart." Given the present state of our society, it's no surprise that we find communications in the grip of an oppressive and contradictory system of mass control. Nowhere is this more evident than in the community struggle for access to the airwaves and the corporate/government campaign to crush it. I have been invited to speak at today's Festival of Resistance to bring news from the free radio movement, about how winning community access to the airwaves will provide an advantage in the battle to defend public spaces and civil powers from further downsizing by the business world—an advantage much needed in the larger liberation struggle being waged here and around the world.

To begin building a better world, we must first achieve democracy—the process by which whole communities may meaningfully participate in decision making. And to make intelligent, well formed decisions, we must be able to receive, produce, debate, and share information openly and freely. It is for this reason that a public access media system is a non-negotiable demand in the struggle for democratic society.

Democracy depends on public spaces and public forums, because it is precisely there that we have the power to exercise our rights and freedoms. The founders of this country envisioned a pluralistic society where every citizen's right to communicate would be protected, not squelched, by the government. In today's information age, however, speech cannot be limited to street corner shouting and leafleting—a miserably inadequate way to reach one's community. For democratic society to exist, to exercise speech in the

MICROBROADCASTERS MARCHING TO THE HEADQUARTERS OF THE NATIONAL ASSOCIATION OF BROADCASTERS, THE SWORN ENEMY OF MICRO.

ways meant by the framers of the Constitution, communities must have access to the town square of the information age—the airwaves—itself public property, and thus a space where our free speech should be fully exercised and protected. But this is not the case.

COMMERCIALISM AND CIVIL SOCIETY

The problem is commercialism—the unrelenting forces that shape society according to the conditions most favorable to business. Almost every aspect of our lives—our work, food, housing, education, and culture—is dominated, in one form or another, by the pro-business mission of commercialism. In our present age, business is defined by massive corporations. Since Reagan, commercial influence on law has accelerated corporate mergers. The new monolithic entities that result control more economic and political power than many of the earth's countries. Indeed, commercial corporations, not nation-states, are emerging as the new global superpowers—and their goal as businesses is to make the most possible amount of money in the shortest possible time, regardless of the human or ecological consequences.

U.S. COMMUNICATIONS HISTORY

Nowhere have U.S. citizens lost greater control of its public sphere than in the government's management of the airwaves. To study the history of radio policy in this country is to study how business interests gradually gain control over a priceless public resource without benefitting civil society. Understanding how our society can suffer such blows while still claiming to be a democracy is well worth considering and may even suggest tactics to reverse the trend.

Radio was introduced to the Western world by Guglielmo Marconi in 1895. By 1907 interest in the technology had reached the general population, and by 1912 hundreds of pioneers began broadcasting in the United States. In August of that year Congress passed the Radio Act of 1912, which required all broadcasters to first acquire a license.

Under the Radio Act of 1912, noncommercial radio flourished. Tens of thousands of individuals took to the airwaves. By the 1920s, noncommercial stations outnumbered commercial stations by a ratio of two-to-one. To cope with the explosion of interest, Congress passed the Radio Act of 1927, thereby creating the Federal Radio Commission (FRC), prototype of today's FCC. The purpose of the FRC was to regulate the airwaves "in the public interest, convenience, and necessity."

From 1927 onward, however, the federal government began interpreting its mandate to serve "public interest" in ways utterly inconsistent with that of other branches of government. In the case of libraries, schools, parks, and highways, for example, regulating in the "public interest" means preserving those spaces from the presence of business. In the case of the airwaves, this interpretation has been reversed, but not without resistance. As Robert W. McChesney points out, "Between 1928 and 1935, some elements of American society actively opposed the emerging commercial set-up and attempted to have a significant portion of the ether set aside for noncommercial and non-profit utilization."[1]

"Declaring that the 'public interest, convenience, and necessity' was better served by 'general public service' (i.e. commercial) stations" writes micro-radio lawyer Robert Perry, "than by 'special interest' and 'propaganda' (i.e., noncommercial) stations, the FRC gave noncommercial stations fewer hours than commercial stations. The FRC also limited broadcast radio licenses to three-month terms, effectively requiring noncommercial stations to expend their limited financial resources fending off license renewal challenges from commercial stations every three months."[2] The FRC's pro-business interpretation of "public interest" served to privatize the airwaves. Noncommercial radio virtually disappeared between 1927 and 1934, shrinking down to barely 2 percent of all radio airtime by 1934.

The passage of the Federal Communications Act of 1934 maintained the seemingly democratic language of the 1927 Act; regulation of the airwaves would be carried out to serve the "public interest, convenience, and necessity," and what was once the FRC then became the FCC. In the 65 years since its inception, the FCC has taken several steps to attempt to fulfill its mandate to serve civil society. To the benefit of commercialism, however, each of these steps has long since been eliminated. At a glance:

1. FAIRNESS DOCTRINE Genuine democracy requires an informed public that has access to a diverse range of controversial and contrasting views. Thus, in 1949 the FCC adopted the Fairness Doctrine, requiring radio stations to provide reasonable coverage of opposing views on issues of relevance to the community. During the Reagan years, the Fairness Doctrine was eliminated.

2. PUBLIC AFFAIRS PROGRAMMING Genuine democracy requires media that reflects the cultural diversity and local issues that characterize a community. Thus, the FCC required that 8 percent of AM radio airtime and 6 percent of FM radio airtime be dedicated to public affairs programming that was nonentertainment oriented. As a condition of license renewal, the FCC also required that stations actually study the communities in which they were broadcasting in order to access the needs of the people living there. During the Reagan years, these requirements were all eliminated.

3. MICROPOWER BROADCASTING Genuine democracy is based on broad public participation, a condition made possible not by political representation, but by direct public access. Beginning in 1948, the FCC permitted public access to the airwaves by issuing "Class D" low power broadcasting licenses to community groups, colleges, and churches. As a result, noncommercial radio flourished for the first time since the 1920s. In 1978, under pressure from an ambitious National Public Radio organization that hoped to consolidate audiences, the FCC enacted a ban on all broadcasting under 100 watts, with no cases of waivers granted to this day.

TELECOMMUNICATIONS REFORM ACT

The general drift toward complete corporate control of the airwaves reached a new extreme with the passage of the Telecommunications Reform Act of 1996. The Act's defining feature is the toleration of a higher limit of media outlets—radio and TV stations—that any one corporation can own. It also eases restrictions preventing these huge media conglomerates from merging into one another—creating enormous, monolithic powers. As microradio scholar Larry Soley observes, "[A]lmost 4,000 or nearly 40 percent, of the nation's roughly 10,300 commercial radio stations have been traded in deals collectively worth $32 billion, with the largest radio station group owners being the most aggressive purchasers. The 10 largest group owners today control 1,134 commercial radio stations, up from 652 prior to passage of the Telecommunications Act of 1996. The Dallas investment firm, Hicks, Muse, Tate & Furst Inc., is the group leader, with over 400 stations, followed by CBS with 175 stations. According to Broadcast Investment Analysts, there are nearly 15 percent fewer radio station owners than there were prior to the passage of the act. Two group owners, CBS and Chancellor Media, today have nearly 53 percent of radio listeners in the top 10 markets, with CBS having 27 percent and Chancellor having 25.2 percent. CBS holds nearly 50 percent of the news/talk listening audience in those markets."[3] And it goes on and on. Corporations get the licenses, controlling both access and content. Any lingering obligation to serve "public interest" is completely paved over, and the notion of democracy itself begins to sound vague, abstract. Media corporations are not in business to make democracy possible but, rather, to capture the largest possible audience, whose attention they then sell like scrap metal to the advertisers.

This scenario and the policies that protect it provide a clear portrait of the corporate agenda: maintaining the face of a democratic society while enacting laws and policies, enforced by government, that decrease the public arena, redefine citizenship in terms of consumerism, and provide unfettered conditions for corporations to evolve with the rights of individuals and the power of nation states. In the resulting free-for-all of corporate mergers, "the public interest" is duly served with a variety of entertainment options, while the spectrum of political and social information reaching public awareness narrows to the point of meaninglessness. The notion of a public discussion pursuing any real increase in social welfare, freedom, or self-determination is impossible, because there are no longer any public venues through which to express such thoughts.

"In the current media environment," says Robert Perry, "speech is merely another commodity to be bought and sold, valued primarily for it's revenue potential." The resulting blackout on local issues, core political speech, and cultural diversity has not occurred without formidable resistance. Over the past five years, a national movement has been mushrooming in opposition to corporate control of communications. This is a movement made up of hundreds of community groups who operate unlicensed clandestine radio stations in much the same spirit that Rosa Parks sat in the front of the bus: to resist and challenge a dehumanizing and unconstitutional system.

NETWORKS OF ALTERNATIVE COMMUNICATION

Everywhere that oppressive restrictions become formerly institutionalized by either government or business, there one finds resistance, underground networks, and liberation struggles. Among grassroots groups, there is a growing consensus to use our precious few resources finding *alternatives* to corporate media, rather than attempting to revolutionize the system through head-on confrontation. "Media wealth is too concentrated, too solidified, and too integrated into the corporate-government elite to make social change within the existing system possible," says Project Censored Director, Peter Phillips.

Realizing that corporate power will continue to deny civil society the kinds of information and access that make participatory democracy possible, the Zapatistas have proposed the formation of an "intercontinental network of alternative communication" as a way of sharing movement news, organizing, and celebrating the art and culture of resistance. In his video message to the *Freeing the Media* gathering that took place in New York City two years ago, Subcommandante Marcos said, "In August 1996, we called for the creation of a network of independent media, a network of information.... We need this network not only as a tool for our social movements but for our lives: this is a project of life, of humanity—humanity which has a right to critical and truthful information." [4]

Alongside the invaluable online activism now proliferating via the Internet, the growing network of microradio broadcasters is emerging as an energetic force in building viable, community-oriented alternatives to the corporate agenda. Around the country, hundreds of communities are creating small *aguascalientes*, centers of civil resistance, by operating low-watt radio stations where they can express their cultures, their languages, and their politics with complete freedom—and in complete opposition to corporate control of the public airwaves. "There are literally thousands of Americans who seek to penetrate the Iron Curtain created by the FCC to prevent any significant diversity of voices and opinions from being expressed over the airwaves" says Lou Hiken, attorney for Stephen Dunifer and Free Radio Berkeley.

The network of clandestine microbroadcasters is not a new development. Laurence Soley says it started in Hitler's Germany, when the resistance movement there used unlicensed radio as a strategy against the Nazis. In fact, Soley suggests that the presence of clandestine radio corresponds to the degree of repression in a given country. The more people feel a restriction of information and speech, the more that they take to the airwaves. The situation in the U.S. has become so problematic that it has moved beyond the mere *presence* of clandestine stations, toward an increasingly organized and sophisticated national effort. Like the civil rights movement of the 1960s, free radio activists

MICRORADIO ACTIVISTS OUTSIDE FCC HEADQUARTERS, OCTOBER 5, 1998.

are becoming adept at coordinating multiple tactics—demonstrations, strategy conferences, legal battles, media campaigns, educational tours, and increasing civil disobedience—to reclaim public access to the airwaves without threat of raid by Federal Marshals.

MICROBROADCASTERS IN THE STREETS

On October 4 & 5, 1998, for example, hundreds of activists gathered in Washington, DC for a national microradio conference and protest of federal communications policies and the corporate forces that shape it. Over the weekend, microradio activists sent a team of lobbyists to meet with representatives on Capitol Hill, launched a new DC station (Radio Libre), staged a panel at the Freedom Forum that was broadcast to 86 countries, and conducted dozens of interviews with the mainstream press, resulting in coverage in the *Washington Post*, NPR, MSNBC, and many others. The weekend culminated with a massive march and puppet parade from Dupont Circle to FCC headquarters, and then on to the headquarters of the National Association of Broadcasters (NAB)—the pro-industry group that most intensely pressures the FCC to eliminate microbroadcasting. DC cops on motorcycles blocked intersections and stopped traffic so that marchers could parade with three huge Bread and Puppet Theater-esque puppets showing FCC Chairman "Kennardio" in the likeness of Pinnochio being controlled by a bigger puppet, a TV-headed monster (The NAB), which, in turn, was being puppeteered by an even larger, more heinous looking beast: the corporate media monolith. The march came to a head when microbroadcasters overpowered NAB agents (attempting to keep marchers off headquarters' property), hauled the NAB flag down from the top of a high pole, and rose up in its place a pirate radio flag. The action filled the air with cheers of joy, and resulted in two arrests.

The entire two-day program was organized by volunteers with next to no resources. Full housing and deliciously prepared food were provided to most conference goers for a one-time registration fee, five bucks in most cases. The weekend in DC is just a small example of the degree of dedication, commitment, and planning now being waged by activists dead set on reclaiming the airwaves for democratic purposes.

MICRORADIO IN THE COURTROOM:
THE CASE OF FREE RADIO BERKELEY

Until now, the FCC has done everything possible to avoid having the constitutionality of their regulations questioned. For more than two years, the micropower radio movement was watching the case of Stephen Dunifer and Free Radio Berkeley, hoping that Judge Claudia Wilken would consider the FCC's ban unconstitutional and rule in favor of the broadcasters. But on Tuesday, June 16, 1998, shock waves rippled through the micropower radio movement as a short message from Stephen Dunifer coursed through e-mail networks across the Internet. Dunifer's message read: "We just received notification that Federal Judge Claudia Wilken has granted the FCC motion for summary judgement for a permanent injunction against myself and all others acting in concert with me." Two days later Dunifer's station, Free Radio Berkeley, was off the air.

Free Radio Berkeley first took to the airwaves in the spring of 1993. In November 1993, the FCC busted the station, fining Dunifer $20,000 for broadcasting without a license. In the legal battle that ensued, the FCC sought a court injunction against Dunifer, an injunction which Judge Claudia Wilken denied on January 30, 1995 for two reasons: first, because Dunifer had raised significant constitutional challenges; and, second, because the FCC was unable to prove that any harm would result if Free Radio Berkeley continued to broadcast.

Judge Wilken did not shut down Dunifer, because his constitutional challenges were overruled. In fact, throughout Judge Wilken's 20-page decision, she manages to completely *avoid* answering the constitutional questions that Dunifer raises as his defense. Instead, Judge Wilken bases her ruling against him on a technical Catch-22: that Dunifer never applied for a license. "This ruling is not based on the merits of Mr. Dunifer's criticism of the FCC's refusal to license microbroadcasters… Mr. Dunifer does not have standing as required by Article III of the United States Constitution to challenge the Class D regulations as they have been applied to him; because he has never applied for a license."[5]

Dunifer's attorneys are contesting Judge Wilken's decision. On Monday, June 29, they filed a Motion to Alter Judgement and requested a hearing for August 7. Their motion argues that Wilken is in error, and the logic of applying for a license and a waiver as prerequisites to challenging the constitutionality of the FCC's microradio ban is like demanding that Rosa Parks ask for a waiver to sit on the front of the bus. "The obstacle course that the F.C.C. has established for licensing full-power commercial broadcasters is so daunting and overwhelming," writes Lou Hiken, "that no microstation could ever pass muster in that context. It is as if the government demanded that mothers taking splinters out of their childrens' fingers comply with the regulatory requirements for an institution engaging in heart surgery."[6]

As stated in Dunifer's June 29, 1998 Motion to Alter Judgment, Judge Wilken's decision means that "all those who have awaited the opportunity to have a federal court resolve on the merits the constitutional issues surrounding access to the airwaves have been told that they must refrain from broadcasting for the months and years that it will take them to apply to the FCC for waivers and to receive the certain denials that will be issued. That is a cruel hoax upon thousands of Americans who want nothing more than the right to speak over their own airwaves..."[7]

Dunifer was not granted a hearing on August 7, 1998. Judge Wilken said that she did not require oral presentations in order to determine if she would amend her judgement. Whether or not she does, public unrest over the ban on microradio will continue to mount until some form of community access to the airwaves has been realized. Dunifer's civil disobedience, like that of Rosa Parks, has ignited a mass movement. As a result of his activism, communities all over America are claiming a seat in the front of the airwaves, challenging the injustice of the FCC's licensing scheme. The FCC have shut down 250 stations in the past 10 months, but new stations keep emerging.[8]

STEAL THIS RADIO, NYC

With the presence of several underground stations and the support of activist groups like the New York Free Media Alliance, Paper Tiger Television and the Center for Constitutional Rights, New York City has become an active front in the free media struggle. At the center of the local resistance is Steal This Radio (STR), a 20-watt station that has been broadcasting at 88.7 FM for three years on the Lower East Side.

In March 1998, Steal This Radio was visited by Judah Mansbach, a notorious FCC agent responsible for shutting down countless microstations. Following Mansbach's visit, STR decided to temporarily go off the air until the station was able to strike first against the FCC with a full-scale legal/media assault. That action began on April 15, 1998, when STR held a demonstration and press conference at the site where George Washington took oath as first President of the United States (directly across from the New York Stock Exchange). That afternoon, Steal This Radio's lawyers initiated the lawsuit by submitting formal papers in Federal court.

Steal This Radio's case is called *Free Speech vs. the FCC* and is represented by two brilliant lawyers, Robert Perry (independent) and Barbara Olshansky (Center For Constitutional Rights). Their legal offensive establishes that the airwaves are a public forum and, as such, are a venue where free speech should be protected by the Constitution. The FCC's condition that broadcasters take to the airwaves at 100 watts or more is one that involves an investment of hundreds of thousands of dollars—resources no community group has at its disposal. (Free speech lawyer Alan Korn compares the situation to being in a public park but only being permitted to exercise free speech if you own a 24-karat gold box to stand on.) STR's case also argues that the FCC's procedure for raiding stations and seizing equipment is illegal, even under the FCC's own statute, the Communications Act of 1934. "In other words," says Perry, "it's the FCC that is breaking the law."

Despite the government's aggressive campaign against low power broadcasting, Olshansky and Perry are optimistic. Unlike Dunifer's *defensive* case against the FCC, STR's case is *offensive;* and, also unlike Dunifer's case, which challenged the FCC 's regulations *as applied to him in his unique set of circumstances*, Steal This Radio's challenge attacks the FCC's licensing scheme as a whole, asserting that it is unconstitutional on its face, not just as applied to STR. For these reasons, Steal This Radio's case has the potential to bring down the whole FCC licensing scheme and breakthrough the corporate control of the airwaves.

PETITIONS FOR RULEMAKING

Outside the courtroom, microbroadcasters are also using channels opened by the FCC themselves to alter regulation. There are presently several petitions before the FCC which seek to open the airwaves to varying degrees of public access. Two of these petitions are meaningless tokens: RM-9208 proposes low power license of 1 watt or less (which basically means shouting distance), and RM-9246 proposes "Event Broadcast Stations" to provide temporary stations access to the airwaves. The third petition, RM-9242, is more sophisticated. Proposed by J. Rodger Skinner, it proposes the creation of three new classes of low power stations: one of up to 50 watts, one 50 watts to 3 kilowatts, and a third for the creation of temporary stations. In order to insure that these stations are a true organ of community, the petition proposes that license holders live within a 50-mile radius of the station and that no licensee would be permitted to own more than 3 stations nationwide. In this petition, micropower stations are called "secondary service stations" and are designated "to those types of of broadcasters who do not wish to conform to a more structured and/ or regulated form of broadcasting." Good as this may sound, this petition too is seriously flawed. Skinner proposes this license as being deferential to commercial interests,"[T]he licensee must vacate the channel," writes Skinner, "if a full-power station becomes short spaced . . . due to an antenna site move or power increase, or application by a . . . primary service applicant." Skinner's idea here is not to create sovereign community stations but, rather, to provide a temporary slot for folks who are planning to "upgrade" to a "full-power" station.

Even though these are the only three petitions that the FCC have formally presented for public comment, new regulations are by no means constrained by these three petitions alone. Thanks to the National Lawyers Guild Committee for Democratic Communications (CDC), a proposal that genuinely expresses a noncommercial, self-determined, public interest orientation has been crafted. The CDC are the in-for-the-long-haul, free media activist lawyers who've been fighting with microbroadcasters ever since 1989. Their mission is to focus "on the rights of all peoples to have a worldwide system of media and communications based upon the principle of cultural and informational self-determination." As an alternative to the three petitions which the FCC presented for public commentary, the CDC propose, and have won wide support for, new regulation that would permit:

1. Noncommercial service
2. Only one station per owner
3. Local ownership, no absentee owners
4. That stations shall be locally programmed. However, recorded materials (such as music, poetry, documentaries, features, etc.) may be used. Sharing of program materials and resources among micro and community stations is strongly encouraged.
5. That owners be individuals, unincorporated associations, or non-profit organizations. For-profit corporations, partnerships, joint ventures, or other organizations may not be owners.
6. That stations may be established on any unused frequency within the FM broadcast band down to 87.5. Second adjacent channel would be the closest spacing allowed.
7. That maximum power shall be 50 watts urban and 100 watts rural. In the event of interference due to power level, a station shall have the option to reduce power to remedy the situation or be shut down.
8. That a microstation shall fill out a simple registration form, and send one copy with an appropriate registration fee to the FCC and a second copy to the voluntary body set up by the micropower broadcast community to oversee the micropower stations.

9. That equipment shall meet a basic technical criteria in respect to stability, filtering, modulation control, etc.

10. That registration shall be valid for four years.

11. That there shall be no specific public service requirements imposed by the FCC.

12. That problems, whether technical or otherwise, shall be first referred to the local or regional voluntary micropower organization for technical assistance or voluntary mediation. The FCC shall be the forum of last resort.

13. That when television broadcast stations go digital, leaving Channel 6 free, it shall be allocated as an extension to the bottom of the FM band strictly for low-power community FM service. Radio receivers manufactured or entering the country after that allocation must meet this band extension.

14. That microbroadcasting of special events (demonstrations, protests, rallies, festivals, concerts, etc.) do not need to be registered but are encouraged to meet all technical specifications.

Intense and sustained pressure from microbroadcasters' civil disobedience strategies, lawsuits, and media campaigns are clearly impacting the FCC. Confirmation of this came two weeks after the October protests, when FCC head William Kennard stood before the sworn enemies of microbroadcasting, the National Association of Broadcasters (NAB), and signalled his intention to soon lift the microradio ban. At the time of this writing, the FCC seem on the verge of releasing for public comment a Notice of Proposed Rulemaking (NPRM) for new low-power radio system, the first step in the legalization process. Few people are optimistic about any initial proposals coming from the FCC. With intense pressure on him from the NAB, it is widely thought that Kennard will hand over microradio to microbusiness and to act primarily in the interests of minority entrepreneurs. "Given Kennard's orientation toward minority enterprise," says Franck, "the risk is that the FCC will simply set up a lower tier of small commercial stations onto the FM band." It's up to the movement to keep the pressure on until a genuinely progressive noncommercial NPRM is presented.

PROMETHEUS RADIO PROJECT

"Until our free speech is permitted over the airwaves at up to 100 watts, the movement will continue to fight, to organize, to attack the FCC in the courts and in the media, and engage in civil disobedience by starting as many new stations as possible," said Pete tri Dish, co-founder of the Prometheus Radio Project, a new group formed to raise public awareness about the coming legalization of microradio and how community groups can start up their own neighborhood station. For information about holding a free workshop in your area, contact: prometheusrp@earthlink.net or call (215) 474-6459.

MICRORADIO EMPOWERMENT COALITION

The Prometheus Radio Project is also spearheading the effort to win new regulation and has launched a Microradio Empowerment Coalition to mobilize widespread public support for *noncommercial* community access to the airwaves. The Coalition is seeking people to sign its statement of purpose and send letters to their representatives in Congress, requesting support for noncommercial regulation, cc-ing each FCC commissioner:

William Kennard (wkennard@fcc.gov)
Susan Ness (sness@fcc.gov)
Harold Furchgott-Roth (hfurchtg@fcc.gov)
Michael Powell (mpowell@fcc.gov)
Gloria Tristani (tristan@fcc.gov)

Federal Communications Commission
12000 M Street, NW, #548
Washington, DC 20554

Such support is crucial if the FCC is to act against the wishes of big business.

MICROBROADCASTING AND REVOLUTION

"Democracy functions insofar as individuals can participate meaningfully in the public arena," writes Chomsky, "while running their own affairs, individually and collectively, without illegitimate interference by concentrations of power." With this definition in mind, it's disturbingly clear that we live in a dysfunctional democracy at best, where public arenas and the means to participate in them are as segregated as Rosa Parks' bus. Corporate powers control communications and decision making, while civil society is marginalized, community speech banned, and our active powers of citizenship are perversely redefined to mean our passive choice as shoppers.

Mainstream media have become the *Niña*, *Pinta*, and *Santa Maria* of commercialism, forcing upon the shores of our consciousness a permanent invasion of unwanted, coercive, and alienating messages. They carry with them the unspoken ideology that representation is reality, ownership is identity, and that to consume is to connect. As a counter-offensive to this degrading assault on our everyday lives, the most effective use of our resources may not be to engage the commercial media system head-on but, rather, to concentrate on building sustainable venues and alternative networks. For those with computers the Internet provides immediate possibilities for entering such a network, possibilities being realized through the efforts of groups like Tao Communications in Toronto and others elsewhere. For those without access, for those who cannot read, for those with few resources, for those who struggle, micropower radio is a powerful weapon, a source, an invitation, a resistance, a connection...

Like Rosa Parks, we are not willing to wait for court cases or petition results to sit in the front of the airwaves. As enormous corporations merge and rival nation states for real global power, regaining control of communications at the local level represents a genuine revolution, a grassroots insurgency to advance our basic human freedoms and to place public access to communications at the heart of our everyday lives. Like the Zapatistas, we will continue to organize, continue to agitate, continue to seek one another out at meetings, over the airwaves, and in the streets until we have won the freedom and the resources to realize genuine democracy, a necessary victory, but not an end, in the struggle to build a better world.

NOTES

Aguascalientes literally means "hot water."

In the Zapatista democracy struggle, *Aguascalientes* refers to the civilian cultural resistance centers that serve surrounding communities by providing a space for political meetings, cultural events, dialogue and *"encuentros"* with civil society, as well as being places that contain schools, women's cooperatives, and health clinics.

The first *Aguascalientes* was destroyed by federal troops after they occupied the township of Guadelupe Tepeyac on February 5, 1995. In 1994 it was the site of the Democratic National Convention where 6,000 people from Mexico and all over the world gathered to meet with the Zapatistas and dialogue about the possibility of building an international movement of resistance "for humanity and against neoliberalism."

Here in the U.S., microradio stations serve many of the same functions as the Zapatistas' civil resistance centers—providing space for political discussion, cultural events, organizing, dialogue, and exchange. In this light, microradio stations are our *Aguascalientes* of the airwaves.

1. Robert W. McChesney, *Telecommunications, Mass Media, & Democracy: The Battle for the Control of U.S. Broadcasting, 1928-1935* (Oxford University Press, 1993): 3f.

2. Robert Perry and Barbara Olshansky, quoted from "The First Amended Complaint, *Free Speech vs. the FCC*, May 12, 1998." Full text see: http://artcon.rutgers.edu/papertiger/nyfma. Much of the info here on U.S. communications history was gleaned by studying their papers.

3. Quoted from Larry Soley's July 2, 1998 affidavit, "Free Speech vs the FCC."

4. See my article with Kate Duncan, *Z* magazine, October 1997. Video message available from Paper Tiger TV. For complete text of the Zapatista proposal and transcript of Marcos's video message, see the Open Media Pamphlet, *Zapatista Encuentro* (Seven Stories Press, 1998; call (800) 596-7437)

5. Quoted from Judge Claudia Wilken's June 16 decision. For the complete text see: http://www.368Hayes.com/wilkenrules.html.

6&7. From Dunifer's June 29, 1998 Motion to Alter Judgment. For full text see: http://www.368Hayes.com/microradio.mtn_to_alter.html

8. Statistic taken from FCC Chairman Kennard's October 16, 1998 speech to the NAB. For complete text see: http://www.fcc.gov/commissioners/kennard/speeches

SPECIAL THANKS... for input, ideas, and inspiration from Peter Franck, Robert Perry, Barbara Olshansky and the Center for Constitutional Rights, Jessica Glass, Mike Eisenmenger, Stephen Provisor, and Crystal and the National Commission for Democracy in Mexico, and all the radio rebels at Steal This Radio.

GREG RUGGIERO is an editor and publicist at Seven Stories Press in New York City. He is a plaintiff in the *Free Speech vs. the FCC* lawsuit and an active member of the New York Free Media Alliance and the Prometheus Radio Project.

CDC is seeking public feedback and support for its proposal for new FCC regulations creating a truly local and noncommercial system of low power radio. For CDC's current proposal and other micropower legal info contact: (415) 648-8450; http://www.radio4all.org/cdc.

NATIONAL LAWYERS GUILD COMMITTEE
FOR DEMOCRATIC COMMUNICATIONS
CDC is seeking public feedback and support for its proposal for new FCC regulations creating a truly local and noncommercial system of low power radio. For CDC's current proposal and other micropower legal info contact: (415) 648-8450; http://www.nlgcdc.org/.

CENTER FOR CONSTITUTIONAL RIGHTS (CCR)

CCR represents the landmark microradio case *Free Speech vs. the FCC*. Founded in 1966 by lawyers who represented civil rights demonstrators in the South, CCR is committed to the creative use of law as a positive force for social change: 666 Broadway, 7th Floor, NY, NY 10012; (212) 614-6464; e-mail: CCR@igc.apc.org.

NEW YORK FREE MEDIA ALLIANCE (NYFMA)

NYFMA's Web page archives some of the many legal papers and briefs by Robert Perry and Barbara Olshansky in the *Free Speech vs. the FCC case*. The site also contains a photo essay of the October 1998 protest in Washington, DC and other information from the free media movement: http://nyfree.media.xs2.net.

FEDERAL COMMUNICATIONS COMMISSION (FCC)

Will new microradio rules truly serve "the public interest," or will the government cave once again to the forces of "private interest," i.e., commercialism? The government has not publicly decided what it will do yet. Help them make up their mind for noncommercial regulation of the airwaves: http://www.fcc.gov/.

RADIO FOR ALL

The grand nexus of microradio Web sites and movement information. Check it out: http://www.radio4all.org/

TAO COMMUNICATIONS

Host to an array of on-line movement networks and Web sites. Check out their amazing Internet site and the many listserves they help maintain. Tao gets my vote for Media Agitator of the Decade Award. See for yourself: http://www.tao.ca/.

PAPER TIGER TELEVISION

Videos of microradio workshops, demos, press conferences, Subcommandante Marcos' video communiqué, and other subjects that "smash the myths of the information industry." Activism + imagination + love = Paper Tiger. Send for their great catalog: 339 Lafayette, #6, NY, NY 10012; (212) 420-9045; http://www.papertiger.org.

FREE RADIO BERKELEY

Interested in starting your own station? Here's where you can get equipment. Contact Stephen Dunifer and Free Radio Berkeley to find out about equipment, and other vital info:1442 A Walnut Street #406 Berkeley, CA 94709; e-mail:frbspd@crl.com.

PROMETHEUS RADIO PROJECT

Noncommercial micropower radio referral, consultation, and advocacy for the 21st century. Find out what's involved in starting your own station. Call: (212) 946-5251; e-mail: prometheus@earthlink.net.

Microradio: The Struggle for America's Airwaves

BY LOUIS N. HIKEN

THE IMPORTANCE OF RADIO

On December 8, 1998, a loss of electrical power silenced newspapers and television programming in San Francisco for five to eight hours. Most households were able to listen to radio programming, which described the progress of repairs throughout the day, because virtually every household had a battery-operated radio.

In his book *Free Radio: Electronic Civil Disobedience* (Westview Press, 1999), Lawrence Soley describes the ubiquitous presence of radios in homes throughout the world:

> Of the major mass media—television, newspapers, magazines, and radio—radio is the most important and influential worldwide. Radio has over twice the penetration of television and nearly four times the penetration of newspapers. There is only one television set for every 6.7 persons in the world, but there is one radio receiver for every three people, making radio far more available. On average, U.S. adults listen to radio about 2.8 hours daily. Overall, there are about 5.6 radio receivers per household with about 96 percent of Americans listening to these radio receivers weekly. [page 1]

Sadly, much of radio programming today exemplifies what Bruce Springsteen mockingly said about television: "57 channels and nothing on." I have spent the last five years representing Stephen Dunifer, aka Free Radio Berkeley (FRB) in his fight against the FCC, so I am painfully aware that the owners of the airwaves are directly responsible for the homogeneity, and mediocrity of commercial radio programming.

FREE RADIO BERKELEY

In 1993, a skilled radio engineer and designer named Stephen Dunifer created a microradio transmitter (fondly called "the brick" for its size and shape) that could broadcast with about 5 to 25 watts of power for less than $100 dollars. The simplicity of the transmitter, the accessibility of the parts needed to assemble it, and the accuracy of its signal created a breakthrough in microradio technology. What had previously cost broadcasters several thousands of dollars to accomplish could now be produced for less than a few hundred dollars.

But Stephen was more than just a radio technician. He was also a political activist, a card-carrying member of the International Workers of the World (IWW), and a strong advocate for the freedom of speech. Stephen didn't keep his transmitter hidden away but made it available to thousands of potential radio broadcasters throughout the world—offering demonstrations to show how they could best be operated.

Within months of its creation, the "brick" became the vehicle for creating a radio station called "Free Radio Berkeley" (FRB). A collective of broadcasters and DJs set up a 24-hour-a-day radio station. The producers of the weekly programs for FRB ranged in age from 14 to 78 years old, representing every race, sexual orientation, and political perspective imaginable. FRB was an ideal exercise in democratic communication.

Ultimately, this democratic communication compelled the FCC to pursue Dunifer as they attempted to silence FRB. Speech, music, and entertainment unfiltered by the corporate sponsors that dominate the radio spectrum threatened the FCC. As columnist Alexander Cockburn wrote in the *Los Angeles Times* and the *Anderson Valley Advertiser*, "There's nothing that so horrifies the Federal Communications Commission as freedom of speech, particularly when it's not backed by the billions now usually required to exercise that right on the airwaves."

At the time Dunifer began broadcasting, there were only a handful of microradio stations throughout the United States. The FCC had taken the position that microradio was not a viable concept worthy of consideration, and the media described people like Dunifer as "pirates" who were stealing the airwaves from licensed broadcasters.

The FCC was finally able to temporarily stop Dunifer from broadcasting in 1998, five years after he created "the brick." By then, there were approximately a thousand "pirate" stations broadcasting in virtually every state in the country. Hundreds of Dunifer's transmitters had been sent to people throughout the world, from Haiti to Chiapas. Some had even been purchased directly by UNESCO for use in underdeveloped nations. The FCC had, in the meantime, initiated rulemaking proceedings and looked into the propriety of legalizing Low Power FM stations (LPFMs). Public consciousness had shifted to the point that corporate interests that had stolen the people's airwaves were largely recognized as the true "pirates" of the airwaves. The microradio broadcasters had come to be correctly perceived as citizen soldiers, taking back what was rightfully theirs. At this point, there are more than 15 federal lawsuits pending in U.S. District Courts both attacking the monopolization of the airwaves by the National Association of Broadcasters (NAB) and seeking to legalize microradio.

To understand the scope and implications of this struggle, some knowledge of radio history is helpful.

A SHORT HISTORY

Robert W. McChesney, in his insightful history *Telecommunications, Mass Media, and Democracy: The Battle for the Control of U.S. Broadcasting, 1928-1935* (Oxford University Press, 1993), outlines the events of the seven-year period during which the corporate interests that now dominate the radio spectrum seized exclusive control of the airwaves from the American public. The forerunners of what is now the National Association of Broadcasters (NAB) created such a formidable obstacle course that obtaining radio licenses today remains a Herculean task. Fifty-five years later, there are only a handful of noncommercial radio stations with significant access to the public.

When Ben Bagdikian wrote his seminal work *The Media Monopoly* (Beacon Press, 1983), he could not have imagined passage of the Telecommunications Act of 1996 and its escalating impact. With one stroke of the pen, Congress created a virtual Gold Rush of radio monopolization. At this point, fewer than 10 corporations possess the licenses for over 50 percent of the radio spectrum. Even the FCC has been stunned by the consolidation of ownership into the hands of such a small number of wealthy corporations.

In a paper presented to the NAB convention in Las Vegas, in April of 1998, Peter Franck and Alan Korn of the Committee on Democratic Communications of the National Lawyers Guild made the following point:

> The First Amendment had to be added to the Constitution before it could be ratified to insure that the United States would have a robust democracy. A robust democracy requires broad channels of discussion and debate on all of society's issues and concerns. It requires a media system which is open to the widest possible range of views, and in which all citizens can effectively express and communicate their ideas, thoughts and concerns, as well as receive and consider the thoughts, ideas, and concerns of their fellow citizens.

The Communications Act of 1934 says that it is enacted " . . . so as to make available, so far as possible, to all the people of the United States, without discrimination on the basis of race, color, religion, national origin, or sex, a rapid, efficient, nationwide and worldwide wire and radio communication service with adequate facilities at reasonable charges." Today's allocation of licenses hits far from the mark envisioned by the Congress of 1934. The chasm between the function of commercial speech and democratic dialogue has never been greater. While commercial speech values efficiency, acceptability, and commonality, democratic expression values investigation, debate, and confrontation. Fifty years ago, the U.S. Supreme Court opined:

> A function of free speech under our system of government is to invite dispute. It may indeed best serve its high purpose when it induces a condition of unrest, creates dissatisfaction with conditions as they are, or even stirs people to anger. Speech is often provocative and challenging. It may strike at prejudices and preconceptions and have profound unsettling effects as it presses for acceptance of an idea. That is why freedom of speech, though not absolute, is nevertheless protected against censorship or punishment, unless shown likely to produce a clear and present danger of a serious substantive evil that rises far above public inconvenience, annoyance, or unrest. There is no room under our Constitution for a more restrictive view. For the alternative would lead to standardization of ideas either by legislatures, courts, or dominant political or community groups (*Terminiello v. Chicago*).

It would be difficult to envision a greater "standardization of ideas" than the current content of licensed radio broadcasting (although the homogeneity of television broadcasting might outdo even radio). As a result of disenfranchising the poor, people of color, women, and other minorities, the FCC has ensured the most undemocratic use of the airwaves imaginable. By delegating licenses exclusively to wealthy commercial broadcasters, the FCC has abandoned in full its obligation to carry out the mandates set forth in the Communications Act, namely:

a) to allocate licenses in the public convenience, interest, and necessity;

b) to study new uses for radio, provide for experimental uses of frequencies, and generally encourage the larger and more effective use of radio in the public interest;

c) to limit broadcasters to the minimum amount of power necessary to carry out the communications desired.

While a handful of "public radio stations" (i.e. NPR, with a budget of $60 million; Pacifica, with a budget of $8 million) adopt the mantle of speaking for "the people," the reality is quite different. We are a pluralistic nation, and we do not speak with one or two voices. If people are to have any opportunity to communicate their views outside the confines of their own homes, there must be outlets for local participation and dialogue. And that requirement is missing from the current regulatory scheme.

MICRORADIO VS. THE MEGAWATT STATIONS

The American people are essentially voiceless. While we are free to express our beliefs and opinions in the privacy of our homes or in the public parks, we do not have the resources to make our views known throughout our broader geographical communities. Few individuals possess the wealth needed to own a television station or newspaper. Yet radio, which is a resource requiring little capital investment, is denied us by the FCC. We can only express our views when and if the owners of media permit us to do so. This insidious form of censorship renders us voiceless at the times when and in the places where we need it most. Experiences with the propaganda surrounding the Gulf War, the impeachment charade, and the pre-packaged documentaries fed us by the homogenized media demonstrate more than ever the need for the American people to regain their own voice.

It is not a coincidence that media control happens to be the exclusive dominion of the wealthy. Just as the leaders of the defense industries and the Pentagon constitute an interlocking board of directors, marked by a revolving door that renders the institutions indistinguishable from one another, so it is with the NAB and the FCC. For decades, the FCC commissioners have been chosen from the ranks of those accountable to the NAB. They hold common interests and attitudes, and their allegiances are to the same masters. What benefits commercial licensees deprives the public of a truly democratic means of communication. The frantic attempts by Congress and corporate America to find some way of controlling the Internet is only the most obvious example of the degree to which those entities are threatened by unfiltered speech. Obscenity and pornography over the Internet does not concern our politicians so much as the dispersal of our uncensored opinions.

In reality there is, or should be, little competition between microradio stations and megawatt stations. Whereas megawatt stations broadcast far and wide, microradio statios are limited to a small geographical patch. Therefore, microradio stations should serve local communities and provide a vehicle for two-way communication. Japanese engineer and activist, Tetsuo Kogawa, argues that microradio should be viewed as a two-way system of communication. He feels that a microradio station should be no more powerful than is necessary to reach people within bicycle range of the transmitter. "In that way," he explains, "you can be assured of community participation in whatever is being broadcast over the air. If people feel that they are not interested in what is being broadcast, they don't have to participate in the dialogue. But if they do have an opinion, they can bicycle over to the station and express it in a timely way."

The multiplicity of voices represented through microradio serves a qualitatively different function than the 150,000 watt stations designed to afford easy listening entertainment and advertisements on behalf of their corporate owners. Furthermore, low power broadcasters don't have the personnel or other capacities required to investigate world issues. They tend to report what is happening in their own areas and why it is of importance to their community. Yet experience has shown that among most microradio broadcasters, there is a broad exchange of tapes and productions from other stations, thereby permitting a much wider distribution of ideas and concerns than would ever have been generated by one small station. In many parts of the country, the microradio stations are the ones that broadcast news about city council meetings, community gatherings, high school sports events, and the like. Megawatt broadcasters have no interest in such non-remunerative topics.

A recent book edited by Stephen Dunifer and Ron Sakolsky, *Seizing The Airwaves: A Free Radio Handbook* (AK Press, 1998), presents speeches and articles from numerous proponents of microradio. They describe the justifications and, indeed, the necessity of fighting for the right to communicate over the airwaves. The book also includes the technical information required to accomplish this objective. While the courts continue to scrape the bottom of the procedural barrel to justify the silencing of the American people, and while the FCC and its handlers, the NAB, continue to mouth outmoded comments about spectrum scarcity and chaos, the public is ever more cognizant of the corporate rip-off that has taken place. Virtually every newspaper in the country has run articles about the monopolization of the airwaves; the majority of the commissioners on the FCC have publicly acknowledged the devastating impact that the Telecommunications Act of 1996 has had on radio ownership; and technological advances have themselves rendered much of the dialogue obsolete. In fact, the availability of direct broadcast satellite systems, cable feeds, digital frequency systems, high speed Internet connections (offering audio and visual programming on demand, and a variety of other advances are significantly altering the nature of the fight.)

In the meantime, Americans are faced with the ongoing difficulty of expressing themselves over airwaves controlled by and for commercial corporate interests. The formula might be as simple as a Labor movement slogan of the 1920s: "Take it easy, but take it." The Web site (www.radio4all.com) carries an up-to-the-moment description of the activities of dozens of micro-radio stations throughout the country. These broadcasters have learned a principle that Frederick Douglass summarized a century ago: "Power cedes nothing without struggle; it never has and it never will."

LOUIS HIKEN is an attorney in private practice in San Francisco, California. He is a member of the National Lawyers Guild Committee on Democratic Communications, and currently represents Stephen Dunifer, a.ka Free Radio Berkeley, in the legal battle against the FCC.

CHAPTER 7

Voices of International Journalists and Scholars

PROJECT CENSORED is pleased to present the Voices of International Journalists and Scholars as alternative perspectives on important global news stories. Writers selected this year were presenters at the International Conference on the Ownership and Control of the Media held in Athens, Greece in May 1998.

On the Fiftieth Anniversary of the Universal Declaration of Human Rights

BY RAMSEY CLARK
(Baghdad, Iraq, December 9, 1998)

"The world has never had a good definition of the word liberty, and the American people, just now, are much in want of one. We all declare for liberty, but in using the same word we do not all mean the same thing." So observed Abraham Lincoln at, for him, the darkest moment of the American Civil War. He had just received reports of the massacre of 800 Union soldiers, former slaves whose ancestors were brought from Africa in chains. They were the first such unit to be engaged in combat. Caught and overwhelmed at Ft. Pillow, Tennessee, on the Mississippi River by a much larger Confederate cavalry force under Nathan Bedford Forrest, every man was killed. Forrest reported that "the river ran red for hundreds of yards." After the war, Forrest was a founder of the Ku Klux Klan and engaged in racist violence for two decades.

Four score and four years after the Ft. Pillow massacre, in the Preamble to the Universal Declaration of Human Rights on December 10, 1948, the U.N. General Assembly found that "a common understanding of these rights and freedoms is of the greatest importance," and proclaimed its declaration in order to provide "a good definition."

The Universal Declaration was dominated by the experience, concerns, interests, and values of a narrow segment of the "people of the United Nations," the governments of the rich nations, primarily the United States, England, and France. It emphasized political rights developed over centuries from their histories with little concern for economic, social, and cultural rights. Still it was and remains an important contribution in the continuing struggle for justice.

In the fifth paragraph of its preamble, the Declaration notes the United Nations has affirmed "... the dignity and worth of the human person and the equal rights of men and women and have determined to promote social progress and better standards of life in larger freedom." Article 1 provides "All human beings are born free and equal in dignity and rights." Article 5 states, "No one shall be subjected to torture or to cruel, inhuman, or degrading treatment or punishment." Article 25 declares, "Everyone has the right to a standard of living adequate for the health and well-being of himself and of his family, including food, clothing, housing, and medical care..."

The United States government pays lip service to the Declaration, but its courts have consistently refused to enforce its provisions, reasoning it is not a legally binding treaty or contract, but only a declaration. This ignores the fact that international law recognizes the provisions of the Declaration as being incorporated into customary international law binding on all nations.

The most fundamental, dangerous, and harmful violation of the Universal Declaration of Human Rights on its fiftieth birthday is economic sanctions

THIS MODERN WORLD by TOM TOMORROW

YOU KNOW, I REALLY DON'T UNDERSTAND WHAT WE WOULD GAIN BY ATTACKING IRAQ AGAIN...

YES, OUR OBJECTIVES ARE MURKY AT BEST--SINCE WE ARE, FRANKLY, UNLIKELY TO ELIMINATE EITHER SADDAM HUSSEIN'S MUCH-BALLYHOOED WEAPONS OF MASS DESTRUCTION OR THE MAN HIMSELF...

IN ALL LIKELIHOOD, WE'D SIMPLY END UP MASSACRING A SUBSTANTIAL NUMBER OF INNOCENT CIVILIANS WHOSE ONLY CRIME WAS TO HAVE BEEN BORN INTO THE WRONG SOCIETY...

THOUGH UNFORTUNATELY, IF HISTORY IS ANY INDICATION, THE REALITY OF THAT SLAUGHTER WOULD BE HIDDEN FROM THE AMERICAN PUBLIC BEHIND A WALL OF MILITARY EUPHEMISMS AND HIGH TECH VIDEO DISPLAYS!

imposed on entire populations. The United States alone blockades 11 million Cubans in the face of the most recent General Assembly resolution, approved by 157 nations, condemning the blockade, with only the United States and Israel in opposition. The entire population of Cuba has had the "right to a standard of living adequate for health and well-being... including food, clothing, housing, and medical care" deliberately violated by the United States blockade.

Security Council sanctions against Iraq, which are forced by the United States, have devastated the entire nation, taking the lives of more than 1,500,000 people, mostly infants, children, chronically ill, and elderly, and harming millions more by hunger, sickness, and sorrow. The sanctions destroy the "dignity and rights" of the people of Iraq and are the most extreme form of "cruel, inhuman, and degrading treatment," which are prohibited by the Declaration.

Despite the cruelest destruction of the most basic human rights and liberties of all the people in Iraq, including rights to medicine, safe drinking water, and sufficient food, the United States government, with the major mass media in near perfect harmony, proclaims itself the world's champion of liberty and human rights. The problem, as Lincoln surely knew, is not merely one of definitions. It is a problem of power, will, and accountability. The United States intends to have its way and serve its own interests, with Iraq, Cuba, Libya, Iran, the Sudan, and many other countries whatever the consequences to the liberties and rights of those who live there.

The United States' control over and its concerted action with the mass media enables it to demonize such countries, its victims, for "terrorism," threats to world peace, and human rights violations at the very time it rains Tomahawk cruise missiles on them and motivates and finances armed insurrections and violence against them. At the same time, the United States increases its own staggeringly large prison industry, more than a million persons confined, including 40 percent of all African-American males between 17 and 27 years old in the State of California. Simultaneously, the U.S. spends more on

its military than the 10 largest military budgets of other nations combined, sells most of the arms and sophisticated weapons still increasing worldwide, while rejecting an international convention to prohibit land mines and an international court of criminal justice. And the U.S. maintains and deploys the great majority of all weapons of mass destruction existent on earth, nuclear, chemical, biological, and the most deadly of all—economic sanctions.

It is imperative that clear definitions of all fundamental rights of people be clearly inscribed in international law, including economic rights which are most basic to human need and on which all other rights are dependent, and rights to freedom from military aggression by a superpower or its surrogates.

But without a passionate commitment by the people of the United States and other major powers to stop their own governments from violating those definitions of human rights, hold them accountable for their acts, and to prevent their own media from seducing them into acceptance or complacency, there will be no protection for the poor and powerless and no correspondence between the words of rich and powerful nations and their deeds.

We can be thankful for the Universal Declaration of Human Rights, but together the people of the world must do better to define and protect the humanity of the people.

RAMSEY CLARK, the Former Attorney General of the United States, can be reached at:

International Action Center
39 West 14th Street, #206
New York, NY 10011
Tel: (212) 633-6646 Fax: (212) 633-2889
http://www.iacenter.org

The Telltale Silence of the Post-Oslo Palestinian Press

BY RONI BEN EFRAT,
Editor of *Challenge* magazine
(Lecture for the conference: "A 21st Century Dialogue: Media's Dark Age?" Athens, Greece, May 24-28, 1998, Organized by: Women for Mutual Security)

The Palestinian Authority oppresses its people and intimidates its press. In what follows I shall give nine examples of this intimidation. Let me say at the start that this fact should not come as a surprise. "Oppression" may be said to be a corollary of the Oslo agreement. The logic is simple: The strong side, Israel, took advantage of its strength, cutting a deal that gave the weak side, the PLO, as little as possible.

The designers of Oslo set up a situation where a great many people were bound to oppose the deal they had gotten. Although they lacked the foresight to make real peace, they did foresee the opposition to the nasty, brutish thing that they *did* make, and they were careful, therefore, to provide the new non-state with a huge police force and plenty of rifles. Imprisonment without trial is the norm. Torture is carried out wholesale. Numerous security organizations vie with one another in extortion, and "Big Brother" is everywhere.

The curbing of the press is merely a part of this general picture. The most alarming aspect in the story has been the speed with which the press agreed to lay down its weapon, the pen.

THE FIRST ACTS OF OPPRESSION

The press was the first to be hit. Arafat arrived in Gaza on July 1, 1994. Twenty-seven days later, forces of the Palestinian Secret Security invaded the offices of *Al-Nahar*, then the second largest daily newspaper in the Territories. They forbade the distribution of *Al-Nahar* in the West Bank, Gaza, and East Jerusalem. According to the Oslo accords, they had no jurisdiction in Jerusalem, or the West Bank, except for Jericho at the time. But when it comes to oppression, Israel gives the Palestinian Authority (PA) a free hand. No explanation was given, but it was understood that the closing of *Al-Nahar* had to do with the paper's pro-Jordanian tendency. The rest of the Palestinian press hardly covered the event. Palestinian human rights activist Bassem Id, then of B'tselem, initiated a protest demonstration, and eight journalists showed up. Perhaps the other Palestinian papers thought it wouldn't happen to them since they weren't "pro-Jordanian." The epilogue: *Al-Nahar* began publishing again after several weeks, but it soon collapsed financially. (For the full story see *Challenge # 27*).

Four months later it was the turn of the biggest Palestinian daily, *Al-Quds*, also published in Jerusalem. On November 18, 1994, the PA forces killed fourteen Palestinians during a demonstration at a Gaza mosque. The opposition party Hamas held a mass rally protesting the massacre. Gaza's Chief of Police, General Ghazi Jibali told the press he estimated 5000 people in attendance. To his consternation, the biggest Palestinian daily, *Al-Quds* preferred the estimate of a foreign press agency, which had counted 12,500. Jibali's response was to keep *Al-Quds* from entering the Gaza Strip. He simply blocked the papers at the Erez checkpoint for a number of days, claiming that heavy rain and floods were preventing their distribution. I interviewed the chief editor of *Al-Quds*, Maruan Abu Zuluf, concerning the strange weather in Gaza. He firmly adhered to his right to publish whatever he saw fit. (See *Challenge 4* 29: "Gaza Weatherman"). Ever since that incident, however, *Al-Quds* has never dared to publish a word contradicting the official Palestinian line. Not even a paid ad.

The third incident involved an independent Palestinian opposition paper called *Al-Uma*, which was also located in Jerusalem. In the '80s its owners, members of the Khatib family, had put out a left-wing daily, *Al-Mithaq*, but Israel had closed it down. In January 1995, however, Israel granted the Khatibs a license for *Al-Uma*. Four months later the paper published an unflattering cartoon of Arafat. Thirty armed Palestinians, members of Preventive Security, entered the print shop and confiscated the plates.

The angry editors alerted human rights organizations. Palestinian figures signed a petition. On May 3, 1995 the offices of *Al-Uma* were burned. The Khatibs never went back to publishing *(Challenge # 32).*

SELF-CENSORSHIP

Since these incidents, the PA has licensed quite a few new media projects. Some of these function as mouthpieces for the Authority—for example, *Al Khayat al Jadida* or the radio station, Sout Falastin. All practice strict self-censorship. This may seem odd at first, because the Authority itself, with super-democratic panache, forgoes all official censorship. On June 25, 1995, Arafat signed the Palestinian Press Law, which guarantees the right to freedom of opinion and a free press. It does contain, nonetheless, several vague and potentially restrictive provisions. Article 37(3), for example, prohibits the publication of anything that "may cause harm to national unity." (*Human Rights Watch,* op. cit.) In reality, censorship Arafat-style has proved to be more zealous and harsh than Israel's ever was. To quote the Authority's radio director, Ali Khayan: "The opposition can express its own opinions, but some things are not allowed because we need time to explain what it means to be democratic." *(*See *Challenge # 32.)*

Under Israeli occupation Palestinian journalists did indeed suffer from oppression. There are stories of chief editors under house arrest who edited major dailies from their homes. Numerous journalists were kept in administrative detention for renewable periods of six months at a time. But such measures did not intimidate them. When they got out, they went back to their work. Today it is different. Why?

FIRST, THERE ARE NO RULES.

During the period of direct Israeli occupation, every Palestinian editor had to send the entire paper to the censor. (The Israeli media, in contrast, only have to send articles that relate to security). The censor would return the Arab paper, marking what had to go. The censor decided what was fit to print. There was no guesswork, and there were no personal reprisals.

Today, Palestinian editors have to guess what *might* not be accepted, and if they guess wrong, they find themselves in trouble. According to the data of *Human Rights Watch* /Middle East (Vol. 9, No. 10, Sept. 1997), in the first two years of self-rule, 25 journalists and photographers "guessed wrong." One of them was Fayez Nora-Din, a photographer for Agence France Press. He photographed some boys washing a donkey in the sea at Gaza. This was a bad guess. The Special Intelligence Service detained him for ten hours on May 13, 1996. They beat and whipped him, accusing him of being in the pay of French intelligence in order to "harm the image of the Palestinians." The donkey, it seems, should have been a Jaguar.

In the report cited above, *Human Rights Watch*/Middle East gave many examples of self-censorship. Most of the journalists were afraid to give the researchers their names. "The problem," said one, "is not that Arafat doesn't want this or that item to be published. The problem is, journalists are afraid that *maybe* he won't like it—so they just stay quiet."

"Frankly," said another, "we wish the Authority would tell us exactly what we can and cannot publish. That would be easier. It seems that it is impossible to talk about the security apparatus, or violations relating to trials, prisons, and torture, or the president. The president is sacred."

The latest story of this kind is that of Abbas Momani, a photographer working both for Reuters and *Al-Quds*. The Authority had attributed the death of Hamas bombmaker Muhi a-Din Sharif, "Engineer #2," to a dispute within Hamas. It claimed that Hamas leader Adel Awadalla had killed Sharif. Shortly after the Authority made this accusation, photographer Momani received a phone call telling him to go to a flat in Ramallah. Here he received a videocassette, in which a masked man claiming to be Adel Awadalla denied having killed Sharif. He brought the cassette to his manager, Paul Holms, and they discussed whether or not to air it. Holms took full responsibility, and the video was distributed and broadcast on April 8. The Authority found the video believable enough to change its story, blaming Adel's brother instead. (See *Challenge # 49*.) But it also closed the Reuters office in Gaza. On April 9, photographer Momani received an order to come for investigation to the office of

Preventive Security Chief, Jibril Rajoub. When Rajoub heard, however, that Paul Holms was going to accompany him, he canceled the meeting. Instead, Momani was arrested by another security branch the next day—then released. On May 5, he was arrested again, this time by Rajoub's men. Four days later, at 3 A.M. he escaped by jumping from a third-floor window of the interrogation building, breaking his leg, and in this condition he managed to reach the hospital. His brother came to help him, and Momani told him how they had hung him by his legs from the ceiling and whipped him with electric cables. (The report was later confirmed by human rights activist, Bassem Id.) They had wanted him to confess, said Momani, that he had made the video. His brother helped him leave the hospital for another flat, but here Rajoub's men caught up with him, arresting him again. As to how they treated him after that, we do not yet know—he was released on May 14, a day before this writing. According to the Israeli weekly, *Kol Ha-Ir*, neither of Momani's employers, Reuters or *Al-Quds*, reported his first arrest. The Palestinian media didn't cover it either. After his escape, most continued to ignore the issue. Journalists Michal Schwartz and Diana Mardi, from our "sister paper" in Arabic, *Al-Sabar*, contacted Paul Holms of Reuters. He told Schwartz that the agency was following his case, and that it had put out a statement on May 6 for "whoever wanted to publish it." Mardi asked the editor of *Al-Quds*, Maher al-Sheikh, why his paper had failed to print a word on the matter, seeing that Momani is one of their journalists. He answered: "Our paper doesn't publish news of that sort." Mardi pressed him: "Of what sort"? The editor answered: "News concerning arrests on the part of the PA." "Why not?" she asked him. He answered: "Because we are afraid. We are afraid of the authorities." (From an interview on May 11, 1998, published in *Al-Sabar*.)

The Momani story brings us to the second reason for self-censorship:

THE JOURNALIST STANDS ALONE.

Momani stood alone.

Here is an earlier example. At midnight on December 24, 1995, *Al-Quds* was about to print an article on page eight about Arafat's meeting with the Greek Orthodox Patriarch. A phone call came, in which editor Maher Alameh was instructed to move the piece up to page one. (How, by the way, could the Authority have known exactly what was to be printed on which page?) In a moment of exceptional courage and resolution, Alameh refused. He was arrested and imprisoned in Jericho for five days. Not a single Palestinian newspaper, including *Al-Quds*, reported the case. (*Human Rights Watch*/Middle East, op. cit.). After Alameh's release, he refused to talk about the matter.

In the post-Oslo situation, when you stick your neck out as Alameh did, you're practically alone. Pre-Oslo you were a hero, part of a fighting people. Solidarity was widespread. The atmosphere was such that if you hadn't served time in an Israeli prison, something was wrong with

you. Since the entry of the Palestinian Authority, however, most opposition factions have been co-opted, or are looking for ways to be co-opted. The atmosphere is one of fear and despair. No lawyer can protect you when you are taken in the middle of the night to be interrogated in Jericho, nor does it help if you work for a foreign news agency. The agencies want to keep their offices running. This (partially) explains why journalists, who were in the forefront of the *Intifada*, have retired into the woodwork.

OTHER KINDS OF MEDIA

Does this mean that Palestinians don't know what's happening? No. They can get information from Israeli radio and television. Ever since the Oslo process began, however, Israel's media have either avoided or played down Arafat's violations of human rights. The Israeli establishment measures him by the strength with which he curbs the opposition. It is remarkable, for example, how quickly most of the Israeli press adopted, one after another, the Authority's changing versions of how Hamas Engineer #2 was killed, although no account has withstood the slightest examination. (See *Challenge* #49.)

Despite the lack of an uncompromising press, alternative Palestinian channels have opened occasionally, but they too have encountered interference.

The Palestinian National Council (PNC) is an elected Parliament. Each member represents a constituency. One cannot simply arrest him or her without, as it were, gagging a whole group of voters. This fact provides PNC members with a measure of freedom to speak. It was the Council, for example, which exposed the astonishing scope and depth of corruption in the Authority. *(Challenge #43 and #45)* The Palestinian papers did not dare publish what the elected representatives had revealed. Journalist Amin Abu Warda told *People's Rights* (a human rights monthly of the organization, Land and Water): "The print media avoided reporting on Council sessions right from the start. Editors consistently censored reports about the sessions, especially when the members criticized Arafat or his associates." (March 1997) But outside media could and did. Stories appeared in *A I-Sabar* and *Challenge,* and later in the Hebrew daily *Haaretz. The Haaretz* article was translated into Arabic, and circulated in the Territories like an underground leaflet.

The Council legislators fought for the right to have their sessions broadcast directly. They finally won this at the beginning of 1997. Viewers watched with interest, too much perhaps. All through March, April, and May when corruption was on the agenda, all kinds of static broke out on the screen. The manager of the broadcasting company, Da'ud Kuttab, complained about this to the *Washington Post.* He found himself in jail for a week. The broadcasts have not resumed.

Another path that seemed relatively free was that of local cable TV. The channels carry many open discussion programs, in which people can speak out. During the recent Gulf Crisis, these talk shows were very popular and militant.

They too were forced to close, however, after the U.S. pressured Arafat to stop showing solidarity with Iraq.

The story of the Palestinian press is sad, if not demeaning. But one can hardly expect to find a free and thriving press alongside a regime that is basically scared of its people. The press will stand on its feet only when Palestinians face the fact that their current leadership cannot be reformed and that peace must be renegotiated. Only then will it be possible for a democratic sovereign state to emerge, one with enough self-confidence to tolerate pictures of children washing donkeys in the sea of Gaza.

RONI BEN EFRAT is the editor of *Challenge* magazine and can be reached at:
Challenge
Ma'agalei Yavne 7/23
Jerusalem: 93582, Israel
Tel & Fax: 972-2-6792270
e-mail: odaa@p-ol.com

The Attempted Character Assassination of Aristide

BY BEN DUPUY
(Presented at the International Conference on the Ownership and Control of the Media, May 26, 1998, Athens, Greece)

Haiti, it is well known, is the only country in world history which carried out a successful slave revolution. It began in 1791, on the heels of the French Revolution. The man who led the slave armies through most of our 13-year liberation war was a former slave named Toussaint Louverture.

While much can be said about his military genius, Toussaint was above all a master in the art of what we might call "diplomatic guile." In other words, he sometimes pretended to go along with his powerful adversaries—variously the French, English, and Spanish—to get what he wanted, which was the abolition of slavery (at least in its classical form).

One who has deeply studied and borrowed from Toussaint's tactics is Jean-Bertrand Aristide. Just as Toussaint attempted to advance his people's interests by sometimes fighting against the French, then sometimes working with them, Aristide has been locked into a similar dance with Haiti's principal adversary in this century: the United States.

The debate about the viability or correctness of using Toussaint's tactics in the 20th century can be left for another time. But one thing is certain: President Aristide has fallen in and out of favor with leading sectors of the U.S. ruling class and government on several occasions, and this offers a very revealing case study of how the mainstream corporate media has alternately demonized and glorified him as a leader, not depending on his support from or attachment to the masses, but according to his professed attitude toward U.S. business interests and U.S. government dictates.

Let us briefly review a little history.

First we must remember that Jean-Bertrand Aristide emerged in Haiti as a liberation theologian with an anti-imperialist message. "Capitalism is a mortal sin" was one of the refrains of the fiery sermons he would deliver at a church located in the La Saline slum of Port-au-Prince, Haiti's capital.

Although his prestige in Haiti was growing, the U.S. corporate press made little mention of him, even though the U.S. Embassy in Haiti was watching his rise very carefully.

Of course, the U.S. mainstream media could no longer ignore him when he announced he was running for president in October 1990, thereby unleashing the euphoric uprising known as the "Lavalas," or the flood.

The initial portrayal of Aristide by the mainstream in that pre-election period can be summed up by the description given by Howard French of *The New York Times* on November 12, 1990: Aristide was "a mix of [Iran's Ayatolla] Khomeini and [Cuba's Fidel] Castro."

But of course, it was hard to frontally attack a man who came to power not through a revolution, but through elections which the U.S. government had sponsored and paid for.

All the mainstream press could do after Aristide's overwhelming victory on December 16, 1990 was to attempt to intimidate him. *The New York Times* in a December 18 editorial warned Aristide that he had "acquired a duty to respect the constitutional procedures that assured his victory" and "to be patient, and to preach patience," cautioning that he "can now become either the father of

Haitian democracy, or just one more of its many betrayers."

Well, we know who ended up betraying Haitian democracy. The U.S. government, through its CIA, would work with Duvalierism to overthrow Aristide after less than eight months in power, with a bloody coup on September 30, 1991.

Rather than condemning the coup, the mainstream press began attacking Aristide. "Returning President Aristide to Haiti is going to be difficult for reasons to which he himself has greatly contributed," stated a *Washington Post* editorial on October 6, 1991. "The president is a hero to the desperate people who live in the slums of Port-au-Prince . . . . He has organized them into an instrument of real terror . . . . He has left the country deeply polarized between his followers and the substantial numbers of people who have reason to fear them." The next day, the *Post* reported that Aristide had a "seeming disregard of legal structures" and cited "independent observers and diplomats" who charged that he "repeatedly has used explicit and implicit threats of mob violence."

"Mob violence." If you look through the mainstream press clippings for the period right after the coup, you will see this refrain throughout. According to Katie Orenstein of *The Latin American Review*, "during the two-week period after the coup, *The New York Times* spent over three times as many column inches discussing Aristide's alleged transgression than it spent reporting on the ongoing military repression. Mass murders, executions, and tortures that were later

reported in human rights publications earned less than 4 percent of the space than *The Times* devoted to Haiti in those weeks."

Throughout the coup, the mainstream press never stopped casting suspicion on Aristide. Negotiations with the putschists began and Aristide was always portrayed as "intransigent" and "inflexible," even though he was making all the concessions and the putschists were scuttling every deal. But Haitians in the diaspora maintained constant demonstrations in support of Aristide and against the coup. The Democrats took advantage of this movement to find support for Bill Clinton's 1992 election.

This is where there emerged a difference between the two factions of the U.S. ruling class. President George Bush and the Republicans were perfectly happy to leave Aristide permanently in exile and work with their old allies, the Haitian military and Duvalierists, in Haiti. But the Democrats, who are supposed to be more "enlightened," calculated that the generals would never provide real stability and would never have legitimacy. So the Clinton Administration decided that they would try to co-opt Aristide and force him to accept what is known in Haiti as "the American plan." The essence of this plan is to discard justice and reconcile with Duvalierist criminals, and structurally adjust the Haitian economy: that is, privatize profitable state enterprises, lower tariff walls, lay off state employees, mainly from schools and hospitals, and slash social subsidies and price-supports.

Of course, even if Aristide accepted the deal, Washington felt he could not really be trusted, so U.S. troops would have to militarily occupy the country as an insurance policy.

That is how the Governors Island Accord was constructed in the summer of 1993, whereby U.N. peacekeepers would land in Haiti prior to Aristide's return on October 30, 1993.

Well, the Republicans didn't like this arrangement at all. Neither did the "invisible government" in the U.S., that is the Pentagon and the CIA. Therefore, the CIA began pumping up a death squad in Haiti known as the FRAPH, which they called a "counterweight" to the Lavalas.

The FRAPH and CIA coordinated their strategies. First, the FRAPH staged a demonstration with a few dozen thugs at the Port-au-Prince wharf on October 11, 1993, so that the Pentagon had an excuse to withdraw its troop carrier, the Harlan County, which was to offload 200 U.S. and Canadian soldiers. The following week, Brial Latell, the CIA's chief Latin American analyst, launched an offensive in the U.S. Congress and mainstream media to portray Aristide as "mentally unstable" and a "murderer and psychopath," while the coup's leader General Raoul Cedras and his cohorts came from "the most promising group of Haitian leaders to emerge since the Duvalier family." Henry Kissinger went on TV to call Aristide "a psychopath." Right-wing politician Patrick Buchanan called him "a bloodthirsty little socialist."

Some of the liberal dailies, like *The New York Times*, made a half-hearted attempt to cast doubt on the right-wing attack and the CIA's characterization of Aristide, but most of the television networks faithfully regurgitated the lies.

Despite the "invisible government's" temporary victory in stopping Aristide's return in 1993, Haiti kept coming back to haunt the U.S. Repression continued and refugees kept flooding out of the country, eventually forcing the Clinton Administration to re-examine how to return Aristide to Haiti under U.S. supervision. This time the Clinton Administration opted for a massive military invasion of 20,000 U.S. troops on September 19, 1994.

When President Aristide agreed to this intervention, along with the structural adjustment program, there was a major shift in the portrayal of Aristide. He was warily praised as a "statesman" who had "matured" and become more "realistic." He was the prodigal son.

"I think the best thing that has happened to Aristide and his administration-in-exile is that they have had a crash course in democracy and capitalism, and come to understand that too much revolution scares away investors. Small countries can't afford too much social experimentation," said former Ambassador Robert E. White, a Carter Center agent, shortly after the invasion in the *Boston Globe*.

Time magazine also spoke candidly about Clinton Administration reasoning:

"For the next 17 months or so, the U.S. must pin its hopes on Aristide. His 1990 election victory gives him an aura of legitimacy no other Haitian figure can come close to matching [one remark: 67.5 percent of the vote usually gives legitimacy, not its aura]; the U.S. can hardly pretend to be restoring Haitian democracy if it backs anyone else. If he is a leftist and no admirer of the U.S., well, in a perverse way, that makes American intervention easier to defend against possible cries of Yanqui imperialism. Instead of overthrowing a populist reformer to install a military dictatorship friendly to the U.S., Washington will be doing the exact opposite."

Two or three months after his return, since there was no revolution, the corporate media was thinking they had won him over. Listen to a December 1, 1994 *Washington Post* article. As is the U.S. "objective" style, they quote an official to give the spin: "'He is doing more than we ever dreamed he would. He is doing everything right,' gushed a senior U.S. official who had long privately expressed doubts about Aristide. 'It's like a dream.'"

But the dream didn't last for long. As 1995 progressed, friction between Aristide and the U.S. began to surface. For example, on March 28, three days before President Clinton was to visit Haiti, a putschist political figure, Mireille Durocher Bertin was publicly assassinated. The hit was never solved but its highly professional execution suggests it was a CIA operation carried out to smear Aristide and embarrass Clinton.

In the U.S. mainstream press, Bertin was lionized as an "opposition figure" and "an expert in international law." Listen to the beginning of a March 31 Associated Press dispatch movingly titled, "Her Last Days" by Michelle Faul: "She was setting up an opposition party running her busy law office, redecorating her home, writing and publishing a newsletter, and making time to educate her four children." They never say that she defended the slaughter of over 5,000 people by Haitian soldiers and FRAPH thugs during the coup. Indeed, she sat on the leadership committee of the death squad FRAPH.

Soon the laments for Bertin became a full-fledged trial of the Aristide government, which was accused of the murder. U.S. government officials said that the killing was "masterminded" by Haitian Interior Minister Mondesir Beaubrun, who vehemently denied the charge.

Leading the attack were coup supporters like reactionary columnist Robert Novak, who claims in an April 3, 1995 column to have unearthed an "enemies list compiled by President Aristide's supporters." Novak went on to assert that "it is common knowledge in Haiti that a shadow government is headed by notorious former prime minister Rene Preval" who oversees a "commando unit greatly feared by the political opposition" as well as "the flow of weapons to the commando units" through the coastal town of St. Marc. His insinuation was that the supposed "commando unit" rubbed out Bertin.

One might dismiss Novak's accusations of a 30-person "hit list" and other things as the mere rantings of the conservative fringe. But the same day, the Associated Press reported that Bertin "was among more than 100 people on a hit list discovered by the U.S. government days before the slaying." Other reports speak of a 96-person list. The simultaneous discovery of supposed "hit lists" point to a typical U.S. government/mainstream media coordinated campaign.

On April 4, the *Washington Post* launched another missile. Writer Douglas Farah said he was not "suggesting Aristide knew of or sanctioned the killing," but noted that Aristide's "unwillingness to take steps against Beaubrun, despite heavy U.S. pressure and the advice of some of his closest advisers, has revived old questions about the president's willingness to tolerate abuses among those who have shown loyalty to him." The assumption here, of course, is that Beaubrun is guilty! No trial, no evidence, just the accusation of the U.S. government and its media.

Other conflicts began to develop as Aristide disbanded the Army, resisted U.S. plans to double the size of the police force, and dragged his feet on privatizing the state enterprises. In October 1995, Aristide's pro-neoliberal Prime Minister Smarck Michel quit in frustration. "Relations between Mr. Aristide's government and the United Nations coalition that brought him back to power have been fraying since Prime Minister Smarck Michel stepped down," said *The New York Times*. "Mr. Michel resigned and was replaced by Mrs. Werleigh after failing to persuade Mr. Aristide to carry out an agreement signed with Haiti's creditors to privatize nine state companies."

Then on November 7, Aristide's cousin, Deputy Jean-Hubert Feuille, was assassinated. When Aristide ordered Haitian authorities to arrest former Haitian dictator General Prosper Avril for possible involvement in the murder, the U.S. intervened to protect Avril. The U.S.'s meddling set the stage for a dra-

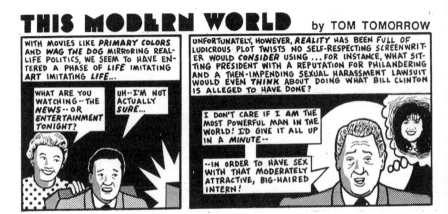

THIS MODERN WORLD by TOM TOMORROW

WITH MOVIES LIKE *PRIMARY COLORS* AND *WAG THE DOG* MIRRORING REAL-LIFE POLITICS, WE SEEM TO HAVE ENTERED A PHASE OF *LIFE* IMITATING ART IMITATING *LIFE*...

WHAT ARE YOU WATCHING -- THE *NEWS* -- OR ENTERTAINMENT TONIGHT?

UH--I'M NOT ACTUALLY SURE...

UNFORTUNATELY, HOWEVER, *REALITY* HAS BEEN FULL OF LUDICROUS PLOT TWISTS NO SELF-RESPECTING SCREENWRITER WOULD *CONSIDER* USING ... FOR INSTANCE, WHAT SITTING PRESIDENT WITH A REPUTATION FOR PHILANDERING AND A THEN-IMPENDING SEXUAL HARASSMENT LAWSUIT WOULD EVEN *THINK* ABOUT DOING WHAT BILL CLINTON IS ALLEGED TO HAVE DONE?

I DON'T CARE IF I AM THE MOST POWERFUL MAN IN THE WORLD! I'D GIVE IT ALL UP IN A *MINUTE* --

--IN ORDER TO HAVE SEX WITH THAT MODERATELY ATTRACTIVE, BIG-HAIRED INTERN!

matic speech Aristide gave at the Port-au-Prince cathedral on November 11.

Standing before U.S. and U.N. officials, Aristide assailed their policies in Haiti. "The game of hypocrisy is over," he said. He condemned the failure of the U.N. occupation forces to help disarm anti-democratic forces, particularly the rich and powerful in their big houses. "We say again that peace must reign here, and for this peace to reign, there must be no accomplices," Aristide said, referring to the U.S./U.N. troops. "The big guns of the international community are here to accompany the Haitian police to disarm all the criminals, all the terrorists, all the extremists," Aristide said. "If not, I'm going to tell them it's over... I'm saying now, whosoever tries to block the legal operation of disarmament, if they're Haitian, we'll arrest them, if they're not Haitian, we'll send them back to their parents," he said in the mostly Creole speech.

Well, you can imagine the U.S. government and corporate press reaction. The November 19 *The New York Times* reported on "Mr. Aristide's tirade," saying that "foreign officials who have been working closely with the Aristide government in efforts to build democracy here after nearly three decades of dictatorship (dictatorships which the U.S. government supported economically and militarily) described themselves as shocked and even betrayed by the President's unexpected behavior."

The Times' editorial on November 26 entitled "Mr. Aristide's Deadly Rhetoric" said that he had:

> "alarmingly reverted to the demagogic political style that scarred his Presidency before the 1991 military coup that forced him into exile. That earlier performance, which included incitements to mob violence, planted reasonable doubts about his commitment to the rule of law and fanned suggestions he was not fit to run the country. Mr. Aristide's latest outburst . . . has already cost at least 10 lives and threatens to destroy

Haiti's best chance ever at democracy . . . With this episode of deliberately provoked terror, Mr. Aristide has shaken the fragile tranquillity painstakingly developed since Washington helped bring him back to Haiti 14 months ago . . . . America's ally in Haiti is democracy, not any individual politician. If Mr. Aristide means to prove his critics right and destroy Haiti's chance for democracy, he should not have American help."

Democracy is threatened not because the U.S. and U.N. occupying forces have shielded *Tonton Macoutes* (as Duvalierist thugs are called) and putschist criminals from arrest and prosecution, allowing them to hide and use their vast arsenals of weapons to create the worst climate of violence and insecurity which the country has ever seen. It is not because World Bank and International Monetary Fund austerity policies have ruined farmers, destroyed small businessmen, and impoverished a country that was already the poorest in the Western Hemisphere. It is because of "Mr. Aristide's tirade" and those unruly "Haitian mobs."

In these same articles and editorials, the mainstream press clamored in unison that Aristide and his supporters might want him to recoup the three years he spent in exile. "He may go back on his pledge to the United States and try to extend his term past its scheduled end next February," warned *The New York Times*. The New York *Daily News* said

that Aristide was "becoming tiresome. The man who had to be prodded to say thanks to the 20,000 Yanks who restored him to power now is talking about ignoring his pledge—and the Haitian constitution—to step down early next year. Coming on top of some inflammatory rhetoric that helped spark a riot, the comments suggest that maybe the CIA was right to fear that Aristide is unstable. Regardless, he is flat out wrong."

Now who gives the U.S. government and its hireling press the right to interpret the Haitian Constitution? Where in the Constitution does it say that the clock is ticking on a President's term when he is removed from power by a bloody coup? The Constitution says nothing about what to do in case of a coup, and if a determination is to be made, it should be by the Haitian people, not Washington and its subservient media.

To make a long story short, the Lavalas Political Organization (OPL), the party which was formed to support the national democratic Lavalas agenda, made a deal with the U.S., betrayed Aristide, and ran Rene Preval for President. Aristide finally acquiesced and turned over power to Preval on February 7, 1996, with the parting shot of establishing diplomatic relations with Cuba.

In the two years since that time, Aristide [has] established the Aristide Foundation for Democracy, which has launched a credit union, a food cooperative, and a children's radio station among other things. Many mass meetings take place at the Foundation's large auditorium.

He also founded a new party, the Fanmi Lavalas, which largely won legislative and municipal elections held on April 6, 1997. The OPL has refused to accept the election results and has launched what Aristide has called "a coup d'état which is revised, corrected, and improved." The result is that the country has been without a Prime Minister since last June and without even a caretaker government since last October. The OPL has blocked in the Parliament every Prime Minister proposed by President Preval.

But if you read the mainstream press, who do they say is responsible for Haiti's deadlock? You guessed it. Jean-Bertrand Aristide.

For example, "Aristide: An Obstacle to Haiti's Progress" was the title of a June 29, 1997 news/analysis piece by the *Miami Herald*'s Haiti correspondent Don Bohning. "The one-time-priest-turned-politician... is simultaneously the country's most popular figure and one of the biggest obstacles to its progress. And there are those who see him as a threat to democracy itself."

Why is Aristide now seen as such an "obstacle" when he is out of office? Because he has become an outspoken critic of neoliberalism. In a bipartisan U.S. Congressional report from June 1997, which *The Herald* and other mainstream media heavily publicized, Aristide is taken to task.

The lack of a strong leader—particularly given Aristide's renewed prominent role in economic and political questions—poses a serious threat to U.S. interests in privatization and economic reform in Haiti. Aristide's criticisms—which offer no constructive suggestions as to how to reform Haiti's moribund economy currently suffering between 70 and 80 percent unemployment—are based on anti-U.S. and anti-international community slogans which suggest a re-emerging nationalism.

And, for the U.S. government and mainstream media, there is no greater sin than being a nationalist, well, except being a bloodthirsty little socialist.

Meanwhile, President Preval, who has embraced the neoliberal austerity package, has become the new darling. Take this June 11, 1996 *Herald* report: "I think President Preval has done a fantastic job. He has really taken the bull by the horns and said 'either we are going to sit around and do nothing, or we will move forward on economic reforms,'" and official of a multilateral aid organization said. "You really get a feeling that things are moving. It's not the usual lethargy." Or here is Don Bohning's February 13, 1997 glowing portrait of Preval in the *Miami Herald:* "Relaxed and informal, he responded to questions candidly with an occasional flash of humor." Other characterizations: "Low-key and unpretentious," or "Preval's modesty and low-key personality." In recent months, as the crisis has dragged on, the press has criticized Preval for not acting strongly enough on behalf of the "American plan" and against Aristide.

When one follows the guidelines, one is rewarded. Depart from them, and you will feel the whip. This is why they now attack Aristide regularly for blocking everything in Haiti because he no longer plays along. Take for example a March 20, 1998 *Miami Herald* article by Bohning entitled "Political Impasse Puts Elections at Risk in Haiti." He claims that Aristide's Fanmi Lavalas has "refused to go along" with elections in Haiti.

This isn't only bad spin, it's just plain false. The Fanmi Lavalas has been calling for elections to continue. And how can it block elections? Aristide's party has no members in the executive branch or in the Parliament. And it should have members in the parliament because it won several seats in the April 6 election, but the OPL has not allowed them to participate, calling them illegal. They are legal according to the Provisional Electoral Council that governs such matters. The mainstream press doesn't castigate and vilify the OPL, even though this party has blocked three different attempts to ratify a new Haitian Prime Minister. If OPL were aligned with Aristide, you would see it in the headlines and on your TV every day.

The sheer volume of misinformation is so vast that it is difficult to show or repudiate anything more than a small fraction. There are so many other lies and distortions to denounce. But I will finish with the latest and most insidious mainstream media campaign.

To show the insidious nature, I just want to offer an anecdote. When we were coordinating President Aristide's participation in this conference—airfares, hotels, and the like—we encountered some financial obstacles. One of the conference organizers, who will remain nameless, asked, "Why are we going through all of this? Doesn't Aristide have money?" Here is a very conscious, engaged, and progressive person helping to organize a conference to combat the big media's lies, who has unconsciously absorbed the media's lies. This shows you the power we are up against.

Their new campaign involves portraying Aristide as a "millionaire," who is corrupt and manipulative and living in a palace. Take the lead of this April 5, 1997 Reuters piece: "Ensconced in a luxury villa behind pink walls, Haiti's former president Jean-Bertrand Aristide still wears the mantle of a champion of the poor as he snipes at the government of his successor and one-time ally." The article goes on to cite Aristide's "self-enrichment that past leaders indulged in" and "a substantial house and swimming pool."

A May 14, 1998 article in the *Los Angeles Times* is another good example of the smear job being attempted. The article relies chiefly on two Aristide critics. "After he came back in 1994, Aristide got the taste of power," said Gerald Dalvius, an opposition politician who has announced his presidential aspirations for 2000. "Now he only believes in power. Maybe he looked for the money to get the power or maybe to make more money."

"In every case, I believe power changes people, but in the case of Aristide more than any other, power aggravated the true personality," said Gerard Pierre-Charles, leader of the OPL." Pierre-Charles also compared Aristide to Duvalier, accused him of being "fascist," of smuggling arms into Haiti, and then "blamed Aristide for the political impasse that has paralyzed Haiti."

In short, Aristide is a devil in the eyes of the U.S. government and the mainstream press because he criticizes their plans for Haiti. He is the "obstacle," the great manipulator, the "threat to democracy." Well, the real manipulator, the real threat to democracy is the corporate media and more generally the capitalist system of which it is a pillar. In *Corporate Media and the Threat to Democracy* professor Robert W. McChesney tells us that "fewer than 10 colossal vertically integrated media conglomerates now dominate U.S. media," companies like Time Warner, Disney, News Corporation, Viacom, and TCI.

I think most of the participants in this conference are already pretty clear about the undemocratic, distorting, and falsifying nature of the corporate mainstream media. But what is to be done? How to fight back?

To our way of thinking, there is no way to "reform" the mainstream media to make it more reliable or truthful. It is not just a bad approach or policy. The mainstream media, just like the state, functions to preserve and defend the interests of monopoly capitalism, and can only function that way.

We might win some media battles, build some media alternatives, denounce the lies, and raise consciousness about the corporate media in various ways. We print *Haãti Progräs* each week as some kind of antidote to and analysis of all the lies they spread each week.

However, the only real solution is to take control of the means of communication from the increasingly tiny ruling class that also owns all the means of production. A truly democratic media will only result from the revolutionary change of capitalist society. Let us all use the media resources in our reach to fight toward that end.

BEN DUPUY is the Former Ambassador-at-Large of President of Haiti.

The Role of AmeriCares: A Wolf in Sheep's Clothing

BY SARA FLOUNDERS

The strangulation of Iraq through sanctions is a policy shrouded in official lies. The devastating consequences have been ignored by the major corporate media. Sanctions are held in place globally through more than 10 U.N. Security Council resolutions and backed up by a U.S. military presence in the Gulf that costs $50 billion a year and deploys aircraft carriers, jet fighters, and satellite reconnaissance. Various pieces of U.S. legislation defining the economic blockade devote hundreds of lines to threats of imprisonment and massive fines. And when all else fails, there are always dirty tricks and cynical media lies.

The NBC-TV news magazine *Dateline* on June 29, 1998 gave people in this country an astounding view of Iraq under sanctions, a view totally different from what I experienced a few weeks earlier as a delegate of the Iraq Sanctions Challenge. Anchor John Hockenberry, whose camera team had accompanied a shipment of medicine to Iraq organized by the group AmeriCares, centered the report on Iraqis dancing the night away in happy abandon at discos, purchasing luxury items, building palaces, "new ones all the time," and watching pirated copies of *Titanic*.

The messages of this television special on the AmeriCares' shipment came through loud and clear: "Conditions are not as bad as my imagination led me to expect"; "people figure out how to get around the sanctions"; "the food situation is under control"; "it's not as bad as it could be"; there are "periodic shortages of medicine and anesthesia," but "we're not seeing sick, profoundly ill children." The special ended with reassuring phrases: "They will get by.... Life goes on."

NBC-TV did not even refer to the well-known nutritional studies by U.N. agencies on the actual conditions in Iraq. "Famine threatens four million people—one-fifth of the Iraqi population." (United Nations Food and Agriculture Organization, December 1995) "Thirty-two percent of children under

the age of five years old—approximately 960,000—are chronically malnourished, a rise of 72 percent since 1991." (UNICEF, 1997). "Since the onset of sanctions there has been a six-fold increase in the mortality rate for children under five and the majority of the country's population has been on a semi-starvation diet." (United Nations World Health Organization, March 1996).

Why didn't the horror of the sanctions get through? Why was NBC so interested in the AmeriCares trip? Could it have something to do with the fact that NBC is owned and controlled by General Electric (GE), the largest military weapons manufacturer in the world? Selling U.S. wars and military adventures is the bottom line for GE's major stockholders.

The goal of the Iraq Sanctions Challenge was to rip the veneer off the bland word "sanctions" and expose the full horror of that systematic strangulation of a whole country. The 84 participants who went to Iraq with four tons of medicine on May 6-13, 1998, and the thousands of supporters who raised funds and support for the effort, did so as a challenge to the criminal sanctions laws and were willing to risk severe legal consequences.

The other shipment of medical supplies, sponsored by AmeriCares, was taken to Iraq just a few days earlier, on April 28. On the surface both seemed to be humanitarian efforts to bring desperately needed medical supplies to Iraq. But the two trips provide a classic example of the difference between form and essence.

The AmeriCares shipment was a sophisticated effort to reinforce and prolong the sanctions by blaming the Iraqi government for the resulting starvation and disease. This U.S. group was positioning itself to be "humanitarian" for continuing the sanctions. The publicity at the time of that shipment sought to create the impression that a few tons of supplies, if taken past the Iraqi government and directly to the hospitals, would alleviate the crisis. Later, the *Dateline* show went even further to deny there was a crisis.

A closer look at AmeriCares gives an understanding of how humanitarian assistance can function as an arm of the most brutal forms of U.S. foreign policy.

Since the sanctions were first imposed on Iraq in August 1990, the U.S. State Department's official position has been that food and medicine are not included in the restrictions. But these officials know very well that it takes more than a cup of rice to survive. All of Iraq's billions of dollars in hard currency deposited in banks around the world were frozen, all credits were frozen, and all exports—from oil to dates—that could earn hard currency were restricted. The Iraqi dinar became a worthless currency as inflation soared past 2,000 percent.

Iraq's infrastructure was devastated by 110,000 aerial sorties flown during the forty days of bombing in 1991. It could not be rebuilt, as no spare parts have been allowed in. Commerce with the outside world is shut down. Industries are denied materials, putting millions out of work. Food production has plummeted without fertilizers, pesticides, or preservatives.

Meanwhile, the U.S. Department of Justice threatens anyone in the U.S. who dares break the sanctions with 12 years of imprisonment. Even the simplest shipment of food or medicine entails highly restrictive licenses and bureaucratic delays of many months.

Around the world, millions of people have sent supplies and confronted the policy of starvation with militant demonstrations. Trade unions, human rights, religious, and progressive grassroots organizations in many countries have used their modest resources in a collective expression of solidarity and defiance.

In the U.S. many thousands of people were involved in the grassroots campaign of the Iraq Sanctions Challenge. For the first time since the war, a broad coalition was formed that included significant religious organizations, Catholic, Protestant, Muslim, along with political and activist groups. The Iraq Sanctions Challenge involved or was in communication with almost every U.S. group concerned about conditions in Iraq.

Just days before the May 6th departure, as centers around the country were organizing major send-off rallies and press events challenging the sanctions, came news of an unexpected shipment of medical supplies to Iraq from AmeriCares. For over seven years this organization had not sent supplies or even issued a press release on the Iraqi health crisis. Major media publicity about the shipment at first raised expectations and enthusiasm. Was the political climate on the sanctions issue changing? Its real purpose soon became clear.

The organizers of the AmeriCares shipment announced they were abstaining from any political discussion critical of the U.S. role in the sanctions policy. Their shipment was "strictly humanitarian." However, their criticism of Iraq was highly political and reinforced the U.S. State Department line.

Their public statements condemned Saddam Hussein for "manipulating U.N. humanitarian programs" and called on Iraq to cooperate with the U.N. Security Council. They declared the medicine they were taking would be delivered directly to hospitals so it would not be stolen or appropriated by the military.

The shipment's arrival on April 28th provoked wide media coverage in the U.S. Both *CBS Evening News* and *ABC World News Tonight* did special reports, describing the aid as "pioneering." ABC's Peter Jennings enthused, "this is the first time since the Gulf War that American aid of any kind has been flown in."

Even though all flights to Iraq had been banned for more than seven years, AmeriCares was given permission to fly its shipment of medicine directly to Baghdad. The flight was arranged in coordination with the Royal Jordanian Air Force. The U.N. Security Council granted special permission. At the last minute, when the Iraqi government refused to allow any military aircraft to land in Baghdad, AmeriCares was able to quickly charter two other planes to take the supplies. Even though the U.N.

Security Council requires one-month advance notice of the exact coordinates and type of aircraft applying to fly to Iraq, AmeriCares was able to get the approval for this change in plans in one day.

AmeriCares claims its medicines were all donated by major U.S. pharmaceutical firms. In contrast, pharmaceutical companies that had pledged to contribute to the Iraq Sanctions Challenge were threatened by the U.S. Department of Justice that such a donation would be in violation of U.S. law, and that they would face prosecution and fines.

Instead of facing threats of imprisonment like the delegates of the Iraq Sanctions Challenge, the AmeriCares delegation was applauded by the Clinton Administration, which released the following statement on April 28th: "The United States Government was pleased to assist AmeriCares in its effort to undertake this mission...We remain deeply disturbed by the manipulation of U.N. humanitarian programs by Saddam Hussein, and again call upon the Iraqi regime to cooperate with U.N. Security Council Resolution 1153, which authorizes increased humanitarian aid to the people of Iraq."

AmeriCares distributed to the media a letter of support from the Security Council (NSC). The letter to AmeriCares founder and chair Robert C. Macauley was signed by Eric P. Schwartz, the Special Assistant to the President and the Director for Democracy, Human Rights, and Humanitarian Affairs of the NSC. It said, "On behalf of the Administration allow me to express appreciation to you and the entire AmeriCares organization for your efforts in organizing this important mission." (AmeriCares Web site, http://www.americares.org.)

The White House was genuinely grateful because this mission attempted to upstage the efforts of many thousands of people across the U.S. who had, at great sacrifice and risk, collected several million dollars worth of medical supplies for Iraq in order to graphically demonstrate the conditions of famine and plague artificially created by the sanctions.

The AmeriCares shipment was clearly a cynical, one-shot publicity stunt by an organization that functions as an arm of U.S. foreign policy. A call to the national office of AmeriCares in New Canaan, Connecticut, two months after their much-publicized shipment confirmed they do not plan to send any additional supplies or assistance to Iraq. This is a group that brags it is the world's largest private relief organization.

AmeriCares is a highly political organization. Barbara Bush, wife of former CIA director and U.S. President George Bush, is its ambassador-at-large. Its 16th annual fund-raising party was held this year on the USS Intrepid, an aircraft carrier converted into a military museum and docked on the Hudson River in New York City. The co-chairs of the gala were George and Barbara Bush. George's brother, Prescott Bush Jr., is on AmeriCares' board of directors.

The dinner honored Amoco President William Lowrie and Mayo Foundation President Dr. Robert Waller (AmeriCares Honors Amoco President, Mayo Foundation, AmeriCares press release, May 14, 1998, #1443). Amoco, one of the largest oil companies in the world, is a direct beneficiary of the Gulf War. It has provided over $46 million to AmeriCares Foundation.

AmeriCares describes itself on its Web site as the "humanitarian arm of Corporate America. Overseeing AmeriCares operations is an Advisory Committee composed of some of the leading minds in business, medicine, and government, including support from all of the living Presidents."

The founder and chair of AmeriCares is Robert C. Macauley, president of Virginia Fibre, a multimillion-dollar paper manufacturing company. He went to Yale with George Bush and has been his buddy since childhood (*Houston Chronicle* October 1, 1994). Macauley says the inspiration for AmeriCares came from Pope John Paul II at a 1982 Vatican meeting. Its first mission that same year was an airlift and distribution network in Poland, which had become indebted to Western banks and was reeling from the social and political effects of food price increases demanded by its creditors (AmeriCares Web site).

Throughout the 1980s AmeriCares continued to play an active role in Eastern Europe in coordination with the Reagan Administration and the Vatican, spreading the influence of its corporate patrons in a region where socialist economic planning was crumbling (AmeriCares Web site).

Since then, the AmeriCares "mission" has spread to over 40 countries worldwide. Its literature describes how, just hours after U.S. troops took over Kuwait City at the end of the Gulf War, an Ameri-Cares, Boeing 707 cargo jet arrived carrying a team of physicians from the White House and the Mayo Clinic.

The timing of the recent planeload of supplies to Iraq is hardly the first controversy over a shipment from Ameri-Cares. Sandinista officials accused AmeriCares of being a CIA front and part of the secret network of private groups used by Marine Corps Lt. Col. Oliver North to deliver aid to the Contras. In 1988 the embattled Sandinista government in Nicaragua rejected an airlift of newsprint donated by AmeriCares to the right-wing opposition daily newspaper, *La Prensa*. It had been timed to arrive just before the elections. The newspapers that supported the Sandinista government were unable to buy newsprint at that time because of a U.S.-imposed embargo, but Vice President George Bush's staff called the Nicaraguan Embassy to try to expedite the shipment to *La Prensa*. Two years earlier, AmeriCares had delivered 200 tons of newsprint to *La Prensa* during another crisis created by the U.S. (*Washington Post*, April 14, 1988)

AmeriCares has also delivered supplies to Contra terrorists based in Honduras. AmeriCares' tax returns revealed donations of cash and materials to the brother of Contra leader Adolfo Calero (New York *Newsday*, April 13, 1988). The Nicaraguan Freedom Fund, a front organization of Rev. Sun Myung Moon's Unification Church, channeled $350,000 to AmeriCares (*The New York Times*, August 13, 1985)

The AmeriCares Web site shows that its shipments seem to find their way to wherever the CIA is most active. Special "humanitarian supplies" have been shipped to contra forces in Afghanistan and their rear bases in Pakistan. An airlift was organized for U.S.-supported forces in Eritrea and Tigre during the war in Ethiopia. During the civil war raging in the Balkans, aid was sent to Croatia, Bosnia, and Kosovo.

AmeriCares often acts as an arm of U.S. foreign and domestic policy by reinforcing and supplying the most reactionary organizations. It controls the distribution network to millions of people in desperate need. This strengthens the infrastructure and influence of groups with a political agenda supportive of U.S. corporate goals. Millions of dollars worth of supplies flooding into a region during a war crisis or famine can exert enormous political influence. As *Forbes* enthused, "AmeriCares is a splendid example of what a free-enterprise approach can accomplish in charity (*Forbes* March 29, 1993)."

A look at AmeriCares' advisory board shows links to both the U.S. government and right-wing organizations in the United States. Besides its links to George Bush, AmeriCares' board includes former U.S. Treasury Secretary William Simon, former U.S. Secretary of State Zbigniew Brzezinski, General Colin Powell, and former U.S. Secretary of State Lawrence Eagleburger.

But the most important link between AmeriCares, the CIA, and ultra-right organizations was J. Peter Grace, Jr. the chair of AmeriCares from 1982 until his death in 1995. J. Peter Grace was the chair of the American Institute for Free Labor Development, the CIA's labor front, and a director of both Kennecott Copper Co. and First National City Bank, now Citigroup. His prominent role in the organization of the fascist coup that overthrew the Allende government in Chile is well documented. He is also connected to the Liberty Lobby, a racist think tank and militarist lobbying group based in Washington, DC. He served as chair of Radio Free Europe, Radio Liberty Fund (CAQ *Information Bulletin*, #25, 1986). Grace was the key figure in Project Paperclip, which brought nine hundred Nazi scientists to the U.S. after World War II, many of whom had been found guilty of experimentation on humans (C.G. Lasby, *Project Paperclip*, Atheneum, NY, 1975).

The connection between top financiers, Cabinet-level Treasury officials, and right-wing, racist organizations didn't begin with William Simon and J. Peter Grace. It reflects the way corporate rule is enforced through the interconnection of government agencies, religious institutions, media outlets, and secret organizations.

It is important for the progressive movement to grasp the significance of AmeriCares' cynical public relations shipment to Iraq. It is connected in a living way to the global struggle that pits those fighting for basic union rights and national self-determination against a handful of extremely wealthy corporate rulers.

AmeriCares' shipment to Iraq during a critical time of growing opposition to the continuing war of aggression shows that the U.S. government is determined to continue the sanctions. It is just one of the many covert ways the corporate-military-political complex manipulates public debate to maintain and justify the murderous policy against Iraq.

The anti-sanctions movement should appreciate how deeply threatened U.S. government officials and corporate rulers are by the growing awareness and resistance of grassroots organizations in the U.S. The Iraq Sanctions Challenge not only brought aid to Iraqi children, it challenged the criminal role of top U.S. government officials. The greatest military power on earth fears the anger of world opposition. A simple act of solidarity is a powerful weapon.

SARA FLOUNDERS is Co-Coordinator of the International Action Center (IAC), an organization that mobilizes opposition to U.S. militarism and war. She initiated the Anti-Sanctions Project of the IAC and the Depleted Uranium Education Project and was an organizer of the Iraq Sanctions Challenge. She has edited and produced the Books: *The Children Are Dying: The Impact of Sanctions on Iraq* (1996), *Metal of Dishonor: Depleted Uranium* (1997), *NATO in the Balkans: Voices of Opposition* (1998), *Challenge to Genocide: Let Iraq Live* (1998).

THIS MODERN WORLD

by TOM TOMORROW

Panel 1: IT'S TIME FOR ANOTHER EXCERPT FROM THE TRAVEL JOURNALS OF *SPARKY THE PENGUIN!* THIS WEEK: SPARKY GOES TO THE *WHITE HOUSE CORRESPONDENTS' DINNER!*

WHY ARE ALL THESE PEOPLE TRYING TO LOOK LIKE ME?

Panel 2: "THERE IS LITTLE EVIDENCE HERE TONIGHT OF THE SUPPOSEDLY ADVERSARIAL RELATIONSHIP BETWEEN POLITICIANS AND THE MEDIA...WHEN THE PRESIDENT TAKES THE PODIUM, HE JOKES ABOUT HIS RECENT TROUBLES AS IF TALKING TO A ROOMFUL OF 2,600 CLOSE FRIENDS..."

I'VE BEEN SO BUSY, I HAVEN'T READ A NEWSPAPER SINCE THE *POPE* WENT TO *CUBA!*

WHAT HAVE YOU ALL BEEN *WRITING* ABOUT?

HA HA

HA HA

Panel 3: "OF COURSE, THIS IS LESS A POLITICAL EVENT THAN A CELEBRITY *CIRCUS--* A SURREAL CONFLUENCE OF POLITICIANS, MOVIE STARS AND THE JOURNALISTIC ELITE, ALL MEMBERS OF AN EXCLUSIVE CLUB TO WHICH *FAME* IS THE ONLY ADMISSION REQUIREMENT...GUESTS RANGE FROM SHARON STONE TO HENRY KISSINGER TO GORDON LIDDY TO JON BON JOVI--"

HELLO I'M FAMOUS!

PLEASED TO MEET YOU! I'M FAMOUS AS WELL!

Panel 4: "--TO *PAULA JONES*, WHO IS APPARENTLY TRYING TO PARLAY HER FIFTEEN MINUTES OF FAME INTO A CAREER AS A TEAM *MASCOT* FOR THE FAR RIGHT--SORT OF A *PHILLY PHANATIC* FOR THE ANTI-CLINTON CONTINGENT..."

GO-O-O-O *TEAM!!*

Panel 5: "AFTER THE DINNER, COCKTAIL PARTIES ABOUND...WITH PREENING, STATUS-CONSCIOUS ATTENDEES DISTRACTEDLY PRETENDING TO CONVERSE WHILE CONTINUOUSLY SCANNING THE CROWD OVER EACH OTHERS' SHOULDERS..."

KIND OF LIKE A HIGH SCHOOL PROM--EXCEPT THAT SAM DONALDSON IS ONE OF THE COOL KIDS...

UM, YES, I AGREE-- WAR IS BAD...

SAY--IS THAT PAULA !?

Panel 6: "IN THIS CROWD, IT REALLY DOESN'T MATTER WHAT SOMEONE HAS DONE TO *BECOME* FAMOUS--JUST THAT THEY *ARE* FAMOUS...CONTEXT IS *IRRELEVANT* AT THE WHITE HOUSE CORRESPONDENTS' DINNER, WHILE SHAMELESS SUPERFICIALITY IS THE *DOMINANT MOTIF...*"

--WHICH, OF COURSE, PRETTY MUCH SUMS UP WHITE HOUSE CORRESPONDENTS *THEMSELVES...*

OH, WHO CARES WHAT *YOU* THINK?

YOU'VE NEVER BEEN ON TELEVISION!

TOM TOMORROW © 5-20-98

CHAPTER 8

Fear in the News

BY DAVID ALTHEIDE

Tucked inside Judy's Gucci bag is a tiny .38-caliber revolver. It eases her mind. "Things are crazy out there," the Scottsdale, Arizona woman says. "I just want to have options." Judy is one of the latest Arizonans to get a permit to carry a concealed weapon. And she is fairly typical: affluent, white, suburban.

Since July 1994, more than 35,000 Arizonans have obtained concealed-weapon permits. A computer analysis of permit holders reveals that the highest rates of weapons purchased are not in parts of "the Valley" where neighborhoods are filled with crack houses, gangs, and violence. They are in upscale suburban neighborhoods like Sun City West, North Phoenix, Scottsdale, Ahwatukee and Mesa..." (*The Arizona Republic*, March 17, 1996; A1).

The fear industry in the United States is going great guns. Fear is everywhere, and formal agents of social control are in the thick of it. The News and Entertainment Media, numerous social control organizations (e.g. the police, FBI), security and alarms businesses, and the massive insurance conglomerates have come together as a self-perpetuating super complex which survives by the reporting of fear.

Despite the fact that the crime rate is down, and that the majority of the people of the United States are safer and more secure than at any other time in history, the "information industry" has promoted the perception that we are unsafe and insecure. "Sources" for the news media and popular culture bombard citizens with daily images that depict a hostile environment, one crawling with criminals, threats to our safety, especially to our children. Entertainment programs fuel the furor about crime and danger. "Reality" shows offering reenactments of the arrests of "most wanted" criminals, for example, can be found on primetime TV. You can watch the tube as you eat, and "know" that, while you eat, the bad guys are being caught. Knowing this, you can finish your meal in peace.

But the anxiety prevails. Numerous opinion polls document this: 78 percent of Americans think they are subjected to more risk today than their parents were 20 years ago, according to a 1994 poll by the Centers for Disease Control (National Center for Health Statistics, Centers for Disease Control, Marsh and McLennan).

The belief that Americans are at greater risk of danger is strong in Arizona, where I live. Arizonans express what one pollster termed a "fear rate" 8 percent higher than national surveys. When asked if there is an area within a mile of their home in which they would be afraid to walk at night, half of those polled said yes. Older people tended to be more fearful than younger respondents, and those with higher income (over $75,000 per year) less fearful than lower income counterparts. Pollster Michael O'Neil concluded, "If one were to look only at local media, one would be prone to conclude that 'the Valley' is in the grips of fear of a new and major crime wave." That half the [Arizona] population feels inhibited within a mile of their home is, in itself, a serious indication of the public's level of concern about crime." (O'Neil Associates, *Valley Monitor*, February 11, 1994).

As predicted by a number of researchers more than two decades ago, the line between news and entertainment has disappeared. Researchers have argued for decades that media coverage affects perceptions about safety. Crime, violence, drugs, and gangs have become staples of news reports as well as entertainment media. Drama, action, violence, and conflict, especially dramatic TV news visuals, are one avenue to improved ratings and profits.

As Shaw argues, "For all their protesting and clamoring for positive news, surveys—and TV ratings—also show that people seem more interested in negative news, sensational news, news about crime and violence and corruption than in what we customarily think of as 'positive' news. To remain in business, the news media must—to some extent—give people what they want. The better, more responsible news media are also supposed to give people what they need—and while few people say they want or need more cynicism, it continues to mount" (*The Arizona Republic*, April 28, 1996).

I have been investigating news reports with several students about fear in general and various crimes in particular in several major news papers and TV networks (e.g., ABC), namely in *The Arizona Republic*. In a procedure called "tracking discourse," we have charted how "fear" is used with other terms (e.g., children) and how this changes over a 10-year period (1987-1996).

There are four general conclusions to be drawn from our work to date: First, the use of the word "fear" has dramatically increased particularly with headlines. Second, it is associated with different topics over time (e.g., crime, violence) and is increasingly associated with the words: children, schools, and community. Third, despite the relative safety and security of most people in American society, there are very few reports that examine why there is so much emphasis on fear. Fourth, fear promotes more public reliance on formal agents of social control.

FEAR AS ENTERTAINMENT

While reportage of concern is important, the news media also promote fear because it is entertaining. "Fear" is one of the most pervasive "discourses" used in "public," in the mass media and popular culture. It is much broader than a specific term like "crime." Indeed, crime reporting is more popular today because it reflects "fear" and is presented in these terms.

1. FEAR HAS INCREASED A basic question for this research concerned how much coverage *The Arizona Republic* (AR) has given to "fear" over a several year period. Figure 1 provides a basic description of fear in headlines and text in the AR from 1987-1996. The use of fear about doubled in both categories:

Headlines: 123 in 1987 and 232 in 1996;

Text: 1379 in 1987 and 2209 in 1996.

The use of "fear" in headlines and text increased from 30-150 percent for most newspapers in our study analyzed over a 7-10 year period, with the peak year in 1994. Many of these increases were associated with more emphasis on crime reporting.

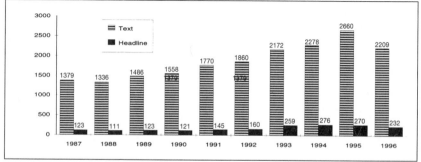

FIGURE 1: Instances of fear in text and headlines, *The Arizona Republic*, 1987–1996.

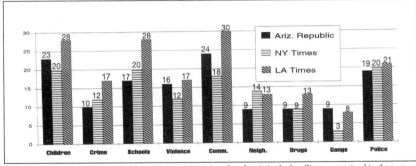

FIGURE 2: Percentage of times text focuses on certain topics when fear is in the headline or contained in the text, *New York Times*, *Los Angeles Times*, *Arizona Republic* (Average for 1994–1996).

2. FEAR IS ASSOCIATED WITH CERTAIN TOPICS While crime and violence are part of the "fear story," there is more to it. Our analysis went well beyond crime and violence to include other topics, as well as to examine the portrayal of fear in various ways. The constant coupling of crime and other aspects of urban living with the word "fear" have produced a unique perspective about the effectiveness of our environment. The purpose of tracking discourse is to delineate the nature and extent of this perception. As noted previously, reports were sought across sections on a dozen topics that have been useful in earlier analyses of media formats and emphases (e.g., violence, crime, community, neighborhood, schools, drugs, gangs, retribution, children, terrorism, environment, and immigrants; Altheide, 1997). On an average day, a thorough reader of *The Arizona Republic* would read 6-7 reports containing "fear," and about 1 headline a day with the word "fear" in it. Over a three-year period, more than 21 percent of these reports associate "fear" in some way with many of the topics presented in Figure 2.

Topics become associated with "fear" through a process: problems (and associated terms) have a "meaning career," often beginning as something that is "deviant" or "immoral," later becoming more accepted, although not necessarily desirable. One example from previous work is "cancer," a term which seldom appears in conjunction with "fear" in mass media reports today (Altheide, 1997). This is not because cancer is no longer feared. On the contrary, it is so overwhelmingly undesired, yet familiar, that it has been recast repeatedly into other discourses, such as medicine, health, and education. This has occurred because the "sources" for reports about cancer tend not to be police officers or public officials, but professionals trained in medicine, public health, and education. However, the "fear" of cancer has been "appropriated" by politicians who link cancer as a metaphor to refer to crime:

CRIME, LIKE CANCER, SPREADS IF LEFT UNCHECKED

"Scottsdale is nervous. Its residents are worrying more and more about crime.

"The recent carjacking at the upscale Scottsdale Fashion Square only sent anxieties even higher. Crime, in tiny Scottsdale? It's not supposed to be this way" (*The Phoenix Gazette*, November 26, 1993).

Even cancer pales in seriousness compared to the way crime is often depicted. Consider the case of some residents living in the Los Angeles suburb of Westminster. Even though they have been living on top of a toxic waste dump that oozes black sludge into homes and swimming pools, the residents aren't too concerned about cancer rates which tend to increase with such pollution. Despite concerns by health officials that "it's not a major immediate threat, but our risk assessments show there could be some chronic long-term effects . . . . There is an elevated risk of cancer, and we believe something needs to be done to eliminate the waste," residents argued that living in this toxic area was less dangerous than crime.

"Despite the [Superfund] stigma, the Westminster tract is an ordinary neighborhood of mostly middle-aged, middle-class working folk, many of whom have lived in their simple stucco homes for 10 to 30 years. The families say they are too busy making ends meet and too relieved that their community is relatively free of crime to worry about the curious black slime that appears on hot summer days" (*Los Angeles Times*, August 25, 1991).

Although children, crime, and schools have remained in the top three categories of our studies since 1987, it is apparent that tremendous changes occurred in the coverage of selected topics and the way they have come to be associated with "fear." This is common with the mass media across the United States, but the extent of change is noteworthy. For example, in 1987, we found 8 and 7 stories, respectively, of violence and crime occurring within 10 words of fear. By 1996 the association of "fear" with "violence" and "crime" had increased six-fold!

A good example is the coverage of children. Figure 2 provides information about *The Arizona Republic*, as well as the *Los Angeles Times* and *The New York Times*. The chart permits a comparison of text and headlines involving children, violence, crime, and gangs.

From 1994-96 children are associated with a lot of news coverage about fear. The association of the words "crime," "children," "schools," and "community" are the most common. In 1994, more than *half* of all reports with "fear" in the headlines included one or more of the following words: children, crime, schools, violence, community, or police (data not provided here)! Specifically, the three-year average (1994-96) for the AR of all the reports with fear in the headlines involved: children (18 percent), schools (17 percent), and community (24 percent). The comparable figures in the AR for crime were 10 percent, violence 16 percent, and gangs 9 percent. Figures for the *Los Angeles Times* were even higher, e.g., 28 percent of all reports with headlines between 1994-96 included reference to children and/or schools!

The news media's association of children with fear may promote "third person" or "altruistic fear"—concern for those whom you love or for whom are responsible—among audience members. Topics for public interest are creatively manipulated by various claims-makers with self-serving interests, and "protecting children" has become a political theme used to justify greater social "controls." Children are being used as symbols, internationally and locally, as part of a war waging rhetoric. Just prior to the U.S. bombardment of Iraq in 1997, President Clinton argued that this was being done to force Saddam Hussein to comply with international rules. As one writer noted,

"He even absurdly brought kids into the equation in the confrontation with Iraq late last year over Saddam Hussein's expulsion of U.N. weapons inspectors. Clinton insisted the inspectors must be allowed to do their jobs because 'the safety of the children of the world depends on it' (*Los Angeles Times*, June 23, 1998).

Our natural human inclination to want to make the world safe for our children is used as part of the justification to "wage war," in marked contrast to anti-war speakers and protesters during the Vietnam War who argued that "war is not healthy for children and other living things." This makes children a part of the *territorial framework* of our public discourse, as are other topics, problems, and issues, presented as "news."

REACTIVE FEAR Suffering, misfortune, distress, and inconvenience are the stuff of contemporary news but they are not "the problem." The problem characteristics are part of a format organized around a narrative that begins with a general conclusion that "something is wrong" and we know what it is! An example of audiences participating in a newspaper's morality play is the following letter to the editor published in the AR on November 16, 1995:

HOW LONG MUST WE LIVE IN PLACE WHERE FEAR IS DICTATOR?
I was appalled and sickened by the senseless killing of a kind, decent man who did the right thing by helping a trick-or-treater on his own

block. A 15-year-old who had no business carrying a gun (Does the NRA really support such craziness?) shot him. I didn't know this 41-year-old humanitarian, but I do know that he could have been me, or my husband, or any one of you. He did what adults are supposed to do: He protected children! He did not cower in a society plagued with violence and fear. How can we continue to live in our community, where fear is the dictator and love the enemy? How can we raise our children to be decent, helpful human beings if it means them risking their lives?

PROACTIVE FEAR Less common than "reactive fear" is fear in anticipation of some event or activity. Fear as a resource is provided by news organizations producing reports within the problem frame of the entertainment format. Audience familiarity with a general scenario lends familiarity and credibility to a specific event. The idea here is that one does something in order to avoid being a victim or to avoid engaging in an activity or issue *already tainted* by fear. Paradoxically, Ferraro (1995: 63) notes that when people take steps to alter lifestyle and avoid situations, they actually increase their perceived risk. For example, 37 percent of state residents interviewed in a recent poll for *The Arizona Republic* and KSAZ-TV (Channel 10) said they had changed their routine in the past six months just to reduce their risk of being a crime victim.

FEW REPORTS ABOUT EXAGGERATION OF FEAR There are very few news reports about why so many people express fear in opinion polls. These reports tend not to be "news reports" per se, but "perspective" pieces, which are very analytical. More often than not, these reports, like most academic analyses of risk, conclude that our society is relatively safe and healthy.

An important part of the context of fear is the worldview people have about the danger and risk factors in their lives. We get a lot of reports about risk, and many people take them to heart. There are very few articles like the report cited above by David Shaw of the *Los Angeles Times* "Afraid in America: Media Hyping Risks; Cancer, Fat, Crime, Just Few Phobias," that try to put fear in perspective.

WHAT WE FEAR MOST ISN'T NECESSARILY WHAT'S MOST DANGEROUS "Events that are common in our daily lives are underestimated in terms of the risk they present to us," said Mary Wilson, a Harvard Assistant Professor in Public Health. "Strange and bizarre things that conjure up images of the unknown cause great anxiety. We end up spending enormous amounts of money on problems that may pose a trivial risk."

As Europe forks out $2.4 billion to defend itself against "mad-cow disease," which may have infected 10 humans, psychologists and risk-management experts try to understand what makes people afraid. Those fears drive public policy, and picking the "wrong" ones can distract us from bigger killers.

HELPLESSNESS FUELS SCARINESS Risks over which people have no control, or no sense of control, are scarier. Airline passengers feel they can do nothing if their plane crashes. Car drivers can do nothing if they crash into a guardrail at 60 miles an hour, but the sense of being in control is greater behind the wheel. "A lot of natural disasters are regular," said psychologist Frederick Koenig at Tulane University. "If you understand what it is, you don't have unstabilized or paralyzing kind of fear." (AR, "Worst Fears Not Always Deadliest: Misdirected Fright Drives Public Policy," April 5, 1996.)

Analysts revel in noting that one's risk of getting cancer from cigarettes (one in three) is seldom at the cognitive forefront as a smoker denounces the lack of police protection in his neighborhood. Nevertheless, we continue to receive a preponderance of news reports about topics that are relatively infrequent, and relatively few about those problems that are more likely to harm us.

This is certainly the case in terms of crime vs. cancer. The death rate from cancer in Maricopa County is 121, compared to the crime rate of 88 (both per 100,000 population). Yet crime is constantly big news, as are the formal agents of social control who claim they can "do something about it," while "soldiers" against cancer receive scant mention.

Crime rates have been steadily *decreasing* in Maricopa County for several years, but the number of news reports about crime have increased. The Maricopa County Sheriff, Joe Arpaio, has become a household name in Arizona and much of the country as hundreds of news reports mention his "tent-city jail," "posse patrols of mall parking lots," and other visible crime-fighting" activities. His 85 percent popularity rating according to opinion polls is one of the highest registered by local opinion takers. By contrast, Regents' Professor George Robert Petit barely appears in any news index. He and his cancer research group at Arizona State University have discovered natural compounds that have proven in some cases to be 95 percent effective in combating certain kinds of cancer, yet they have received scant media attention.

CONSEQUENCES OF FEAR REPORTING: POLICE, PRISON, PROTECTION There are several important consequences of the expanding use of fear in the mass media. First, it contributes to very negative social definitions by citizens, including promoting mistrust of officials and fellow citizens, especially in the context of crime and danger. Second, other issues receive less attention and therefore become less significant for citizens to support public policy decisions to deal with them. Police, prisons, and protection dominate public policy. According to the General Social Survey, in 1972, 46.3 percent of respondents felt they could trust others. This percentage has steadily declined to 34.4 percent in 1994 (National Opinion Research Center, 1996). Despite a gradual decline in news media usage over the last few years, Americans have been voracious news consumers over the last decade and a half, with some 60 percent claiming to read articles about violent crime in the newspapers, 71 percent viewing violent TV news reports daily. Poll data are consistent with Graber's (1980: 50) panel study of Chicago-area news readers, who demonstrated a high recall of crime related news reports. Indeed, people who watch TV news daily (particularly women) are less likely to trust others (General Social Survey, 1994). The relevance of these first two consequences for Arizona are quite apparent: Arizonans worry about crime to the exclusion of almost every other issue, according to a poll conducted for *The Arizona Republic* and KSAZ-TV (Channel 10).

Crime was identified by 48 percent of those polled as the most pressing concern in Arizona, eclipsing the economy and education. Other high-profile issues, such as health care and taxes, barely registered. Although nearly half of those surveyed now say crime is the big issue, only 3 percent felt that way in 1991.

That's an alarming development to Esther Wiegand, a north-central Phoenix resident. "There are too many guns," said Wiegand, aged 80. "They are too simple to get. There are too many kids getting them. I read about in the paper. They [authorities] should see to it that kids are off the street."

There are other consequences as well, including more reliance on police and formal agents of social control. Surette (1998: 237) observes: "If you influence the symbol-creating and symbol-defining engine of a society, you create the social reality of that society. And if a particular perspective of social reality gains control of a social construction engine, other constructions will never be truly competitive."

While crime is commonly the referent for "fear," there are many other topics associated with the encompassing theme of fear. It is commonplace for people to turn to the "state" to help resolve fears and "solve" the particular problem, e.g., the "crime problem." As we were reminded during the Nazi rise to power, a frightened society is a dangerous society. Citizens become less reflective, and more "proactive," seeking to attack the source of their fears.

Another consequence, then, is that as a discourse of fear pervades our symbolic environment, formal agents of social control (FASC) become more influential in public policy decisions and are more visible across the social spectrum. This means that other forms of discourse, other perspectives on social problems are not likely to be considered.

It is a truism in social science research that perceptions matter regardless of their actual truth. An axiom for most social scientists is what has been called the "self fulfilling prophecy" or the "definition of the situation": "A situation defined as real is real in its consequences." The physical and symbolic experiences—including mass media and popular culture—provide the symbolic order of the meaning of everyday life. If we believe that the world is scary and that danger lurks everywhere, that we should adopt "fear" rather than "common sense" as an orientation, then we will act on that basis, and ironically, may help produce the very situations we "feared" and avoided.

THE OPTIONS There are many options, but they all begin with awareness of the problem, and this can only be aided by new approaches to research. In general, a big part of the problem is that the entertainment formats used by virtually all mass media promote the discourse of fear to make them "interesting" to audiences. These messages interact with other communications in our symbolic environments and soon people expect others to "talk the talk" about fear, to take it for granted, and to deal with it in appropriate ways. Horror stories about past events become the key to "priming" our cognitive maps when the next crime or crisis is reported. Each new fear-trauma thus reflects the scores of previous media images. The "obvious" and increasingly, the preferred, way to deal with news-fear usually involves using formal agents of social control, who serve their own interests by promoting a certain spin on problems and issues, and offering narrow singular solutions. With this practice, the mass media in general, and the news media in particular play an important role in clouding significant social issues.

A responsible news media can take action to move away from fear-oriented "infotainment." This is actually being done by Austin TV station KVUE. Station management examined how crime news was being covered and agreed essentially with several decades of social science research that much of the coverage was sensational, dramatic, and had no social value whatsoever. Accordingly, they set forth five rules of thumb for covering crime news:

1) Does action need to be taken?
2) Is there an immediate threat to safety?
3) Is there a threat to children?
4) Does the crime have significant community impact?
5) Does the story lend itself to a crime-prevention effort?

In response, many in the "information industry" as well as newspaper writers criticized them for breaking the ranks of crass sensationalism, and in some cases, they were chided for not presenting all the news. The strongest claim was that their ratings would fall and that people would switch channels to the traditional blood-and-guts that leads local TV newscasts across the country. To KVUE's credit, and perhaps their relief, the ratings have held and their new brand of TV journalism has become more popular and other stations across the country are talking about change. This is all very encouraging. It is possible to take more control of our social environment, but much of this action begins not with "cleaning up the streets" as much as focusing on our symbolic environment, understanding how our meaning machines are operating, and trying to provide some options.

DAVID ALTHEIDE is a Regent's Professor in the College of Public Programs School of Justice Studies Arizona State University. E-mail: David.Altheide @asu.edu

REFERENCES

Altheide, David L., "The News Media, The Problem Frame, and the Production of Fear," *The Sociological Quarterly* 38 (4, 1997): 647-668.

Hawthorne, NY: Aldine de Gruyter, 1991.

Ferraro, Kenneth F. *Fear of Crime: Interpreting Victimization Risk*. Albany, NY: State University of New York Press, 1995.

Graber, Doris, *Processing the News: How People Tame the Information Tide*. New York: Longmans, 1984

Snow Robert P., *Media Worlds in the Postjournalism Era*.

Surette, Ray, *Media, Crime and Criminal Justice: Images and Realities*, 2nd. Belmont, CA:West, 1998.

Warr, Mark, "Fear of Rape Among Urban Women," *Social Problems* 32, 1985: 238-250.

The Junk Food News Stories of 1998

BY CATHY COLEMAN with research assistance and editorial support from CHANTILLE HICKMAN AND SUZANNE Z. MURPHY

It should come as no surprise that the Number One Junk Food News story of 1998 was President Clinton's sex life. What is surprising is the landslide by which it won the poll: not one of the other 24 stories nominated even came close in garnering votes, it seems that our diet of sensationalized stories was more imbalanced than ever.

Once again, the members of the Organization of News Ombudsmen were asked to rate their choices for the most over-reported, insignificant stories of the year. Their choices for the Top 10 Junk Food News stories are as follows:

1. President Clinton's sex life, including Monica Lewinsky, Linda Tripp, Kathleen Willey, Vernon Jordan, the cigar, and The Dress.
2. Spice Girls
3. *Titanic*
4. Paula Jones
5. The British Royal Family
6. JonBenet Ramsey
7. John Glenn
8. Jerry Springer
9. Viagra
10. Jerry Seinfeld

Few stories in history can compare to "Zippergate," as the President's alleged affair with a young White House intern has come to be called. Not only have the airwaves and headlines been deluged with tawdry details of what is reputed to have transpired in the Oval office, but the ancillary characters have stolen more than their share of the spotlight. (Did we really need to hear where Willey claims Bill touched her? Or the embarrassing details of an ambitious young woman's infatuation, divulged to a so-called "friend" in confidence?) One ombudsman extracted Ms. Lewinsky from this category, giving her, not one, not two, but three separate nominations of her own. Everyone's favorite special prosecutor, Ken Starr, barely missed the Top 10 Dishonor Roll, proving once again that money—even $40 million—can't buy you popularity.

As for other stories (yes, Virginia, there was other junk food) a British singing quartet stole the media show like no one since the Beatles more than 30 years ago. We had almost daily updates on their clothes, songs, and pregnancies.

An historical event was fictionalized and re-created in opulence exceeding the original version. While it's unlikely that the hype about the 1998 movie version of the sinking of the Titanic will survive past this century, it is entirely possible that the amount of press coverage given to the making of the movie, the director, the stars, and their personal lives, far exceeds the press coverage given to the tragedy itself over the past 86 years.

Paula Jones' reappearance in our JFN chapter is a testimony to her perseverance, and her craving for the limelight. One respondent's poignant plea regarding this subject was, "Please go away!"

The British Royal family is back in the Top 10 because we ex-patriots just can't seem to get enough of them. News stories about Diana flow on and on, even long after her death, and the privacy of her sons, which she guarded so carefully, is crumbling. From the shadow of his late ex-wife, Prince Charles appears to be flourishing as the press eagerly reports any morsels regarding his relationship with his paramour, Camilla.

Some tragedies are unfortunately dragged through the Junk Food grinder because of mysteries that enshroud them. JonBenet Ramsey's story is destined to live longer than did the sweet victim herself, since the media periodically dredges it up and massages facts and fantasy into quasi-news. This is another case of the media expanding their viewership through misfortune and mystery.

As the country struggled though the sex scandal in the White House and debated whether or not the President should be impeached, one distinguished senior citizen was diverting attention from our woes and giving us something to cheer about. John Glenn's return to the space program was more nostalgic than heroic. People may have been thrilled by and for him, but reports of his anti-gravity blood pressure readings held little interest in contrast to his prior "giant step for mankind."

The collective segué into the news of wonder-drug Viagra warms the hearts of marketing experts. How wonderfully it all fits: "Zippergate," an aging astronaut, and the potency pill coming together in a kind of junk news trinity.

In the glamorized world, while Oprah Winfrey battled "Cattle," other celebrities grabbed our attention with their decadence or dissipation or just plain cuteness. We read about Tim Allen's DUI, Robert Downey's drug conviction. We read anything and everything about Leonardo DiCaprio. But the two who captured spots in the elite Top 10 were the vilified Jerry Springer and the glorified Jerry Seinfeld. The demise of the Seinfeld show received unprecedented attention and was treated almost like a state funeral, with people gathering at each other's homes to mourn in unison while watching the final episode. Advertisers paid more per second than even the Superbowl can command, and magazine covers bemoaned our "collective" loss. Fans of the show wondered what was left to life—how could they go on?—leaving the rest of us scratching our heads and wondering what we had missed. And Jerry Springer is the man everyone loves to hate, but someone must be watching in order for him to stay on top of the ratings, even have a movie released about himself.

Other stories under consideration for the dubious honor of JFN's Top 10 were Monica Lewinsky (although technically she is part of the #1 JFN story of the year) former nanny Louise Woodard; Mark McGuire's use of steroids; the baseball home run race; Beanie Babies; convicted killer Karla Faye Tucker's execution by the state of Texas; celebrity deaths (Sinatra, Bono, Kennedy, Hartman, Farley); the threat of a Y2K crisis; inner-city crime; and school shootings. The last two topics underscore the meaning of JFN. It is not necessarily the subject that determines whether the stories benefit us in some substantive way. Rather, it is the sensationalized coverage, the over-dramatization, and the just plain old over-reporting that, like the sugar rush, fills us up but lets us down.

The ombudsmen who responded to our survey were in almost unanimous agreement: The media itself is to blame for the proliferation of Junk Food News. Competition for ratings and audience was the most frequently cited reason, but television was also accused.

The following comments from individual ombudsmen are in answer to the question, "Why do the media tend to sensationalize stories such as those you cited above?"

ROGER JIMENEZ, *La Vanguardia*, Barcelona, Spain:
"The history is as usual. TV's effect is strong on media."

CARL JENSEN, Project Censored Founder:
"This year the national news media outdid themselves with Junk Food News. There were so many deserving issues, it was difficult to limit the choices to ten. Equally sad, the top JFN story, Clinton's sex life, gave the prestigious establishment press an opportunity to rival the sensational tabloid press with pornographic material. And they did."

HARRY THEMAL, (retired) *The News Journal*, Wilmington, Delaware:
"In almost all of these, all media are following each other. No one wants to be left behind with any details, no matter how flimsy or spurious they may be. You must add to the media mix the many talk and other entertainment shows, the jokesters, the political cartoonists, and everyone else who loves to feed on sensational subjects. These have eliminated the line between news and entertainment. On the number one topic, Clinton et. al., you must add the bad predictions and findings of the commentators and pollsters, who predicted the Republican sweep in the elections and then pulled back, but not far enough at the end. Add to that the hypocrisy of those who spent a lot of time reporting on the public's being fed up with all the impeachment and sex scandal news and then continue to report on it at length. The public was just as hypocritical, claiming it was tired of it all but savoring every new disclo-

THIS MODERN WORLD

by TOM TOMORROW

sure. Finally there's the sanctimoniousness of the 'serious' press, which was obviously being leaked information by the special prosecutor but condemning the Drudge Report for the same thing."

SHEILA SYKE, *The Salt Lake Tribune*, Salt Lake City, Utah:
"Lazy journalists do not look into and report on worthwhile issues such as health care, where's money for Social Security, and conflict of interest among politicians, but they can rant on and on and on and on about sex. There are too many 'tabloid talk shows' posing as news shows (i.e., *Hard Copy, 20/20, Extra!*, and on and on)."

DENNIS FOLEY, *The Orange County Register*, Santa Ana, California:
"Media emphasis on 'celebrity' news is, I fear, driving out substantive news and is alienating people from becoming involved in the public life that makes for healthy communities. Media have a responsibility to build community, not just entertain people for profit."

MARK HOPKINS, (former) *Voice of America*, Washington DC:
"It's the combination drive for ratings (t.v.) and apprehension of editors (all media) that they would be left behind, caught short etc. on stories that seem to burgeon in the popular wind. Editors' news judgments, which would well minimize some of the more salacious or sensational stories, are set aside in a rush to be covered."

JERRY FINCH, *Richmond Times-Dispatch*, Richmond, Virginia:
"Perhaps some of the nominees played bigger in California than Virginia. Allen's DUI—was that a big thing somewhere? And sorry, you can't measure the impact of inner-city crime on the basis of some FBI statistics."

EMERSON STONE, *Freelance*, Greenwich, Connecticut:

"They do it: (A) because others do and (B) they fear being left behind in rating/circulation and (C) many of today's journalists grew up in a world spattered with this sort of stuff, and they think it's news and (D) they've forgotten (if they ever knew) that the press needs to give people what they need, not what they want (entertainment is for the latter), and (E) a myriad of other reasons (excuses)."

PAUL GIACOBBE, *WJAR-TV*, Warwicic, Rhode Island:

"Because people want to hear about them, sensationalizing attracts attention to your coverage of the story."

APPENDIX B

The Year's Most Under-Reported Humanitarian Stories

BY DOCTORS WITHOUT BORDERS/MÉDECINS SANS FRONTIERES

The following is Doctors Without Borders/Médecins Sans Frontières' list of the Top 10 Under-Reported Humanitarian Stories of 1998. The organization compiled the list to call attention to human crises that were largely ignored by the U.S. press in the past year.

"There has been a precipitous drop in the quantity and quality of international news coverage in recent years," said Joelle Tanguy, executive director of the U.S. office of Doctors Without Borders. "Save for some outstanding journalistic efforts, the items on the Top 10 list have gone sadly under-covered. Without adequate information, we lack the ability to form responsible personal and societal responses to events that affect many and may one day affect us."

The devastating famine in southern Sudan, the growth of multidrug-resistant diseases, and a cholera epidemic that swept East Africa were among the 10 major stories that failed to receive widespread media attention. A full list follows. Doctors Without Borders is the world's largest independent international medical relief agency, working in more than 80 countries. In 1998, over 2,000 Doctors Without Borders volunteers brought aid to the world's "hot spots," such as Kosovo and the areas affected by Hurricane Mitch. But most of their work occurred in places that fall outside the glare of the media's spotlight.

"My friends and neighbors have no idea of the magnitude of the tragedy in Sudan," said Lisabeth List, R.N., a Doctors Without Borders volunteer from Dallas, Texas, who spent four months running a feeding center for severely malnourished children in Sudan's Bahr el Ghazal province.

Doctors Without Borders' U.S. office compiled the opinionated list from events witnessed firsthand by its volunteers. The list includes crises that occurred during 1998, such as the mutilation of civilians in Sierra Leone and a mass exodus of people fleeing the fighting in the capital of Guinea-Bissau. It also includes catastrophes that have evolved over many years, such as the environmental destruction of the Aral Sea basin in countries of the former Soviet Union, the explosion in the number of the world's children who spend their days on the street, and the vast spread of the AIDS epidemic.

1998'S TOP 10 HUMANITARIAN NEWS STORIES
UNDER-REPORTED BY THE U.S. MEDIA

#1. MILLIONS SUFFER FROM ENVIRONMENTAL ILLS IN ARAL SEA BASIN. Five million people in parts of Uzbekistan, Kazakhstan, and Turkmenistan live in a toxic environmental wasteland due to the destruction of the Aral Sea and pollution of the surrounding land. A canal system built in the 1960s to irrigate cotton fields of Central Asia has diverted as much as three-quarters of the water destined for the Aral Sea, leaving former fishing towns more than 60 miles from the sea. Some 35,000 square kilometers of what was once sea is now highly salinated and polluted land, and toxic salt storms commonly blow through the communities in the region. The economy has been devastated, leading to the collapse of health care structures. The region has one of the highest levels of anemia in the world and one of the highest levels of tuberculosis in the former Soviet Union.

#2. 2.6 MILLION FACE FAMINE IN SUDAN The famine in southern Sudan produced mortality rates that in some areas equaled or exceeded those reported in Ethiopia during the crisis of 1985. During one week in mid-July, 120 people were dying each day in the area of Ajiep (pop. 17,000), in the province of Bahr el Ghazal, and many other villages recorded catastrophic death rates. Not only were there no blockbuster concerts in support of the victims, few people seemed to know about the famine at all.

#3. DRUG-RESISTANT DISEASE GROWS INTERNATIONALLY Resistance to the drugs that treat tuberculosis, malaria, sleeping sickness, and other infectious diseases is growing rapidly. Some strains of malaria—which infects 300 to

500 million people a year and kills nearly 3 million—are resistant to most of the available drugs. The most resistant malaria in the world occurs on the Thai-Cambodian and Thai-Burmese borders. Most international pharmaceutical companies, however, have eliminated research programs for malaria, so it is unlikely that there will be many new drugs to combat resistant malaria within the next 5 to 10 years.

#4. PAN-AFRICAN CHOLERA EPIDEMIC SWEEPS 14 COUNTRIES In the aftermath of the El Niño floods, Africa faced one of its most geographically far-reaching cholera epidemics since the widespread reemergence of the disease in the 1960s. The disease leap-frogged across 14 countries during the winter of 1997-98, infecting at least 168,011 people and killing more than 7,000. Experts at the World Health Organization (WHO) say that official figures most likely represent fewer than half the victims. Cholera also swept through Latin America in 1998, infecting 38,169 people and causing more than 300 deaths.

#5. RISE IN NUMBER OF STREET CHILDREN FOLLOWS GLOBAL ECONOMIC SLUMP The growing global economic crisis increased the number of children who live on urban streets, straining the coping mechanisms of societies from Romania to Rwanda to Guatemala. The problem, once mainly a result of migration from rural to urban areas, is compounded by internal armed conflict and sudden economic collapse around the globe. In Madagascar's capital, Antananarivo, more than 6,000 children who live and sleep on the street receive no public services and face frequent police harassment. In the Philippine capital of Manila, repression of the estimated 75,000 street children is on the rise. Many of the children have families but poverty compels them to beg for money on city streets where they often face arrest. For Manila's 5,000 to 7,000 "full-time" street children with no family, neither prison nor public rehabilitation centers offer care for the serious trauma, such as sexual abuse, that many have suffered.

#6. CIVILIANS MUTILATED IN SIERRA LEONE The February 6, 1998 ouster of the leaders of a coup that had taken control of Freetown eight months earlier sent rebels into northern and eastern Sierra Leone, where fighting ensued. Within weeks, Freetown's Connaught Hospital was receiving hundreds of civilians suffering from ghastly mutilations, such as arms and ears severed by machetes. The kidnapping and harassment of aid workers ensured little international presence in the affected areas. The defeated soldiers' effort to sow intimidation worked; it was so dangerous that journalists could not cover the story from the areas where the atrocities took place. Only months later, when a human rights report of the atrocities was issued, did the public first learn about the situation.

#7. WOMEN DEPRIVED OF HEALTH CARE IN KABUL, AFGHANISTAN In July 1998, international relief agencies were expelled from Kabul, the capital of Afghanistan, after months of unsuccessful negotiations with Taliban authorities. The Taliban had placed severe restrictions on women's access to health (to the point of forcibly removing 12 women from a hospital on October 19, 1997) and attempted to ghettoize non-governmental organizations in an unequipped facility far from the populations they served. Before their expulsion, international aid groups had achieved some success in providing necessary care in this country with one of the world's highest rates of maternal mortality. At the end of 1998, Afghan women remained trapped in a vicious paradox: They cannot be treated by male physicians, yet women have been barred from medical education.

#8. AIDS RAVAGES SUB-SAHARAN AFRICA While sporadic reports indicated that AIDS was spreading rapidly in Africa, news stories tended to focus on the AIDS problem in individual countries, obscuring the tremendous breadth of the epidemic. No one but the relief workers on the ground was prepared for the October 27 report by the United Nations, which said that, in several Sub-Saharan nations, one in four adults is infected with HIV. Ninety-one percent of the world's deaths from AIDS have occurred in the 34 Sub-Saharan countries and in some urban centers more than one-third of pregnant women test positive for HIV. Given the scope of the epidemic and local health systems' ill-preparedness, medical aid groups are juggling not only the prevention and treatment, but also the profound societal problems stemming from social stigmatization.

#9. HUNDREDS OF THOUSANDS FLEE WAR IN GUINEA-BISSAU A civil war raged from June to November 1998 in this tiny African nation. By the end of June, between 200,000 and 300,000 people (one-fourth to one-fifth of the country's population) had fled the capital, Bissau City, as a result of the conflict which broke out on June 7 between troops loyal to president Joao Bernardo Vieira and insurgents. Many people who were displaced toward the cities located along main roadways are still too afraid to return to their homes, despite a peace process that is now underway. With Senegal and Guinea closing their borders for long periods during the conflict, the passage of fuel, food, and medical supplies was often halted, frustrating attempts to aid the displaced people.

#10. SLEEPING SICKNESS MAY AFFECT 300,000 PER YEAR Epidemiologists estimate that more than 300,000 people per year are infected with sleeping sickness—a disease that is deadly if left untreated. Found in 36 African countries, the disease hits Angola, Uganda, Sudan, and the Democratic Republic of Congo the hardest. One of the main difficulties associated with sleeping sickness is that a key drug used to treat the later stage of the disease, the arsenic derivative melarsoprol, which is injected intravenously, causes death in 5 percent of the cases in which it is used. In addition, patients are showing resistance to melarsoprol. The best drug to treat late-stage sleeping sickness, eflornithine, is no longer manufactured because its high price puts it out of reach to the people who need it in the developing world.

Interviews with **JOELLE TANGUY**, executive director of Doctors Without Borders, can be arranged by calling (212) 655-3763 or (212) 655-3764. Doctors Without Borders' medical professionals are available to discuss the issues included in the Top 10 list. Contact Barbara Kancelbaum, (212) 655-3763 or Kris Torgeson, (212) 655-3764.

THIS MODERN WORLD

by TOM TOMORROW

Panel 1:

SINCE JOURNALISTS ON SHOWS LIKE *THE McLAUGHLIN GROUP* ARE PRIMARILY INTERESTED IN BECOMING *MARKETABLE COMMODITIES*--

EXIT QUESTION! HOW LOW WILL YOUR LECTURE FEES *PLUMMET* IF I KICK YOU OFF THIS SHOW?

ER--

PLEASE DON'T.

Panel 2:

--PERHAPS THEY SHOULD START MERCHANDISING THEMSELVES IN *EARNEST*... WITH A LINE OF *ACTION FIGURES*, FOR INSTANCE...

LOOK OUT! HERE COMES *ELEANOR CLIFT* WITH SPRING-LOADED *CONVENTIONAL WISDOM*!

HAH! JOHN McLAUGHLIN'S *INVECTIVE BOLTS* WILL *CLOBBER* HER!

Panel 3:

...OR A SPINOFF *RAP ALBUM*...

YO! MY NAME'S MOR-*TAHN* AND I'M FULLA *PREDICTIONS*-- AND I REALLY DON'T CARE IF THEY'RE *FACT* OR *FICTION*!

GOT THAT RIGHT.

WORD.

Panel 4:

...OR--WHO KNOWS?-- MAYBE EVEN A WACKY, CATCHPHRASE-LADEN *ANIMATED SERIES*...

WILL THE CAMPAIGN FINANCE HEARINGS RESULT IN SUBSTANTIVE REFORM?

FRED *BARNES*?!

HEY--DON'T HAVE AN *ANEURYSM*, MAN...

TOM TOMORROW © 12-10-97

APPENDIX C

Less Access to Less Information By and About the U.S. Government

XXX, A 1998 Chronology: January-June
and XXXI, A 1998 Chronology: June-December
By the AMERICAN LIBRARY ASSOCIATION (ALA) Washington Office

INTRODUCTION

For the past 17 years, this ongoing selective chronology has documented efforts to restrict and privatize government information. It is distributed as a supplement to the *ALA Washington Office Newsletter* and as an electronic publication at http://www.ala.org/washoff/lessaccess. While government information is more accessible through computer networks and the Freedom of Information Act, there are still barriers to public access. Continuing revelations of Cold War secrecy show how government information has been concealed, resulting in a lack of public accountability and cost to taxpayers.

There is the growing tendency of federal agencies to use computer and telecommunication technologies for data collection, storage, retrieval, and dissemination. This trend has resulted in the increased emergence of contractual arrangements with commercial firms to disseminate information collected at taxpayer expense, higher user charges for government information, and the proliferation of government information available in electronic format only. This trend toward electronic dissemination is occurring in all three branches of government. While automation clearly offers promises of savings, will public access to government information be further restricted for people who cannot afford computers or pay for computer time?

On the other hand, the Government Printing Office (GPO) Access system and the Library of Congress THOMAS system have enhanced public access by providing free online access to government databases.

ALA continues to reaffirm its long-standing conviction that open government is vital to a democracy. A January 1984 resolution passed by ALA's Council stated that "there should be equal and ready access to data collected, compiled, produced, and published in any format by the government of the United States."

With access to information a major ALA priority, library advocates should be concerned about barriers to public access to government information. Previous chronologies were compiled in two ALA Washington Office indexed publications, *Less Access to Less Information By and About the U.S. Government: A 1981-1987 Chronology*, and *Less Access to Less Information By and about the U.S. Government: A 1988-1991 Chronology*. The following selected chronology continues the tradition of a semi-annual update.

JANUARY

Department of Energy Will Adopt "Culture of Openness"

U.S. Secretary of Energy Federico Peña announced that the culture of keeping secrets in the Department of Energy will end and a "culture of openness" will be adopted. Hundreds of thousands of declassified documents were released, and two new rule changes were announced to expand and streamline whistle-blower protection for contract employees. Energy officials said the classification reform will reverse a Cold War-era rule that automatically classified all information relating to the department's nuclear program. As a result of this rule, the number of classi-fied documents would make a pile 23 miles high if placed in one stack. Shoddy record keeping makes it expensive and difficult to find many documents. (Steven Trimble, "Peña Declares End to Secrecy at Energy," *Federal Times*, January 12, 1998: 9)

Director's Resignation Complicates Plans for 2000 Census

The resignation of Census Director Martha Farnsworth Riche complicates the government plan to conduct an accurate census in 2000, and intensifies doubts in the Census Bureau's ability to avoid the problems of the expensive 1990 Census, which missed 10 million Americans, and miscounted 6 million.

The Census is used to determine which states will gain or lose seats in the House of Representatives, how state and federal legislative districts are drawn, and how billions of dollars in federal aid are disbursed. Riche's plan to use statistical sampling to estimate the portion of the population missed by traditional counting methods ran into trouble in Congress.

Republicans have attacked sampling as illegal because the Constitution calls for an "actual enumeration" of all residents of the United States. Additionally, many Republicans are concerned that sampling would result in a population estimate that included larger numbers of minorities, potentially redrawing electoral districts in a way that would favor Democrats and threaten Republican control of the House.

Riche said that she was tired of "putting out fires" at the Bureau of the Census. Some fear that Riche's resignation will make it difficult, if not impossible, to prevail over Republican opposition to sampling. (Steven Holmes, "Weary of Political Sniping, the Census Bureau Chief Resigns," *The New York Times*, January 13, 1998: A11)

Open Meeting Law Violated by Health Care Advisory Committee

According to the General Accounting Office (GAO), a government technology advisory committee has been meeting behind closed doors in apparent violation of the federal open-meeting law.

The advisory committee, which determines which new medical proce-

dures should be covered by Medicare, and reports to the Health Care Financing Administration, includes members from the private sector as well as government employees. It should have been open to anyone in the public who wanted to attend. The health care agency, in a letter to GAO, acknowledged the panel was in apparent violation of open-meeting laws and pledged that it would be revamped to include only government employees, who are allowed to meet privately.

"This is very troubling," said Ari Fleischer, press secretary to the House Ways and Means Committee. "It again raises questions about the administration engaging in secret deliberations involving health care decisions." (John E. Harris, "White House Advisory Panel Meeting in Secrecy," *Washington Post*, January 17, 1998: A8)

Defense Department Destroys Evidence of Soldier's Identity

Evidence suggests that the bones buried in 1984 at Arlington National Cemetery may be those of Air Force 1st Lt. Michael J. Blassie, whose airplane was shot down in 1972.

From the time a South Vietnamese recovery team found an identity card, a wallet and other items near a crash site in the jungles of Vietnam in 1972, a U.S. government forensic laboratory in Hawaii believed, but could not prove, that the remains belonged to Blassie. The assessment was not revealed to Blassie's family.

In 1980, a Defense Department board reviewing the status of soldiers missing in action reclassified the remains, marked X-26, as "unidentifiable." To preclude the possibility that the identity of the soldier could be questioned, the X-26 file was destroyed, and the ID and wallet are missing.

In 1984 under pressure from Vietnam veterans groups, the Defense Department picked the remains of X-26 to place at the cemetery. Only recently did Blassie's family receive documentation explaining the evidence the government originally had in its possession. (Dana Priest, "Unknown Soldier May Be Identifiable, Pentagon Says," *Washington Post*, January 21, 1968: A12) (Ed. Note: In May officials decided to exhume the remains of the Vietnam-era soldier buried in the Tomb of the Unknowns for DNA testing to see if his identity could be determined.)

Judge Rules Air Force Can Invoke State Secrets Privilege

The 9th Circuit Court of Appeals in San Francisco rejected efforts by a group of former government employees to prove they were poisoned while working at a mysterious Air Force base in Nevada. About two dozen former Groom Dry Lake base employees, led by two widows of civilian workers, sued the Air Force and the Environmental Protection Agency three years ago under the Resource Conservation and Recovery Act of 1976. The January 8 opinion, written by Judge Pamela Ann Rymer, said that the state secrets privilege invoked by the Air Force secretary made discovery and trial on the claims of environmental crimes "impossible." Notwithstanding a plaintiff's ability to produce unclassified or even nonprivileged evidence, if the "very subject matter of the action" is a state secret, "then the court should dismiss the plaintiff's action based solely on the invocation of the state secrets privilege." (*Kasza v. Browner*, 96-15535.)

Lead defense attorney Jonathan Turley, a law professor at George Washington University National Law Center, said the suit sought information about chemicals workers may have been exposed to so they can seek appropriate medical treatment. The lawsuit alleged that workers were subjected to rare and deadly industrial toxins when the Air Force burned hazardous wastes in open trenches in the late 1970s and early 1980s, and the government is covering it up. The government's response neither confirmed nor denied the allegations, but instead declared them off-limits. When the EPA conducted an investigation of the site, 100 miles north of Las Vegas, President Clinton signed a special exemption from the EPA's duty to publicly disclose what it found—an exemption that has been renewed annually, according to the *Washington Post*. (Gail Diane Cox, "Secrets Privilege Scuttles USAF Suit: Claims by Ex-Employees Gutted by 9th Circuit," *National Law Journal*, January 26, 1998: A06)

FCC Requires Long-distance Carriers to Provide Information About Rates

The Federal Communications Commission (FCC) acted to require long-distance carriers, beginning July 1, to notify pay telephone users of their rate before the call is connected. High prices for pay phone long-distance calls are among the FCC's biggest source of complaints, having received 5,000 angry letters in the past two years. The agency cited complaints of rates upwards of $5 per minute and higher.

However, the new regulations will not necessarily result in lower pay phone rates. Because pay phone providers compete to offer service in airports, hotels, restaurants, and other locations, they must promise even higher commissions, which leads to higher rates. "Unfortunately, operator services from pay phones are a rare example of competition leading to higher prices for consumers," said FCC Commissioner Gloria Tristani. (Mike Mills, "Long-Distance Pay Phone Rates Must Be Disclosed," *Washington Post*, January 30, 1998: G1)

FEBRUARY

White House Changes Strategy to Guard Internal Documents

In 1997 the White House strategically released entry logs, telephone records, notes, and other internal documents in part to preempt information from congressional critics. The White House has assembled many of the same types of records about the president's alleged relationship with Monica Lewinsky, and turned them over to Independent Counsel Kenneth Starr.

But information about White House visits and presidential phone calls made public last year is now being guarded with fierce protectiveness. According to White House officials, the change in strategy reflects the different nature of the perceived threat. "They've been much more circumspect," said White House press secretary Michael McCurry speaking of the lawyers who control the flow of information. Key questions that presumably could be answered by White House documents have been left unaddressed in the public arena. (Peter Baker, "White House, Changing Tactics, Guards Records," *Washington Post*, February 3, 1998: A7)

National Archives Must Reevaluate Decision to Give Away Films

U.S. District Judge T.S. Ellis III ruled the National Archives' decision to give away 56 boxes of film that documented the American occupation of Okinawa was "arbitrary and capricious. "The disposal decision was based on an erroneous factual premise," he wrote. The "conclusion that the films lack sufficient 'value to warrant continued preservation' [is], to say the least, unreliable."

The decision was a victory for Seiko Green, an Arlington, Virginia researcher, who argued that the films were historically unique and should be preserved. The judge stopped short of ordering the Archives to keep the 2,815 films, but he told the government to reevaluate the collection's significance. Thus, Green and other historians will get a chance to prove the films are valuable before the Archives can proceed with a plan to give the collection to a local government in Japan.

"Only some of the millions of records generated by federal officials...meet the tests of permanent value," said John W. Carlin, archivist of the United States. "We concluded that these films do not...But we will respect the court's opinion by giving them a fresh evaluation." (Brooke Masters, "Researcher Wins Lawsuit Against National Archives," *Washington Post*, February 5, 1998: D4)

Librarians and Archivists Warn of the Fragility of Electronic Government Records

According to the *U.S. News & World Report*, the ability of current and future generations to hold the government accountable is at great risk. As the records of government are increasingly held on computer disks, CD-ROMs, and magnetic tapes, there is a growing recognition of the fragility of these storage mediums and concerns about the continued availability of the hardware and software needed to read them.

Modern record keepers such as archivists and librarians warn that electronic storage mediums are turning out to be far less durable than parchment and old-fashioned top-quality paper. The danger extends to records related to health and human survival, such as studies of disease transmission or the location of toxic-waste sites.

But the nation's cultural legacy is at risk since new music, animated art, and early drafts of literature and academic works are created and stored in computers. President of the Council on Library and Information Resources Deanna Marcum says that librarians and archivists must think about preservation as soon as new knowledge is generated—deciding what to save, putting information into a common, standard format, and recording what machinery and software were used to encode the data. (Laura Tangley, "Whoops, there goes another CD-ROM," *U.S. News & World Report*, February 16, 1998: 67-8)

More Data Needed to Ensure Equity in Access to Organs for Transplants

In developments related to an item in a previous Less Access chronology, Health and Human Services Secretary Donna Shalala sent a letter to Congress advising that the administration plans to revamp the nation's system for allocating livers to people awaiting transplants.

The question of who gets available organs has become one of the most contentious medical and economic dilemmas in organ transplants. Currently, livers for transplant are first made available to patients within a local region, even if they are not as ill as patients elsewhere.

Shalala wrote that she is preparing regulations that will establish goals so that priority will be based on need. The goals would include improved equity of access through more sharing and greater availability of data from transplant centers so patients can make better informed decisions. (Rick Weiss, "HHS to Revise Liver Allocation for Most-Needed Transplants," *Washington Post*, February 27, 1998: A2)

White House Spokesman Avoids Gathering Facts

A seven-page article in the *Washington Post Magazine* described how White House press secretary Mike McCurry avoided helping reporters with information on the charges of sexual encounters in the White House. The author maintains that McCurry stayed away from fact gathering, leaving that to the lawyers, while he struggled to maintain credibility with both the press and the president. (Howard Kurtz, "Spin Master," *Washington Post Magazine*, March 8, 1998: 11)

Discrepancies Found in Records of Campaign Contributions

According to a study by the Project on Government Oversight, hundreds of thousands of dollars in PAC contributions are unaccounted for, improperly listed, or otherwise missing from Federal Election Commission (FEC) data. The watchdog group reviewed the FEC files of nearly 500 candidates in the 1996 election and found that only four of those candidates accurately reported the PAC contributions.

The report stressed that the discrepancies appeared to be due to flaws in the FEC's current disclosure system, not an attempt by candidates to conceal contributions. FEC officials said they could eliminate some of the problems by making some record-making changes and implementing other reforms. (Amy Keeler, "Report Slams Misleading PAC Records," *Roll Call*, March 9, 1998: 3)

Department of Justice Agrees to Release FBI Crime Lab Reports

The Department of Justice agreed to release some 200,000 pages of FBI crime lab reports and pay $300,000 to settle a lawsuit with veteran FBI agent and lab chemist Frederic Whitehurst. The settlement was in response to Whitehurst's claim that the Department spread false and derogatory information about him for being a whistleblower. He promises to use the documents to search for errors in the FBI laboratory's past work.

Whitehurst, 50, gained notoriety when he publicly criticized the lab's handling of evidence in several major cases, including the World Trade Center and Oklahoma City bombings. In April he reached a $1.16 million settlement with the FBI for legal fees and the annual payments he would have earned had he reached the normal FBI retirement age of 57. As part of the settlement, Whitehurst voluntarily resigned from the agency. He is now leading a project at the National Whistleblower Center, an advocacy and research group in Washington, DC.

The government did not acknowledge any wrongdoing in either settlement. While the Justice Department's inspector general found that many of Whitehurst's allegations could not be substantiated, enough of his criticisms proved accurate, requiring substantial changes in laboratory policies and practices. (Roberto Suro, "Whistle-Blower to Get Documents," *Washington Post*, March 12, 1998: A13)

CIA Releases Bay of Pigs Report After 37 Years of Secrecy

After 37 years of secrecy, the Central Intelligence Agency's internal report on the fiasco at the Bay of Pigs in April 1961 has been released.

The CIA's top-secret report on the U.S.-sponsored invasion of Cuba is a case study of the costs of secrecy. Written by Lyman Kirkpatrick, the 150-page report represented the agency's only investigation of the swift defeat of the CIA-organized brigade of 1,500 Cuban exiles. For years, not a word of the report, "The Inspector General's Survey of the Cuban Operation," was declassified.

According to the article, CIA Director George Tenet deserves credit for declassifying the controversial document. The CIA has moved to exempt some 100 million pages of documents from its massive secret archives as a result of President Clinton's 1995 executive order that all national security documents more than 25 years old be declassified. Says the author, "By holding history hostage to the dictates of secrecy, the CIA effectively refused to address its mistakes and denied the American people the ability to learn those lessons as well." (Peter Kornbluh, "The CIA Secret Kept for 37 Years," *Washington Post*, March 15, 1998: C1)

APRIL

Editorial Says "Government Keeps Too Many Secrets"

An editorial in the *Washington Post* asserted that the "government keeps too many secrets. It keeps material classified far too long. Excessive secrecy is expensive, breeds popular distrust of government and withholds from historians, researchers, and the voting public information that is important." The editorial supported pending legislation sponsored by Senator Daniel Patrick Moynihan (D-NY) that would establish a minimum standard of openness that would bind presidential administrations.

The editorial staff observed that classifying information "has been governed primarily by executive orders that individual presidents could change whenever they chose. This has allowed some presidents to impose draconian secrecy rules, while others have more relaxed rules without input from Congress or the courts." ("The Secrecy Legislation," *Washington Post*, April 10 1998: A22)

State Data Disarray Hampers Evaluation of Revised Welfare Law

Eighteen months after Congress revised the nation's welfare law, it is becoming clear that the data the government requires states to collect is in such disarray that it is impossible to determine whether the law is working. Serious computer problems and other complications have hampered the federal government in determining the extent to which states are complying with the law by getting welfare recipients into jobs.

The data is the only means by which Congress can measure which states have effective programs. Tens of millions of dollars are at stake since Congress could dock states if they fail to move a proportion of their caseload into jobs. Also in question are large federal bonuses to be shared by those states that are most successful at getting welfare recipients into jobs where they stay and advance. But states can define their caseloads differently, use varying definitions, and choose which information to submit to compete for the bonus. When the federal government starts comparing data, it is comparing the statistical equivalent of apples with oranges.

Director of Legislative Affairs at the Association of Welfare Agencies Elaine Ryan said that the Department of Health and Human Services did not tell states what information to collect until September 1997, and then required them to collect it dating to July. "I do wonder what the heck they are doing," she said. "It's really frustrating."

State officials say they are overwhelmed with gathering all the numbers required by the federal government. On the other hand, Senator Paul Wellstone (D-MN) is among the legislators who argue that the federal government knows too little about what is happening to the millions of families who have left the welfare rolls recently. "As responsible policy makers, I would think we would want to know how many of these families are reaching economic self-sufficiency," Wellstone said. "The fact of the matter is, very few states can tell me. No one knows." (Barbara Vobejda and Judith Havemann, "States' Welfare Data in Disarray," *Washington Post*, April 13, 1998: A1)

Unions Charge Army Imposing Gag Order on Job Information

Union officials representing employees of the U.S. Army Training and Doctrine Command at Fort Rucker, Alabama and Fort Bliss, Texas, allege that gag orders are being used to deny access to information about possible reductions in force (RIF) to meet downsizing goals.

The Metal Trades Council claims it has been denied information and access to meetings about whether a RIF will be necessary. They complain that employees needed to know whether their positions were targeted in a RIF before they could decide whether to take a buyout or early retirement.

The unions contend that this is a violation of the law as well as a violation of the unions' bargaining agreement. The unions point to a March 2 video teleconference held by Command officials where documents referenced "what's not allowed." The Army permits: 1) No announcement of RIFs or position cuts to work force or union; 2) No discussion with the union or work force of total reductions; and 3) No announcement of RIF date. Army officials would say only that a RIF notice had not been announced. (Lisa Daniel, "Army 'Gag Order' Alleged," *Federal Times*, April 20, 1998: 10)

Vice President Announces Expansion of Community Right to Know About Toxic Chemicals

On April 21 Vice President Gore announced a major expansion of every community's right to know about potentially harmful chemicals released into the air, land, and water. Three new initiatives will accelerate the collection and dissemination of basic public health data on the most commonly used industrial chemicals, and will require closer scrutiny for those posing the greatest risk to children.

"The public needs to know more," Vice President Gore said. "People have a right to basic health effects data about chemicals they may be exposed to at home, at work or in the environment...Yet for the majority of industrial chemicals, these data are simply not available." The administration will implement measures to fill the data gaps. (The White House, Office of the Vice President, "Toxics: Expanding The Public's Right to Know," April 21, 1998)

National Archives Destroys Naval Records; Procedures to Change Following Misunderstanding

The National Archives and Records Administration (NARA) released a 28-page report detailing its 1997 destruction of a vast collection of Naval Research Laboratory records. According to the report, NARA destroyed 4,200 bound scientific notebooks and approximately 1.5 million pages of correspondence and technical memos.

The records covered the development of radar and sonar and the early days of the U.S. space program. The NARA investigation blamed a breakdown in communication between the Archives and the Navy. The report said the

Archives thought the records could be destroyed unless they met all the specified criteria for their retention, while the Naval Research Laboratory thought the records would be kept if any of the criteria were met.

Henceforth, NARA will send the originating agency a notice by certified mail when records are scheduled for destruction. The report is on the National Archives Web page at: http://www.nara.gov/records/nrlrept.html. (Associated Press, "Archives error destroys naval records," *Washington Times*, April 25, 1998: A3)

Controversial Tobacco Document Pulled from Congressional Web Site

After mounting thousands of secret tobacco industry papers on their public Web site, the House Commerce Committee removed a controversial 104-page memo after R.J. Reynolds Tobacco Company (RJR) officials objected it being made public.

The memo described how RJR's lawyers suppressed research on the health hazards of smoking over a 30-year period. The Committee held back 400 documents from the public in response to tobacco industry pleas that the papers contained trade secrets or were entitled to confidentiality because they had been prepared by outside lawyers now working for the companies.

Over 39,000 secret tobacco industry papers were released on the committee's public Web site after a Supreme Court decision upholding a Minnesota judge's ruling the papers should be made public. Subsequently, the committee posted the documents online at http://www. house.gov/commerce (Henry Weinstein, "Tobacco Memo Pulled from House Web Site," *Washington Post*, April 27, 1998: A4)

"Good and Bad News" Locating Congressional Hearings Online

Finding Congressional committee hearings online is confusing because the House and Senate have gone their separate ways in providing electronic access to them. There is little consistency between committee Web sites, House and Senate information systems, and between GPO Access and THOMAS, the two main electronic gateways to Congressional information.

One bright spot is the Government Printing Office, which, in conjunction with the Senate, is putting up complete hearing records with transcripts, prepared statements, answers submitted to questions and other materials for three Senate committees: Appropriations, Environment and Public Works, and Governmental Affairs. Plans are underway to provide online hearing records for all Senate committee by the end of the year.

The author includes a table of the various activities of the committees and Congress outlines the "good news/bad news" about accessing these materials online. (James McDonough, "Committee Hearings Online Present a Confusing Face,"

Electronic Public Information Newsletter, May 1998: 33-35)

OMB Oversight Faulted on Implementation of Electronic Freedom of Information Law

OMB Watch, a non-profit research and advocacy group, released a report about federal agency implementation of the Electronic Freedom of Information Act (EFOIA) 1996 amendment requirements. The study indicates that, overall, agency compliance with the EFOIA amendments has been overwhelmingly inadequate. The three overriding reasons for this conclusion are the following:

1. Congress has not provided the necessary funding to implement the amendments.

2. The Office of Management and Budget (OMB) has not provided adequate guidance or assistance to agencies during the implementation process.

3. By failing to comply fully with the EFOIA amendments, agencies have yet to make public access to government information a priority.

The report observes that, with agencies delaying implementation, the public is denied important access to electronic files. Unlike paper files, electronic data can be delivered instantaneously to the public through the Internet, making research easier and less time-consuming.

While critical of the majority of federal agencies, the report applauds several agencies or departments that have been exemplary at implementing EFOIA. For example, the Department of Defense and the Federal Communications Commission maintain excellent home pages to make research easy and information accessible. The Small Business Administration and the National Science Foundation provide forms to submit FOIA requests online, accelerating the public's access to federal government information. Others such as the Veteran's Administration accommodate a variety of low-tech and high-tech users by using audio-visual and text-only sites. To receive a copy of the study, "Arming the People," contact OMB Watch at (202) 234-8494. (James McDonough, "OMB Watch Takes Feds to Task," *Electronic Public Information Newsletter*, May 1998: 38)

Archivist Announces Measures to Make it Easier for Public Contributions to Archival Decisions

Archivist of the United States John W. Carlin has announced measures to make it easier for the public to participate in deciding which government agency records are worth keeping and for how long. The measures include the following:

➤ Federal Register notices from the National Archives and Records Administration (NARA) requesting public comments on records proposed for destruction will be more informative and descriptive;

➤ The public will have more information on which to evaluate proposals and make comments; and

➤ The public may now request copies of the disposal schedules and appraisal memorandums prepared by NARA staff members, as well as evaluations that contain additional information concerning the nature and value of the records covered by a proposed schedule.

While no federal records are authorized for destruction without the approval of the Archivist of the United States, Carlin says, "Now we are making it easier for records users in the public to making sound contributions about what to 'sort out.'" (John W. Carlin, "Which Records Should We Keep? How the Public Can Help Decide," *The Record: News from the National Archives and Records Administration*, May 1998: 3)

Citizen Tries to Make Patent Database Freely Available

Carl Malamud, president of the non-profit Internet Multicasting Service, has challenged the federal government to make the Nation's patent and trademark database freely available. In a letter to Vice President Al Gore and Commerce Secretary William Daley he said that he would make the database available himself if the government fails to do so by July 1, 1998.

"I'm going to buy the trademark data and will build the user base as big as I can in a year," Malamud said. "At the end of the year, I'll pull the rug out from the users and give them Al Gore's e-mail address."

Malamud's organization has successfully mounted various other databases, including Securities and Exchange Commission (SEC) documents and various databases, including information from the General Services Administration, the Federal Election Commission, the Federal Reserve Board, and the Government Printing Office. His organization ran the SEC and patent databases for 18 months. Subsequently the SEC took over the Web site, which now receives more than 500,000 hits a day.

Regarding Malamud's latest initiative, Bruce Lehman, the commissioner of the Patent and Trademark Office, said, "We'd do this tomorrow if we had the funding. What Mr. Malamud wants to do is permit people to download the entire database. If he can do that we'd be out all $20 million we now receive in fees. Why would anyone want paper?"

Dan Duncan of the Information Industry Association was also critical of the idea. "The government should be very cautious of going into the provision of new information services of this magnitude when there are already private providers in the marketplace." Malamud's "crusade" highlights the continuing dispute between those who advocate widely distributing government databases that are created at taxpayer expense and the thriving private information industry that remarkets and resells the information to business customers and libraries. (John Markoff, "U.S. Is Urged to Offer More Data on Line," *The New York Times*, May 4, 1998: D6)

CIA Urges Congress to Reject Release of Secret American Files on Human Rights Violators

In testimony before a subcommittee of the House Committee on Government Reform and Oversight, CIA official Lee Strickland urged Congress to reject proposed legislation that would speed the release of secret American files. Such a release could help identify human rights violators throughout Latin America Strickland argued. He also said that under the proposed Human Rights Information Act, "sources will be imperiled and the mission of the CIA 'to support the Congress and the president' will be disadvantaged." He asserted that the ability of the agency to recruit foreigners, gather secrets, and do business was on the line. The legislation would require the CIA, State Department, Justice Department, Pentagon, and other federal agencies to lean toward openness. (Reuters, "CIA Opposes Release of Secret Files," *Washington Post*, May 12, 1998: A07)

Census 2000 Tests Disappointing

The results of the "dress rehearsal" for the 2000 Census were disappointing because only 53 percent of those receiving mailed questionnaires responded. Despite a major advertising campaign by the Census Bureau in the areas of California, South Carolina, and Wisconsin, where the test was conducted, the returns fell far short of the anticipated 66 percent. Census officials said that many American resist attempts to be counted due to widespread distrust of government, especially among minority and immigrant groups. (August Gribbin, "Compilers of 2000 Census Face Diminishing Returns," *Washington Times*, May 18, 1998: A12)

House Urges President to Make Documents Public

The House of Representatives passed a non-binding resolution demanding that President Clinton make public all legal documents involved in his effort to invoke executive privilege in the Monica Lewinsky investigation, an assertion he has not even publicly acknowledged. The White House "brushed off" the House vote. White House spokesman James Kennedy said, "The President has and will continue to abide by his constitutional obligations."

The House voted 259 to 157 to approve the resolution which did not go as far as some wanted because it did not seek to limit the use of executive privilege in such circumstances. (Peter Baker and Juliet Eilperin, "House Demands Clinton Release Executive Privilege Documents," *Washington Post*, May 22, 1998: A16)

Democrats Join in Urging President to Cooperate with Congressional Investigations

A majority of House Democrats joined Republicans in urging President Clinton and Administration officials to cooperate more with a growing number of congressional investigations. At issue is the administration's China policy, which came a month before the president visited China.

Presidential aides said that Clinton hopes to quell the rapidly escalating controversy over last February's approval of a waiver to U.S. policy concerning sending an American satellite into space on a Chinese rocket. White House aides said the president would divulge information, something his congressional critics said he has failed to do. The White House planned to send documents to the House that will show there was nothing wrong with President Clinton's approval of the technology transfer. (Juliet Eilperin and John Harris, "Democrats Ask Clinton's Cooperation In Probes," *Washington Post*, May 22, 1998: A)

Intelligence Agencies Use "Perception Management Program" to Spread Misinformation

Federal intelligence agencies are studying ways to use computers and the Internet to shape and disseminate information designed to form public opinion internationally. They are turning to computers to develop more sophisticated ways of manipulating and delivering digital photos, video clips, and recorded sound to portray fictitious events which can in turn be broadcast to foreign countries via the Internet.

For decades, as part of its "perception management program," intelligence agencies have created misinformation to try to cause political or military change without direct political or military involvement in countries where the United States has vested interests, such as Iraq and North Korea. The Office of Information Warfare, created in August 1996 with a staff of seven analysts, now has a staff of 100 and a dedicated collection team established within the Defense Intelligence Agency focused solely on information operations and information warfare.

An unidentified congressional staff member said use of the Internet and video-editing tools to shape public opinion in places such as Iraq "should be just another part of the intelligence toolkit." For example, intelligence agencies may wish to convince a world leader that a massive invasion is imminent by broadcasting manipulated video news clips showing the presence of a much larger military force than actually exists. The hope, said the congressional source, is that by "having such a capability, we would avoid having to actually deploy troops."

However, since the Internet knows no borders, there may be risks involved, including possible breaches of intelligence regulations which spell out what the intelligence community can and cannot do within U.S. borders. "Because it involves national security, the risks are worth it," the congressional source said.

Randall Whitaker, an analyst at the Air Force Research Laboratory, said delivering propaganda via the Internet is risky. Whitaker wondered, "Who's more at risk: the deceivers or the receivers?" (Daniel Verton, "Spies turn to high-tech info ops: PCs, Internet used for manipulating images, public opinion," *Federal Computer Week*, May 25, 1998: 1)

Classified Report is Central to Congressional Resolution

According to an Air Force intelligence assessment, there are accusations that U.S. security was harmed by a classified report when engineers from Loral Space and Communications gave the Chinese a technical study on the cause of the 1996 crash of a Chinese rocket carrying an American satellite.

Officials of the Department of Defense have refused to make the report available to Congress, or elaborate publicly on what kind or how much damage was done to U.S. security, citing an ongoing Justice Department investigation into the case. The absence of details has left an opening for many heated assertions. The House of Representatives voted 364 to 54 to bar further U.S. satellite exports to China. Those arguing that a damaging transfer of space launch technology has occurred do not have significant evidence. (Bradley Graham, "Chinese Missile Gain Questioned," *Washington Post*, May 31, 1998: A1)

GAO Report Shows Lobbyists Disclosure Law Working

A General Accounting Office (GAO) report shows an increase of nearly two and a half times the number of organizations and individuals that have registered as lobbyists since the enactment of the Lobbying Disclosure Act of 1995. GAO found that the law, passed to close loopholes and improve disclosure, forced 10,612 new lobbyists to disclose their activities during the first year the law was in effect. Senator Carl Levin (D-MI), who authored the reform, said, "The new law provides a much more complete picture of who is lobbying whom on what issues and for how much money. The dramatic increase in registration brings much needed sunshine to the lobbying business." (Francesca Contiguglia, "GAO Finds That Lobbyist Registration Has Soared," *Roll Call*, May 14, 1998: 14)

Wartime Japanese Ambassador Acts as Unwitting Source of Information to Allied Forces

Documents recently released by the National Archives and Records Administration show how Japan's wartime ambassador to Germany was an unwitting source of critical information to the United States.

From 1941 until the fall of Berlin, the reports Ambassador Hiroshi Oshima telegraphed to the Foreign Office in Japan were intercepted by the United States. These reports provided a methodical account of German defenses along the Atlantic coast in the critical months leading to the Allied invasion along the coast of Normandy. The reports were intercepted, decoded, translated and delivered to U.S. military leaders within hours.

The transcripts of the intercepts, marked "Top Secret Ultra," are part of a bonanza of World War II secret files declassified by presidential directive over the past several years. The information that Oshima provided supplemented other data the Allies received from German cable traffic yet to be declassified. (Charles Fenyvesi, "Japan's Unwitting D-Day Spy," *Washington Post*, May 26, 1998: A10)

White House Urges Agencies to Use Plain Language in Government Writing

The White House issued a memorandum to the heads of executive departments and agencies directing them to make the use of plain language in government writing a top priority.

The statement said that using plain language sends a clear message about what the government is doing, what it requires, and what services it offers. "Plain language saves the government and the private sector time, effort, and money." The National Partnership for Reinventing Government will issue guidance to help government employees comply with the directives and to explain more fully the elements of plain language. (The White House, Memorandum for the Heads of Executive Departments and Agencies, "Plain Language in Government Writing," June 1, 1998.)

Federal Government Slow in Fixing Possibility of Year 2000 Computer Breakdowns

The federal government is facing a significant risk of critical computer breakdowns because several Cabinet agencies have slowed in their progress on computer repairs for 2000.

For example, the Department of Health and Human Services faces a shortage of skilled programmers to work on Medicare computers. The Defense Department has found problems thwarting quick repairs to certain missile missions planning software. The Treasury Department is facing uncertainty with the system that processes government-wide financial data because of scheduling delays involving a private-sector contractor.

The government's pace of repair work has alarmed many computer industry analysts and has come under attack by Republicans on Capitol Hill. Representative Steve Horn (R-CA), chair of a House subcommittee that has been examining the Clinton Administration's 2000 efforts, asserted that the current rate of repairs means that more than 40 percent of the critical systems will not be fixed by a March 1999 deadline set by the White House. Technology specialists warn that government computer crashes could ripple through society. (Rajiv Chandrasekaran and Stephen Barr, "Agencies Note Difficulties in Speeding Fix of 2000 Computer Bug," *Washington Post*, 3 June 3, 1998: A2)

Intelligence Agencies Fail to Forecast India's Nuclear Explosions

Intelligence agencies failed to forecast India's nuclear explosions in May in large part because of a "mind-set" leading officials to conclude that the Indian government would not risk the consequences of fulfilling a campaign promise to conduct tests. Clinton Administration officials learned of the tests when they were announced by the Indian government.

Retired Admiral David Jeremiah has been appointed by CIA Director George Tenet to head a review panel investigat-

ing American's multibillion-dollar spy agencies' failure to predict India's first nuclear tests in 24 years. Jeremiah told a news conference that the country's spy agencies should have ordered "increased coverage" of India after a hard-line party came to power in March. Calling the lapse "a serious problem," Jeremiah said his report offered a series of recommendations for more efficient management of the 13 agencies that make up the U.S. intelligence community. He said no officials should be fired for the failure. While he summarized some of his findings for reporters, the report was classified. (Walter Pincus, "Spy Agencies Faulted for Missing Indian Tests," *Washington Post*, June 3, 1998: A18)

Former Secretary of Energy Cites Reprisals Against Whistleblowers

During a May 19 deposition in connection with a lawsuit by an Energy Department whistleblower, former Energy Secretary Hazel O'Leary acknowledged long-standing practices of reprisal against whistleblowers. "Once they have raised a concern or an allegation with respect to safety or integrity, they find themselves facing a very strong and impenetrable stone wall," O'Leary said. Typically, whistleblowers were called "the crazies" and had their security clearance withdrawn, thus preventing the individuals from working in other federal entities or for contractors. O'Leary said she tried to eliminate retaliation against whistleblowers during her tenure.

The lawsuit involves Joseph Carson, a

safety manager and critic of the agency, who sued to block his transfer from the Department of Energy's nuclear facility in Oak Ridge, Tennessee to Germantown, Maryland. According to his attorneys and the Government Accountability Project, Carson investigated and criticized the closing and erasing of files on documented safety deficiencies at Oak Ridge, as well as suppressing findings of a "chilled atmosphere" about reporting safety concerns at the facility. The hearing will continue at the end of June in District of Columbia District Court. (P.J. Shuey, "Former Energy Chief Defends Whistle-blower," *Federal Times*, June 8, 1998: 9)

Obey Decries Difficulty in Finding Accurate Pending Bill

According to a *Roll Call* editorial, when the transportation bill came to the House floor in April, it was impossible for anyone to tell from published documents what was included in the bill. According to Representative David Obey (D-WI), only one accurate copy of the bill existed. It was in the House Rules Committee where Members would page through it to find out whether their pet projects were included or not. Citizens and the press were purposely left in the dark except when Members of Congress made the information public.

Obey observed, "Knowledge is power and the lack of knowledge is powerlessness. If only the inside fixers know what is going on, you might as well not have a Congress." According to *Roll Call*, "If knowledge is power and power corrupts, then what we have in Congress is info-corruption, especially when Congress's information practices are measured against the promises of openness solemnly enunciated when the GPO first took power." ("Info-Corruption," *Roll Call*, June 8, 1998: 4)

Government Performance and Results Act Information Questioned

According to House Republican leaders, the Government Performance and Results Act has not produced reliable information for Congress to use in budget or policy decisions. The 1993 statute was intended to show taxpayers what they get for their money as federal agencies develop "strategic plans," set goals, develop measures of progress, and write annual reports on how well they performed.

In a letter to the White House, Republican leaders expressed fear that the reform effort could end up as just another bureaucratic paperwork drill. They also said that too many agencies lack data about their programs, such as payment error rates or timeliness of service, making it difficult to plan reasonable steps to improvement.

House Democrats contend that Republicans played politics with the Results Act this year by handing out failing grades to most agencies in an attempt to embarrass the administration and Vice President Gore as he prepares for the 2000 presidential campaign. (Stephen Barr, "GPO Sees No Results in Results Act," *Washington Post*, June 9, 1998: A4)

Secret Navy Data Declassified

Vice President Gore announced the declassification and release of secret and restricted Navy data. The data, of scientific and commercial value, will help increase public understanding of marine life, improve weather forecasting and climate change research, and identify valuable ocean resources. Additionally, the Department of Defense will improve marine safety by producing computer-based nautical charts to replace the paper charts used by mariners for centuries. (White House press release. "Public Access to Military Data and Technology," June 12, 1998)

Agencies Find it Difficult to Comply with Electronic Freedom of Information Law

Backlogs in processing traditional paper-based requests under the Freedom of Information Act are hindering some federal agencies from complying with the requirements of the 1996 Electronic Freedom of Information Act (EFOIA). At a hearing of the House Subcommittee on Government Management, Information and Technology, chaired by Rep. Steve Horn (R-CA), a FBI spokesman said the agency has a backlog of nearly 11,900 requests for information. Technical difficulties in Web site development have also stymied agencies from EFOIA compliance, said Richard Huff, co-director of the Justice Department's Office of Information and Privacy.

Patrice McDermott of OMB Watch, an organization that monitors public access to government records, said that of the 57 federal agencies her organization had surveyed recently, none had complied fully with EFOIA. She cited three reasons for the lack of compliance: lack of Congressional funding, lack of guidance to agencies from the Office of Management and Budget, and the failure of agencies to make access to federal information a priority. "The goal of EFOIA should be to make so much information publicly available online that Freedom of Information Act requests become an avenue of last resort," McDermott said. (L. Scott Tillett, "Feds find EFOIA a tough act to follow," *Federal Computer Week*, June 15, 1998: 18)

The FBI Makes Secrets Available on the Internet

The FBI quietly posted more than 1,600 pages dating back to the 1940s on its Web site (http://www.fbi.gov/), although most contain blacked-out passages and missing names. The agency plans to put up to 1.3 million documents online, including some on famous people, unidentified flying objects, and alleged alien abductions. (Courtney Macavinta, "FBI posts the real 'X files,'" CNET News.Com, June 19, 1998, http://www.news.com/News/Item/0,4,233343,00.html.)

Patent Database to Be Freely Available on the Internet

The Clinton Administration announced that it would make the full database of United States patents since 1976 and trademark text and images starting from the late 1800s freely available on Internet at http://www.uspto.gov/. The project will create the largest online government database, made up of more than 21 million documents. This decision will fuel the fierce debate between public interest advocates who argue that government information should be available electronically and commercial companies that purchase the data from government agencies to resell for a profit. ("U.S. Plans Free Public Access to Patent Database on the Web," *San Jose Mercury News*, June 25, 1998: 4C)

Thusands of Nixon Records Destroyed

In early June the National Archives and Records Administration shredded more than 70,000 pages of documents about former President Richard M. Nixon. Then the shreds were stuffed into 126 burn bags and incinerated at the Pentagon. The records, not classified or related to national security, were logs summing up what have been deemed to be "private/personal" or "private/political" conversations on the former president's White House tapes. The documents were covered by a federal court order that requires the Archives to return to the Nixon estate all the "personal and private" conversations scattered throughout his original White House tapes.

Archivist John Carlin is trying to decide what to do with the fragile, original tapes. It is estimated that it would take five years to edit the 3,700 hours of tape. Additionally trying to edit out the 819 hours of "personal" discussions would probably destroy most of the original tapes including segments concerning the Watergate scandal. Some archival specialists suggest a bonfire for the original tapes, too. "Cutting and splicing them is going to be a monumental waste of time," one said. "Once you start cutting, you've destroyed the tapes." (George Lardner, "Nixon Logs Burn to Ashes," *Washington Post*, July 1, 1998: A21)

[Ed. Note: Previous chronologies reported on earlier developments about the Nixon tapes.]

CIA Breaks Promises to Release Cold War Files

Citing lack of funds and personnel, George Tenet, director of the Central Intelligence Agency (CIA), announced that the agency will not release secret records about most of its major Cold War covert operations in the foreseeable future. The CIA promised five years ago to declassify thousands of files on 11 major paramilitary and political operations carried out under Presidents Truman, Eisenhower, and Kennedy. Some documents from two of the operations have been published: the 1961 Bay of Pigs invasion of Cuba and the 1954 coup against the Guatemalan government. But Tenet's statement made it clear that the agency never undertook a serious effort to declassify the remaining nine operations.

Information about the nine operations make up a secret history of American power used against foreign government.

The CIA also promised six years ago to release records of its coup in Iran in 1954. It belatedly acknowledged last year that most of those files had been destroyed in the 1960s. Tenet said the CIA had released 227,000 pages to a government panel on the assassination of President Kennedy and reams of information for the official histories of the State Department of the 1950s and 1960s. These releases took precedence over the voluntary effort to declassify covert actions.

Page Putnam Miller, director of the National Coordinating Committee for the Promotion of History, said, "There are no resources now for this project." A CIA spokeswoman said about 150 people work on declassification, handling requests from the White House, Congress, State Department, and requests under the Freedom of Information Act. She said the amount of money spent on the effort could not be revealed because it was secret. (Tim Weiner, "CIA, Breaking Promises, Put Off Release of Cold War Files," *The New York Times*, July 15, 1998: A13)

Tobacco Documents Made More Accessible to the Public

Important information about the health hazards of tobacco and the tobacco industry's effort to induce children to smoke were hidden by the industry for decades. President Clinton directed Secretary of Health and Human Services Donna E. Shalala to coordinate a public health review of tobacco industry documents and develop a plan to make the documents more accessible to researchers and the public at large. The plan would: (1) propose a method for coordinating review of the documents and making available an easily searchable index and/or digest of the reviewed documents; (2) propose a plan to disseminate widely the index and/or digest as well as the documents themselves, including expanded use of the Internet; and (3) provide a strategy for coordinating a broad public and private review and analysis of the documents to gain critical public health information. (White House press release, "President Clinton Makes Tobacco Documents More Accessible to the Public," July 17, 1998)

FBI Exemption to Declassified Order Revealed

In 1995 when President Clinton signed an executive order directing the automatic declassification of millions of government secrets more than 25 years old, he did not mention that the Federal Bureau of Investigation would have a blanket exemption. FBI officials defended the previously undisclosed exemption, saying it was essential because of the size of its files—6.5 million cubic feet—where classified and unclassified files are mingled, often without labels that show those supposed to concern national security. No other government agency, including the CIA and the super-secret National Security Agency, won an exemption. "It sounds like we pulled a real coup," one FBI agent said.

The arrangement came to light in court papers in June and was laid out in detail in a memo obtained by the *Wash-*

ington Post under the Freedom of Information Act. Critics of government secrecy said that the exemption was legally questionable because it has no cut-off date and because the FBI used federal privacy law instead of any national security concerns to justify it. It is uncertain how and why the special arrangement for the FBI came about. "The understanding was that there was a distinction between making something public and removing any classification from it," said former National Security Council staff member Morton Halperin. "These files were not going to be automatically put in a public library after 25 years. They would still be subject to law enforcement and privacy reviews. So therefore this [automatic declassification] was not a big threat to them." (George Lardner, "FBI Won Exception to Presidential Order Declassifying Secrets," *Washington Post*, July 19, 1998: A03)

Judge Tells FDA Not to Block Drug Data

U.S. District Judge Royce Lamberth ruled that the Food and Drug Administration's ban on the distribution to doctors of scientific journal articles and textbooks violates constitutional protections for commercial speech. At issue is medical information concerning unapproved uses for pharmaceutical companies' products. FDA officials argued that the ban is necessary to insure that companies do not promote products by providing incomplete or biased information, or gain approval for a drug for a narrow use and then promote many other

uses through the distribution of favorable scientific information. The Clinton Administration is likely to appeal the ruling. (John Schwartz, "FDA Is Told Not to Block Drug Data," *Washington Post*, July 31, 1998: A23)

AUGUST

Bill Would Open Nazi Records

Congress passed S. 1379, The Nazi War Crimes Disclosure Act, establishing the Nazi War Criminal Interagency Working Group to locate, identify, inventory, recommend for declassification, and make available to the public all classified Nazi war criminal records of the United States. The Act will make it much easier for historians, researchers, and the public to view the documents dating to the Cold War years that followed World War II. Several federal agencies, including the CIA, the State Department, and the Department of Defense, refused to declassify the documents, citing national security. (Associated Press, "Bill Would Open Nazi Crimes Files," *Boston Globe*, August 7, 1998: A14)

[Ed. Note: The President signed P.L. 105-246 on October 8, 1998.]

Declassification Ordered of Selected Cold War Documents

A report from the Interagency Security Classification Appeals Panel (ISCAP) showed that the panel reversed agency decisions and declassified Cold War records more than 80 percent of the time. Information was declassified in full or in part in 81 out of the 96 documents presented to it, while agency classification actions were upheld in the case of 15 documents. ISCAP was established in 1995 when President Clinton signed Executive Order 12958, the first effort since the end of the Cold War to reassess the balance between open government and the need to maintain secrets vital to national security. The panel resolves appeals from Executive Branch classification decisions, and can be reached by e-mail at iscap@arch1.nara.gov. (White House press release, "Federal Panel Orders Declassification of Selected Cold War Documents," August 26, 1998)

SEPTEMBER

Sen. Moynihan Thinks Secrecy is for Losers

In his book, *Secrecy: The American Experience*, Sen. Daniel Patrick Moynihan (D-NY) offered advice to public officials considering whether or not to keep information confidential: When in doubt, put it out. Moynihan drew on the work of the Commission on Protecting and Reducing Government Secrecy (1995-97), which he chaired, to write a history of official secrecy in America.

Moynihan wrote that a case can be made that secrecy is for losers—both people and policies. He asserted that Richard Nixon's rage at the publication of the top-secret Pentagon Papers in 1971 eventually led to the Watergate break-in and ultimately his resignation. Additionally, he believes that the covert Bay of Pigs fiasco in 1961 "arguably led to the

Cuban missile crisis of 1962," the most dangerous moment of the Cold War.

Moynihan argued that overclassification stifles analysis and debate (the reason the CIA did not foresee the collapse of the Soviet Union); it deters self-criticism that is fundamental to democracy; and it feeds suspicions of conspiracy. He said that the benefits of publication are rarely weighed when classifiers worry about the harm that may result from disclosure of information. Knowledge is power, Moynihan concluded, and if other people have less knowledge, the official has more power. (Robert L. Turner "Putting the Word Out on 'Secrecy,'" *Boston Globe*, September 29, 1998: C2)

JFK Assassination Records Released

The Assassination Records Review Board released its final report in late September after releasing thousands of previously secret government records about the assassination of President Kennedy. Because the Board decided to interpret an "assassination record" very broadly, the documents reveal significant new insights into Cold War foreign policy and how some agencies operated during crises. For historians, the value of this federal undertaking was seen not only in the released documents, but also in the broad implications of openness for declassification policy.

While the Board weighed the public's right to know with the need to protect sensitive national security information, statute mandated a "presumption of disclosure." Agency heads could only appeal to the President to keep closed those records that the Board decided should be kept open. The Final Report of the Assassination Records Review Board is available from the Government Printing Office (S/N 05200301472-6, $24) or online at http://fedbbs.access.gpo.gov /libs/arrb_pdf.htm (Page Miller, "Assassination Records Review Board Issues Final Report with Recommendations for Increasing Openness," *NCC Washington Update*, September 30, 1998)

OCTOBER

Military Required to Remove Information from Public Web Sites

Deputy Secretary of Defense John Hamre issued a directive on September 25 requiring all Department of Defense organizations to remove certain information from public military Web sites. Plans for military operations, movements of military units, and personal data such as Social Security numbers, phone numbers, and addresses of military personnel family members were included. The threat of terror attacks against military people and installations was the justification for the directive.

The impact of the directive was not immediately clear since few, if any, military Web sites have content that has not cleared for release. However, the new directive might make it more difficult to decide what may be released. Among the materials that may go under wraps are maps, biographies of, and speeches by civilian officials. "By looking at various

speeches, you might find that the person might reference his parents and where they live," a spokesman said. "If you connect bios with the speeches, you could get personal information about civilian officials." However, removing maps from Web sites would not do much for security because maps appear in guidebooks that are available to the public. The Defense Department recognizes that the information on its Web sites is public information and that the public could obtain it by going to a military installation or filing a Freedom of Information Act. But making information so easily accessible on the Internet concerns Defense officials.

Internet freedom advocates expressed concern that officials may use threats to personnel as an excuse to keep legitimate information from the public. "If this is taken as an excuse to take out budget information, information on weapons systems, and so on it would be a travesty on the American people," said William Arkin, an independent defense analyst. The Pentagon's main Web site at http://www.defenselink.mil branches into separate Web sites for each military branch and some individual units and ships. Some bases have independent sites. (Gopal Ratnam, "Defense Reviews Sensitivity of Web Site Data," *Federal Times*, October 12, 1998: 4)

House Members Angry at Secrecy Surrounding Huge Omnibus Appropriations Bill

Numerous rank and file Members of Congress criticized the House leadership for secretly stuffing millions of dollars in controversial projects into the $520 billion omnibus appropriations bill that was prepared as the 105th Congress moved toward adjournment. Republicans were angered when their leadership blocked them from examining the details of the pending funding legislation. "We have negotiated a bill we can't read with people we don't trust and spent money we don't have for things we don't need," Rep. Steve Largent (R-OK) said of the funding bill that passed the House on October 20. Republicans were particularly angry with Speaker of the House Newt Gingrich (R-GA) and Appropriations Chair Robert Livingston (R-LA) for allegedly "hiding" the details of the 40-pound, 4,000-page bill until just hours before the final vote.

On the Senate side, Sen. John McCain (R-AZ) said, "The process by which the bill was created is deplorable. Negotiations were conducted behind closed doors, out of sight of the public as well as the vast majority of Members of Congress. Decisions were made and then reversed without notice." Sen. Daniel Patrick Moynihan (D-NY) criticized Congressional leaders for writing nearly one-third of the $1.7 trillion budget behind closed doors. "We are beginning to resemble a kind of bastard parliamentary system in which the real decisions are made in a closed room by three or four people," he said. Republicans were equally infuriated that the budget plan was available for only a few to see. (Jim VandeHei and Ethan Wallison, "Budget Fight Ends, But Few Are Happy," *Roll Call*, October 22, 1998: 1)

Automatic Declassification of Government Documents Halted

Automatic declassification of classified records more than 25 years old was halted by a provision inserted into the defense authorization bill for Fiscal Year 1999 (P.L. 105-261). Decried by critics as a major blow to secrecy reform, the law directs government agencies to revert to a page-by-page review of all classified records more than 25 years old. This painstaking and time consuming review is required until the Department of Energy and the National Archives develop procedures determining which of their documents are "highly unlikely" to contain "Restricted Data" or "Formerly Restricted Date," as nuclear secrets are called.

As he signed H.R. 3616, President Clinton stated: "I am disappointed that the Congress, in a well-meaning effort to further protect nuclear weapons information, has included an overly broad provision that impedes my Administration's work to declassify historically valuable records. I am committed to submitting the plan required under this Act within 90 days. In the meantime, I will interpret this provision in a manner that will assure the maximum continuity of agency efforts, as directed by my Executive Order 12958, to declassify historically valuable records." (Page Putnam Miller, "President Critical of Restrictive Declassification Provision in Defense Authorization Act," *NCC Washington Update*, Vol. 4, No. 42, October 26, 1998, http://www.h-net.msu.edu/~ncc/)

Defense Department Blacks Out General Pinochet Biographic Sketch

When the U.S. Defense Intelligence Agency released a biographic sketch of General Augusto Pinochet, it blacked out everything on the page other than the date, his name, and his position as the President and Chief of the Military Junta in Chile. The document, released under the Freedom of Information Act, is one page of thousands of secret documents buried in Washington. A picture of the black page was featured in *The New York Times*. (Peter Kornbluh, "Op-Art: Defense Intelligence Agency," *The New York Times*, October 26, 1998: A25)

Head of CIA Publications Review Board Takes Pride On What He Has "Left In"

John Hollister Hedley heads the five-member publications review board that decides what former employees of the Central Intelligence Agency (CIA) can publish about the agency. He hates to be called a censor, but his job is to decide how much the CIA will permit to be revealed about the inner workings of the agency. He has even cut information from a cookbook of recipes prepared by CIA agents and their spouses.

During the past three years, Hedley has distinguished himself by what he has left in, not by what he has taken out. He has helped establish new standards of openness that have allowed former spies, analysts, and agency officials to go farther than ever before in describing their clandestine careers. "I think we need to open up, and I think we can have it both ways," said Hedley. "I do not think you endanger the protection of that which needs to be protected while you open up and are much more transparent than we've been, in terms of what kind of people we are, and what we do, and how we do it." (Vernon Loeb, "Drawing the Company's Line," *Washington Post*, October 13, 1998: A13)

National Security Archive Mounts Collection of Declassified Documents

The world's largest non-governmental collection of declassified documents is the National Security Archive Web site (http://www.seas.gwu.edu/nsarchive/). The National Security Archive, an independent non-governmental research institute and library located at The George Washington University in Washington, DC, collects and publishes declassified documents acquired through the Freedom of Information Act. It has assembled a particularly impressive collection documenting government misadventures in Latin America over the past four decades. Other topics range from nuclear weaponry and the militarization of space to the White House meeting of President Nixon and Elvis Presley. (David Futrell, "Top Secret Documents Put Starr's Stuff to Shame," *Newsday*, October 18, 1998: B15)

CIA Refuses to Reveal Names of Human Rights Violators

In a newly declassified report written by its inspector general, the Central Intelligence Agency (CIA) refused to give human rights investigators in Honduras the names of Honduran military officers suspected of executing a leader of counterinsurgency operations in 1983. Despite deletions, the report acknowledged for the first time that the CIA knew at the time of "death squad" activities linked to Honduran military personnel with whom the U.S. government had close ties. The report also acknowledged that CIA officials failed to fully reveal the extent of human rights violations in Honduras to agency headquarters or to Congress.

The agency's deletions of names again ignited a debate over legislation that would have required the CIA to disclose information even if it revealed the identity of confidential intelligence sources. The Senate narrowly defeated legislation that would have prohibited the CIA from withholding information about an individual's involvement in human rights abuses "solely because that individual was or is an intelligence source." The bill also established an expedited declassification process for documents sought by human rights investigators in Honduras and Guatemala and created a panel to review declassification decisions made by the CIA. (Vernon Loeb, "CIA Won't Name Hondurans Suspected of Executing Rebel," *Washington Post*, November 4, 1998: A2)

Switch from Paper to Electronic Distribution of 2000 Census Data Raises Information Issues

The Census Bureau is planning to mount most of the 2000 Census data on the Internet, with little being distributed in paper. Although the plan is likely to result in a profusion of private-sector packaging of government information, there appears to be little concern about whether the quality and veracity of government data could be compromised by marketers who may enhance the materials in their zeal to tailor it for business clients. Others express concerns about the Internet being used as the primary method for disseminating federal statistics without a national policy for cyberspace information storage and retrieval. "What the Census Bureau is doing is just the tip of a much bigger iceberg," said Gary Bass, executive director of OMB Watch, an organization that monitors public access to government records. "The government doesn't have a plan for regulating its data. [Federal officials] can't, or shouldn't, be putting it out there willy-nilly because what they are releasing affects us all."

Although some experts worry about policy implications, entrepreneurs are eager to download information produced by the Census Bureau, repackage it, and sell it at a profit. Mike Bergman, a Census Bureau spokesman, said, "The idea is to put this new system in place and allow people to do the sophisticated number-crunching themselves online." Bureau officials said their Web site (http://www.census.gov) is already among the most popular in the world. Don Wynegar, chief of marketing services at the bureau said, "Once we have the data up on our Web site, it will generate opportunities for middlemen to repackage the data and sell it. Millions of people who have access to the Internet will be able to dial us up. There will be numerous vendors looking for ways to use the materials. We're giving it away." (Sam Fulwood, "U.S. Counting on Web to Be Census Source Data: Bureau Plans to Post Most of Its 2000 Enumeration Data on the Internet," *Los Angeles Times*, Home Edition, November 15, 1998: 28)

National Archives Becomes Trove of Declassified World War II Documents

Recently declassified National Archives documents from the World War II era could provide a rich source of clues for researchers, historians, and politicians as to what happened to Jewish assets and bank accounts in the United States during and after the war. The creation of the U.S. Holocaust Assets Presidential Advisory Commission and the Clinton Administration's plans to declassify additional American intelligence records have added additional hope that bringing together scattered declassified documents that may lead to long-lost fortunes: plundered gold and assets of conquered countries and slain victims, as well as the unclaimed bank accounts, assets, and insurance policies of Nazi victims. (Desson Howe, "A Wealth of New Information

on Holocaust," *Washington Post*, November 18, 1998: B01)

EPA Decides to Withhold Disaster Information from the Internet

The 1990 Clean Air Act requires facilities that use large amounts of extremely hazardous substances to prepare Risk Management Plans (RMP), including worst-case accident scenarios. The Environmental Protection Agency, (EPA) which implements the law, has decided not to proceed with a plan to put the complete scenarios on the Internet. Intense pressure from Congress, law-enforcement agencies, and the chemical industry apparently caused the change in policy. EPA said that it had been eager to place the disaster scenarios on the Internet, but now it will post some basic information about chemicals at the plants, including which chemicals are being stored and used and emergency-response plans for those places. Some Members of Congress, the FBI, and the CIA opposed the plan, maintaining that broadly available disaster information could be used by terrorists. Environmental groups said the publicly accessible database would help Americans identify threats in their backyards, and that the more public information that is available about chemicals in neighborhoods, the more pressure there will be to reduce the use of these chemicals. (Seth Borenstein, "EPA Keeps Data on Disaster Scenarios Off Internet," *Philadelphia Inquirer*, November 19, 1998: A13)

Supreme Court Stops Case Because of Secrecy

On November 2 the Supreme Court declined to hear two cases brought by employees at a top-secret Air Force base near Groom Lake, Nevada. The plaintiffs, former workers and two widows of men who worked at the base, claim they were exposed to high levels of hazardous waste. A district court had dismissed the cases, finding that a trial would be impossible because of the Air Force's right to keep secret national security information. Among the secret information the Defense Department, the co-defendant with the Environmental Protection Agency, was allowed to withhold from the plaintiffs was whether hazardous materials were generated, stored or disposed of at the base known as Area 51. Both widows claimed that the death of their husbands was job-related. The case is *Stella Kasza et. al. vs. EPA et. al.*, 98-5405, U.S. Supreme Court, Nov. 2, 1998. (Christy Harris, "Secrecy Stops Widows' Claims," *Federal Times*, November 23, 1998: 4)

Controversy Could Lead to Less Accurate Census

Controversy continues to surround the method of counting the population to be used in the 2000 Census. Trying to correct an undercount of about 4 million people in the 1990 Census, Census Bureau officials have planned to use statistical sampling to reduce the disproportionate undercount of racial minorities in the 2000 Census. Some members of the Census Monitoring Board, a congressionally-appointed bipartisan board, have suggested the Census Bureau eliminate "scientific sampling" from the 2000 Census by using Medicaid, food stamp, driver's license and similar files. Resisting the suggestion, Census Bureau officials said that for years they have been testing the feasibility of gathering, matching and verifying data from federal, state and local agencies. They have found that some state officials fail to release needed records, and files they could use with special permission often were dated, error-riddled and incomplete for census use. Officials said relying extensively on administrative records would raise costs and take more time than the agency now has.

For various reasons some Members of Congress and others oppose sampling, which the Census Bureau says would be more accurate and less costly than the traditional methods. Additionally, sampling twice has been ruled illegal. These rulings have been appealed and the Supreme Court heard arguments on sampling's legality on November 30. Justices are expected to rule on the issues by July 1999. The cases are *Department of Commerce vs. House of Representatives*, No. 98-404, and *Clinton vs. Glavin*, No. 98-564. (August Gribbin, "Census officials see problems with suggestion to use files," *Washington Times*, November 24, 1998: A4)

Annual Report on Declassification Identifies Lingering Problems

At the end of August, the Information Security Office released its annual report for Fiscal Year 1997 concerning its implementation of Executive Order 12958 on national security policy and declassification of government records. Although positive trends were highlighted, it also identified lingering problems.

The report said start-up and compliance among the major classifying agencies has been uneven. Additionally, the rate of declassification at several agencies is lagging because of an apparent unwillingness to alter an extremely cautious approach to declassification. Several agencies will not declassify any information that has not undergone a line-by-line review by several reviewers, notwithstanding the age of the documents or their subject matter. Resource limitations are having a clear impact on agency compliance and oversight. In some instances, declassification activity has been so prolific that it exceeds the ability of agency systems and resources to process the records for public access, or even the ability to advise other agencies and the public about what information has been declassified. The "Information Security Oversight Office: 1997 Report to the President" is available at the Web site of the Federation of American Scientists at http://www.fas.org/sgp/isoo/isoo97.html (Page Putnam Miller, *NCC Washington Update*, Vol. 4, No. 46, December 1, 1998)

Nixon Papers Controversy Continues in New Trail

A long-delayed trial to determine the "just compensation" due to former President Nixon's estate opened in a federal court. The Nixon lawyers say that the former president's White House tapes and papers have a "fair market value" of up to $213 million dollars. Government lawyers sought to show that Nixon never intended to sell them and could not have done so without years of laborious processing. A Nixon attorney said that Congress abrogated an agreement to donate his records to the National Archives when Congress passed a law in 1974 confiscating Nixon's records and thwarting his hopes of having them housed in a traditional presidential library. Congress acted to prevent Nixon from destroying his tapes and to provide the public "with the full truth" about the abuses of power that forced him from office. (George Lardner, "Nixon Agreement on Donating Papers Cited," *Washington Post*, December 4, 1998: A10)

Federal Agency Holds Secret Information about Princess Diana

In the process of denying a Freedom of Information Act request, the National Security Agency (NSA) revealed that it had a 1,056-page file on the late Princess Diana. An NSA spokesperson said that the documents had been classified top secret "because their disclosure could reasonably be expected to cause exceptionally grave damage to the national security."

The super-secret spy agency was involved in an additional controversy in Europe. Last January a report released by the European Parliament concluded, "within Europe, all e-mail, telephone, and fax communications are routinely intercepted by the United States National Security Agency." The report focused on a system called ECHELON through which NSA and its spy partners in Britain, Canada, New Zealand, and Australia share communications intercepted worldwide and divide the huge task of analyzing the "take." "Each of the five [countries] supply 'dictionaries' to the other four of key words, phrases, people and places to 'tag,' and the tagged intercept is forwarded straight to the requesting country," according to the report.

Steven Aftergood, of the Federation of American Scientists, said he could not understand why the ECHELON controversy has gone unnoticed in the United States. He acknowledged that the lack of interest might result from the fact that law prohibits NSA from targeting American citizens for communications intercepts, here or abroad. (Vernon Loeb, "NSA Admits to Holding Secret Information On Princess Diana," *Washington Post*, December 12, 1998: A13)

Democrats and Republicans Clash over FBI Documents

Democratic Members of Congress have accused Republican Judiciary Committee members of trying to increase support for President Clinton's impeachment based on unproven and "misleading" information. The materials at issue are sealed FBI documents containing unsubstantiated allegations about the president that were not included in the public material accompanying Independent Counsel Kenneth Starr's report to Congress.

Democrats on the House Judiciary Committee were furious over the inspections of the sealed documents. They accused Republicans of circulating unfounded rumors about the president and of failing to tell Democrats that the sealed documents were available in an area for "secured" information in the Gerald R. Ford congressional building. Jim Jordan, spokesman for the Committee's Democrats, said, "The material was withheld of the committee...because it's unsubstantiated, ambiguous, and misleading."

Sam Stratman, spokesman for Committee Chair Henry Hyde (R-IL), said the inspections to the sealed documents were proper. He added that when the House formally created its impeachment inquiry in October, it granted every member access to all the documents accumulated by Starr, including those not made public. (Amy Goldstein and Juliet Eilperin, "Democrats, GOP Clash over FBI Documents," *Washington Post*, December 19, 1998: A36)

CIA Fights Release of Budget Information

A *Washington Post* editorial criticized the Central Intelligence Agency (CIA) for actively opposing a lawsuit requesting the CIA's intelligence budget request for 1999. The editorial encouraged the CIA to reconsider its position, arguing that "the government's unwillingness to disclose the budget request smacks of reflexive government secrecy and of an unreadiness of the agency to subject itself to the most rudimentary public accountability."

In 1997 and 1998 the CIA did release aggregated intelligence budget information in response to a Freedom of Information Act lawsuit by the Federation of American Scientists. In 1996 the bipartisan Commission on the Roles and Capabilities of the United States Intelligence Community recommended that the disclosure of both budget requests and appropriations every year could be done "in a manner that does not raise a significant security concern."

CIA Director George J. Tenet filed a statement opposing this latest lawsuit, stating that disclosure of the 1999 figures, along with previously disclosed figures for 1997 and 1998, "provides a measure of the administration's unique critical assessment of its own intelligence programs." Tenet also argued that release of such budget information "reasonably could be expected to cause damage to the national security and would tend to reveal intelligence sources and methods." ("A CIA Secret," *Washington Post*, December 28, 1998: A24)

APPENDIX D

Project Censored's Alternative Media/Activist Resource Guide

Project Censored is pleased to announce that the 1999 resource guide has grown so extensively that it is being published as a separate volume, *The Progressive Guide to Alternative Media and Activism*, now also available from Seven Stories Press. The complete guide includes much not included here: a lengthy section of alternative weeklies, regional activist groups, entries from Canada, and dozens more of the listings that make the guide an invaluable resource both for journalists looking for outlets, and for activists seeking to reach out to affinity groups. The abbreviated version of the guide presented here has been edited down to two sections: 1) nationally distributed alternative print or Internet publications, 2) and news services and activist organizations. Our goal is to maintain an up-to-date listing of progressive/alternative media in support of building a stronger alternative media information system in the United States. Information on omissions and errors should be sent to Project Censored's e-mail address: censored@sonoma.edu.

or by mail to:
Project Censored's Resource Guide Team
Sonoma State University
1801 East Cotati Avenue
Rohnert Park, CA 94928

NATIONAL ALTERNATIVE PUBLICATIONS

ABOUT...TIME MAGAZINE
283 Genesee Street
Rochester, NY 14611
(716) 235-7150

This monthly focuses on issues of international, national and regional importance reflecting the African-American experience.

ADBUSTERS: A MAGAZINE OF MEDIA AND ENVIRONMENTAL STRATEGIES
1243 West Seventh Avenue
Vancouver, British Columbia
V6H 1B7 Canada
(604) 736-9401 Fax (604) 737-6021
adbusters@adbusters.org
adbusters.org/adbusters/

Strategies for fighting mind pollution from advertising.

ADVOCATE, THE
6922 Hollywood Boulevard, Suite 1000
Los Angeles, CA 90028
(213) 871-1225 Fax (213) 467-6805
newsroom@advocate.com
www.advocate.com

Leading national gay and lesbian news magazine.

AFSCME LEADER
1625 L Street, NW
Washington, DC 20036-5687
(202) 429-1144 Fax (202) 429-1084
www.afscme.org

Activist newsletter of the American Federation of State, County, and Municipal Employees.

AGAINST THE CURRENT
7012 Michigan Avenue
Detroit, MI 48210
(313) 841-0161 Fax (313) 841-8884
efc@igc.apc.org
www.igc.apc.org/solidarity

Promoting dialogue among activists, organizers, and serious scholars of the left, from the general perspective of "socialism from below."

AKWESASNE NOTES
P.O. Box 196
Rooseveltown, NY 13683-0196
(518) 358-9531
notes@glen-net.ca

News of Mohawk and other indigenous peoples.

ALBION MONITOR
P.O. Box 1733
Sebastopol, CA 95473
(707) 823-0100
editor@monitor.net
www.monitor.net/monitor

Primarily covering environmental News and human rights and politics. Syndicated and other copyrighted material available to subscribers only.

ALLIANCE FOR COMMUNITY MEDIA
666 11th Street, NW, Suite 806
Washington, DC 20001-45429
(202) 393-2650 Fax: (202) 393-2653
acm@alliancecm.org
www.alliancecm.org

Journal covering topics such as: legal, community, censorship, technical, professional, advocacy—for cable access, Internet, and electronic media.

ALTERNATIVE PRESS INDEX
P.O. Box 33109
Baltimore, MD 21218-0401
(410) 243-2471 Fax (410) 235-5325
altpress@igc.apc.org
www.altpress.org/

Includes coverage of practices and theories of socialism, labor, feminism, ecology, anarchism, anti-racism—print and electronic available.

ALTERNATIVE PRESS REVIEW
P.O. Box 1446
Columbia, MO 65205-1446
(573) 442-4352
jmcquinn@mail.coin.missouri.edu

Promoting and supporting alternative, liberating media.

ALTERNATIVES
1800 30th St., Suite 314
Boulder, CO 80301-1032
(303) 444-6684 Fax (303) 444-0824
peacock@rienner.com
www.rienner.com

Alternative views in international relations, politics, and Third World study.

ALTERNATIVES
1718 M Street, NW, #245
Washington, DC 20036
(202) 588-9888 Fax (202) 588-1818
NLGJA@aol.com
www.nlgja.org

News and reports from the National Gay and Lesbian Journalists Association.

AMERICAN EDITOR, THE
11690 B Sunrise Valley Drive
Reston, VA 20191-1409
(703) 453-1122 Fax (703) 453-1133
asne@asne.org
www.asne.org

Discusses topics related to the current state and future of newspapers and journalism in this country.

AMERICAN JOURNALISM REVIEW
8701 Adelphi Road
Adelphi, MD 20783
(301) 405-8803 Fax (301)405-8323
editor@ajr.umd.edu
www.ajr.org

This review and reports on American journalism and provides information for professional journalists.

AMERICAN PROSPECT
P.O. Box 383080
Cambridge, MA 02238
(617) 547-2950 Fax (617) 547-3896
prospect@epn.org
epn.org/prospect.html

A bi-monthly publication covering areas of concern such as political, social, and cultural issues.

AMERICAN WRITER
113 University Place, 6th floor
New York, NY 10003
(212) 254-0279 Fax (212) 254-0673
nwu@nwu.org
www.nwu.org/nwu

Tracks developments in the media/ information industry and the labor movement that concern working writers and reports on union activities.

AMICUS JOURNAL
40 West 20th Street
New York, NY 10011
(212) 727-2700 Fax (212) 727-1773
amicus@nrdc.org
www.nrdc.org/eamicus/back/maga.html

Focuses on thought and opinion on
environmental affairs.

ANTIPODE
238 Main Street
Cambridge, MA 02142
(800) 835-6770 Fax (617) 547-0789
www.staff.uiuc.edu/~dwilson2/antipod.
html

Marxist, socialist, anarchist, anti-racist,
and feminist analysis of environmental
and geographical issues.

ARAB AMERICAN NEWS
5461 Schaefer Road
Dearborn, MI 48121
(313) 582-4888 Fax (313) 582-7870
osama@visitus.net
www.arabameriannews.com

The *Arab American News* is a
nationally circulated, bilingual weekly
newspaper serving the nation's three
million Arab Americans.

ARMS SALES MONITOR
307 Massachusetts Avenue, NE
Washington, DC 20002
(202) 675-1018 Fax (202) 675-1010
llumpe@fas.org
www.fas.org/asmp/

Highlights U.S. government policies on
arms exports and conventional weapons
proliferation.

ASIANWEEK
809 Sacramento Street
San Francisco, CA 94108
(415) 397-0220 Fax (415) 397-7258

A nationally circulated publication
with a "community" focus, covering
news of Asian Americans.

BEAT WITHIN, THE
450 Mission Street, #204
San Francisco, CA 94105
(415) 243-4364
www.pacificnews.org/yo/beat/

A weekly newsletter of writing and art
by incarcerated youth.

BEYOND TV
2311 Kimball Street
Silver Springs, MD 20910
(301) 588-4001 (301) 588-4001
apluhar@tvp.org
www.tvp.org

Quarterly newsletter aimed at empow-
ering parents to use television wisely.

BIRACIAL CHILD
2870 Peachtree Road
P.O. Box 12048
Atlanta, GA 30305
(404) 350-7877 Fax (404) 350-0819

A quarterly geared toward parents of
biracial children and the broad
subjects and issues that these
children face.

BLACK CHILD
P.O. Box 12048
Atlanta, GA 30355
(404) 350-7877 Fax (404) 350-0819

A bi-monthly geared toward African American parents and the broad subjects and issues that black parents face.

BLACK ISSUES IN
HIGHER EDUCATION
10520 Warwick Avenue, Suite B-8
Fairfax, VA 22030-3136
(703) 385-2981 Fax (703) 385-1839

Bi-weekly—the nation's only news magazine dedicated exclusively to minority issues in higher education.

BLACK MASKS
P.O. Box 2
Bronx, NY 10471
(212) 304-8900 Fax (212) 304-8900

One of the most extensive bi-monthly publications devoted to the Black performing and visual arts in the United States.

BLACK RENAISSANCE/
RENAISSANCE NOIRE
601 North Morton Street
Bloomington, IN 47404
(800) 842-6796 Fax (812) 855-8507

Essays, fiction, reviews, and art work that address the full range of contemporary Black concerns.

BLACK SCHOLAR
P.O. Box 2869
Oakland, CA 94618-0069
(510) 547-6633 Fax (510) 547-6679
blkschlr@aol.com

An independent intellectual journal of the African-American experience.

BLK
P.O. Box 83912
Los Angeles, CA 90083-0912
(310) 410-0808 Fax (310) 410-9250
newsroom@blk.com
www.blk.com

News magazine for black, lesbian, and gay community.

BODY POLITIC, THE
P.O. Box 2363
Binghamton, NY 13902
(607) 648-2760 Fax (607) 648-2511
annebower@delphi.com
www.bodypolitic.org/

A national abortion and health care rights news service.

BOSTON REVIEW
E53-407, MIT
Cambridge, MA 02139
(617) 253-3642 Fax (617) 252-1549
bostonreview@mit.edu
www.bookwire.com/bbr-home.html

Combines commitments to public reason with literary imagination.

BOYCOTT QUARTERLY
P.O. Box 30727
Seattle, WA 98103-0727
boycottguy@aol.com

Comprehensive coverage of boycotts across the political spectrum and around the world.

BRAZZIL
2039 North Avenue
Los Angeles, CA 90042-1024
(213) 255-8062 Fax (213) 257-3487
brazzil@brazzil.com
www.brazzil.com

In-depth articles deal with politics, economy, behavior, ecology, tourism, literature, arts, and culture in general.

BREAKTHROUGH
P.O. Box 1442
San Francisco, CA 94114

A magazine of international and domestic politics and activism.

BRIARPATCH
2138 McIntyre Street
Regine SK S4P 2R7
Canada
(316) 525-2949 Fax (306) 565-3430

Alternative view on issues, events and Aboriginal and women's rights.

BRILL'S CONTENT
521 5th Avenue, 11th Floor
New York, NY 10175
(800) 829-9154 or (212) 824-1900
Fax (904) 445-2728
www.brillscontent.com

A monthly magazine based on the idea that consumers of news and information in this Information Age should know how what they watch, read, or log on to is produced and how much they can rely on it.

BROADCASTING AND
CABLE MAGAZINE
1705 DeSales Street, NW, Suite 600
Washington, DC 20036
(202) 659-2340 Fax (202) 429-0651
www.broadcastingcable.com

A newsweekly on broadcasting and cable issues.

BROKEN PENCIL
P.O. Box 203, Station P
Toronto, ON M5S 2S7
Canada
(416) 340-0878 Fax (416) 340-0878
halpen@interlog.com
http://www.interlog.com/~halpen/

Reprints of the best of the underground press and original features.

BULLETIN OF CONCERNED
ASIAN SCHOLARS
1515 Webster Street, # 305
Oakland, CA 94612
(510) 451-1742 Fax (510) 835-9631
tfenton@igc.org
csf.colorado.edu/bcas/

Challenging accepted formulas for understanding Asia, the world, and ourselves.

BULLETIN OF THE
ATOMIC SCIENTISTS
6042 South Kimbark Avenue
Chicago, IL 60637
(773) 702-2555 Fax (773) 702-0725
bullatomsci@igc.apc.org
www.bullatomsci.org

Covers international security, military affairs, nuclear issues.

BULLETIN, THE
2642 College Avenue
Berkeley, CA 94704
(510) 540-0749 Fax (510) 849-1247
pbiusa@igc.apc.org
www.igc.org/pbi/index/html.

Provides in-depth information on a monthly basis to subscribers with more extensive knowledge about the regions in which PBI works.

BUSINESS ETHICS
2845 Harriet Avenue, #207
P.O. Box 8439
Minneapolis, MN 55408
(612) 879-0695 Fax (612) 879-0699
BizEthics@aol.com
condor.depaul.edu/ethics/bizethics.html

The mission of BE is to promote
ethical business practices.

CALIFORNIA PRISON FOCUS
2489 Mission Street, #28
San Francisco, CA 94110
(415) 452-3359
coreman@igc.org
www.igc.org/justice.cpf

A newsletter that spreads information
about control unit prisons, conditions
in California, and provides a voice for
the prisoners.

CALIFORNIA PRISONER, THE
P.O. Box 1019
Sacramento, CA 95812-1019
(916) 441-4214 Fax (916) 441-4297

Newspaper of the Prisoner's Rights
Union, committed to restoring
fundamental civil rights to prisoners
and their families.

CALYPSO LOG
870 Greenbrier Circle, Suite 402
Chesapeake, VA 23320
(757) 523-9335 Fax (757) 523-2747
cousteau@infi.net
www.cousteau.org

Focused on protection and
improvement of the quality of life
for future generations.

CAPITAL EYE
1320 19 Street, NW, #620
Washington, DC 20036
(202) 857-0044 Fax (202) 857-7809
info@crp.org
www.crp.org

Covers money-in-politics at the federal,
state, and local levels.

COVERTACTION QUARTERLY
(CAQ)
1500 Massachusetts Avenue,
NW, #732
Washington, DC 20005
(202) 331-9763 Fax (202) 331-9751
caq@igc.org
www.caq.com

Investigative journalism exposing
malfeasance and covert activities in
government, corporations, and other
areas affecting the public.

CENSORSHIP NEWS
275 7th Avenue, 20th Floor
New York, NY 10001
(212) 807-6222 Fax (212) 807-6245
ncac@ncac.org
www.ncac.com

Contains information and discussion
about freedom of expression issues.

CHILD OF COLORS
2870 Peachtree Road
P.O. Box 12048
Atlanta, GA 30305
(404) 350-7877 Fax (404) 350-0819

Quarterly magazine dealing with issues
facing and of concern to parents and
children of color.

CHRISTIAN SCIENCE MONITOR
1 Norway Street
Boston, MA 02115-3195
(617) 450-2000
orders@csmonitor.com
www.csmonitor.com

An 87-year-old daily newspaper
covering national and international
news.

CHRONICLE OF
HIGHER EDUCATION, THE
1255 23rd Street, NW
Washington, DC 20037
(202) 466-1000 Fax (202) 296-2691
editor@chronicle.com
www.chronicle.com

The number one news source for
college and university faculty.

CHRONICLE OF
PHILANTHROPY, THE
1255 23rd Street, NW, 7th Floor
Washington, DC 20037
(202) 466-1200 Fax (202) 466-2078
editor@philanthropy.com
www.philanthropy.com

Published bi-monthly, this newspaper
of the non-profit world is the number
one news source for charity leaders and
fund raisers.

CIVIL LIBERTIES
125 Broad Street
New York, NY 10004
(212) 549-2500 Fax (212) 549-2646
www.aclu.org

Issues of civil liberties including
online information on Internet free
speech issues.

COLORLINES
4096 Piedmont Avenue #319
Oakland, CA 94611
(510) 465-9577 Fax (510) 465-4824
colorlines@arc.org
www.arc.org

A magazine which focuses on race,
culture, and organizing within
communities of color.

COLUMBIA JOURNALISM REVIEW
700 Journalism Building
New York, NY 10027
(212) 854-1881 Fax (212) 854-8580
www.cjr.org

Assesses the performance of
journalism and stimulating continuing
improvements in the profession.

COMMUNITIES MAGAZINE
P.O. Box 169
Masonville, CO 80541
(970) 593-5615 Fax (970) 593-5615
communities@igc.org
www.ic.org

Focus on "intentional communities,"
including ecovillages, co-housing,
urban housing cooperatives, shared
living and other projects.

COMMUNITY MEDIA REVIEW
666 11th Street, NW, Suite 806
Washington, DC 20001
(202) 393-2650 Fax (202) 393-2653
AllianceCM@aol.com
www.thesphere.com/ACTV/acm.html

A newsletter reporting on political and
regulatory issues in the media; reports
on emerging information systems.

COMPARATIVE STUDIES:
SOUTH AFRICA, ASIA, &
THE MIDDLE EAST
P.O. Box 90660
Durham, NC 90660
(919) 687-3614
Ki.acupub.duke.edu
www.duke.edu/web/dupress

Comparative studies of South Asia,
Africa, and the Middle East.

CONGRESSIONAL QUARTERLY
WEEKLY REPORT
1414 22nd Street, NW
Washington, DC 20037
(202) 887-8500 Fax (202) 728-1863
voter96.cqalert.com

A world-class provider of information on
government, politics, and public policy.

CONSCIOUS CHOICE
920 North Franklin Street, Suite 202
Chicago, IL 60610-3119
(312) 440-4373 Fax (312) 751-3973
cc@consciouschoice.com or aliess@
consciouschoice.com
www.consciouschoice.com

Promotes sustainable patterns of
living, environmental issues and
natural alternatives, natural health,
living and vegetarian nutrition.

CONSUMER REPORTS
101 Truman Avenue
Yonkers, NY 10703-1057
(914) 378-2000 Fax (914) 378-2992
www.consumerreports.org

Consumer's Union is a non-profit
organization that has been testing
products on behalf of consumers for
more than 60 years.

CO-OP AMERICA QUARTERLY
1612 K Street, NW, Suite 600
Washington, DC 20006
(800) 58-GREEN or (202) 872-5307
Fax (202) 331-8166
info@coopamerica.org
www.coopamerica.org

Teaches consumers how to use their
spending power to support socially
and environmentally responsible
businesses and promote social
and economic justice.

CORPORATE CRIME REPORTER
1209 National Press Building
Washington, DC 20045
(202) 737-1680

Legal weekly covering issues of
corporate and white-collar crime.

COUNTER MEDIA
1573 North Milwaukee Avenue, #517
Chicago, IL 60622
(312) 243-8342
lquilter@igc.apa.org
www.cs.uchicago.edu/cpsr/
countermedia/

Covers protests, actions, and issues
ignored by conventional media sources.

COUNTERPOISE
1716 Williston Road
Gainesville, FL 32608
(352) 335-2200
willett@gnv.fdt.net
www.jessamyn.com/srrt/aip/
counterpoise.html

Sponsored by the Alternatives in
Print Task Force of the Social
Responsibilities Round Table of the
American Library Association.

COUNTERPUNCH
P.O. Box 18675
Washington, DC 20036
(202) 986-3665 Fax (202) 986-0974
counterpunch@erols.com
www.newsun.com/counter.html

DC-based investigative newsletter on power and evil in Washington.

CRONE CHRONICLES: A JOURNAL OF CONSCIOUS AGING
Box 81
Kelly, WY 83011
(307) 733-8639
www.feminist.com/crone.html

A grassroots publication written by and for honest, outrageous, and wise older women who are challenging stereotypes by living authentically.

CUBA UPDATE
124 West 23rd Street
New York, NY 10011
(212) 242-0559 Fax (212) 242-1937
cubanctr@igc.apc.org
www.eden.com/fineprint/40289.html

Cuba Update provides accurate, accessible news coverage and discussion of important issues almost impossible to find elsewhere.

CULTURAL ENVIRONMENT MONITOR, THE
3508 Market Street, Suite 30-030
Philadelphia, PA 19104
(215) 204-6434 Fax (215) 387-1560
cem@libertynet.org
www.cemnet.org

A publication which covers the activities of members and affiliates of CEM and prints articles on related topics.

CULTURAL SURVIVAL QUARTERLY
96 Mt. Auburn Street
Cambridge, MA 02138
(617) 441-5400 Fax (617) 441-5417
csinc@cs.org
www.cs.org/csq/csq.html

World report on the rights of indigenous peoples and ethnic minorities.

CULTURE WATCH
1904 Franklin Street, Suite 900
Oakland, CA 94612
(510) 835-4692 Fax (510) 835-3017
masildatactr@tmn.com
www.egc.org/culturewatch/

Monthly newsletter which tracks and monitors the political and social agenda of the religious right.

DARK NIGHT FIELD NOTES
P.O. Box 3629
Chicago, IL 60690-3629
(773) 373-7074 Fax (773) 373-7188

A quarterly publication covering issues related to the recognition and liberation of indigenous peoples.

DAYBREAK
P.O. Box 315
Williamsville, NY 14231-0315
(716) 645-2548 Fax (716) 645-5977

Forum of information sharing around issues which impact indigenous peoples worldwide.

DEFENSE MONITOR
1779 Massachusetts Avenue, Suite 615
Washington, DC 20036
(202) 332-0600 Fax (202) 462-4559
info@cdi.org
www.cdi.org

Opposes policies that increase the
danger of war.

DEMOCRATIC LEFT
180 Varick Street, 12th Floor
New York, NY 10014
(212) 727-8610 Fax (212) 727-8616
dsa@dsausa.org
www.dsausa.org/index.html

A quarterly review of socialist issues
and activities.

DE TODO UN POCO
2830 5th Street
Boulder, CO 80304
(303) 444-8565 Fax (303) 545-2074
tmoore@igc.apc.org

Issues in Central America, Mexico,
the Caribbean, and U.S. influence in
the region.

DIOXIN DIGEST
150 South Washington Street #300
Falls Church, VA 22040-6806
(703) 237-2249 Fax (703) 237-8389
cchw@essential.org
www.essential.org/cchw&sustain.org/
hcwh

A free publication providing
information on dioxin and other
chemical toxins.

DISSENT
521 Fifth Avenue, Suite 1700
New York, NY 10017
(212) 595-3084 Fax (212) 595-3084
dissent@igc.org
www.igc.org/dissent

Quarterly democratic socialist and
left-liberal argument.

DOLLARS AND SENSE:
WHAT'S LEFT IN ECONOMICS
1 Summer Street
Somerville, MA 02143
(617) 628-8411 Fax (617) 628-2025
dollars@igc.epc.org
www.igc.org/dollars

Reports on issues of social justice and
economic policy.

DOMES
P.O. Box 413
Milwaukee, WI 53201
(414) 229-4707 Fax (414) 229-4848

Quarterly provides for a balance of
views on the Middle East.

DOUBLETAKE
1317 West Pettigrew Street
Durham, NC 27705
(919) 660-3669 Fax (919) 660-3688
dtmag@aol.com
www.duke.edu/doubletake/

Publishes work in the documentary
tradition including fiction, non-fiction,
reportage, poetry, and photography.

E: THE ENVIRONMENTAL
MAGAZINE
P.O. Box 5098
Westport, CT 06881
(203) 854-5559 Fax (203) 866-0602
Emagazine@prodigy.net
emagazine.com

Independent national environmental
magazine.

EARTH FIRST! JOURNAL
P.O. Box 1415
Eugene, OR 97440
(541) 344-8004 Fax (541) 344-7688
earthfirst@igc.apc.org
www.envirolink.org

Reports on the radical environmental
movement and hard-to-find information
about strategies to stop the destruction
of the planet.

EARTH ISLAND JOURNAL
300 Broadway, Suite 28
San Francisco, CA 94133-3312
(415) 788-3666 Fax (415) 788-7324
journal@earthisland.org
earthisland.org/ei/

International environmental news
magazine focusing on socio-economic,
political issues affecting Earth's
ecosystems.

ECOLOGIST, THE
55 Hayward Street
Cambridge, MA 02142
(617) 253-2889 Fax (617) 258-6779
ecologist@gn.apc.org
gold.net/ecosystem/ecol.htm

Covers ecological issues and supports
small-scale agriculture and
democratized political power.

EEO BIMONTHLY
1800 Sherman Place, Suite 300
Evanston, IL 60201-3769
(847) 475-8800 Fax (847) 475-8807

National Equal Employment
Opportunity Career Journal, addresses
the career development needs of
today's diverse professional multi-
ethnic work force.

EL INFORMADOR HISPANO
2229 N. Main Street
Fort Worth, TX 76106
(817) 626-8624 Fax (817) 626-8635

Promotes professional development of
the Latino media in the United States.

EL MUNDO
630 20th Street
Oakland, CA 94612
(510)763-1120 Fax (510) 763-9670

A national Spanish language
publication.

EL SALVADOR WATCH
19 West 21st Street, Room 502
New York, NY 10010
(212) 229-1290 Fax (212) 645-7280
cispesnatl@igc.org
www.cispes.org

A grassroots organization dedicated to
supporting the Salvadoran people's
struggle for self-determination and
social and economic justice.

EL PREGONERO
5001 Eastern Avenue
Hyattsville, MD 20782
(301) 853-4504 Fax (301) 853-3349

Hispanic tabloid newspaper.

EMERGE: BLACK AMERICA'S
NEWS MAGAZINE
One B.E.T. Plaza
1900 West Place, NE
Washington, DC 20018
(202) 608-2093 Fax (202) 608-2598
emergmag@compuserv.com
emerg@aol.com or emergmag.com or
emergmag@aol.com

News analysis and commentary from
the African-American perspective.

ENVIRONMENTAL HEALTH
MONTHLY
150 South Washington Street #300
Falls Church, VA 22040
(703) 237-2249 Fax (703) 237-8389
cchw@essential.org
essential.org/cchw & sustain.org/hcwh

A monthly digest of reprinted
environmental, medical, and scientific
articles on a particular topic.

ETHIOPIAN REVIEW
8715 Ramsgate Avenue
Los Angeles, CA 90045
(404) 325-8411 Fax (404) 325-8411

Directed toward those of African-
American/Caribbean/African ethnicity.

EVERYBODY'S: THE CARIBBEAN-
AMERICAN MAGAZINE
1630 Nostrand Avenue
Brooklyn, NY 11226
(718) 941-1879 Fax (718) 941-1886

A general interest Caribbean/American
monthly magazine.

EVERYONE'S BACKYARD
P.O. Box 6806
Falls Church, VA 22040-6806
(703) 237-2249 Fax (703) 237-8389
cchw@essential.org
essential.org/cchw

The Journal of the Grassroots
Movement for Environmental Justice.

EXTRA!
130 West 25th Street
New York, NY 10001
(212) 633-6700 Fax (212) 727-7668
info@fair.org
www.fair.org

Provides media criticism featuring
articles on biased reporting, censored
news, media mergers, and more.

FACTNET NEWSLETTER
P.O. Box 3135
Boulder, CO 80307-3135
factnet@factnet.org
www.factnet.org

Protecting freedom of mind by exposing
cults and mind control.

FACTSHEET 5
P.O. Box 170099
San Francisco, CA 94117-0099
(415) 668-1781
seth@factsheet5.com
factsheet.5.com

Guide to the 'zine revolution; resources
and reviews of thousands of underground publications.

FAT!SO?
P.O. Box 423464
San Francisco, CA 94142-3464
(800) OHFATSO
marilyn@fatso.com
www.fatso.com

For people who don't apologize for their size.

FELLOWSHIP MAGAZINE
P.O. Box 271
521 North Broadway
Nyack, NY 10960
(914) 358-4601 Fax (914) 358-4924
fellowship@igc.org
www.nonviolence.org/for/fellowship

Seeks to replace violence, war, racism, and economic injustice with nonviolence, peace, and justice.

FEMINIST MAJORITY REPORT
1600 Wilson Boulevard #801
Arlington, VA 22209
(703) 522-2214
www.feminist.org

News and reports on politics, culture, women's health, reproductive rights, events, career opportunities, and the multi-dimensional nature of feminism.

FIFTH ESTATE
4632 Second Avenue
Detroit, MI 48201
(313) 831-6800

Longest-running English-language anarchist publication in U.S.

FILIPINAS MAGAZINE
655 Sutter Street, Suite 333
San Francisco, CA 94102
(415) 563-5878 Fax (415) 292-5993

Covers Filipino-American interests and affairs.

FILIPINO EXPRESS, THE
2711 Kennedy Boulevard
Jersey City, NJ 07306
(201) 333-5709 Fax (201) 434-0880

Weekly—targeting Asian/Pacific Islanders.

FILIPINO REPORTER
350 5th Avenue,
Suite 610 Empire State Bldg.
New York, NY 10018
(212) 967-5784 Fax (212) 967-5848

English-language weekly of particular interest to Asian/Pacific Islanders.

FIRE INSIDE, THE
100 McAllister Street
San Francisco, CA 94102
(415) 255-7036 ext. 4
Fax (415) 552-3150
ccwp@igc.org
www.prisonactivist.org/ccwp

A quarterly newsletter covering issues related to incarcerated women.

FIRST THINGS: A JOURNAL OF RELIGION AND PUBLIC LIFE
156 5th Avenue, Suite 400
New York, NY 10010

Dedicated to advancing a religiously-informed public philosophy for the ordering of society.

FOOD FIRST NEWS
398 60th Street
Oakland, CA 94618
(510) 654-4400 Fax (510) 654-4400
foodfirst@igc.apc.org

www.foodfirst.org
An information and reader action guide for ending world hunger and poverty.

FOOD NOT BOMBS MENU
3145 Geary Boulevard #12
San Francisco, CA 94118
(800) 884-1136
foodnotbombs@earthlink.net
www.eci.com/dave/fnb.html

The menu reprints flyers, letters, and news reports about Food Not Bombs, Homes Not Jails, the free radio movement, and other information about the direct action community.

FOOD & WATER JOURNAL
389 VT Route 215
Walden, VT 05873
(802) 563-3300 Fax (802) 563-3310

A quarterly magazine which advocates for safe food and water.

FORWARD
45 East 33rd Street
New York, NY 10016
(212) 889-8200 Fax (212) 447-6406

National/Weekly—Dedicated to social justice and helping generations of immigrant Jews enter American life.

FREE INQUIRY:
THE INTERNATIONAL SECULAR
HUMANIST MAGAZINE
P.O. Box 664
Amherst, NY 14226
(716) 636-7571 Fax (716) 636-1733
www.secularhumanism.org

A quarterly magazine which celebrates reason and humanity.

FRONTIERS NEWS MAGAZINE
P.O. Box 46367
West Hollywood, CA 90046
(213) 848-2222 Fax (213) 656-8784
webmaster@frontiersweb.com
www.frontiersweb.com

A comprehensive magazine for and about lesbian/gay issues and rights.

FUNDING EXCHANGE
666 Broadway #500
New York, NY 10012
(212) 529-5300
fexexc@aol.com

It works to increase funding for social issue media.

GENEWATCH
5 Upland Road, Suite 3
Cambridge, MA 02140
(617) 868-0870 Fax (617) 491-5344
crg@essential.org
www.essential.org/crg

A publication that provides information and opinions about the social and environmental aspects of genetic engineering.

GEO—GRASSROOTS
ECONOMIC ORGANIZING
83 Charles Lane
Storrs, CT 06268
(860) 429-6194
krimerm@uconnvm.edu

A bi-monthly newsletter dedicated to educating the public about how to organize effectively.

GLAADLINES

150 West 26th Street, Suite 503
New York, NY 10001
(212) 807-1700 Fax (212) 807-1806
glaad@glaad.org
www.glaad.org

An on-line resource for promoting
fair, accurate, and inclusive media
representation of lesbian, gay, bisexual,
and transgendered people.

GLOBAL PESTICIDE CAMPAIGNER

49 Powell Street, Suite 500
San Francisco, CA 94105
(415) 981-1771 Fax (415) 981-1991
panna@panna.org
www.panna.org/panna

Environmental, health, and other
information about pesticides, ecological
pest control, and sustainable
agriculture.

GOVERNMENT INFORMATION INSIDER

1742 Connecticut Avenue, NW
Washington, DC 20009
(202) 234-8494 Fax (202) 234-8584
ombwatch@rtk.net
www.ombwatch.org/ombwatch.html

A magazine which focuses on
government secrecy and the public's
right to know.

GRASSROOTS FUNDRAISING JOURNAL

P.O. Box 11607
Berkeley, CA 94712
(510) 704-8714 Fax (510) 649-7913
chardn@aol.com
www.chardonpress.com

Grassroots Fundraising Journal is a
how-to magazine providing information
on all aspects of fundraising for groups
working for social change.

GROUNDWORK TIDES CENTER

P.O. Box 14141
San Francisco, CA 94114
(415) 255-7623

Covers community organizing and
direct action on environmental and
social justice issues.

GUILD NOTES

126 University Place, 5th Floor
New York, NY 10003
(212) 627-2656 Fax (212) 627-2404
nlgno@nlg.org
www.nlg.org

A newsletter of the national lawyer's
guild.

HA!

P.O. Box 1282
Carrboro, NC 97510
gmonster@email.unc.edu
www.unc.edu/~cherylt

A 'zine which is a venue for women's
voices and self-expression.

HEALTH QUEST: THE PUBLICATION OF BLACK WELLNESS

200 Highpoint Drive, Suite 215
Chalfont, PA 18914
(215) 822-7935 Fax (215) 997-9582

Focuses specifically on health and
wellness in the African-American
community.

HEART & SOUL
33 East Minor Street
Emmaus, PA 18098
(610) 967-5171

National/Bi-Monthly—Addresses total
well-being of body, mind, and spirit for
African-American women.

HIGH COUNTRY NEWS
P.O. Box 1090
Paonia, CO 81428
(970) 527-4898 Fax (970) 527-4897
editor@hcn.org
www.hcn.org

Bi-weekly tabloid covering natural
resource and community change issues
in the western United States.

HIGH GRADER MAGAZINE
P.O. Box 714
Colbalt, ON P0J 1C0
Canada
(705) 679-5533 Fax (705) 679-5033

News reporting and offbeat cultural
comments from a working-class
perspective.

HIGHTOWER LOWDOWN, THE
P.O. Box 20065
New York, NY 10011
(212) 741-2365 Fax (212) 979-2055
spectator@newslet.com

A twice-monthly populist newsletter
featuring Jim Hightower.

HIP MAMA
P.O. Box 9097
Oakland, CA 94613
(800) 585-6262
hipmama@sirius.com
www.hipmama.com

A 'zine for progressive families covering
the culture and politics of parenting.

HISPANIC ENGINEER
729 East Pratt Street, Suite 504
Baltimore, MD 21202
(410) 244-7101 Fax (410) 752-1837

This quarterly is dedicated to promotion opportunities for Hispanic
Americans in science and technology.

HUMAN RIGHTS TRIBUNE
8 York Street, Suite 302
Ottawa, Ontario K1N 5S6
Canada
(613) 789-7407 Fax (613) 789-7414
hri@hri.ca
www.hri.ca

Web site has links to human rights,
web sites worldwide, job postings
from human rights organizations,
databases, etc.

HUNGRY MIND REVIEW
1648 Grand Avenue
St. Paul, MN 55105
(612) 699-2610 Fax (612) 699-0970
hmreview@winternet.com
www.bookwire.com/hmr

A quarterly book review magazine
geared toward the iconoclastic reader
who frequents independent bookstores.

I.F. MAGAZINE
2200 Wilson Boulevard, Suite 102-231
Arlington, VA 22201
(703) 920-1580 Fax (703) 920-0946
rparry@ix.retcom.com
www.delve.com/consort.html

I.F. Magazine is a bi-monthly
publication of investigative journalism.

IMAGES
150 West 26th Street, Suite 503
New York, NY 10001
(212) 807-1700 Fax (212) 807-1806
gladd@gladd.org
www.gladd.org

A quarterly publication focusing on
images and representations of gays,
lesbians, bisexuals, and transgender
people in the media.

IN THESE TIMES
2040 North Milwaukee Avenue,
2nd Floor
Chicago, IL 60647-4002
(773) 772-0100 Fax (773) 772-4180
itt@inthesetimes.com
www.inthesetimes.com

Provides independent news and views
you won't find anywhere else.

INDEPENDENT FILM &
VIDEO MONTHLY, THE
625 Broadway, 9th Floor
New York, NY 10012
(212) 807-1400 Fax (212) 463-8519
www.aivf.org

A monthly publication covering issues
and events related to independent films
and videos.

INDEPENDENT POLITIC NEWS
P.O. Box 170610
Brooklyn, NY 11217-0610
(718) 624-1807 Fax (718) 643-8265
indpol@igc.apc.org

Builds a unified, independent,
progressive alternative to the
corporate-controlled Democratic
Republican political and economic
system.

INDIA CURRENTS
P.O. Box 21285
San Jose, CA 95151
(408) 274-6966 Fax (408) 274-2733

Devoted to the exploration of the arts
and culture of India as it exists in the
United States.

INDIAN COUNTRY TODAY
(LAKOTA TIMES)
1920 Lombardy Drive
P.O. Box 2180
Rapid City, SD 57709
(605) 341-0011 Fax (605) 341-6940

Most influential and widely read Native
American newspaper in the United
States. (Also has a regional section
covering the Pine Ridge Reservation.)

INDUSTRIAL WORKER
103 West Michigan Avenue
Ypsilanti, MI 48197-5438
(734) 483-3548 Fax (734) 483-4050
ghq@iww.org
www.parsons.iww.org/~iw/
index_text.html

The Industrial Worker is the monthly
newspaper of the industrial workers of
the world, or Wobblies.

INFOACTIVE KIDS
1511 K Street, NW, Suite 518
Washington, DC 20005
(202) 628-2620 Fax (202) 628-2554
cme@cme.org
www.cme.org/cme

For the child advocacy, consumer,
health, and educational communities
as well as a resource for journalists
covering children and media topics.

INFUSION: TOOLS FOR ACTION
AND EDUCATION NEWSLETTER
P.O. Box 425748
Cambridge, MA 02142
(617) 725-2886
cco@igc.apc.org
www.cco.org

Provides news, analysis, action guides,
and organizing tips and resources for
progressive campus activists.

INSIGHT
3600 New York Avenue, NE
Washington, DC 20002
(202) 636-8810 Fax (202) 529-2484
76353.2113@compuserve.com
www.insightmag.com

Our focus is simple: Report news
others won't or can't. We follow the
story wherever the facts lead and
regardless of who's involved.

INTELLECTUAL FREEDOM
ACTION NEWS
50 E. Huron Street
Chicago, IL 60611
(800) 545-2433 ext. 4221
crobinson@ala.org
www.ala.org/alaorg/oif/ifan_pub.html

A monthly publication dedicated to
freedom of thought, freedom of the
written and spoken word, and freedom
of expression.

INTELLIGENCE REPORT
400 Washington Avenue
Montgomery, AL 36104
(334) 264-0286 Fax (334) 264-8891
www.splcenter.org/klanwatch.kw-
4.html

Reports on white supremacist
organizations and extreme
anti-government groups.

INTERNATIONAL EXAMINER
622 S. Washington Street
Seattle, WA 98104
(206) 624-3925 Fax (206) 624-3046

Published since 1974, the International
Examiner is the oldest English-
language Asian community newspaper.

INTERRACE
2870 Peachtree Road
P.O. Box 12048
Atlanta, GA 30305
(404) 350-7877 Fax (404) 350-0819

Provides information relating to issues
of relevance to interracial/ multiracial
people, couples, families and
transracial adoptive families.

IRE: INVESTIGATIVE REPORTERS
AND EDITORS
138 Neff Annex
Columbia, MO 65211
(573) 882-2042 Fax (573) 884-5544
www.ire.org

IRE's goal is to assist other investigative reporters in their pursuit of stories.

ISSUES IN SCIENCE AND
TECHNOLOGY
1636 Hobart Street, NW
Washington, DC 20009
(202) 965-5648 Fax (202) 965-5649
kfinnera@nas.edu
www.nas.edu

A journal which covers all areas of
science, technology, health, and related
policy issues in the United States.

IUE NEWS
1126 16th Street, NW
Washington, DC 20036
(202) 785-7200 Fax (202) 785-4563
info@iue.org
www.iue.org

An official publication of the
International Union of Electronic,
Electrical, Salaried, Machine and
Furniture Workers, AFL-CIO.

JEWISH TELEGRAPHIC AGENCY
330 Seventh Avenue
New York, NY 10001-5010
(212) 643-1890 Fax (212) 643-8498

Information about the lives, fate, and
well-being of Jews of all countries and
serves as a link among the various
Jewish communities worldwide.

JEWISH WEEK, THE
1501 Broadway, Suite 505
New York, NY 10036
(212) 921-7822

In seeking to build and strengthen
Jewish community while championing
an aggressive and independent press—
its first loyalty is to the truth.

JOURNAL OF BLACKS IN
HIGHER EDUCATION, THE
200 West 57th Street, 15th floor
New York, NY 10019
(212) 399-1084 Fax (212) 245-1973

Higher education journal on
Black Americans.

JOURNAL OF
COMMUNITY PRACTICE
School of Social Work, CB #3550
Chapel Hill, NC 27599
(800) 342-0678 Fax (800) 895-0582

A journal of organizing, planning,
development, and change.

JOURNAL OF
PRISONERS ON PRISONS
P.O. Box 54 University Centre
Winnipeg, MB R3T 2N2
Canada
www.synapse.net/~arrakis/jpp/jpp.html

A journal composed of contributions by
prisoners and former prisoners.

JOURNALISM AND MASS
COMMUNICATION QUARTERLY
Washington, DC 20052
(212) 994-6226 Fax (212) 994-5806
aejmc@scu.edu
www.aejmc.sc.edu

A scientific research publication about
journalism and mass communication.

KICK IT OVER
P.O. Box 5811, Station A
Toronto, ON M5W 1P2
Canada

Advocating Anarchism as a form of
social organization based on personal
responsibility and mutual co-operation.

KINESIS
#301-1720 Grant Street
Vancouver, B.C. V6A 2G2
Canada
(604) 255-5499 Fax (604) 255-5511
Kinesis@wes.net

A journal of news, features, art reviews, commentary of and for women to work actively for social change.

KOREA TIMES
4525 Wilshire Boulevard
Los Angeles, CA 90010
(213) 692-2043 Fax (213) 738-1103

A monthly bilingual publication for reaching Korean families in the United States as a family journal for parents and their children.

LABOR NEWS FOR
WORKING FAMILIES, I.I.R.
2521 Channing Way #5555
Berkeley, CA 94720
(510) 643-6814 Fax (510) 642-6432
socrates.berkeley.edu/~iir/workfam/home.html

Highlights union policies and benefits including family leave, child care, elder care, flexible work.

LABOR NOTES
7435 Michigan Avenue
Detroit, MI 48210
(313) 842-6262 Fax (313) 842-0227
labornotes@igc.org

Focuses on news and information for workplace activists.

LAMBDA BOOK REPORT
P.O. Box 73910
Washington, DC 20056
(202) 462-7924 Fax (202) 462-5264
LBREditor@aol.com

Trade news publishing information for Gay and Lesbian writers.

LATIN AMERICAN PERSPECTIVES
1150 University, Suite 107
Riverside, CA 92517
(909) 787-1571 Fax (909) 787-5685

An academic journal on Latin American issues.

LEFT BUSINESS OBSERVER
250 West 85th Street
New York, NY 10024-3217
(212) 874-4020 Fax (212) 874-3137
dhenwood@panix.com
www.panix.com/~dhenwood/
LBO-home.html

A journal of news and analysis.

LEFT CURVE
P.O. Box 472
Oakland, CA 94604
(510) 763-7193
leftcurve@wco.com
www.ncal.verio.com/~leftcurv

An artist-produced magazine addressing problems of cultural forms emerging from problems of modernity.

LEGAL TIMES
1730 M Street, NW, Suite 802
Washington, DC 20036
(202) 457-0686 Fax (202) 457-0718
legaltimes@legaltimes.com
www.americanlawyer.com

A weekly legal newspaper.

LIBERTY
55 West Oak Ridge Drive
Hagerstown, MD 21740
(301) 791-7000

A magazine of religious freedom.

LIBRARIANS AT LIBERTY
1716 SW Williston Road
Gainesville, FL 32608
(352) 335-2200

Librarians at Liberty aims to give
people working in libraries and related
fields an unconstrained opportunity to
express professional concerns.

LM MAGAZINE
P.O. Box 769, Murray Hill Station
New York, NY 10156
im@informinc.co.uk
www.informinc.co.uk

A loud-mouthed free speech magazine
which dares to publish what others are
frightened to whisper.

LRA'S ECONOMIC NOTES
145 West 28th Street, 6th Floor
New York, NY 10001
(800) 875-8775 Fax (212) 714-1674
gregt@ira.ny.com
www.lra/ny.com

A journal of labor, economics, and
politics for labor policy makers.

LUNA MEDIA SERVICES
P.O. Box 1265
Eureka, CA 95502
(707) 839-8974
lunanews@humboldt1.com
www.lunatree.org

A monthly update of Julia Butterfly's
one plus year sit in her heroic vigil to
save the last remaining old growth
redwoods of Northern California.

MASALA
87 Fifth Avenue, Suite 603
New York, NY 10003
(212) 627-2522 Fax (212) 627-5657
A quarterly covering issues of interest
to Asians and Pacific Islanders.

MEDIA BYPASS
P.O. Box 5326
Evansville, IN 47716
(812) 477-8670 Fax (812) 477-8677
newsroom@4bypass.com
www.4bypass.com

A national magazine from alternative
sources.

MEDIA CONSORTIUM, THE
2200 Wilson Boulevard, Suite 102-231
Arlington, VA 22201
(703) 920-1580 Fax (703) 920-0946
rparry@ix.netcom.com
www.delve.com/consort.html

An independent, investigative news
company.

MEDIA CULTURE REVIEW
77 Federal Street, 2nd floor
San Francisco, CA 94107
(415) 284-1420 Fax (415) 284-1414
congress@igc.org
www.mediademocracy.org/
MediaCultureReview

Media Culture Review is the award-
winning 'zine published by the Institute
for Alternative Journalism. Now online.

MEDIA REPORT TO WOMEN
10606 Mantz Road
Silver Spring, MD 20903-1247
(301) 445-3231
sheilagib@aol.com

Reports and commentary about the media's depiction of women and girls.

MEDIA WATCH
P.O. Box 618
Santa Cruz, CA 95061-0618
(408) 0423-6355 Fax (408) 423-6355
mwatch@cruzio.com
www.mediawatch.com

Media Watch works to challenge media bias through education and action.

MIDDLE EAST REPORT
1500 Massachusetts Avenue, NW, Suite 119
Washington, DC 20005
(202) 223-3677 Fax (202) 223-3604
merip@igc.org
www.merip.org

A journal offering an independent critical voice on the Middle East—welcomes, and will pay for current, related photographs.

MILITARY AND THE ENVIRONMENT
222-B View Street
Mountain View, CA 94041
(415) 904-7751 Fax (415) 904-7765
cpro@igc.apc.org

Aimed at educating the public about current issues and legislation related to the military and its impact on the environment.

MINORITY BUSINESS ENTREPRENEUR (MBE)
3528 Torrance Boulevard., Suite 101
Torrance, CA 90503-4803
(310) 540-9398 Fax (310) 792-8263

A multi-ethnic, bi-monthly business magazine.

MOMENT
4710 41st Street, NW
Washington, DC 20016
(202) 364-3300 Fax (202) 364-2636

A bi-monthly publication covering Jewish issues.

MONTHLY REVIEW
122 West 27th Street
New York, NY 10001
(212) 691-2555 Fax (212) 727-3676
mreview@igc.apc.org
www.peacenet.org

An independent socialist magazine

MOTHER JONES
731 Market Street, Suite 600
San Francisco, CA 94103
(415) 665-6637 Fax (415) 665-6696
query@motherjones.com
www.motherjones.com

The magazine of investigative journalism; now with the on-line sister "mojowire."

MOUTH: VOICE OF THE DISABILITY NATION
61 Brighton Street
Rochester, NY 14607-2656
(716) 244-6599 Fax (716) 244-9798

Mouth speaks the unspeakable, questions the unquestionable, follows the money in the $100 billion disability exploitation industry.

MS. MAGAZINE
230 Park Avenue
New York, NY 10169
(212) 445-6100
ms@echonyc.com
www.womweb.com

The founding magazine of the feminist movement, ad-free, national, and international focus on issues affecting women.

MSRRT NEWSLETTER:
LIBRARY ALTERNATIVES
4645 Columbus Avenue South
Minneapolis, MN 55407
(612) 694-8572 Fax (612) 541-8600
cdodge@sun.hennepin.lib.mn.us
www.cs.unca.edu/~davidson/msrrt

A newsletter of news, commentary, and networking information for activist librarians and cultural workers.

MULTINATIONAL MONITOR
P.O. Box 19405
Washington, DC 20036
(202) 387-8034 Fax (202) 234-5176
monitor@essential.org

A journal which tracks corporate activity, especially in the Third World.

NABJ JOURNAL
3100 Taliaferro Hall,
University of Maryland
College Park, MD 20742-7717
(301) 405-8500 Fax (301) 405-8555

Publication of the National Association of Black Journalists, the largest media organization of people of color in the world.

NACLA REPORT ON
THE AMERICAS
475 Riverside Drive, Suite 454
New York, NY 10115
(212) 870-3146 Fax (212) 870-3305
nacla@nacla.org
www.nacla.org

NACLA analyzes the major political, social and economic trends in Latin America.

NAJA NEWS
1433 E. Franklin Avenue, Suite 11
Minneapolis, MN 55404
(612) 376-0441 Fax (612) 376-0448

A quarterly newsletter of the Native American Journalists Association.

NATION, THE
72 Fifth Avenue
New York, NY 10011
(212) 209-5400 Fax (212) 982-9000
info@thenation.com
www.thenation.com

Investigative journalism, a leading forum for leftist debate; home of Radio Nation and The Nation Institute.

NATIONAL CAMPAIGN FOR
FREEDOM OF EXPRESSION
QUARTERLY
918 F Street, NW, #609
Washington, DC 20004
(800) 477-6233 or (202) 393-2787
Fax (202) 347-7376
ncfe@artswire.org
www.artswire.org/~ncfe

An educational and advocacy magazine for artists, arts organizations, audience members, and concerned citizens for fighting censorship.

NATIONAL CATHOLIC REPORTER
P.O. Box 419281
Kansas City, MO 64141
(816) 531-0538 Fax (816) 968-2280
lesliewirp@aol.com
www.natcath.com

An independent, catholic newsweekly covering events related to the church.

NATIONAL GREEN PAGES
1612 K Street, NW, Suite 600
Washington, DC 20006
(800) 58-GREEN or (202) 872-5307
Fax (202) 331-8166
info@coopamerica.org
www.greenpages.org

A directory of thousands of responsible businesses, products, and services—a wonderful resource—published yearly.

NATIONAL MINORITY POLITICS
13555 Bammel N. Houston, #227
Houston, TX 77066
(281) 444-4265 Fax (281) 583-9534

A monthly publication by and about African-Americans and Hispanics with a conservative political bent.

NEA TODAY
1201 16th Street, NW
Washington, DC 20036
(202) 822-7207 Fax (202) 822-7206
NEAToday@aol.com
www.neatoday.com

Provides insights on educational challenges facing the U.S. today.

NEIGHBORHOOD WORKS, THE
2125 West North Avenue
Chicago, IL 60647
(773) 278-4800 Fax (773) 278-3840
tnwedit@cnt.org
www.cnt.org/tnw/

A bimonthly magazine that seeks out those people, projects and issues that demonstrate substantial principles at work in urban areas.

NETWORK NEWS, THE
1325 G Street, NW
Washington, DC 20005
(202) 347-1140 Fax (202) 347-1168

A bi-weekly newsletter focusing on women's health and related subjects.

NEW CITIZEN, THE
34 Wall Street, #407
Ashville, NC 28801
(704) 255-0182 Fax (704) 254-2286
cml@main.nc.us
www.main.nc.us/cml/

Links media literacy with the concepts and practices of citizenship—provides media analysis and criticism.

NEW DEMOCRACY
P.O. Box 427
Boston, MA 02130
(617) 566-9637
Newdam@aol.com
users.aol.com/newdem

Founded to help people in their struggle against capitalism, to shape the world with anti-capitalist values of solidarity, equality, and democracy.

NEW PARTY NEWS
88 Third Avenue, Suite 313
Brooklyn, NY 11217
(718) 246-3713 Fax (718) 246-3718
newparty@newparty.org
www.newparty.org

The New Party is a grassroots-based democratic political party now in active formation in a dozen states.

NEW REPUBLIC, THE
1220 19th Street, NW
Washington, DC 20036
(202) 331-7494 Fax (202) 331-0275
tnr@aol.com
magazines.enews.com/magazines/tnr

America's leading weekly journal of
political opinion.

NEWS INDIA
244 Fifth Avenue
New York, NY 10001
(212) 481-3110 Fax (212) 889-5774

The only four-color English language
weekly serving the million-strong
Asian Indians settled in the United
States.

NEWS MEDIA AND THE LAW
1101 Wilson Boulevard, Suite 1910
Arlington, VA 22209
(703) 807-2100 Fax (703) 807-2109
www.rcfp.org/rcfp

A quarterly magazine which covers
issues related to news reporting and the
media, and the legal issues therein.

NEWS MEDIA UPDATE
1101 Wilson Boulevard, Suite 1910
Arlington, VA 22209
(703) 807-2100 Fax (703) 807-2109
www.rcfp.org/rcfp

A twice-monthly newsletter regarding
current media issues.

NEWS ON EARTH
P.O. Box 20065
New York, NY 10011
(212) 995-8527 Fax (212) 979-2055
spectator@newslet.com
www.newslet.com/washingtonspectator

A politically independent newsletter
that reports on the vital issues of the
day and tells the real story about what
is going on in Washington.

NEWSLETTER ON INTELLECTUAL FREEDOM
50 East Huron Street
Chicago, IL 60611
(312) 280-4223 Fax (312) 280-4227
nperez@ala.org
www.ala.org/oif.html

Newsletter of the ALA's (American
Libraries Association) office of
intellectual freedom.

NEWSPAPER GUILD, THE
501 Third Street, NW
Washington, DC 20001
(202) 434-7177 Fax (202) 434-1472
www.newsguild.org/

This is the newsletter for the
Newspaper Guild—CWA's
(Communications Workers of America)
30,000 members in the U.S. and
Canada.

NEWSPRINTS
P.O. Box 19405
Washington, DC 20036
(202) 387-8030 Fax (202) 234-5176
newsprints@essential.org
essential.org/newsprints/newsprints.ht
ml

Publishes leads the national dailies
and network news shows miss.

NEWSWATCH MONITOR
c/o School of Communication, Simon
Fraser University
8888 University Drive
Burnaby, BC V5A 1S6
Canada
(604) 291-4905 Fax (604) 291-4204
censored@sfu.ca
newswatch.cprost.sfu.ca

A quarterly newsletter which reports on
Canada's media performance.

NEW TIMES
1950 Sawtelle Boulevard, Suite 200
Los Angeles, CA 90025
(310) 477-0403 Fax (310) 478-9875
editior@newtimesla.com
www.newtimesla.com

A place to get the real truth about L.A;
this weekly has taken on such topics as
the city's poor enforcement of anti-slum
laws, horrid safety conditions in the
building of L.A.'s new metro system,
and many more alternative issues.

NEXUS
P.O. Box 177
Kempton, IL 60946-0177
(888) 909-7474 or (815) 253-6464
Fax (815) 253-6454
nexususa@earthlink.net
www.icom.net/~nexus/

Since Nexus recognizes that humanity
is undergoing a massive transformation,
it seeks to provide 'hard-to-get'
information so as to assist people
through these changes.

NONVIOLENT ACTIVIST, THE
339 Lafayette Street
New York, NY 10012
(212) 228-0450 Fax (212) 228-6193
wri@igc.apc.org
www.nvweb/wrl/nonviolence.org/

Political analysis from a pacifist
perspective.

NUCLEAR MONITOR, THE
1424 16th Street, NW, Suite 404
Washington, DC 20036
(202) 328-0002 Fax (202) 462-2183
nirsnet@igc.apc.org
www.nirs.org

A publication of the Nuclear
Information & Resource Service.

NUCLEAR RESISTER, THE
P.O. Box 43383
Tucson, AZ 85733-3383
(520) 323-8697
nukeresister@igc.org

Information about and support for
imprisoned anti-nuclear activists.

OBJECTOR, THE: A MAGAZINE OF
CONSCIENCE AND RESISTANCE
955 Sutter #514
San Francisco, CA 94102
(415) 474-3002 Fax (415) 474-2311
cccowr@peacenet.org
www.libertynet.org/ccco/

Magazine of the Central Committee for
Conscientious Objectors.

OFF OUR BACKS:
A WOMEN'S NEWSJOURNAL
2337-B 18th Street, NW
Washington, DC 20009
(202) 234-8072 Fax (202) 234-8092

National and international news on
feminist issues.

OMB WATCHER
1742 Connecticut Avenue, NW
Washington, DC 20009-1171
(202) 234-8494 Fax (202) 234-8584
ombwatch@rtk.net
ombwatch.org/ombwatch.html

Focuses on budget issues and activities
at the Office of Management and
Budget in Washington.

ORGANIZING
5600 City Avenue
Philadelphia, PA 19131
(215) 878-4253 Fax (215) 879-3148

Dedicated to coverage of community
organizations who are actively
participating in local affairs.

OUR STRUGGLE/NUESTRA LUCHA
DEMOCRATIC SOCIALISTS OF
AMERICA
P.O. Box 162394
Sacramento, CA 95816
(916) 361-9072
www.jps.net/lryder\index
campsd@csus.edu

Newsletter of Anti-Racism, Latino,
African American Commissions.

OUR TIMES
P.O. Box 182
New Glasgow, NS B2H 5E2 Canada
(902) 755-6840 Fax (902) 755-1292
ourstory@web.net
www.ourtimes.web.net

Focuses on social change through
unionism and democratic socialism.

OUT MAGAZINE
110 Green Street, Suite 600
New York, NY 94942-10012
(212) 334-9119 Fax (212) 334-9227
outmag@aol.com

A general interest gay and lesbian
magazine.

OUTLOOK
#3-6184 Ash Street
Vancouver, BC V5Z 3G9 Canada
(604) 324-5101 Fax (604) 325-2470

Supports multiculturalism, self-determination of people all over the world.

PAPERWORKER
3340 Perimeter Hill Drive
Box 1475
Nashville, TN 37202
(615) 834-8590 Fax (615) 831-6791

Official publication of the International
Paperworkers' Union.

PATHFINDER
P.O. Box 649
Luck, WI 54853
(715) 472-4185 Fax (715) 472-4184
nukewatch@win.bright.net

Encourages a non-violent change for
an environment free of the nuclear
industry and weapons of mass
destruction.

PBI/USA REPORT
2642 College Avenue
Berkeley, CA 94704
(510) 540-0749 Fax (510) 849-1247
pbiusa@igc.apc.org
www.igc.org/pbi/index/html.

Provides quarterly updates to the supporters of PBI (Peace Brigades International) in the U.S. about the work of their peace teams in seven regions of the world.

PEACE MAGAZINE
736 Bathurst Street
Toronto, ON M5S 2R4 Canada
(416) 533-7581 Fax (416) 531-6214
mspencer@web.net
www.peacemagazine.org

Issues and activities of movements for peace and nonviolence around the world.

PEACEWORK
2161 Massachusetts Avenue
Cambridge, MA 02140
(617) 661-6130 Fax (617) 354-2832
pwork@igc.apc.org
www.afsc.org/nero/nepw.html

Intended to serve the movements for nonviolent social change, particularly in the Northeast.

POCLAD—PROGRAM ON CORPORATIONS, LAW & DEMOCRACY, THE
P.O. Box 246 South
Yarmouth, MA 02664-0246
(508) 398-1145 Fax (508) 398-1552
people@poclad.org

A quarterly publication that instigates democratic conversations and actions that contest the authority of corporations to govern.

PORTLAND SKANNER
2337 North Williams Avenue
P.O. Box 5455
Portland, OR 97227
(503) 287-3562 or (800) 755-COPYT

Takes on hard issues affecting Blacks and other minorities, and offers positive role models for youth—stories not usually covered by the media.

POZ MAGAZINE
1279 Old Chelsea Station
New York, NY 10113-1279
(212) 242-2163 Fax (212) 675-8505
edit@poz.com
www.poz.com

Focusing on quality of life issues for anyone impacted by AIDS and HIV.

PR WATCH
3318 Gregory Street
Madison, WI 53711
(608) 233-3346 Fax (608) 238-2236
stauber@compuserve.com
www.prwatch.org

Investigates corporate and government propaganda. The editors also wrote *Toxic Sludge is Good For You: Lies, Damn Lies and the Public Relations Industry.*

PRINCETON
PROGRESSIVE REVIEW
315 West College
Princeton, NJ 08544
progrev@princeton.edu
www.princeton.edu/~progrev

A journal of news analysis and
occasional cultural critique, voicing
social justice—subscriptions are
online.

PRISON LEGAL NEWS
2400 NW 80th Street, Suite 148
Seattle, WA 98117
(206) 781-6524
pwright@prisonlegalnews.org
www.prisonlegalnews.org

PLN reports court rulings involving
prisoner's rights as well as providing
news and commentary on criminal
justice issues.

PROBE
139 W. 13th Street, #6
New York, NY 10011-7856
(212) 647-0200 Fax (212) 463-8002
probenewsletter.com

Investigative and interpretive newsletter promoting science and rationality as
key elements in a democratic society.

PROGRESSIVE LIBRARIAN
P.O. Box 2203
Times Square Station
New York, NY 10108
(973) 623-7642
www.libr.org

A journal for critical studies and
progressive politics.

PROGRESSIVE POPULIST, THE
P.O. Box 150517
Austin, TX 78715-0517
(512) 447-0455
populist@usa.net
www.populist.com

Promotes the idea that people are more
important than corporations.

PROGRESSIVE REVIEW, THE
1739 Connecticut Avenue, NW
Washington, DC 20009-8922
(202) 232-5544 Fax (202) 234-6222
ssmith@igc.org
http://emporium.turnpike.net/P/ProRev/

This is Washington's most unofficial
source. It provides Green, populist
perspectives.

PROGRESSIVE, THE
409 East Main Street
Madison, WI 53703
(608) 257-4626 Fax (608) 257-3373
progressive@peacenet.org
www.progressive.org

The Progressive discusses peace,
politics, social justice, and
environmental concerns from a
liberal point of view.

PUBLIC CITIZEN MAGAZINE
1600 20th Street, NW
Washington, DC 20009
(202) 588-1000 Fax (202) 588-7799
pnye@citizen.org
www.citizen.org

Consumer rights, safety issues,
corporate and business accountability,
environmental issues, and citizen
empowerment.

PUBLIC EYE, THE
120 Beacon Street, Suite 202
Somerville, MA 02143-4304
(617) 661-9313 Fax (617) 661-0059
publiceye@igc.apc.org
www.publiceye.org/pra/

The Public Eye is a quarterly
newsletter featuring an in-depth
analysis and critique of issues
pertaining to the U.S. political right
wing.

QBR: THE BLACK BOOK REVIEW
625 Broadway, 10th Floor
New York, NY 10012
(212) 475-1010 Fax (212) 475-1433

Presents a national African-American
book review of the caliber to support
and strengthen the influence of
African-American literary culture.

QUILL
16 South Jackson Street
P.O. Box 77
Greencastle, IN 46135-0077
(765) 653-3333 Fax (765) 653-4631
spj@spjhq.org
www.spj.org

A national magazine that reports on
journalism.

RADICAL AMERICA
237-A Holland
Somerville, MA 02144
(617) 628-6585 Fax (617) 628-6585

Publication of the Alternative
Education Project.

REAPPRAISING AIDS
7514 Girard Avenue, #1-331
La Jolla, CA 92037
(810) 772-9926 Fax (619) 272-1621
philpott@wwnet.com
www.wwnet.com/~philpott/
ReappraisingAIDS

Scrutinizes the AIDS virus from an
alternative and sometimes controversial
perspective.

RELIGION WATCH
P.O. Box 652
North Bellmore, NY 11710
(516) 785-6765
relwatch1@aol.com
www.religionwatch.com

A monthly newsletter which monitors
trends in contemporary religion.

RESPONSIVE PHILANTHROPY
2001 S Street, NW, Suite 620
Washington, DC 20009
(202) 387-9177 Fax (202) 332-5084
info@ncrp.org
www.ncrp.org

Committed to making philanthropy more
responsive to socially, economically and
politically disenfranchised people.

**RETHINKING SCHOOLS
NEWSPAPER**
1001 East Keefe Avenue
Milwaukee, WI 53212
(800) 669-4192 or (414) 964-7220
Fax (414) 964-7220
RS Business@aol.com
www.rethinkingschools.org

Provides an alternative to mainstream
educational materials, committed to
issues of equity and social justice.

REVOLUTIONARY WORKER
Box 3486, Merchandise Mart
Chicago, IL 60654
(773) 227-4066 Fax (773) 227-4097
www.mcs.net/~rwor

The weekly newspaper of the
Revolutionary Communist Party, USA.

RFD: A JOURNAL FOR GAY MEN
EVERYWHERE
P.O. Box 68
Liberty, TN 37095
(615) 536-5176

A reader-written journal for gay men
focusing on country living, and
encouraging alternative lifestyles.

RIGHTS
666 Broadway, 7th Floor
New York, NY 10012
(212) 614-6464 Fax (212) 614-6499

Covers issues involving freedoms
guaranteed by the Constitution and
Bill of Rights.

RYERSON REVIEW OF
JOURNALISM
350 Victoria Street
Toronto, ON M5B 2K3 Canada
(416) 979-5000 x7434
Fax (416) 979-4216
hattp:www.acs.ryerson.ca

A progressive review from Ryerson
Polytechnic University in Canada.

S.O.A. WATCH (GEORGIA)
P.O. Box 3330
Columbus, GA 31903
(706) 682-5369 Fax (706) 682-5369
www.derechos.org/soaw/

S.O.A. WATCH (WASHINGTON)
P.O. Box 4566
Washington, DC 20017
(202) 234-3440 Fax (202) 234-3440
www.derechos.org/soaw/

Tracks and reports on activities at the
School of the Americas.

SECRECY & GOVERNMENT
BULLETIN
307 Massachusetts Avenue, NE
Washington, DC 20002
(202) 675-1012 Fax (202) 675-1010
saftergood@igc.apc.org
www.fas.org/sgp/

Reports on new developments in
government secrecy policies.

SE JOURNAL
P.O. Box 27280
Philadelphia, PA 19118-0280
(215) 836-9970 Fax (215) 836-9972
SEJoffice@aol.com
www.sej.org

Written primarily by journalists for
journalists, its purpose is to provide
information and guidance on covering
the environmental beat.

SOCIAL JUSTICE ACTION
QUARTERLY
430 Keap Street
Brooklyn, NY 11211
(718) 218-7005
johnpotash@hotmail.com

Activist social work newspaper
promoting organizing and mobilizing
for social equity.

SOCIAL POLICY
25 West 43rd Street, Room 620
New York, NY 10036-7406
(212) 642-2929 Fax (212) 642-1956
socpol@igc.apc.org
socialpolicy.org

Social Policy is a magazine about
social movements. It breaks new
ground with its in-depth and thoughtful
analysis of public policy in America.

SOJOURNERS
2401 15th Street, NW
Washington, DC 20009
(202) 328-8842 Fax (202) 328-8757
sojourners@sojourners.com
www.sojourners.com/sojourners

A grassroots network for personal,
community, and political
transformation rooted in prophetic
biblical tradition.

SOLIDARITY
8000 E. Jefferson
Detroit, MI 48214
(313) 926-5373
71112.363@compuserve.com
www.uaw.org

Official magazine of the United Auto
Workers.

SOUTH ASIA TIMES
38 Westland Avenue, Suite 23
Boston, MA 02115
(617) 536-4606 Fax (617) 536-4606

News and views on South Asia
upholding the causes of democracy,
human rights, freedom of speech,
disarmament, and world peace.

SOUTHERN EXPOSURE
P.O. Box 531
Durham, NC 27702
(919) 419-8311 ext. 26
Fax (919) 419-8315
Southern@igc.apc.org
sunsite.unc.edu/SouthernExposure

Award-winning magazine focused on
fighting for a better South.

SPACE AND SECURITY NEWS
5115 S. A1A Highway, Suite 201
Melbourne Beach,FL 32951
(407) 952-0601
ssn@rmbowman.com
www.rmbowan.com

Covers programs and policy issues
related to space and space exploration.

SPIRIT OF CRAZY HORSE
P.O. Box 583
Lawerence, KS 66044
(785) 842-5774 Fax (785) 842-5796
lpdc@idir.net
www.unicom.net/peltier/index.html

Statements from and updates on
Leonard Peltier's case—also focuses on
native sovereignty and prison issues.

STAY FREE!
P.O. Box 306
New York, NY 10012
(718) 398-9324 Fax (212) 477-5074
stayfree@sunsite.unc.edu
sunsite.unc.edu/stayfree

A magazine which casts a critical eye
on commercialism and pop culture.

STEELABOR
Five Gateway Center
Pittsburgh, PA 15222
(412) 562-2442 Fax (412) 562-2445
www.building.org

News and commentary about members of steelworkers, plus political, economic, and social issues of concern to steelworkers.

STUDENT PRESS LAW CENTER REPORT
1101 Wilson Boulevard, Suite 1910
Arlington, VA 22901
(703) 807-1904 Fax (703) 807-2109
splc@splc.org
www.splc.org

Reports on cases, controversies, and legislation relating to free press rights of student journalists.

SUSTAINABLE TIMES, THE
1657 Barrington Street, Suite 508
Halifax, NS B3J 2A1 Canada
(902) 423-6709 Fax (902) 423-9736

Solutions to employment, environment and global development challenges.

SYNTHESIS/REGENERATION: A MAGAZINE OF GREEN SOCIAL THOUGHT
P.O. Box 24115
St. Louis, MO 63130
(314) 727-8554 Call first
fitzdon@aol.com

A tri-annual magazine focusing on the social aspects of environmentalism.

TASK FORCE CONNECTIONS
973 Market Street, Suite 600
San Francisco, CA 94103
(415) 356-8110 Fax (415) 356-8138

Updates and reports on issues related to AIDS prevention and treatment.

TEACHING TOLERANCE MAGAZINE
400 Washington Avenue
Montgomery, AL 36104
(334) 264-0286 Fax (334) 264-3121
www.splcenter.org

A twice-yearly magazine covering issues related to the Teaching Tolerance Project begun by Morris Dees at the Southern Poverty Law Center.

TEAMSTER MAGAZINE
25 Louisiana Avenue, NW
Washington, DC 20001
(202) 624-6911 Fax (202) 624-6918
ibtcomm@aol.com
www.teamster.org

A magazine which focuses on fighting for the future and the rights of working families.

TEEN VOICES MAGAZINE
P.O. Box 120-027
Boston, MA 02112-0027
(617) 426-5505 Fax (617) 426-5577
womenexp@teenvoices.com
www.teenvoices.com

A magazine that provides an interactive, educational forum that challenges media images of young women and girls.

TELEMEDIUM, THE JOURNAL OF
MEDIA LITERACY
120 E. Wilson Street
Madison, WI 53703
(608) 257-7712 Fax (608) 257-7714

Address issues of media literacy in the
United States.

THIRD FORCE
1218 East 21st Street
Oakland, CA 94606-9950
(510) 533-7583 Fax (510) 533-0923
ctwo@igc.org
www.igc.org/ctwo/

Reports on labor, low income issues,
communities of color, and community
activism and organizing.

TIBET PRESS WATCH
1825 K Street, NW, Suite 520
Washington, DC 20006
(202) 785-1515 Fax (202) 785-4343
ict@peacenet.org
www.savetibet.org

A magazine focusing on the current
situation inside Tibet as well as the
support movement within the United
States.

TIKKUN
P.O. Box 1778, Cathedral Station
New York, NY 10025
(212) 864-4110 Fax (212) 864-4137
www.tikkun.com

A magazine which focuses on topics of
particular interest to the Jewish
community, including culture, politics,
and philosophy.

TOWARD FREEDOM
Box 468
Burlington, VT 05402-0468
(802) 658-2523 Fax (802) 658-3738
Tfmag@aol.com
www.towardfreedom.com

A progressive international news,
analysis and advocacy journal that
helps strengthen and extend human
justice and liberties.

TRADEWOMEN: A MAGAZINE FOR
WOMEN IN BLUE COLLAR WORK
P.O. Box 2622
Berkeley, CA 94702
(510) 548-2099

TRANSITION
25 Francis Avenue, Van Serg Hall B11
Cambridge, MA 02138
(617) 496-2847 Fax (617) 496-2877
transit@fas.harvard.edu

An independent publication from
Harvard University.

TREATMENT REVIEW
611 Broadway, Suite 613
New York, NY 10012-2809
(800) 734-7104 Fax (212) 260-8869
atdn@aidsnyc.org
www.aidsnyc.org/network

Provides an overview of AIDS
treatments in clinical trial and newly
as well as general medical treatment
information.

TRICYCLE: THE BUDDHIST
REVIEW
92 Vandam Street
New York, NY 10013
(212) 645-1143
tricycle@well.com
http://www.tricycle.com

A non-sectarian magazine examining
the juxtaposition of the dharma in
western culture.

TURNING THE TIDE: JOURNAL OF
ANTI-RACIST ACTIVISM,
RESEARCH AND EDUCATION
P.O. Box 1055
Culver City, CA 90232-1055
(310) 288-5003
part2001@usa.net

Exposes the strategies of organized
white supremacists and their roots in
U.S. political and social structures,
promoting anti-racist activism.

TYNDALL WEEKLY REPORT
135 Rivington Street
New York, NY 10002
(212) 674-8913 Fax (212)979-7304

A weekly fax-sheet monitoring the
television networks' nightly newscasts.

UPPNET NEWS
271 19th Avenue South
Minneapolis, MN 55455
(612) 624-4326
uppnet@labornet.org or
jsee@csom.umn.edu
www.mtn.org/jsee/uppnet.html

Official publication of the Union
Producers and Programmers Network,
promoting TV and radio shows pertinent to the cause of organized labor
and working people.

URGENT ACTION NEWSLETTER
P.O. Box 1270
Nederland, CO 80466-1270
(303) 440-0913 Fax (303) 258-7881
sharris@igc.apc.org
www.amnesty-usa.org

The newsletter for Amnesty
International out of the Urgent Action
Program Office.

UTNE READER
1624 Harmon Place, Suite 330
Minneapolis, MN 55403
(612) 338-5040 Fax (612) 338-6043
info@utne.com
www.utne.com

A digest of alternative ideas and
material reprinted from alternative
and independent media sources.

VETERAN, THE
1224 M Street, NW
Washington, DC 20005
(202) 628-2700 Fax (202) 628-5880
www.vva.org

The official voice of Vietnam Veterans
of America.

VILLAGE VOICE
36 Cooper Square
New York, NY 10003
(212) 475-475-3300
Fax (212)475-8944
ads@villagevoice.com
www.villagevoice.com

A weekly newspaper covering regional, national, and international affairs from a New York perspective.

VOCES DE LA FRONTERA
P.O. Box 340195
Austin, TX 78734-0195
(512) 264-0834 Call first
beecreek@aol.com

A bilingual magazine which provides space for maquiladora workers to express themselves and covers independent democratic union struggles.

WAR AND PEACE DIGEST
32 Union Square East
New York, NY 10003-3295
(212) 777-6626 Fax (212) 777-2552
warpeace@interport.net
www.warpeace.org

An anti-nuclear publication promoting peace, social justice, and media reform.

WASHINGTON MONTHLY, THE
1611 Connecticut Avenue, NW
Washington, DC 20009
(202) 462-0128 Fax (202) 332-8413
enews.com/magazines/wash_month/magazines.enews

National opinion magazine covering politics, media, and government.

WE INTERNATIONAL
736 Bathurst Street
Toronto, Ontario M5S 2R4
(416) 516-2600 Fax (416)531-6214
weed@web.net
www.web.net/~weed/

A magazine which examines women's multiple relationships with their environment.

WELFARE MOTHERS VOICE
2711 W. Michigan
Milwaukee, WI 53208
(414) 342-6662 Fax (414) 342-6667

WMV provides a voice to mothers in poverty who receive or have received public support for children.

WHISPERING WIND
53196 Old Uneedus Road
P.O. Box 1390
Folsom, LA 70437-1390
(504) 796-5433 Fax (504) 796-9236

A bi-monthly magazine dedicated to preserving the traditions of the American Indian both past and present.

WHO CARES MAGAZINE
511 K Street, NW, Suite 1042
Washington, DC 20005
(800) 628-1692 or (202) 628-1691
Fax (202) 628-2063
info@whocares.mag
www.whocares.org

A national bi-monthly journal of service and action, it publishes information to help people create, grow, and manage organizations for the benefit of the common good, and to foster a sense of community among social entrepreneurs nationwide.

WHOLE EARTH MAGAZINE
1408 Mission Avenue
San Rafael, CA 94901
(415) 256-2800 Fax (415) 256-2808
wer@well.com

Provides access to tools, ideas, and
practices—reviews books and products
to help people help themselves—
publishes a catalogue.

WHY MAGAZINE
505 Eighth Avenue, 21st Floor
New York, NY 10018
(212) 629-8850 Fax (212) 465-9274

A quarterly publication that challenges
the existence of hunger and poverty,
presenting leading thinkers and
activists with information, insight, and
opportunities for involvement.

WOMEN'S HEALTH LETTER
2245 East Colorado Boulevard,
Suite 104
Pasadena, CA 91107-3651
(626) 798-0638 Fax (626) 798-0639

The thinking woman's guide to
wellness: offers sane and sound health
and healing insights.

WORKBOOK, THE
P.O. Box 4524
105 Stanford SE
Albuquerque, NM 87106
(505) 262-1862 Fax (505)262-1864

Helps people gain access to vital
information that can help them assert
control over their lives.

WORLD POLICY JOURNAL
65 Fifth Avenue, Suite 413
New York, NY 10003
(212) 229-5808 Fax (212) 229-5579
robertsa@newschool.eduworldpolicy.or

A leading quarterly magazine covering
international affairs in the United
States.

WORLD PRESS REVIEW
200 Madison Avenue, Suite 2104
New York, NY 10016
(212) 982-8880
worldpress@worldpress.org
www.worldpress.org

A digest of the global press, a sampling
of newspapers from around the world.

WORLD RIVERS REVIEW
1847 Berkeley Way
Berkeley, CA 94703
(510) 848-1155 Fax (510) 848-1008
irn@irn.org
www.irn.org

Provides the latest news on the worldwide movement to stop destructive
dams and information about
alternatives to large hydro projects.

WORLD WATCH
1776 Massachusetts Avenue, NW
Washington, DC 20036
(202) 452-1999 Fax (202) 296-7365
www.pub@worldwatch.org
www.worldwatch.org

A bi-monthly publication which
informs the general public about the
damage done by the world economy to
its environmental support system.

WORLDVIEWS
1515 Webster Street, #305
Oakland, CA 94612
(510) 451-1742 Fax (510) 835-3017
worldviews@igc.org
ww.igc.org/worldviews

A quarterly review of resources for
education and action.

YES! A JOURNAL OF
POSITIVE FUTURES
P.O. Box 10818
Bainbridge Island, WA 98110
(206) 842-0216 Fax (206) 842-5208
yes@futurenet.org
www.futurenet.org

A journal which helps shape and
support the evolution of sustainable
cultures and communities

Z MAGAZINE
18 Millfield Street
Woods Hole, MA 02543
(508) 548-9063
lydia.sargent@lbbs.org
www/lbbs.org

An independent political magazine of
critical thinking on political, cultural,
social, and economic life in the
United States.

MEDIA ACTIVIST ORGANIZATIONS AND NEWS SERVICES

AFRICA NEWS SERVICE
P.O. Box 3851
Durham, NC 27702
(919) 286-0747 Fax (919) 286-2614
newsdesk@afnews.org
www.africanews.org

Disseminates stories from African news
organizations

ACCURACY IN MEDIA (AIM)
4455 Connecticut Avenue, NW,
Suite 330
Washington, DC 20005
(202) 364-4401 Fax (202) 364-4098
ar@aim.org
www.aim.org

Provides media analysis and
investigation from a radical right
perspective.

ALTERNATIVE MEDIA, INC.
P.O. Box 21308
Washington, DC 20009
(202) 588-9807 Fax (202) 588-9809
mpaulsen@aminc.com

ALTERNATIVE PRESS CENTER
P.O. Box 33109
1443 Gorsuch Avenue
Baltimore, MD 21218-0401
(410) 243-2471 Fax (410) 235-5325
altpress@igc.apc.org
www.altpress.org/

Publishes the Alternative Press Index
and Annotations, a directory of the
independent critical press.

ALTERNET (INSTITUTE FOR
ALTERNATIVE JOURNALISM)
77 Federal Street
San Francisco, CA 94107
(415) 284-1420 Fax (415) 284-1414
www.igc.org/an/

A news service for the alternative
press.

AMERICAN HELLENIC
MEDIA PROJECT
P.O. Box 1150
New York, NY 10028
ahmp@hri.org
www.hri.org/ahmp/

A grassroots, not-for-profit think tank
created to educate the media regarding
American-Hellenic issues.

AMERICAN LIBRARY
ASSOCIATION OFFICE FOR
INTELLECTUAL FREEDOM
50 East Huron Street
Chicago, IL 60611
(312) 280-4223 or (800) 545-2433
Fax (312) 280-4227
oif@ala.org
www.ala.org/oif.html

Organized to educate librarians and the
general public about the nature and
importance of intellectual freedom in
libraries.

AMERICAN SOCIETY OF
JOURNALISTS AND AUTHORS
1501 Broadway, Suite 302
New York, NY 10036
(212) 398-1934 or (212) 997-0947
Fax (212) 768-7414
asja@compuserve.com
www.asja.org

A membership directory , including a
list of 1,000 non-fiction freelance
writers, their telephone, fax, office
and specialty of writing.

ASIAN AMERICAN
JOURNALISTS ASSOCIATION
1765 Sutter Street, Suite 1000
San Francisco CA 94115
(415) 346-2051 Fax (415) 931-4671
aaja1@aol.com
www.aaja.org/

Committed to insuring diversity in
American journalism and expressing
the Asian-American perspective.

ASSOCIATION FOR EDUCATION
JOURNALISM AND MASS
COMMUNICATION
1621 College Street
Columbia, SC 29208
(803) 777-2005

Deals mainly with research topics in
mass communications.

ASSOCIATION OF ALTERNATIVE
NEWSWEEKLIES
1660 L Street, NW, Suite 316
Washington, DC 20036
(202) 822-1955 Fax (202) 822-0929
aan@intr.net
aan.org

A coordinating and administrative
organization for 113 alternative
newsweeklies in the U.S. and Canada.

ASSOCIATION OF AMERICAN
PUBLISHERS
71 Fifth Avenue
New York, NY 10003
(212) 255-0200 Fax (212) 255-7007
jplatt@publishers.org
www.publishers.org/

A national trade association dedicated
to protection of intellectual property
rights and defense of free expression.

BERKELEY MEDIA
STUDIES GROUP
2140 Shattuck Avenue, Suite 804
Berkeley, CA 94704
(510) 204-9700 Fax (510) 204-9710
bmsg@bmsg.org

Focused on public health and
social issues.

BEYONDMEDIA
59 East Van Buren, #1400
Chicago, IL 60605
(312) 922-7780

A video production organization
focused on public awareness of
women's and girl's social change
initiatives.

BLACK WOMEN IN PUBLISHING
P.O. Box 6275, FDR Station
New York, NY 10150
(212) 772-5951
bwip@hotmail.com
www.bwip.org

An employee-based trade association
dedicated to increasing the presence,
and supporting the efforts of African
Heritage women and men in the
publishing industry.

CALIFORNIA FIRST
AMENDMENT COALITION
2701 Cottage Way, Suite 12
Sacramento, CA 95825-1226
(916) 974-8888 Fax (916) 974-880
wzlotlow@cfac.org or tfrancke@cfac.org
www.cfac.org

California journalist's legal notebook
and annual conference to California's
First Amendment Conference.

CAMPUS ALTERNATIVE
JOURNALISM PROJECT
P.O. Box 425748
Cambridge, MA 02142
(617) 725-2886 Fax (617) 547-5067
cco@igc.apc.org
www.cco.org

Supports the work of campus
progressive activists who make their
own printed media.

CENTER FOR COMMERCIAL-FREE
PUBLIC EDUCATION, THE
360 Grand Avenue
P.O. Box 385
Oakland, CA 94610
(510)268-1100 Fax (510)268-1277
unplug@igc.apc.org

Provides support to students, parents,
teachers and others concerned,
organizing across the U.S. to keep
their schools commercial-free and
community controlled.

CENTER FOR INTEGATION AND
IMPROVEMENT OF JOURNALISM
Journalism Department
San Francisco State University
1600 Holloway Avenue
San Francisco, CA 94132
(415) 338-2083 Fax (415) 338-2084
iroman@sfsu.edu
www.journalism.sfsu.edu
www.newswatch.sfsu.edu

A series of model programs designed to
bring ethnic diversity to the country's
newsrooms and promote a fair and
balanced coverage of our multicultural
society.

CENTER FOR INVESTIGATIVE
REPORTING
500 Howard Street, Suite 206
San Francisco, CA 94105-3000
(415) 543-1200 Fax (415) 543-8311
CIR@igc.org
www.muckraker.org/pubs/papertrails/in
dex.html

Exposes abuse of power in bureaucracy
by working with local and national
media focusing on public
accountability.

CENTER FOR MEDIA AND
DEMOCRACY
3318 Gregory Street
Madison, WI 53711
(608) 233-3346 Fax (608) 238-2236
stauber@compuserve.com
www.prwatch.org

The Center specializes in "blowing the
lid off today's multi-billion dollar
propaganda-for-hire industry."

CENTER FOR MEDIA AND
PUBLIC AFFAIRS
2100 L Street, NW, Suite 300
Washington, DC 20037-1526
(202) 223-2942 Fax (202) 872-4014
cmpamm@aol.com
www.cmpa.com/html/2100.html

CMPA bridges the gap between
academic research and the broader
domains of media and public policy.

CENTER FOR MEDIA EDUCATION
1511 K Street, NW, Suite 518
Washington, DC 20005
(202) 628-2620 Fax (202) 628-2554
cme@cme.org
www.cme.org/cme

Publishes "InfoActive Kids" a
quarterly print publication for the child
advocacy, consumer, health and
educational communities.

CENTER FOR MEDIA LITERACY
4727 Wilshire Boulevard, Suite 403
Los Angeles, CA 90010
(213) 931-4177 Fax (213) 931-4474
cml@medialit.org
www.medialit.org

Encouraging critical thinking in
academic environments with videos
and books that focus on democratic
processes.

CENTER FOR PUBLIC INTEGRITY
1634 I Street, NW, Suite 902
Washington, DC 20006
(202) 783-3900 Fax (202) 783-3906
contact@publicintegrity.org
www.publicintegrity.org

Coverage of important national issues
by responsible journalists published in
full form without the traditional time
and space limitations.

CENTER FOR WAR, PEACE AND
THE NEWS MEDIA
10 Washington Place, 4th Floor
New York, NY 10003
(212) 998-7960 Fax (212) 995-4143
war.peace.news@nyu.edu
www.nyu.edu/globalbeat

Dedicated to supporting journalists and
news organizations in their efforts to
sustain an informed citizenry.

CHICAGO MEDIA WATCH
P.O. Box 268737
Chicago, IL 60626
(773) 604-1910
cmw@mediawatch.org
www.mediawatch.org/chicago

Media activist group who publish a quarterly newsletter on vital public information that the mainstream press chooses to omit, distort or ignore.

CITIZENS FOR MEDIA LITERACY
34 Wall Street, Suite 407
Asheville, NC 28801
(704) 255-0182 Fax (704) 254-2286
cml@main.nc.us
www.main.nc.us/cml

CML provides assistance to citizen activists and journalists on issues related to the Freedom of Information Act and Open Records laws.

COMMITTEE TO PROTECT JOURNALISTS
330 Seventh Avenue, 12th Floor
New York, NY 10001
(212) 465-1004 Fax (212) 465-9568
info@cpj.org
www.cpj.org

Monitors violations of press freedom and of journalists' human rights both nationally and internationally.

COMMUNITY MEDIA WORKSHOP
600 South Michigan Avenue
Chicago, IL 60605-1996
(312) 344-6400 Fax (312) 344-6404
commnews@mcs.net
www.newstips.org

CMW provides the link between the news media and community and civic groups to in an effort to make Chicago a better place to live and work.

CONSUMER PROJECT ON TECHNOLOGY
P.O. Box 19367
Washington, DC 20036
(202) 387-8030 Fax (202) 234-5176
love@cptech.org
www.cptech.org

CPT is active in a number of issue areas, including intellectual property, telecommunications, privacy and electronic commerce.

CULTURAL ENVIRONMENT MOVEMENT (CEM)
3508 Market Street, Suite 3-030
Philadelphia, PA 19104
(215) 204-6434 Fax (215) 387-1560
ggerbner@nimbus.Temple.edu

A broad-based international coalition of citizens, scholars, activists, and media professionals who promote democratic principles in the cultural environment.

DEEP DISH TV
339 Lafayette Street
New York, NY 10012
(212) 473-8933
http://www.igc.org/deepdish
deepdish@igc.org

Deep Dish TV is a national satellite network, linking access producers and programmers, independent video makers, activists, and people who support the idea and reality of a progressive television network.

DIVA-TV
(Damned Interfering Video Activists)
12 Wooster Street
New York, NY 10013
divatv@aidsnyc.org
http://www.actupny.org/diva/DIVA-
TV.html

Progressive video producers.

ELECTRONIC FRONTIER
FOUNDATION
1550 Bryant Street Suite 725
San Francisco, CA 94103
(415) 436-9333 Fax (415) 436-9993
eff@eff.org
www.eff.org

A leading civil liberties organization
devoted to maintaining the Internet as
a global vehicle for free speech.

FAIRNESS AND ACCURACY IN
REPORTING (FAIR)
130 West 25th Street
New York, NY 10001
(212) 633-6700 Fax (212) 727-7668
info@fair.org
www.fair.org

A national media watchdog group that
focuses public awareness on "the narrow corporate ownership of the press.

FEMINISTS FOR FREE
EXPRESSION
P.O. Box 2525 Times Square Station
New York, NY 10108
(212) 702-6292 Fax (212) 702-6277
FFE@aol.com
www.well.com/user/freedom

(FFE) is a national organization of
people who share a commitment both to
gender equality and to preserving the

individual's right to read, rent or purchase, media materials of their choice,
free from government intervention.

FREE SPEECH TV (FSTV)
P.O. Box 6060
Boulder, CO 80306
(303) 442-8445 or (303) 442-5693
Fax: (303) 442-6472
fstv@fstv.org
http://www.freespeech.org

National network offering progressive
programming..

FREEDOM FORUM
WORLD CENTER
1101 Wilson Boulevard
Arlington, VA 22209
(703) 528-0800 Fax (703) 522-4831
news@freedomforum.org
www.freedomforum.org

A nonpartisan, international foundation
dedicated to free press, free speech
and free spirit for all people.

FREEDOM OF
EXPRESSION FOUNDATION
171-B Claremont Avenue
Long Beach, CA 90803
(562) 434-2284
crsmith@csulb.edu
www.csulb.edu/~research/Cent/lamend.
html

Publishes a number of studies on
freedom of expression in America and
a newsletter that deals with issues of
the day.

FREEDOM OF INFORMATION CENTER

University of Missouri
127 Neff Annex
Columbia, MO 65211
(573) 882-4856 Fax (573) 884-496
Kathleen_Edwards@jmail.jour.missouri.edu
www.missouri.edu/~foiwww

The Freedom of Information Center collects and indexes materials relating to controls on the flow and content of information to research free-press issues.

FREEDOM OF INFORMATION CLEARINGHOUSE

P.O. Box 19367
Washington, DC 20036
(202) 588-7790
foia@citizen.org
www.citizen.org/public_citizen/litigation/foic/foic.html

Freedom of Information Clearinghouse Guidebook—a citizen's guide to making FOIA requests and appealing agency decisions.

Fund for Investigative Journalism
5120 Kenwood Drive
Annandale, VA 22003
(703) 750-3849
fundfij@aol.com
www.fij.org

FIJ gives grants to journalists seeking help for investigative pieces involving environmental issues, corruption, malfeasance, incompetence and societal ills.

GLOBAL EXCHANGE

2017 Mission Street, Suite 303
San Francisco, CA 94110
(415) 255-7296 Fax (415) 255-7498
gx-info@globalexchange.org
www.globalexchange.org

Global Exchange publishes books and pamphlets on various social and economic topics and helps build public awareness about human rights abuses worldwide.

GLOBALVISION

1600 Broadway, Suite 700
New York, NY 10019
(212) 246-0202 Fax (212) 246-2677
www.igc.org/globalvision/

An independent film and television production company. Specializing in an "inside-out" style of journalism, it has produced *Rights & Wrongs: Human Rights Television* and *South Africa Now* along with other highly acclaimed investigative documentaries.

HIGHTOWER RADIO/ UNITED BROADCASTING

P.O. Box 13516
Austin, TX 78711
(512) 477-5588 Fax: (512) 478-8536
hightower@essential.org
http://essential.org/hightower/

Jim Hightower's progressive-populist national radio network.

HISPANIC EDUCATION AND
MEDIA GROUP, INC.
P.O. Box 221
Sausalito, CA 94966
(415) 331-8560 Fax (415) 331-2636
chalawerber@hotmail.com

Dedicated to improving the quality of
life of the Latino community with a
main focus on high school dropout
prevention and health issues.

HUCK BOYD NATIONAL CENTER
FOR COMMUNITY MEDIA
Kansas State University
105 Kedzie Hall,
Manhattan, KS 66506
(913) 532-6890 Fax (913) 532-5484
huckboyd@ksu.edu
www.jmc.ksu.edu/jmc/files/hbnc/
hbnc.html

The mission of HBNC is to strengthen
local media in order to help create
better, stronger communities in
America.

INDEPENDENT MEDIA INSTITUTE
77 Federal Street
San Francisco, CA 94107
(415) 284-1420 Fax (415) 284-1414
congress@igc.org
www.mediademocracy.org

Protecting and advancing public policy
issues that affect the First Amendment;
IMI's mission is to improve public
access to independent and alternative
journalism.

INDEPENDENT PRESS
ASSOCIATION
P.O. Box 191785
San Francisco, CA 94119-1785
(415) 896-2456 Fax (415) 896-2457
indypress@igc.org
www.indypress.org

As a membership-based association,
we provide technical assistance,
hands-on training, and an online
communications for independent
publishers.

INDEPENDENT TELEVISION
SERVICE
51 Federal Street, Suite 401
San Francisco, CA 94107
(415) 356-8383 Fax: (415) 356-8391
itvs@itvs.org
http://www.itvs.org

Produces independent television
programs for undeserved populations
and audiences.

INSTITUTE FOR MEDIA POLICY
AND CIVIL SOCIETY
910-207 W. Hastings Street
Vancouver, BC V6B 1H6 Canada
(604) 682-1953 Fax (604) 683-8536
media@impacs.bc.ca
www.impacs.bc.ca

IMPACS mission is to build strong
communities by providing training and
education to Canadian civil society
organizations.

INSTITUTE FOR POLICY STUDIES
733 15th Street, NW, Suite 1020
Washington, DC 20005
(202) 234-9382 Fax (202) 387-7915
www.igc.org/ifps

A leading progressive think tank, dedicated to strengthening our country's most important social movements such as those promoting fair trade and sustainable communities.

**INSTITUTE FOR
PUBLIC ACCURACY**
65 Ninth Street, Suite 3
San Francisco, CA 94103
(415) 552-5378 Fax (415) 552-6787
institute@igc.org
www.accuracy.org

IPA serves as a nationwide consortium of progressive policy researchers, scholars and activists-providing the media with quick responses to news releases from major corporate backed think tanks.

INTERNATIONAL ACTION CENTER
39 West 14th Street, Room 206
New York, NY 10011
(212) 633-6646 Fax (212) 633-2889
iacenter@iacenter.org
http://www.iacenter.org

Initiated in 1992 by U.S. Attorney General, Ramsey Clark, and other anti-war activists, IAC coordinates international meetings and teach-ins, holds demonstrations, publishes news releases and produces video documentaries.

**INTERNATIONAL CONSORTIUM OF
INVESTIGATIVE JOURNALISTS**
1634 I Street, NW, Suite 902
Washington, DC 20006
(202) 783-3900 Fax (202) 783-3906
info@icij.org
www.icij.org

ICIJ is a working consortium of leading investigative reporters from around the world that sponsors investigations into pressing issues which transcend national borders.

**INVESTIGATIVE JOURNALISM
PROJECT**
122 Maryland Avenue, NE, Suite 300
Washington, DC 20002
(202) 546-3732 Fax (202) 543-3156

**INVESTIGATIVE REPORTING
FUND, THE (FIRE)**
2 Wall Street, Suite 203
Asheville, NC 28801-2710
(704) 259-9179 Fax (704) 251-1311
calvina@main.nc.us
www.main.nc.us/fire

Keeps the heat on for the public's right to know.

JUST THINK FOUNDATION
80 Liberty Ship Way, Suite 1
Sausalito, CA 94965
(415) 289-0122 Fax (415) 289-0123
think@justthink.org
www.justthink.org

Teaches media educators how to integrate curriculum into classrooms.

L.A. ALTERNATIVE MEDIA NETWORK
8124 West Third Street #208
Los Angeles, CA 90048
(213) 665-5720 Fax (213) 458-6566
sekler@labridge.com
http://home.labridge.com/~laamn

LAAMN is a network of multi-media and media watch activists who have come together to develop a strong presence for the independent, alternative media in Los Angeles.

MEDIA ACCESS PROJECT
1707 L Street, NW
Washington, DC 20036
(202) 232-4300 Fax (202) 223-5302
www.mediaaccess.org/

Promotes the public's First mendment right to hear and be heard on the electronic media.

MEDIA ALLIANCE
814 Mission Street, Suite 205
San Francisco, CA 94103
(415) 546-6334 Fax (415) 546-6218
ma@igc.org
www.media-alliance.org

Review and analysis of San Francisco Bay Area media issues.

MEDIA COALITION/AMERICANS FOR CONSTITUTIONAL FREEDOM
139 Fulton Street, Suite 302
New York, NY 10038
(212) 587-4025 Fax (212) 587-2436
mail@mediacoalition.org
http://www.mediacoalition.org

We defend the American public's First Amendment right to have access to the broadest possible range of opinion and entertainment.

MEDIA & DEMOCRACY INSTITUTE, THE
77 Federal Street
San Francisco, CA 94107
(415) 284-1420 Fax (415) 284-1414
congress@igc.org
www.alternet.org/an/Congress.html
Dedicated to strengthening, supporting and increasing public access to independent and alternative journalism.

MEDIA EDUCATION FOUNDATION, THE
26 Center Street
Northampton, MA 01060
(800) 897-0089 or (413) 584-8500
Fax (800) 659-6882 or (413) 586-8398
mediaed@mediaed.org
www.mediaed.org

Founded to produce and distribute educational videotapes with a critical media perspective.

MEDIA NETWORK/ALTERNATIVE MEDIA INFORMATION CENTER
39 West 14th Street, #403
New York, NY 10011
(212) 929-2663 Fax (212) 929-2732

NATIONAL ASIAN AMERICAN TELECOMMUNICATION ASSOCIATION
346 9th Street, 2nd Floor
San Francisco, CA 94103
(415) 863-0814 Fax (415) 863-7428
www.naatanet.org

Organization seeking to increase Asian and Pacific Islanders participation in the media and the promotion of fair and accurate coverage of our communities.

NATIONAL ASSOCIATION OF BLACK JOURNALISTS
8701 Adelphi Road
Adelphi, MD 20783-1716
nabj@nabj.org
www.nabj.org

Our mission is to strengthen ties among African-American journalists, promote diversity in newsrooms, expand job opportunities and recruiting activities for established African-American journalists and students.

NATIONAL ASSOCIATION OF HISPANIC JOURNALISTS
National Press Building, Suite 1193
Washington, DC 20045
(202) 662-7145 Fax (202) 662-7144
najh@nahj.org
www.nahj.org

NAHJ is dedicated to the recognition and professional advancement of Hispanics in the news industry.

NATIONAL ASSOCIATION OF RADIO TALK SHOW HOSTS
1030 15th Street, NW, Suite 700
Washington, DC 20005
(202) 408-8255 Fax (202) 408-5788
nashe@priority1.net
www.talkshowhosts.com

Provides a resource guide to talk radio world wide.

NATIONAL CAMPAIGN FOR FREEDOM OF EXPRESSION
918 F Street, NW, #609
Washington, DC 20004
(202) 393-2787 Fax (202) 347-7376
ncfe@artswire.org
www.artswire.org/~ncfe/

The NCFE is an educational and advocacy network formed to protect and extend freedom of artistic expression and fight censorship throughout the United States.

NATIONAL COALITION AGAINST CENSORSHIP
275 7th Avenue, 20th Floor
New York, NY 10001
(212) 807-6222 Fax (212) 807-6245
ncac@ncac.org
www.ncac.org

NCAC works to educate members and the public at large about the dangers of censorship and how to oppose it.

NATIONAL CONFERENCE OF EDITORIAL WRITERS
6223 Executive Boulevard
Rockville, MD 20852
(301) 984-3015 Fax (301) 231-0026
ncewhqs@erols.com
www.ncew.org

NCEW is dedicated to the purpose of stimulating the conscience and quality of the editorial.

NATIONAL EDUCATIONAL MEDIA NETWORK

655 13th Street, Suite 1
Oakland, CA 94612
(510) 465-6885 Fax (510) 465-2835
nemn@nemn.org
www.nemn.org

The nation's only media organization dedicated to recognizing and supporting excellence in educational media.

NATIONAL LESBIAN AND GAY JOURNALISTS ASSOCIATION

1718 M Street, NW, #245
Washington, DC 20036
(202) 588-9888 Fax (202) 588-1818
nlgja@aol.com
www.nlgja.org

NLGJA works from within the news industry to foster fair and accurate coverage of lesbian and gay issues.

NATIONAL TELEMEDIA COUNCIL

120 East Wilson Street
Madison, WI 53703
(608) 257-7712 Fax (608) 257-7714
Ntelemedia@aol.com
danenet.widip.org./ntc

NTC is a national non-profit educational organization that promotes media literacy education with a positive, non-judgmental philosophy.

NATIONAL WRITERS UNION

113 University Place, 6th floor
New York, NY 10003
(212) 254-0279 Fax (212) 254-0673
nwu@nwu.org
www.nwu.org/nwu/

NWU's national quarterly, "American Writer," tracks developments in the media/information industry and the labor movement that concern working writers.

NEWS WATCH CANADA

Simon Fraser University
8888 University Drive
Burnaby, BC V5A 1S6 Canada
(604) 291-4905 Fax (604) 291-4024
censored@sfu.ca
newswatch.cprost.sfu.ca/newswatch

Canadian media watch organization and freedom of information advocacy group.

NICAR: NATIONAL INSTITUTE FOR COMPUTER-ASSISTED REPORTING

138 Neff Annex
Columbia, MO 65211
(573) 882-2042 Fax (573) 882-5431
info@ire.org
www.nicar.org

NICAR trains investigative reporters on how to use various data bases for investigative purposes.

PACIFIC NEWS SERVICE

450 Mission Street, Room #204
San Francisco, CA 94105
(415) 438-4755 or (415) 243-4364
Fax (415) 438-4935
pacificnews@pacificnews.org
www.pacificnews.org/ncm

Produces an article per day for reprint in a variety of newspapers worldwide.

PAPER TIGER TV
339 Lafayette Street
New York, NY 10012
(212) 420-9045 Fax: (212) 420-8223
http://www.papertiger.org
E-mail: tigertv@bway.net

Alternative/Progressive TV Production.

PEACENET, LABORNET, ECONET,
CONFLICTNET, WOMEN'S NET
Institute for Global Communications
Presidio Building 1012
P.O. Box 29904
San Francisco, CA 94129
(415) 561-6100 Fax (415) 561-6101
http://www.igc.org
E-mail: mlockwood@igc.org

Information for progressive activists.

PEOPLE'S NEWS AGENCY
7627 16th Street, NW
P.O. Box 56466
Washington, DC 20040
(202) 829-2278 Fax: (202) 829-0462
E-mail: proutwdc@prout.org
www.prout.org/pna

News service and free reprints for
progressive publications.

PEOPLE'S VIDEO NETWORK
2489 Mission Street, #28
San Francisco, CA 94110
(415) 821-6545 or (415) 821-7575
Fax (415) 821-5782
npcsf@igc.apc.org

Films important progressive events and
speeches for rebroadcasting.

PEOPLE'S VIDEO NETWORK
39 West 14th Street
New York, NY 10071
(212) 633-6646 Fax (212) 633-2889
http://www.peoplesvideo.org

Films important progressive events and
speeches for rebroadcasting.

PAUL ROBESON FUND FOR
INDEPENDENT MEDIA/FUNDING
EXCHANGE, THE
666 Broadway, #500
New York, NY 10012
(212) 529-5300
jan.strout@fex.org
www.fex.org\robeson

The PR Fund supports media activism
and grassroots organizing by local,
state, national or international
organizations and individual media
producers by funding radio, film and
video productions.

PROGRESSIVE MEDIA PROJECT
409 East Main Street
Madison, WI 53703
(608) 257-4626 Fax (608) 257-3373
pmproj@itis.com
www.progressive.org/mediaproject.html

It provides opinion pieces from a
progressive perspective to daily and
weekly newspapers all over the
country.

PROJECT CENSORED
Sonoma State Univeresity
1801 E. Cotati Avenue
Rohnert Park, CA 94928-3609
(707) 664-2500 Fax (707) 664-2108
project.censored@sonoma.edu
www.sonoma.edu/ProjectCensored

Project Censored is a faculty/student media research project dedicated to building free democratic news systems.

PUBLIC MEDIA CENTER
446 Green Street
San Francisco, CA 94133
(415) 434-1403 Fax (415) 986-6779

PMC is a non-profit, public interest advertising agency focusing on social, political and evironmental issues.

REPORTER'S COMMITTEE FOR FREEDOM OF THE PRESS
1101 Wilson Boulevard, Suite 1910
Arlington, VA 22209
(703) 807-2100 Fax (703) 807-2109
rcfp@rcfp.org
http://www.rcfp.org

The Committee serves as a major national and international resource in free speech issues.

SOCIETY OF ENVIRONMENTAL JOURNALISTS
P.O. Box 27280
Philadelphia, PA 19118-0280
(215) 836-9970 Fax (215) 836-9972
SEJoffice@aol.com
www.sej.com

Dedicated to supporting environmental journalists and furthering environmental journalism.

SOUTHWEST ALTERNATIVE MEDIA PROJECT
1519 West Main Street
Houston, TX 77006
(713) 522-8592 Fax (713) 522-0953
cyberia@swamp.org
www.swamp.org

A non-profit media center promoting the creation and appreciation of film and video as art forms for a multicultural public.

TELEVISION PROJECT, THE
2311 Kimball Place
Silver Springs, MD 20910
(301) 588-4001 Fax (301) 588-4001
apluhar@tvp.org
www.tvp.org

An organization to help parents understand how television affects their families and community.

THOMAS JEFFERSON CENTER FOR THE PROTECTION OF FREE EXPRESSION, THE
400 Peter Jefferson Place
Charlottesville, VA 22911-8691
(804) 295-4784 Fax (804) 296-3621
freespeech@tjcenter.org
www.tjcenter.org

An organization devoted to the defense of free expression in all its forms.

TV-FREE AMERICA
1611 Connecticut Avenue, NW
Washington, DC 20009
(202) 887-0436 Fax (202) 518-5560
tvfa@essential.org
http://essential.org/orgs/tvfa

An organization that encourages Americans to reduce the amount of television they watch in order to promote richer, healthier and more connected lives, families, and communities.

UNION PRODUCERS AND PRO-
GRAMMERS NETWORK
271 18th Avenue, South
Minneapolis, MN 55455
(612) 624-4326
jsee@csom.umn.edu or uppnet@labor-
net.org
www.mtn.org/jsee/uppnet.html
Organized to promote production and
use of TV and radio shows pertinent to
the cause of organized labor and working people—publishes UPPNET News.

WE INTERRUPT THIS MESSAGE
965 Mission Street, Suite 220
San Francisco, CA 94103
(415) 537-9437 Fax (415) 537-9439
interrupt@igc.org

Interrupt builds capacity in public
interest groups to do traditional media
and publicity work as well as to
reframe public debate and interrupt
media stereotypes.

WOMEN FOR MUTUAL SECURITY
5110 West Penfield Road
Columbia, MD 21045
(410) 730-7483 Fax (410) 964-9248
foerstel@aol.com
www.iacenter.org/wms/

A international network of women's
organizations and individuals
committed to making a paradigm shift
from a hierarchical violent society to a
cooperative and peaceful one.

WOMEN'S INSTITUTE FOR
FREEDOM OF THE PRESS
3306 Ross Place, NW
Washington, DC 20008-3332
(202) 966-7783 Fax (202) 966-7783
wifponline@igc.apc.org
www.igc.org/wifp/

Explores ways to assure that everyone
has equal access to the public, speaking for themselves, so everyone's information can be taken into account in
decision-making.

WORLD PRESS
FREEDOM COMMITTEE
11600 Sunrise Valley Drive
Reston, VA 22091
(703) 715-9811 Fax (703) 620-6790
freepress@wpfc.org

A network of national and international
news media organizations united in the
defense and promotion of freedom.

THIS MODERN WORLD

by TOM TOMORROW

THIS WEEK: A GUIDE TO THE *GLOBAL ECONOMY*!

STEP ONE: INVESTORS INSIST MANUFACTURING JOBS BE MOVED TO LOW WAGE COUNTRIES. OBSEQUIOUS PUNDITS QUICKLY PROFER A FAMILIAR LITANY OF EXPLANATORY BUZZPHRASES.

--FREE MARKETS!

--COMPETI-TIVENESS!

--THE *SHARE-HOLDERS*!

BLAH!

BLAH!

STEP TWO: WIDESPREAD DOWNSIZING LEAVES REMAINING WORKERS IN A STATE OF PERPETUAL INSECURITY. WAGE STAGNATION ENSUES, FURTHER BENEFITTING WALL STREET.

MAN, MY STOCKS ARE GOING THROUGH THE DAMN *ROOF*! I GUESS I WON'T FIRE YOU *THIS* WEEK.

YOU'RE SIMPLY TOO GEN-EROUS, SIR.

WALL STREET JOURNAL

STEP FOUR: MARGIN-ALIZED WORKERS END UP RESCUING THE VERY INVESTORS RESPONSI-BLE FOR THEIR PLIGHT TO BEGIN WITH. BACK TO STEP ONE!

THANKS FOR YOUR HELP, SON! I COULD HAVE LOST A *FORTUNE*!

MAD COW BURGERS™ OUR PRICES ARE CRAZY

GRRR...

STEP THREE: OVERSEAS MARKETS STUMBLE. SUDDENLY, OUTSPOKEN FREE MARKETEERS ARE TRANSFORMED INTO UNABASHED PROPONENTS OF GOVERNMENT INTERVENTION.

A TAXPAYER-FUNDED IMF BAILOUT IS THE *ONLY SOLUTION*!

I QUITE CONCUR! WE CERTAINLY CAN'T EXPECT GLOBAL IN-VESTORS TO TAKE RESPONSIBILITY FOR THEIR *OWN ACTIONS*!

TOM TOMORROW-28-98

APPENDIX E

TOP 5 CENSORED REPRINTS

COMPILED BY TRICIA BORETA AND YVETTE TANNENBAUM

1 CENSORED

Secret International Trade Agreement Undermines Sovereignty of Nations

"BUILDING A GLOBAL ECONOMY"
By Joel Bleifuss; *In These Times;* January 11, 1998

With fast track down, though perhaps not out, the next battle in the pell-mell rush into a globalized economy will be fought over the Multilateral Agreement on Investment (MAI). This proposed treaty extends the free trade provisions of the General Agreement on Tariffs and Trade (GATT) by prohibiting signatory nations from impeding the flow of money and production facilities from one country to another. The treaty, in effect, subordinates the right of elected governments to set national economic policy to the right of transnational corporations and investors to conduct business—investing and divesting—however they see fit.

Since 1995, the Organization for Economic Cooperation and Development (OECD), an alliance of 29 of the world's richest nations, has been quietly negotiating the treaty in Paris. The treaty's strongest supporters, which include the United States, the European Union, and transnational corporations, argue that government regulations that prevent the free movement of money and production facilities are inefficient and costly. Removing these barriers, the treaty's preamble states, "will contribute to the efficient utilization of economic resources, the creation of employment opportunities and the improvement of living standards."

Renato Ruggerio, director general of the World Trade Organization, describes the treaty as "the constitution for a new global economy." But according to Public Citizen's Chantell Taylor, that constitution grants rights only to corporations. "This treaty takes the strongest provisions of GATT, NAFTA, and bilateral trade agreements and expands them in a way that is revolutionary," she says. "This is on the largest scale that these rights for corporations have ever been applied."

Negotiations on the treaty continue, with the final draft due to be released in May. If President Clinton and the other 28 countries agree on a pact, the treaty is likely to reach the Senate for ratification sometime in 1999. Once the 29 OECD countries have ratified MAI, the 157 non-OECD nations will be invited to join. Most will have no choice but to do so. As the State Department explains in a published summary of the treaty's intent, the MAI would serve as "a benchmark for emerging economies wishing to continue to attract foreign investment."

Public interest groups in the United States are beginning to fight the treaty, arguing that, in the name of international fairness, it erodes the prerogative of governments to intervene in the market for the public good. In particular, they point to the section entitled "National Treatment" in the May 1997 draft of the treaty, which was leaked to Public Citizen. This part of the bill would require signatory nations to treat foreign investors exactly the same way that they treat their domestic counterparts. That provision, they say, could undermine a slew of regulations. For example, a European corporation that wants to do business in the United States could contest local statutes that provide set-aside programs for minorities and women, since such laws put foreign corporations at a disadvantage. Ditto for any government policy that grants preferences to small business owners. And in developing countries, the provision could be used to overturn programs that limit foreign ownership in order to keep farmland under peasant control and to stabilize the domestic food supply.

Nor does the treaty allow governments to discriminate between foreign investors based on their country of origin. While this foreign treatment provision of the treaty may seem fair, it would prevent democratically elected governments from imposing sanctions against countries that are gross abusers of human rights or wanton despoilers of the environment. If MAI had been in place in the '80s, for example, the U.S. sanctions against investment in South Africa, which helped bring down the apartheid regime, could have been prohibited. (The bill does contain exemptions for issues of "national security," so that much of the Helms-Burton Act, which puts teeth in the U.S. embargo against Cuba by penalizing corporations that do business there, would remain intact.)

"Performance Requirements"—laws that require that corporations transfer technological knowledge to host countries or achieve a certain level of domestic content—get their own section of the treaty. MAI would ban nearly all of them, threatening community development programs such as the 1977 Community Reinvestment Act, which requires banks to make loans in poor neighborhoods if they open a branch there.

Meanwhile, environmentalists worry about MAI provisions on "uncompensated expropriation." As drafted, MAI could be interpreted to imply that environmental regulations are an expropriation of property, since the regulations limit how a corporation can use its investment. "The expropriation provision is a huge problem because it blurs the legal distinction between the outright seizure of property and regulations that set limitations on the use of property," says Michelle Sforza of the Preamble Center for Public Policy, a Washington, D.C.-based public interest group. "MAI is quite explicit about expanding the definition of expropriation to cover 'regulatory takings' or 'creeping expropriation.'" The Clinton Administration, realizing that this section threatens the environment, recently reopened the topic for further discussion.

To enforce its new economic rules, MAI sets up a dispute resolution process using the North American Free Trade Agreement (NAFTA) as a blueprint. The MAI legal framework would permit both corporate and individual investors to sue sovereign nations for any failure to follow MAI rules "which causes [or is likely to cause] loss or damage to the investor or his investment." (The brackets denote language in the treaty on which there is disagreement among negotiators.) Traditionally, international agreements have only allowed nations to sue other sovereign nations for treaty violations.

In the case of a lawsuit, MAI requires that nations defend their policies before a tribunal chosen from a list of OECD-approved arbitrators. The tribunal would base its findings on the treaty itself, and

will be empowered to provide "compensatory monetary damages," restitution or "any other form of relief." The judgment of the tribunal would be "binding," and a nation that loses a case would be required to enforce the judgment "as if it were a final judgment of its courts."

While MAI permits corporations to sue governments for violating the agreement, the treaty contains no provisions for governments to sue corporations. In fact, the treaty puts almost no demands on corporations. MAI contains no measures to counter anti-competitive business practices (like price fixing) that a treaty actually designed to improve economic efficiency should include.

In Paris, delegates are currently hammering out a number of specific exemptions. Many regulations currently in place are likely to be grandfathered, giving nations time to adjust their policies accordingly. Several nations are also seeking language to protect their country's cultural traditions. France, for example, has asked that "literary and artistic works" be exempted from MAI. The United States adamantly opposes such a blanket exemption, which is designed to prevent Disney or Warner Brothers from buying up the film industries of France or Spain. As it is currently drawn, MAI would prohibit nations from subsidizing their culture industries through tax credits, which would put a major crimp in the Australian and Canadian film industries. Countries, like Canada, that try to insulate their media outlets from U.S. competition could also be affected.

Most Americans (and even many policy makers) have never heard of MAI. But U.S.-based transnational corporations are in the loop, thanks to the United

States Council for International Business (USCIB), the principal U.S. supporter of the treaty. The USCIB, the American affiliate of the International Chamber of Commerce, is comprised of 600 U.S.-based corporations. The group officially opposes the use of economic sanctions as an instrument of foreign policy, codes of conduct on child labor, and a cap on greenhouse gas emissions. USCIB's "Working Group on MAI" reports that it has "helped shape U.S. negotiating positions by providing business views and technical advice on specific policy issues at regular meetings with U.S. negotiators immediately before and after each MAI negotiating session." In addition, the group provides USCIB-affiliated corporations with "direct access to Ambassador Franz Engering, chairman of the OECD's MAI negotiating group."

Last spring, the Clinton Administration, apparently trying to head off opposition from labor and environmental groups, asked its negotiators to include language in the treaty that addressed the critics' concerns. As a result, the agreement will include statements on the environment and labor. Whether those statements will actually be binding, like the NAFTA side agreements, remains to be seen. The State Department's Assistant Secretary for Economic and Business Affairs, Alan Larson, says that members of the Clinton Administration are still undecided about whether or not the United States should support binding side agreements.

For its part, the business community is opposed to environmental or labor standards of any kind. In a July 11 letter, USCIB President Abraham Katz cautioned U.S. Trade Representative Char-lene Barshefsky against doing anything that "would turn this agreement into a vehicle for achieving environmental and labor objectives." The Working Group on MAI has also vowed to "strongly resist efforts to impose new guidelines of codes of conduct on multinational corporations," even voluntary ones.

The national media have been slow to pick up the story. Since treaty negotiations began in 1995, *The New York Times* has only mentioned the treaty once, and that was in a letter to the editor. The *Washington Post* has not covered it at all. One exception has been the *Chicago Tribune*, which ran a story in December.

With funding from the Ford Foundation, the Preamble Center plans to educate the public about the treaty. The group, which does not take an official position for or against the agreement, is sponsoring debates in 20 cities between MAI partisans, either from the USCIB or the Clinton Administration, and MAI opponents such as Public Citizen. Public Citizen is planning to campaign against the treaty in 25 states, and has already joined organizations from 23 other countries in an international anti-MAI coalition. "MAI is an unbalanced agreement that gives rights to corporations and at the same time burdens governments with new obligations to investors," says Public Citizen's Taylor. "It ties the hands of governments to choose their own social and economic policies."

Richard Grossman, the co-founder of the Program on Corporations, Law and Democracy in Provincetown, Massachusetts, believes that the opposition to MAI is operating within too limited a context. "MAI should be resisted in ways that challenge existing corporate privileges, such as their claims to First Amendment protections, that define corporate operations as beyond the sovereignty of the American people," he says. "We are always on the defensive. We are, in effect, saying that the most important factors in our lives are only worthy of being dealt with in side agreements."

Grossman has a point. Yet Washington-based groups are in the nation's capital in order to influence legislation. And with the Republicans in control of Congress, the work of public interest groups is naturally going to be more reactive than proactive. But none of that stops citizens, political parties, and public interest groups outside the Beltway from filling in the broader picture. By putting MAI in context, these groups could push real alternatives to corporate power.

"HUMAN RIGHTS OR CORPORATE RIGHTS? THE MAI CHALLENGE"

By Miloon Kothari and Tara Krause; *Human Rights Tribune*, Vol. 5, Nos. 1-2; April 1998: p. 16-17

This year, as we commemorate the 50th anniversary of the Universal Declaration of Human Rights, we should refrain from self-congratulations. While, over the past five decades, we have created an impressive international human rights law regime, we have also witnessed the parallel evolution of the Bretton-Woods institutions. The globalization which has resulted from that process now threatens to undermine all our human rights gains.

THE MAI IS NOTHING LESS THAN A BILL OF RIGHTS AND FREEDOMS FOR TRANSNATIONAL CORPORATIONS We have, in fact, arrived at a historic juncture where we need to decide whether our international and national systems will be governed by the principles of corporate rights or human rights. There are increasingly strong and vocal forces calling for trade and finance to override the imperatives of local governance and human rights. Nothing typifies trend more than the draft Multilateral Agreement on Investment (MAI), currently being debated for possible adoption later this year by the OECD—the Organisation of Economic Cooperation and Development—the international club of the world's 29 richest countries.

If adopted, this treaty would contribute significantly to a constitution of a single global economy. The MAI is nothing less than a bill of rights and freedoms for transnational corporations and a declaration of corporate rule.

Up until last year, the MAI was for the most part negotiated in secret and benefited from the aggressive advocacy of the International Chamber of Commerce, the U.S. Council on International Business, and other corporate-backed groups. After news about the MAI was leaked, environmental, social justice, labor and development groups rallied all the forces they could muster. It was clear to this coalition that the new trend of corporate globalization embodied in the MAI would routinely brush aside the international law obligations states had assumed over the past years, especially in the areas of human rights and the environment. This expanding NGO coalition has not, however, included many human rights groups.

WHERE ARE THE HUMAN RIGHTS NGOS? The human rights community has traditionally been slow to react to violations of economic and social rights, and it has reacted sluggishly at best to economic and social policies and agreements that have profound implications for human rights. This is what occurred with respect to the Structural Adjustment Programs (SAPs) mandated by the World Bank or the International Monetary Fund (IMF), with the Uruguay Round of the General Agreement on Tariffs and Trade, and with the establishment of the World Trade Organization (WTO).

The pattern is being repeated with the MAI. By its failure to act in concert with other progressive forces, the human rights movement is marginalizing itself. The ease with which the MAI has reached such an advanced stage of preparation, and the power of para-statal agencies that this symbolizes, should act as a wake-up call for human rights NGOs.

WHY IS THE MAI SO DANGEROUS? What is so dangerous about the MAI is that it will force nations to relax or abrogate the obligations they have assumed to protect human rights, environmental, and labor standards in order to attract investment and trade. In this manner, the expanding corporate agenda, of which the MAI is a convenient instrument, will undermine the sovereignty of countries. It will create a global system where accountability and responsibility will theoretically rest with governments but where all the benefits will actually accrue to the investors. Furthermore, the investors and corporations will only respond to the logic and calculus of competitiveness, high investment returns, and the unhindered flow of global capital.

The principles upon which the MAI is based and the prescriptions it details run counter to the principles on which the international human rights regime is based. Essentially, the MAI seeks to codify the free trade agenda, always favoring the rights of transnational investors and corporations over the rights of workers, consumers, communities, and the environment. For example, the MAI lacks binding provisions on corporate responsibilities vis-a-vis labour practices. The most basic contradiction is that, under the MAI, investors—mostly transnational corporations—are given the power to sue governments for lost competitiveness and profits. Investors can always challenge state legislation and regulations, or governmental policies and practices, threatening governments with potentially high damage awards. Local communities, governments, and citizens groups have no similar recourse. They must comply with the free trade regime or face penalties. The MAI provides for a special investor-state dispute settlement mechanism, which is a fast-track international tribunal/arbitration panel, that completely bypasses domestic legal channels.

The MAI can also counter and negate positive measures that states have taken to end discrimination against vulnerable people and communities in relation to the human rights to food, health, housing, land, and work. Necessary measures—such as food subsidies, control of land speculation, agrarian reform, the implementation of health and environmental standards—can be challenged as "illegal" under the MAI. So, too, can measures that provide community control of forests, local bans on use of pesticides and hormone-induced foods, clean air standards, limits on mineral, gas, and oil extraction, bans on toxic dumping.

As well, the MAI specifically abrogates commitments made in Beijing and Istanbul that stipulate that corporations comply with all national codes, social security measures, and international law, including international environmental law. Agreements such as the Kyoto Protocol and the Global Biodiversity convention are thereby put at risk. Rather than reaffirming or acknowledging existing norms and standards, the MAI erodes even non-binding codes of conduct. In other words, the MAI allows the rights of investors to trump individual and collective human rights.

WHO WILL BE MOST AFFECTED? It is easy to see that such discrimination in favor of global capital and investment will lead to the destruction of the natural resource and the common property resource base. Since the principle resources of the developing countries are still in the sectors of agriculture, mining, forestry, and fisheries, the MAI could considerably exacerbate the pressure that these sectors are already experiencing. The most severely affected will be women and children, and vulnerable communities such as marginal farmers, indigenous peoples, fisherfolk, and rural agricultural laborers.

In addition, the MAI would undermine the capacity of local municipalities to govern sustainably and democratically. Recently, for example, the U.S. administration warned that Maryland state legislation implementing sanctions against Nigeria would run counter to GATT rules that bar trade discrimination even against countries with egregious human rights and environmental records.

WHAT SHOULD THE HUMAN RIGHTS COMMUNITY DO? More than the GATT and the NAFTA, the MAI has sent shock waves through civil society groups at all levels and across all regions of the world. Environmental groups have quickly used the framework of multilateral environmental agreements to marshal international law arguments against MAI. Yet human rights groups have been virtually silent. Nonetheless, the tasks before the international human rights community are clear. Human rights NGOs should:

➤ Conduct an immediate technical review of the MAI treaty using the framework of a human rights legal analysis to examine the impact it is likely to have on international norms, standards and enforceability.

➤ Stress that economic, social and cultural rights are equal in importance to civil and political rights, and must be equally respected.

Analyze the impact that multinational non-state actors can have on the realization of all human rights.

➤ Strengthen the U.N. human rights system by lobbying governments to bolster the office of the High Commissioner for Human Rights. The stress Mary Robinson has placed on economic, social, and cultural rights should be welcomed.

➤ Further articulate the content of environmental human rights, stressing the need to work towards the full recognition of the collective human right to a healthy environment, the human right to safe, potable water and other similar survival rights.

➤ Use whatever provisions exist in the MAI, however minor, to counter its destructive powers. For example there is a provision that refers to the U.N. Charter for the maintenance of international peace and security. Are there other cogent arguments, such as *jus cogens*, the concept of public order, or the Vienna Convention on International treaties, that can be exploited for human rights advocacy against the MAI?

MAI ALLOWS THE RIGHTS OF INVESTORS TO TRUMP HUMAN RIGHTS. The MAI, and the mindset it represents, poses a formidable challenge to all groups concerned with protecting the human rights of people and communities. As we approach the third millennium and prepare the commemoration of the UDHR, we must insist that the rapidly globalizing regime of trade and finance conform to international human rights standards. Third party accountability is yet to be defined within the framework and actions of the international human rights regime. Now is the time to take up this task in earnest with the full cooperation of the Office of the High Commissioner of Human Rights. The MAI demands nothing less from us.

*MILOON KOTHARI is the Convener of Habitat International Coalition's Housing and Land Rights Committee. **TARA KRAUSE** is affiliated with the People's Decade for Human Rights Education and Voices 21.

"MAI TIES"

By Bill Dixon; *Democratic Left*; Spring 1998

Sometime in the coming months Americans will be introduced to yet another obscure and controversial economic acronym—MAI, for the Multilateral Agreement on Investment.

The MAI would establish a vast set of protections for foreign investment against "government regulation," making the world a safer place for investors and a more precarious place for everyone else. More radical in scope than NAFTA or GATT, the MAI would push the global economy far closer to a brave new world of transnational *laissez-faire*. With the coming debate over the MAI, the great clash between democracy and free-markets in the era of globalization will emerge more starkly than ever before.

Where NAFTA and GATT sought to end tariffs and establish free-trade, the MAI is designed to protect "foreign direct investment," a broad term for any assets —factories, products, services, currency, stock—that are located in one country but which are owned by a company located in another. The historic increase in foreign direct investment (which has more than doubled on the part of U.S. firms over the past 10 years) is a large part of what the new global economy is all about. Yet foreign investment can carry enormous risks because governments, especially governments in developing countries, sometimes do things that outside investors don't like. Governments, goes the complaint, often set up troublesome and perhaps unnecessary or unfair regulations which are in any case expensive to meet and difficult to challenge in court if you're not a citizen of the country in question. Worse, governments often try to develop their home economies by favoring domestic firms through tariffs and subsidies, tilting the balance against foreign competitors. And then sometimes, in rare moments of crisis and/or inspiration, governments appropriate property or nationalize industries, etc. all without compensating the injured parties at the going rate.

Powerful business interests, in reckoning the profitability of the New World Order, would like to get rid of such risks by instituting a standard set of rules across the globe. They want the ability to move production around without political hassles, repatriate their profits without "unfair" tax burdens, and trade stock and currency in the twinkle of a microchip without the bother of local red tape. Turning that capitalist wish list into world law is a tall order, but then the MAI is one of the most sweeping economic agreements in history.

Begun in the World Trade Organization just after the passage of GATT in 1995, early drafts of the MAI drew staunch criticism from Third World countries and many non-governmental organizations, all of whom warned that the MAI would undermine the sovereignty of government policies by giving too many rights of redress to multinational corporations.

To save the measure from its critics in the WTO, the MAI was sent off to the more sympathetic climate of the Organization of Economic Cooperation and Development (OECD). The 29 member OECD has its origins in the aftermath of World War II, when it was created to administer U.S. aid in the reconstruction of Europe through the Marshall Plan. Since then the OECD has grown into a powerful forum for finance and commerce policies throughout the leading nations of Europe, North America, and East Asia. Unlike previous OECD agreements, however, the MAI would be a binding, enforceable treaty and, more importantly, would quickly reach beyond the wealthy Northern hemisphere neighborhoods of the OECD and into the developing nations where dependence on foreign investment is often a matter of life and death. Yet despite the global ambitions of its proponents, the MAI negotiations stayed behind the closed doors of the OECD, excluding labor and NGO representatives while welcoming the participation of certain select members of the international business community.

Through the two years of the MAI's negotiation the details of specific proposals were kept a tight secret. Finally, in January of 1997 a draft of the agreement was leaked and some of the worst fears of the MAI's critics were confirmed.

The MAI would require "national treatment" for all foreign investors, which means that governments could no longer treat domestic firms differently than foreign ones. Under this provision, for example, there could be no restrictions on what outside firms could own, nor could there be subsidy programs designed to aid or develop domestic industries.

For poorer countries this provision could become tremendously dangerous, since it would threaten to take the enormous questions surrounding virtually any aspect of economic growth—land reform, industry support—out of public policy and into the unaccountable whims of the international market (and more likely, the multinational corporation's boardrooms).

Wealthy and powerful countries, like the U.S. and European Union members, are likely to negotiate exceptions to the national treatment provision. But again the question will be, which domestic interests will benefit from these protections and which will not? Dow Chemical and ADM might be able to keep their subsidies and tax breaks, but what about family farms or minority-owned businesses?

The MAI would also limit "performance requirements," regulations for how firms must do business, which are sometimes used as eligibility criteria for government aid or tax breaks. This could easily threaten to undermine employment policies, particularly affirmative action and anti-discrimination laws. The provision could also be used to challenge government programs aimed at channeling investment into poorer regions. Interestingly, the MAI would limit performance requirements whether or not they discriminate specifically against foreign investors.

The MAI of course bans the "uncompensated expropriation of assets," but in doing so it also casts a very wide net in defining what counts as "tantamount to expropriation." This means that regulations or policies which indirectly cost investors or cause them to forgo an otherwise profitable venture could be challenged as "expropriation." So, while it's true that this measure would forbid the seizure of the means of production by a revolutionary proletariat (which would be an unlikely candidate for MAI membership in any case), MAI proponents also have more immediate targets in mind. This provision is designed to curtail the scope of environmental and consumer laws which corporate interests view as obstacles to business as usual.

A telling case study for this issue is the U.S.-based Ethyl Corporation's suit against the Canadian government. A Canadian law bans the use of MMT, a gasoline additive and known toxin which Ethyl produces. Under the NAFTA protocols which served as a model for the MAI, Ethyl is suing Canada for $251 million, arguing that the regulation is unnecessary and violates their rights as a firm under NAFTA. The case, while still pending, will be an important test for what corporations can claim as their rights under transnational policies like NAFTA, GATT, and the MAI.

The Ethyl case also raises the crucial issue of how the MAI would be enforced. Like NAFTA and GATT, MAI member countries would have the power to pursue claims against each other in front of international panels, which would then have the power to rule on the cases and levy fines and sanctions. Under the MAI, however, corporations themselves could take advantage of "investor to state" procedures which give them the legal standing to sue governments directly. This is what Ethyl is doing against Canada through the more limited investor to state procedures found in NAFTA. Of course, the procedures only go one way, so governments would not enjoy the privilege of targeting corporations for bad conduct. The agreement instead gives multinational corporations a clear upper hand in the grievance process, making it less likely that governments would bother to put up a fight against a MAI complaint. To make matters worse, the agreement remains profoundly ambiguous about the scope of its jurisdiction—exactly when should a law be challenged as a trade issue?

Unlike NAFTA, the MAI contains no language or side-agreements regarding corporate responsibility or even general commitments to environmental protection or public health or labor rights, which among other things means that disputes like the Ethyl case would have very little in the way of actual law on which to base a decision.

The MAI would also mandate granting equal trade status to all MAI members, so that designations like Most Favored Nation, sometimes used in the U.S. to promote human rights, would no longer be optional. Economic sanctions against MAI members because of human rights or labor or environmental issues would be forbidden. Sanctions could only be leveled because of trade issues and even then only through the "due process" of MAI panels.

What will happen when an American public already anxious, skeptical, and angry about the new global economy confronts the most radical version of neoliberalism ever proposed? With the downfall of fast-track authority and the Asian financial crisis still fresh in public memory, not to mention the 1998 elections fast approaching, the fight over the MAI might just provide the Left with a chance to meet the issue of globalization head on. The MAI embodies much of what Americans dislike and mistrust about the corporate-led response to the enormous political and economic changes at work in the world, yet so far the agreement has gone without the slightest public attention in the U.S. Were that to change, the MAI would probably face serious reform or even defeat, but the results may reach even further. After all, the end of the MAI as we know it would signal a historic shift in the politics of globalization, which just might mean brighter prospects for the long march away from the absolute sovereignty of capital and toward greater solidarity and democracy within and across borders.

2 CENSORED

Chemical Corporations Profit Off Breast Cancer

"THE TRUTH ABOUT BREAST CANCER"—PART 1

By Peter Montague; *Rachel's Environment and Health Weekly;* December 4, 1997

BACKGROUND More American women have died of breast cancer in the past two decades than all the Americans killed in World War I, World War II, the Korean War and the Vietnam War combined.[1] The average woman killed by breast cancer loses 20 years of her life. Thus, with approximately 46,000 American women killed each year by breast cancer, we are now losing nearly a million person-years of life each year from breast cancer.[2] The costs of this epidemic are incalculably large.

About 180,000 new cases of breast cancer arise each year among U.S. women.[2] Furthermore, since 1940, the incidence (occurrence) of breast cancer has been creeping upward [1 percent] each year. This relentless increase cannot be explained by an aging population or by better detection such as mammography screening.[2] Since 1940, a woman's chance of getting breast cancer has doubled.[3]

Everyone now accepts that breast cancer has environmental and "lifestyle" causes; two basic facts make this conclusion inescapable: first, breast cancer incidence is five times as high in some countries as in others; secondly, when women migrate from a country with low incidence of breast cancer to a country with high incidence, their daughters acquire the breast-cancer risk prevailing in the high-incidence country.[4] Clearly, something in the environment (air, water, soil, food, or electromagnetic spectrum [for example, x-rays]) is at work here.

Until recently, the search for causes of breast cancer has ranged from nonexistent to lackadaisical—perhaps because of racism (the most rapid rise in breast cancer is occurring among African-American women[2]), or perhaps because in the U.S. women are simply not valued as highly as men. (We know, for example, that in the U.S. women's work is not valued as highly as men's—women earn only 70 percent as much as men for equal work.[5])

For years, breast cancer research (centered at the National Cancer Institute [NCI] in Bethesda, Maryland) has focused not on prevention but on therapy and treatment—earlier detection, better chemotherapy, better radiation, and better surgery.[6] These approaches have allowed many women to survive the disease (most of them without their breasts) but they have done little or nothing to prevent the scourge.

This non-preventive approach has been promoted aggressively by "Breast Cancer Awareness Month," an annual campaign that surfaces every October, sponsored by 17 governmental, professional, and medical organizations, including the National Cancer Institute.[7]

Breast Cancer Awareness Month was initiated in 1985 by a British chemical conglomerate called Imperial Chemical Industries (ICI), now known as Zeneca Pharmaceuticals. Breast Cancer Awareness Month is "focused on educating women about early detection of breast cancer."[7] Breast Cancer Awareness Month has promoted the slogan, "Early Detection is Your Best Prevention," but this is nonsense—if your cancer can be detected it's too late to prevent it. Breast Cancer Awareness Month—with all the authority of those 17 sponsoring organizations—consistently diverts attention away from real prevention.

According to a recent investigative report on Breast Cancer Awareness Month (BCAM) by Monte Paulsen (*Detroit Metro Times*, May 1993), "ICI has been the sole financial sponsor of BCAM since the event's inception. Altogether, the company has spent several million dollars' on the project, according to a spokeswoman. In return, ICI has been allowed to approve—or veto—every poster, pamphlet, and advertisement BCAM uses."[8] Thus the lack of a prevention message from Breast Cancer Awareness Month has not been accidental, and the 17 sponsoring agencies have adopted and endorsed Imperial Chemical's program and message.

Breast Cancer Awareness Month thus reveals an uncomfortably close connection between the chemical industry and the cancer research establishment in the U.S. Imperial Chemical—with revenues of $14 billion—is among the world's largest manufacturers of pesticides, plastics, pharmaceuticals and paper. ICI is also a major polluter. For example, one of its Canadian paint subsidiaries has been held responsible for 30 percent of all the toxic chemicals dumped into the heavily-polluted St. Lawrence River which separates the U.S. from Canada.[9]

In recent years, breast cancer research has begun to focus somewhat more on causes, but until very recently the emphasis has been on "lifestyle" factors—specifically obesity, alcohol, fat in the diet, age at first pregnancy, number of pregnancies, breast feeding, and so forth. Six years ago, 600,000 women wrote letters to Congress saying they wanted federal researchers to cast a wider net in the search for causes of breast cancer.[6] Two years later, *Science* magazine titled a major story, "Search for a Killer: Focus Shifts from Fat to Hormones."[3]

Actually hormones have been at the center of breast cancer research for at least 20 years because everyone agrees that 30 percent of breast cancers can be explained by exposure to naturally-occurring estrogen, the female sex hormone.[10] (Breast cancer may be caused by other things as well, but exposure to natural estrogens in the bloodstream is widely accepted as an important cause.) After a woman's period begins, each month her bloodstream is flooded with natural estrogens If she has a baby, the estrogen flow is interrupted. If she breast-feeds, the estrogen flow is interrupted. When she goes through menopause, the estrogen flow is greatly diminished.

One of the effects of estrogen is to cause cells to grow in the breasts. Many studies have now confirmed that women who start menstruating later than the average and who go through menopause earlier than the average have a reduced likelihood of breast cancer—presumably because they have a reduced exposure to estrogen. Women who have their first child early have a reduced risk. Women who have many children have a reduced risk. Women who breast-feed have a reduced risk.

After a woman goes through menopause, her natural flow of estrogen is greatly reduced. In the past 20 years, about 30 percent of American women aged 50-65 have been taking estrogen replacement pills after menopause.[11] There are real benefits from this "estrogen replacement therapy" (or ERT) — reduced osteoporosis (thinning of the bones) and reduced likelihood of death from heart disease. Unfortunately, taking ERT pills for 10 years increases a woman's chances of getting breast cancer by anywhere from 30 percent to 100 percent, and the longer she takes ERT the worse her outlook for breast cancer.[11,12,13]

In the past 5 years researchers have begun asking, "If some pesticides and plastics and other chlorinated chemicals can interfere with both male and female sex hormones in wildlife and humans,[14] and if 30 percent of breast cancer is known to be caused by naturally-occurring female sex hormones, isn't there a reasonable likelihood that some of these chlorinated chemicals contribute to the rising incidence of breast cancer?" It seems a reasonable enough question.

Researchers Devra Lee Davis and Leon Bradlow with Cornell University formally proposed a hypothesis, suggesting ways in which environmental estrogens (or, as they are sometimes called, xenoestrogens—xeno meaning "foreign") might cause breast cancer.[15] The research world began to buzz with interesting new work, asking whether chemicals that mimic, or block, estrogens might contribute to breast cancer.

It seemed a rather straightforward and obvious scientific question to be asking —and one with great consequences for public health. But to the chemical industry it looked like something more than merely an important public health question. With billions of dollars riding on the outcome, they saw it as a political struggle, less about saving lives than about maintaining profits, power and, above all, control. The Chemical Manufacturers Association (CMA) and its subsidiary, the Chlorine Chemistry Council (CCC), quickly developed a strategy to protect their interests against those of the 180,000 women afflicted by breast cancer each year. (See REHW #495.) They hired a scientist to begin casting doubt on the Davis/Bradlow hypothesis by saying this line of research is a dead end, a huge waste of time and taxpayers' money. (Manufacturing doubt is a strategy that has served the tobacco industry handsomely for 50 years, and the chemical industry has now adopted it—all, of course, in the name of "good science.") And they hired a sleazy, third-rate public relations firm—Mongoven, Biscoe and Duchin of Washington, DC—to develop a plan for discrediting Devra Lee Davis herself—Peter Montague (National Writers Union, UAW Local 1981/AFL-CIO)

[1] David Perlmutter, "Organochlorines, Breast Cancer, and GATT [a letter]," *Journal of the American Medical Association*; Vol. 271, No. 15, April 20, 1994: 1160-1161.

[2] Devra Lee Davis and H. Leon Bradlow, "Can Environmental Estrogens Cause Breast Cancer?" *Scientific American* Vol. 273, No. 4, October 1995: 166-172.

[3] Eliot Marshall, "Search for a Killer: Focus Shifts From Fat to Hormones," *Science* Vol. 259, January 29, 1993: 618-621.

[4] David J. Hunter and others, "Plasma Organochlorine Levels and the Risk of Breast Cancer," *New England Journal of Medicine*, Vol. 337, No. 18, October 30, 1997: 1253-1258.

[5] U.S. Bureau of the Census, *Statistical Abstract of the United States*, 116th edition, Springfield, Virginia: National Technical Information Service, 1996: 426, Table 663.

[6] Eliot Marshall, "The Politics of Breast Cancer," *Science* Vol. 259, January 29, 1993: 616-617.

[7] This information comes from the M.D. Anderson Cancer Center in Orlando, Florida. See http://www.pinkoctober.org/awarenes.html (Note the unique spelling of awareness).

[8] Paulsen quoted in Jim Hightower, *There's Nothing in the Middle of the Road but Yellow Stripes an Dead Armadillos* (New York: HarperCollins, 1997: 215-216. The *Detroit Metro Times* (and Monte Paulsen) can be reached at (313) 961-4060.

[9] Hightower, cited above, 215.

[10] Stephen Safe, "Is There an Association between Exposure to Environmental Estrogens and Breast Cancer?" *Environmental Health Perspectives*, Vol. 105, Supplement 3 April 1997: 675-678.

[11] Louise A. Brinton and Catherine Schairer, "Estrogen Replacement Therapy and Breast Cancer Risk," *Epidemiologic Reviews* Vol. 15, No. 1, 1993: 66-79.

[12] Graham A. Colditz and others, "The Use of Estrogens and Progestins and the Risk of Breast Cancer in Postmenopausal Women," *New England*

Journal of Medicine Vol. 332, No. 24, June 15, 1995: 1589-1593.

[13] Randall E. Harris and others, "Breast Cancer Risk: Effects of Estrogen Replacement Therapy and Body Mass," Journal of the National Cancer Institute, Vol. 84, No. 20, October 21, 1992: 1575-1582.

[14] Theo Colborn and Coralie Clement, editors, Chemically Induced Alterations in Sexual and Functional Development: The Wildlife/Human Connection [Advances in ModernEnvironmental Toxicology Vol. XXI] (Princeton, N.J.: Princeton Scientific Publishing Co., 1992).

[15] Devra Lee Davis, H. Leon Bradlow and others, "Medical Hypothesis: Xenoestrogens As Preventable Causes of Cancer," Environmental Health Perspectives Vol. 101, No. 5, October, 1993: 372-377.

"PROFITING OFF OF BREAST CANCER"

By Allison Sloan and Tracy Baxter; *The Green Guide;* October 1998

THE SPONSORSHIP SCAM October has been National Breast Cancer Awareness Month (NBCAM) since 1985, and this month, in addition to examining our breasts, it's high time we examined the corporate motives behind this event. For, while public education is vital to defeating this disease, NBCAM publicity and events focus exclusively on detection, ignoring any mention of prevention— including possible environmental causes. "The sole mission of NBCAM is to promote the importance of the three-step application to early detection: mammography, clinical breast exam and breast self-exam," says NBCAM's promotional brochure.

Although early detection through routine mammography screening does save some lives, the brochure neglects to mention that medical irradiation, including mammography and other x-rays, is a known cause of breast cancer in younger women. Nor does it mention that 7 of 11 recent studies on the relationship between breast cancer and organochlorine chemicals, including dioxin and pesticides like DDT, found elevated organochlorine levels in breast cancer victims. Why these omissions? Could it be because the founder of NBCAM manufactures carcinogenic chemicals as well as breast cancer treatment drugs?

National Breast Cancer Awareness Month was established by Zeneca Group PLC, a bioscience company with 1997 sales of $8.62 billion. Forty-nine percent of Zeneca's 1997 profits came from pesticides and other industrial chemicals, and 49 percent were from pharmaceutical sales, one-third (about $1.4 billion's worth) of which were cancer treatment drugs. The remaining 2 percent of Zeneca's profits derived from health care services, including the 11 cancer treatment centers Zeneca operates across the U.S. The herbicide acetochlor, considered a probable human carcinogen by the EPA, accounted for around $300 million of Zeneca's 1997 sales. Tamoxifen citrate (Nolvadex™), the most commonly prescribed breast cancer treatment drug on the market, accounted for $500 million.

When asked why prevention is not a priority of NBCAM, Debbie Ashcraft, Zeneca Pharmaceuticals' NBCAM Project Coordinator, replied that the company was hopeful tamoxifen will soon be approved for preventive use by the FDA. An FDA scientific advisory panel voted overwhelmingly in September to recommend approval of tamoxifen for reducing the incidence of breast cancer in healthy women at high risk of developing the disease.

This decision was reached in response to a four-year trial, concluded in April, by the National Cancer Institute of 13,388 "high risk" women. NCI found that tamoxifen decreased the incidence of breast cancer by almost one-half. Unfortunately, women in the tamoxifen group also had twice the incidence of uterine (endometrial) cancer, three times the rate of pulmonary embolisms (blood clots in the lungs), and 50 percent more cases of deep vein thrombosis (blood clots in major veins). Five women in each group died: all five from breast cancer in the placebo group; and three from breast cancer and two from pulmonary embolisms, a side effect of the drug, in the tamoxifen group.

Ironically, the World Health Organization's International Agency for Research on Cancer considers tamoxifen a "probable human carcinogen." It stands to reason that Zeneca, with $1.4 billion in annual sales of cancer treatment drugs, wouldn't be interested in prevention unless, as with tamoxifen, it means further profits, regardless of the potential health risks.

What You Can Do: To reduce your risk of breast cancer, Devra Lee Davis, Ph.D., M.P.H., of the World Resources Institute, advises, "Eat less meat and more vegetables and fruit; exercise regularly; avoid excessive alcohol and animal fat." And perform breast self-exams monthly.

Dr. Davis also urges that we as a society focus on improving workplace and product safety and, foremost, on reducing the use of hazardous materials. As the late Congresswoman Bella Abzug said at the 1997 World Conference on Breast Cancer, "We must take on the nuclear industry, the chemical industry, the makers and users of pesticides and organochlorines, and the other potential sources of poison in our breasts and bodies. And demand action from our governments to legislate, regulate, and discipline transnational corporations and this out-of-control global economy."

Whether women should begin mammography screening at age 40 or 50 remains controversial, but there seems to be consensus that its benefits outweigh its risks for women ages 50 to 70. This decision is ultimately up to each woman and her physician. Three safer detection techniques, involving heat imaging, lasers, and magnetic resonance imaging, are undergoing tests for effectiveness.

RESOURCES: Women's Environment and Development Organization (WEDO), Tel: (212) 973-0325. The Women's Community Cancer Project, Tel: (617) 354-9888. Breast Cancer: Poisons, Profits, and Prevention by Liane Clorfene-Casten, (Common Courage Press, 1996). The Breast Cancer Prevention Program by Samuel Epstein, M.D., and David Steinman (Macmillan, 1997). World Resources Institute Web site: www.wri.org/health/slidhome.html—By Allison Sloan

WE'RE NO DUMMIES In the last two decades, more American women have died of breast cancer than all Americans killed in Korea, Vietnam, and both world wars. Of the 180,000 women diagnosed with breast cancer this year, about 46,000 will die of the disease.

With all the evidence of a full-blown epidemic happening under our noses, why do researchers focus more on detection and treatment than on prevention? The answer might be written on the bottom line. Besides Zeneca's vested interest in breast cancer, General Electric sells upwards of $100 million annually in mammography machines; Du Pont supplies much of the film used in those machines. These companies aggressively promote mammography screening of women in their 40s, despite the risk of its contributing to breast cancer in that age group. Another corporate partner-in-grime, biotech giant Monsanto, sponsors National Breast Cancer Awareness Month's high profile event, the Race for the Cure, but also produces a number of pesticides that have been linked to cancer.

Let's face it: We're no dummies, and it's time to expose companies that, by producing environmental poisons and providing breast cancer services, get us coming and going. The Toxic Links Coalition is staging its 5th annual Cancer Industry Tour, a march on breast cancer profiteers, in San Francisco on October 28. Call (415) 243-8373 ext. 305 for information on a tour in your area.

Kristin Ebbert
Senior Administrator
Managing Editor, *The Green Guide*

"Take your planet personally."
Mothers & Others for a Livable Planet
40 W. 20th Street
New York, NY 10011-4211
Tel: (212) 242-0010, ext. 303
http://www.mothers.org

3 CENSORED

Montsanto's Genetically Modified Seeds Threaten World Production

"A SEEDY BUSINESS"

By Leora Broydo; *Mother Jones Interactive (Mojo Wire)*; April 7, 1998

A new "terminator" technology will make crops sterile and force farmers to buy seeds more often—so why did the USDA invent it?

Plus: *USDA Inc.*: When Public Research Goes Corporate

It's a practice as old as farming itself: As sure as the rooster crows at dawn, farmers save seeds from one growing season and plant them in the next. In South America, poor farmers use knowledge passed down over centuries to select seeds best suited to the local climate and soil. Across the equator their counterparts in South Dakota do it too; 80 to 90 percent of wheat farmers there save seeds from harvests. Those seeds are carefully cleaned and conditioned and then planted. They've been doing it for generations, year after year.

But the practice of seed saving may soon go the way of the steam tractor, and farmers have little say in the matter. A new genetic technology, patented in March, will make it possible for companies to sell seeds that will only work for one growing season, so farmers have to buy each time they plant. Crops will grow as usual, but their seeds in turn will be duds, unable to germinate. Seeds of this kind are expected to come to market by 2004.

Who will challenge this affront to the age-old practice of seed saving? Surely the U.S. Department of Agriculture, long the champion of the American farmer, will stand up to this plot to pad corporate profits and proclaim, "Not on American soil, bucko!" Unlikely. USDA is the inventor.

Using taxpayer money, about $229,000, USDA created the new "technology protection system" with Delta and Pine Land Company, the nation's largest producer of cotton seeds with a 73 percent market share. Together they hold the patent. Public-private partnerships are not at all unusual at USDA—two recent USDA inventions, a spray to prevent salmonella in chickens and a feed that will reduce water-polluting phosphorous content in animal waste, were both developed using private funds—but this one stands out because it was not done to improve food safety, the environment, crop viability, or consumer choice. The research was done, according to the USDA inventor himself, to improve the bottom lines of American corporations.

WHY TERMINATOR SEEDS? How does USDA, a public agency which says its scientific mission is to do research that is "good for the public," justify developing this new biotechnology?

Seed saving may be good for farmers, but it's not good for the chemical and seed companies who are spending billions to develop genetically engineered seed varieties. Although a 1970 law permits U.S. farmers to save proprietary seeds for use on their own farms, companies selling genetically engineered varieties now say that farmers must not reuse their patented varieties at all. They say they can't make ends meet unless farmers pay each and every season.

Biotech seed companies have managed to control the "problem" of seed saving in this country by policing farmers. Monsanto requires that buyers of its Roundup Ready seeds agree to use them only once, and hires Pinkerton investigators to root out violators. However, companies have been unable to do the same in developing countries, where they have little or no patent protection and enforcement is a real headache. How can these companies continue spending millions to develop new high-tech seeds if they can't reach the millions of farmers in the untapped markets of China, India, Pakistan, South America?

USDA to the rescue. "The need was there to come up with a system that allowed you to self-police your technology, other than trying to put on laws and legal barriers to farmers saving seed, and to try and stop foreign interests from stealing the technology," says USDA scientist Melvin Oliver, the primary inventor of the new patent-protecting technique. Oliver says the invention is a way to put "billions of dollars spent on research back into the system."

When the MoJo Wire called back to ask exactly whose billions will be recouped by USDA's invention, Oliver said he had been instructed not to speak to the press any further. USDA refused to say whose idea the new technology was, but Delta and Pine president Murray Robinson was more forthcoming: He told us it was the company's idea.

USDA would not provide a copy of its contract with Delta and Pine, but under the public-private research program, USDA receives licensing fees and royalty payments when its inventions come to market—and USDA scientists personally get a cut of royalties as well.

NEW MARKETS FOR BIOTECH The sheer scope of the invention is remarkable: The patent covers all seeds, both transgenic and everyday conventional varieties. Though it's only been tested on cotton and tobacco thus far, the inventors believe it could work on all major crops. In the past, seed companies have been reluctant to invest in wheat, oat, and rice seed markets, for example, because those crops are self-pollinating, i.e., can't be controlled reproductively; thus farmers can save the seeds, returning to the commercial market to replenish every five years or so. With the new gene technology, those farmers could be forced to buy every year, making bundles for companies in those markets.

"If commercially viable, the new technology could mean huge profits in entirely new sectors of the seed industry," says Hope Shand of the Rural Advancement Foundation International (RAFI), an international public-interest group which dubs the new technology the "terminator" seed. "For farmers, the patented technology will undoubtedly mean greater dependence on the commercial seed market."

The USDA and Delta and Pine plan to license the new technology widely to seed companies, both American and foreign. "We will make this as readily available to our direct competitors as we would to people working in crops that we

have no interest in," says Murray Robinson, president of Delta and Pine. "In the spirit of trying to help everyone we will certainly be open to companies in other countries protecting their technology or their proprietary developments."

While it may seem counterintuitive to share such a coveted technology with our neighbors overseas—especially since it was created to protect American corporate interests—it's really in Delta and Pine's, and USDA's, financial interests to spread it around. Selling licenses to the technology won't increase competition for Delta and Pine one bit. "Seed companies compete on the quality of their seeds," explains Mark Wiltamuth, an agribusiness analyst with investment bank Furman Selz. "This [technology] doesn't add any quality." What it does, says Wiltamuth, is expand long-term growth and licensing opportunities for Delta and Pine.

How much does Delta and Pine stand to make? Because the technology hasn't been commercialized yet, it's hard to say, but previous USDA-private inventions give some idea. In 1994, a patent was filed for a new genetic engineering technique developed with USDA and private funds. Since then, 90 percent of the world's seed companies have taken a license in that technology, including Monsanto, Pioneer Hi-Bred, and Novartis; it is expected to generate $2 million a year in royalty revenues. Given the same return on the new Delta and Pine/USDA invention, it would be $229,000 well spent.

THE FUTURE OF FOOD? The potential impact of the "terminator" seed is magnified by the continuing consolidation of the seed industry. With its continuing buyouts and multi-company deals to share research and distribution networks, the industry is getting mighty tight. Globally, according to RAFI, just 10 seed companies already control about 40 percent of the commercial seed market.

Critics of the new technology worry about the effect its widespread use would have, particularly in developing countries. They see it as a threat to millions of resource-poor farmers who depend on saving seeds, and exchanging seeds with neighbors, for their livelihood. Since the technology will enable multinational seed companies to enter Second-and-Third-World markets, there is also the fear that greater amounts of identical crops will be grown worldwide, increasing monocropping and further eroding agricultural biodiversity. Some even see it as threat to world food security.

"If this were to take place, it would mean every single person in this country, and perhaps all the countries in the world where these seeds were in widespread use, would become dependent on the stability of the international seed supply industry," says Lawrence Busch, a sociology professor at Michigan State University. "The fact is that wars and civil disturbances and catastrophes of a natural variety occur. Those are the kinds of things that can wipe out seed supplies. If farmers can't plant the stuff that they harvest, and become totally dependent on this, you are really raising the ante on the possibility of mass starvation."

Industry sees an entirely different world. It's a place where companies can develop ever-improved seeds and expect farmers to pony up a return on their investment. They say seeds that yield more, require fewer harsh chemicals, and resist what the world has to throw at them—pests, disease, drought—may be our only hope for a withering environment and growing world population. These technologies, they say, may be our only way of averting mass starvation.

"If you're going to be in the game, you've got to go out and be proactive," says Delta and Pine's Robinson. "We have to go and work proactively even with the most disadvantaged countries to say, 'How can we help make you more productive?'"

Will the invention help make farmers more productive? What will it do for agriculture and ecosystems? In USDA's words, "We have no way of knowing at this point." What is clear is that the technology will provide impenetrable patent protection for the products of seed companies like Delta and Pine. It's understandable why any company, in any industry, would want that sort of protection; it's a stroke of brilliance from a business standpoint. The real question is, is this the sort of research that the USDA, an agency which regulates the seed business, should be doing?

As federal research budgets shrink, USDA, like other agencies, looks to the private sector for help. Its public-private partnerships have been an effective way to commercialize the extraordinary discoveries made by USDA scientists, a way to create a revolving fund for future agriculture research. But the private sector, understandably, is only interested in cooperating if the resulting innovations benefit their business; the result is a research environment that is more product-driven. Where does this leave traditional USDA research that serves farmers and consumers, but that promises no new profits for industry?

"The USDA patent on 'terminator' seeds puts us in a quandary, on the line that divides corporate greed and public interest," says Neth Daño of the Southeast Asian Regional Institute for Community Education, a Philippines-based group that works with resource-poor farmers. "Where does the USDA's interest really lie?"

When the sun sets on the 2004 growing season, it's a question many farmers, from Southeast Asia to South Dakota, may be asking themselves.

SIDEBAR: WHEN USDA RESEARCH GOES CORPORATE, THE RESULTS CAN BE VISIONARY, DISTURBING, OR JUST GOOFY

USDA INC.

By Leora Broydo; *Mother Jones Interactive (Mojo Wire)*; April 7, 1998

From permanent press clothing to concentrated orange juice and instant potato flakes, USDA inventions have changed our lives in so many ways. Certainly, they've created a veritable bounty for American industry.

However, until recently, getting USDA innovations from the lab to the market was a difficult process. Corporations were reluctant to enter into cooperative research and commercializing efforts with USDA because the terms were less than user-friendly by private sector standards. For example, the public nature of government research did not jibe well with the confidentiality of the private sector. Also, regulations didn't allow federally owned inventions to be licensed exclusively to one company.

But the Federal Technology Transfer Act of 1986 changed all that. This Reagan-era law says that corporations can provide funding to USDA for research projects. It gives those corporations exclusive licenses on patented inventions that result from a given project. It exempts their work with USDA researchers from the Freedom of Information Act. And, as you'll see below, the law has allowed USDA to enter into all sorts of creative business ventures and partnerships. Indeed, USDA is looking more and more like a Fortune 500 company, and less a cash-strapped public institution, every day.

ALTERNATIVE AGRICULTURAL RESEARCH AND COMMERCIALIZATION CORPORATION

It's hip, it's wow, it's totally now: AARC Corp. is a venture capital firm wholly owned by USDA. It was established in 1992 by the Secretary of Agriculture to boost the development of "environmentally friendly" non-food products from farm and forest materials. AARC gets an annual appropriation from Congress and operates a revolving fund (money made from investments gets reinvested). Investments generally range from less than $100,000 to $1 million. Here a few examples of where its money has gone:

➤ The Gridcore Corp. / Gridcore Systems International, which makes a strong, lightweight building material from plant fibers and turns it into furniture, office dividers, stage sets, and display sets for trade shows.

➤ Natural Fibers Corp., which makes hypoallergenic pillows and comforters from a mixture of syriaca, or milkweed, fiber and goose down.

➤ KEN-GRO Corp., which uses kenaf to produce a soil-free potting mix. This product replaces peat, of which there is a finite supply.

➤ AARC Corp. also invests a nice chunk of change in the Biotechnology Research and Development Corp. (see below), a firm that works with the private sector to commercialize research done by government, university, and other public-sector scientists.

Investment decisions at AARC are made by an 11-person board of directors which includes at least eight members from the private sector who represent processing, financial, producer, and scientific interests. The board reports directly to the Secretary of Agriculture. And while "procedures are in place to avoid conflicts of interest on the part of board members" they haven't always been effective.

In 1995, AARC Corp.'s then chairman Martin Andreas, senior vice president of Archer Daniels Midland and nephew of ADM head Dwayne Andreas, was found to have steered $2.4 million in research money to ADM projects or business interests. Two other AARC Corp. board members, officers of Mycogen and BRDC, were found to have conflicts in $1.4 million in grants.

BIOTECHNOLOGY RESEARCH AND DEVELOPMENT CORPORATION BRDC is USDA's link to the big boys. Since 1992, USDA and its venture capital firm AARC Corp. have given approximately $16 million in grant money to BRDC, a private corporation owned by biotech company Alexion Pharmaceuticals; along with American Home Products; Dalgety, PLC; Dow Chemical Co.; Mallinckrodt Inc.; McDonald's Corp.; and Schering Plough.

BRDC was created primarily as a way to get USDA and public university research into commerical products. It focuses its development work on inventions involving genetic engineering tools, and biological control agents. Profits made from commercializing USDA research are split evenly between BRDC, USDA, and AARC Corp., and BRDC also promises to pay back grant money over time.

Companies like Dow Chemical have invested hundreds of thousands of dollars to be part of BRDC. In exchange, they get access to publicly-funded research going on at USDA and public universities. "This investment lets us access $3.4 million in research and play a significant role in directing that research," a representative of Dow Chemical told USDA's *Agricultural Research* magazine.

To date, BRDC has funded 130 research projects at 37 institutions throughout the country at a cost in excess of $28 million. BRDC funding has resulted in a technology that predicts litter size in pigs, an effective vaccine against cattle shipping fever, and a method of cloning pigs, to name a few. BRDC is based at USDA's National Center for Agricultural Utilization Research (NCAUR) (see below) in Peoria, Illinois, where it has easy access to USDA researchers.

NATIONAL CENTER FOR AGRICULTURAL UTILIZATION RESEARCH Without NCAUR, a USDA research center, there'd be no Super Slurper, no Z-Trim, no Oatrim. Imagine such a world. Since 1980, the center has received more than 108 patents, and licensed 41 percent of them to the private sector. With a base funding of $23 million; 110 research scientists, 160 scientific support personnel, and 50 contract employees, NCAUR's mission is to develop and commercialize new uses of agricultural commodities for industrial and food products. Here are just a few of NCAUR's recent success stories:

FLUFFY CELLULOSE, a high-fiber, low-calorie flour substitute.

Z-TRIM, a natural dietary fiber food ingredient, so named because it has zero calories. A person who normally eats 3,500 calories a day could cut as many as 700 calories by eating the same kinds of food in the same volume, while ingesting about half an ounce of Z-Trim to replace fat.

SUPER SLURPER, an absorbent gel used in a wide variety of products, most notably disposable diapers. The gel is capable of absorbing hundreds of times its own weight in water. The invention has found commercial life in products as varied as seed coatings, wound dressings, automobile fuel filters, and plastic barriers used at construction sites.

FANTESK, a fat-mimicking material that has been used in everything from ice cream and processed meats to adhesives and glues.

"NEW PATENT AIMS TO PREVENT FARMERS FROM SAVING SEED"

By Chakravarthi Raghavan;
Third World Resurgence; #92

In March, an American cotton seed company and the U.S. Department of Agriculture (USDA) announced that they had obtained a patent on a technique that genetically disables a seed's capacity to germinate when planted again. Dubbed by one critic as "Terminator Technology," the technique—if it works as advertised—has profound implications for agriculture, particularly in the Third World. News of the granting of the patent has kicked up a storm.

By year 2000, after a 12,000-year history of farming, farmers may no longer be able to save seed or breed improved varieties.

According to the Canada-based international NGO, RAFI, the problem is not the Millennium Bug but the "Millennium Seed."

On March 3, an American cotton seed company and the U.S. Department of Agriculture (USDA) announced they had received a patent on a technique that genetically disables a seed's capacity to germinate when planted again.

U.S. Patent No. 5,723,765, granted to Delta & Pine Land Co., doesn't just cover the firm's cotton and soybean seed business but, potentially, all cultivated crops.

Under a research agreement with the USDA, the company has the exclusive right to license the new technology to others.

While only cotton and tobacco seeds have been shown to respond to the new technique, the company plans to have what Research Director Hope Shand of RAFI has dubbed, "Terminator Technology" ready for a much wider range of crops shortly after year 2000.

According to USDA spokesman Willard Phelps, the primary targets for the Terminator are "Second and Third World" markets. Priority crops include rice, wheat, sorghum, and soybeans. These are crops largely ignored by agribusiness breeders because they aren't readily hybridized—a tried-and-true biological means of forcing farmers back into the seed market every year.

By and large, profit-hungry seed companies have shunned these crops because the returns don't match those for hybrid crops like maize and many vegetables. With the patent announcement, the world's two most critical food crops—rice and wheat, staple foods for three-quarters of the world's poor—potentially enter the realm of private monopoly.

The patent has taken plant breeders by storm. The technique—if it works as advertised—has profound implications for agriculture.

But the news has also created division. Some of those contacted by RAFI see benefits from the new technology. One crop economist put it this way: "For the first time, private companies will be encouraged to invest in the world's most vital food crops. We can look forward to a new flow of investment into crops whose yields have stagnated or even declined in the '90s. Now such poor people's crops as rice and wheat will get the research support they so desperately need."

The patent's defenders acknowledge that the Terminator Technology will mean a hefty hike in seed costs as farmers who now only buy seed when they change varieties are forced to make annual purchases. But they defend hiking seed prices by saying farmers will only opt for the "sterile" seeds if they offer a big advantage. Otherwise, farmers will keep with the current publicly bred varieties.

RAFI's Hope Shand disagrees. "Don't forget, the Terminator was developed by the public sector (USDA) together with the private sector. There will be enormous pressure on public breeders to adopt the technique in order to feed cash-starved government and university research department with corporate dollars."

Edward Hammond of RAFI concurs, "Biotech companies that are already patenting specific crop genes and traits will probably insist that other breeders licensing their germplasm use the Terminator to protect their monopoly. It won't take long before farmers run out of choices. Either they pay for the Millennium Seed or they replant older varieties from abandoned breeding programs."

THE "GREED GENE" "This is a patent that really turns on the greed gene," says Camila Montecinos of the Chilean-based Center for Education and Technology (CET). "It's too profitable for companies to ignore. We will see pressure on national regulatory systems to marginalise saved-seed varieties and clear the way for the Terminator. One point four billion farm families are at risk."

Aside from skyrocketing seed costs, Neth Daqo of the Philippines-based civil society organization SEARICE sees a threat to the environment and to long-term food security.

"We work with farmers who may buy a commercial variety but its breeder wouldn't recognize it five years later. Women select the best seeds every year and—over a time—the rice melds itself to the farm's own ecosystem. Women also cross the commercial variety with other rice strains to breed their own locally adapted seeds.

"The Terminator could put an end to all this and increase crop uniformity and vulnerability. It poses a threat to the culture of seed sharing and exchange that is led primarily by women farmers. Ultimately, the Terminator technology will severely limit farmer options," says Neth Daqo of SEARICE. "Will we be left with rice varieties that taste like sawdust and which pests and diseases love to devour?"

Camila Montecinos of Chile-based CET is calling for a global boycott of the Terminator Technology. "Governments should make use of the technology illegal," she insists. "This is an immoral technique that robs farming communities of their age-old right to save seed and their role as plant breeders. It should be banned."

To this, corporate breeders argue that the new technology simply does for hard-to-hybridize crops what the hybrid technique did for maize. Hybrid seed is either sterile or fails to reproduce the same quality characteristics in the next generation. Thus, most maize farmers buy seed every year.

"Poor farmers can't afford hybrids either," Montecinos points out, "but there's a key difference. The theory behind hybridization is that it allows breeders to make crosses that couldn't be made otherwise and that are supposed to give the plant higher yields and vigor. The results are often disappointing but that's the rationale.

"In the case of Terminator Technology, there's absolutely no agronomic benefit for farmers. The sole purpose is to facilitate monopoly control and the sole beneficiary is agribusiness."

RAFI will be working with its partners around the world to encourage a global ban on the use of Terminator Technology. "By the time it's ready for market shortly after the year 2000, we hope that the Millennium Seed will succumb to the Millennium Bug," concludes RAFI's Shand.

"MONSANTO: A CHECKERED HISTORY" AND "REVOLVING DOORS: MONSANTO AND THE REGULATORS"

By Brian Tokar; *The Ecologist*; September/October 1998

Monsanto's high-profile advertisements in Britain and the U.S. depict the corporation as a visionary, world-historical force, working to bring state-of-the-art science and an environmentally responsible outlook to the solution of humanity's pressing problems. Whether one is concerned about population growth, the future of agriculture, the quality of our food, or the health needs of an aging population, we are assured that Monsanto will find the answers.

But just who is Monsanto? Where did they come from? How did they get to be the world's second largest manufacturer of agricultural chemicals, one of the largest producers of seeds, and soon—with the impending merger with American Home Products—the largest seller of prescription drugs in the United States? What do their workers, their customers, and others whose lives they have impacted, have to say? Is Monsanto the "clean and green" company its advertisements promote, or is this new image merely a product of clever public relations? A look at the historical record offers some revealing clues, and may help us better understand the company's present-day practices.

Headquartered just outside St. Louis, Missouri, the Monsanto Chemical

Company was founded in 1901 by John Francis Queeny. Queeny, a self-educated chemist, brought technology to manufacture saccharin, the first artificial sweetener, from Germany to the United States. In the 1920s, Monsanto became a leading manufacturer of sulfuric acid and other basic industrial chemicals, and is one of only four companies to be listed among the top ten U.S. chemical companies in every decade since the 1940s.[1]

By the 1940s, plastics and synthetic fabrics had become a centerpiece of Monsanto's business. In 1947, a French freighter carrying ammonium nitrate fertilizer blew up at a dock 270 feet from Monsanto's plastics plant outside Galveston, Texas. More than 500 people died in what came to be seen as one of the chemical industry's first major disasters.[2] The plant was manufacturing styrene and polystyrene plastics, which are still important constituents of food packaging and various consumer products. In the 1980s the U.S. Environmental Protection Agency (EPA) listed polystyrene as fifth in its ranking of the chemicals whose production generates the most total hazardous waste.[3]

In 1929, the Swann Chemical Company, soon to be purchased by Monsanto, developed polychlorinated biphenyls (PCBs), which were widely praised for their nonflammability and extreme chemical stability. The most widespread uses were in the electrical equipment industry, which adopted PCBs as a nonflammable coolant for a new generation of transformers. By the 1960s, Monsanto's growing family of PCBs were also widely used as lubricants, hydraulic fluids, cutting oils, waterproof coatings, and liquid sealants. Evidence of the toxic effects of PCBs appeared as early as the 1930s, and Swedish scientists studying the biological effects of DDT began finding significant concentrations of PCBs in the blood, hair, and fatty tissue of wildlife in the 1960s.[4]

Research in the 1960s and seventies revealed PCBs and other aromatic organochlorines to be potent carcinogens, and also traced them to a wide array of reproductive, developmental, and immune system disorders.[5] Their high chemical affinity for organic matter, particularly fat tissue, is responsible for their dramatic rates of bioaccumulation, and their wide dispersal throughout the North's aquatic food web: Arctic cod, for example, carry PCB concentrations 48 million times that of their surrounding waters, and predatory mammals such as polar bears can harbor tissue concentrations of PCBs more than 50 times greater than that. Though the manufacture of PCBs was banned in the United States in 1976, its toxic and endocrine disruptive effects persist worldwide.[6]

The world's center of PCB manufacturing was Monsanto's plant on the outskirts of East St. Louis, Illinois. East St. Louis is a chronically economically depressed suburb, across the Mississippi River from St. Louis, bordered by two large metal processing plants in addition to the Monsanto facility. "East St. Louis," reports education writer Jonathan Kozol, "has some of the sickest children in America." Kozol reports that the city has the highest rate of fetal death and immature births in the state, the third highest rate of infant death, and one of the highest childhood asthma rates in the United States.[7]

DIOXIN: A LEGACY OF CONTAMINATION The people of East St. Louis continue to face the horrors of high level chemical exposure, poverty, a deteriorating urban infrastructure, and the collapse of even the most basic city services, but the nearby town of Times Beach, Missouri was found to be so thoroughly contaminated with dioxin that the U.S. government ordered it evacuated in 1982. Apparently the town, as well as several private landowners, hired a contractor to spray its dirt roads with waste oil to keep dust down. The same contractor had been hired by local chemical companies to pump out their dioxin-contaminated sludge tanks. When 50 horses, other domestic animals, and hundreds of wild birds died in an indoor arena that had been sprayed with the oil, an investigation ensued that eventually traced the deaths to dioxin from the chemical sludge tanks.[8] Two young girls who played in the arena became ill, one of whom was hospitalized for four weeks with severe kidney damage, and many more children born to mothers exposed to the dioxin-contaminated oil demonstrated evidence of immune system abnormalities and significant brain dysfunction.[9]

While Monsanto has consistently denied any connection to the Times Beach incident, the St. Louis-based Times Beach Action Group (TBAG) uncovered laboratory reports documenting the presence of large concentrations of PCBs manufactured by Monsanto in contaminated soil samples from the town.[10] "From our point of view, Monsanto is at the heart of the problem here in Missouri," explains TBAG's Steve Taylor. Taylor acknowledges that many questions about Times Beach and other contaminated sites in the region remain unanswered, but cites evidence that close investigations of the sludge sprayed in Times Beach were limited to those sources traceable to companies other than Monsanto.

The cover-up at Times Beach reached the highest levels of the Reagan Administration in Washington. The nation's environmental agencies during the Reagan years became notorious for officials' repeated backroom deals with industry officials, in which favored companies were promised lax enforcement and greatly reduced fines. Reagan's appointed administrator of the Environmental Protection Agency, Anne Gorsuch Burford, was forced to resign after two years in office and her special assistant, Rita Lavelle, was jailed for six months for perjury and obstruction of justice. In one famous incident, the Reagan White House ordered Burford to withhold documents on Times Beach and other contaminated sites in the states of Missouri and Arkansas, citing "executive privilege," and Lavelle was subsequently cited for shredding important documents.[11] An investigative reporter for the *Philidelphia Inquirer* newspaper identified Monsanto as one of the chemical companies whose executives frequently hosted luncheon and dinner meetings with Lavelle.[12] The evacuation sought by residents of Times Beach was delayed until 1982, 11 years after the contamination was first discovered, and eight years after the cause was identified as dioxin.

Monsanto's association with dioxin can be traced back to its manufacture of the herbicide 2,4,5-T, beginning in the late 1940s. "Almost immediately, its workers started getting sick with skin rashes, inexplicable pains in the limbs, joints and other parts of the body, weakness, irritability, nervousness, and loss of libido," explains Peter Sills, author of a forthcoming book on dioxin. "Internal memos show that the company knew these men were actually as sick as they claimed, but it kept all that evidence hidden."[13] An explosion at Monsanto's Nitro, West Virginia herbicide plant in 1949 drew further attention to these complaints. The contaminant responsible for these conditions was not identified as dioxin until 1957, but the U.S. Army Chemical Corps apparently became interested in this substance as a possible chemical warfare agent. A request filed by the *St. Louis Journalism Review* under the U.S. Freedom of Information Act revealed nearly 600 pages of reports and correspondence between Monsanto and the Army Chemical Corps on the subject of this herbicide byproduct, going as far back as 1952.[14]

The herbicide "Agent Orange," which was used by U.S. military forces to defoliate the rainforest ecosystems of Vietnam during the 1960s was a mixture of 2,4,5-T and 2,4-D that was available from several sources, but Monsanto's Agent Orange had concentrations of dioxin many times higher than that produced by Dow Chemical, the defoliant's other leading manufacturer. This made Monsanto the key defendant in the lawsuit brought by Vietnam War veterans in the United States, who faced an array of debilitating symptoms attributable to Agent Orange exposure. When a $180 million settlement was reached in 1984

between seven chemical companies and the lawyers for the veterans, the judge ordered Monsanto to pay 45.5 percent of the total.[15]

In the 1980s, Monsanto undertook a series of studies designed to minimize its liability, not only in the Agent Orange suit, but in continuing instances of employee contamination at its West Virginia manufacturing plant. A three-and-one-half-year court case brought by railroad workers exposed to dioxin following a train derailment revealed a pattern of manipulated data and misleading experimental design in these studies. An official of the U.S. EPA concluded that the studies were manipulated to support Monsanto's claim that dioxin's effects were limited to the skin disease chloracne.[16] Greenpeace researchers Jed Greer and Kenny Bruno describe the outcome:

> According to testimony from the trial, Monsanto misclassified exposed and non-exposed workers, arbitrarily deleted several key cancer cases, failed to verify classification of chloracne subjects by common industrial dermatitis criteria, did not provide assurance of untampered records delivered and used by consultants, and made false statements about dioxin contamination in Monsanto products.[17]

The court case, in which the jury granted a $16 million punitive damage award against Monsanto, revealed that many of Monsanto's products, from household herbicides to the Santophen germicide once used in Lysol brand disinfectant, were knowingly contaminated with dioxin. "The evidence of Monsanto executives at the trial portrayed a corporate culture where sales and profits were given a higher priority than the safety of products and its workers," reported the *Toronto Globe Mail* after the close of the trial.[18] "They just didn't care about the health and safety of their workers," explains author Peter Sills. "Instead of trying to make things safer, they relied on intimidation and threatened layoffs to keep their employees working."

A subsequent review by Dr. Cate Jenkins of the EPA's Regulatory Development Branch documented an even more systematic record of fraudulent science. "Monsanto has in fact submitted false information to EPA which directly resulted in weakened regulations under RCRA [Resources Conservation and Recovery Act] and FIFRA [Federal Insecticide, Fungicide and Rodenticide Act] . . ." reported Dr. Jenkins in a 1990 memorandum urging the agency to undertake a criminal investigation of the company. Jenkins cited internal Monsanto documents revealing that the company "doctored" samples of herbicides that were submitted to the U.S. Department of Agriculture, hid behind "process chemistry" arguments to deflect attempts to regulate 2,4-D and various chlorophenols, hid evidence regarding the contamination of Lysol, and excluded several hundred of its sickest former employees from its comparative health studies:

> Monsanto covered up the dioxin contamination of a wide range of its products. Monsanto either failed to report contamination, substituted false information purporting to show no contamination or submitted samples to the government for

analysis which had been specially prepared so that dioxin contamination did not exist.[19]

NEW GENERATION HERBICIDES Today, glyphosate herbicides such as Roundup account for at least one-sixth of Monsanto's total annual sales and half of the company's operating income,[20] perhaps significantly more since the company spun off its industrial chemicals and synthetic fabrics divisions as a separate company, called Solutia, in September of 1997. Monsanto aggressively promotes Roundup as a safe, general purpose herbicide for use on everything from lawns and orchards, to large coniferous forest holdings, where aerial spraying of the herbicide is used to suppress the growth of deciduous seedlings and shrubs and encourage the growth of profitable fir and spruce trees.[21] The Oregon-based Northwest Coalition for Alternatives to Pesticides (NCAP) reviewed over 40 scientific studies on the effects of glyphosate, and of the polyoxyethylene amines used as a surfactant in Roundup, and concluded that the herbicide is far less benign than Monsanto's advertising suggests:

> Symptoms of acute poisoning in humans following ingestion of Roundup include gastrointestinal pain, vomiting, swelling of the lungs, pneumonia, clouding of consciousness, and destruction of red blood cells. Eye and skin irritation has been reported by workers mixing, loading and applying glyphosate. EPA's Pesticide Incident Monitoring System had 109 reports of health effects associated with exposure to glyphosate between 1966 and October 1980.

These included eye or skin irritation, nausea, dizziness, headaches, diarrhea, blurred vision, fever, and weakness.[22]

It is important to note that the 1966-1980 dates represent a time period well before Roundup came to be widely used.

A series of suicides and attempted suicides in Japan during the 1980s using Roundup herbicide allowed scientists to calculate a lethal dose of six ounces. The herbicide is 100 times more toxic to fish than to people, toxic to earthworms, soil bacteria, and beneficial fungi, and scientists have measured a number of direct physiological effects of Roundup in fish and other wildlife, in addition to secondary effects attributable to defoliation of forests. Breakdown of glyphosate into N-nitrosoglyphosate and other related compounds have heightened concerns about the possible carcinogenicity of Roundup products.[23]

A 1993 study at the University of California at Berkeley's School of Public Health found that glyphosate was the most common cause of pesticide-related illness among landscape maintenance workers in California, and the number three cause among agricultural workers.[24] A 1996 review of the scientific literature by members of the Vermont Citizens' Forest Roundtable—a group which successfully lobbied the Vermont Legislature for a statewide ban on the use of herbicides in forestry—revealed updated evidence of lung damage, heart palpitations, nausea, reproductive problems, chromosome aberrations, and numerous other effects of exposure to Roundup herbicide.[25] In 1997, Monsanto responded to five years of complaints by the New York State Attorney General that its advertisements for Roundup were misleading; the company altered its ads to delete claims that the herbicide is "biodegradable" and "environmentally friendly," and paid $50,000 toward the state's legal expenses in the case.[26]

In March of 1998, Monsanto agreed to pay a fine of $225,000 for mislabeling containers of Roundup on 75 separate occasions. The penalty was the largest settlement ever paid for violation of the Worker Protection Standards of the Federal Insecticide, Fungicide and Rodenticide Act (FIFRA). According to the *Wall Street Journal*, Monsanto distributed containers of the herbicide with labels restricting entry into treated areas for only four hours instead of the required 12 hours.[27] This is only the latest in a series of major fines and rulings against Monsanto in the United States, including a $108 million liability finding in the case of the leukemia death of a Texas employee in 1986, a $648,000 settlement for allegedly failing to report required health data to the EPA in 1990, a $1 million fine by the state Attorney General of Massachusetts in 1991 in the case of a 200,000 gallon acid wastewater spill, a $39 million settlement in Houston, Texas in 1992 involving the deposition of hazardous chemicals into unlined pits, and numerous others.[28] In 1995, Monsanto ranked fifth among U.S. corporations in EPA's Toxic Release Inventory, having discharged 37 million pounds of toxic chemicals into the air, land, water, and underground.[29]

BIOTECHNOLOGY'S BRAVE NEW WORLD
Monsanto's aggressive promotion of its biotechnology products, from recombi-

nant Bovine Growth Hormone (rBGH), to Roundup Ready soybeans and other crops, to its insect-resistant varieties of cotton, is seen by many observers as a continuation of its many decades of ethically questionable practices. "Corporations have personalities, and Monsanto is one of the most malicious," explains author Peter Sills. "From Monsanto's herbicides to Santophen disinfectant to BGH, they seem to go out of their way to hurt their workers and hurt kids."

Originally, Monsanto was one of four chemical companies seeking to bring a synthetic Bovine Growth Hormone, produced in E. coli bacteria genetically engineered to manufacture the bovine protein, to market. Another was American Cyanamid, now owned by American Home Products, which is in the process of merging with Monsanto. As Jennifer Ferrara describes elsewhere in this issue, Monsanto's 14-year effort to gain approval from the U.S. Food and Drug Administration (FDA) to bring recombinant BGH to market was fraught with controversy, including allegations of a concerted effort to suppress information about the hormone's ill effects. One FDA veterinarian, Richard Burroughs, was fired after he accused both the company and the agency of suppressing and manipulating data to hide the effects of rBGH injections on the health of dairy cows.[30]

In 1990, when FDA approval of rBGH appeared imminent, a veterinary pathologist at the University of Vermont's agricultural research facility released previously suppressed data to two state legislators documenting significantly increased rates of udder infection in cows that had been injected with the then-experimental Monsanto hormone, as well as an unusual incidence of severely deforming birth defects in offspring of rBGH-treated cows.[31] An independent review of the University data by a regional farm advocacy group documented additional cow health problems associated with rBGH, including high incidences of foot and leg injuries, metabolic and reproductive difficulties, and uterine infections. The U.S. Congress's General Accounting Office (GAO) attempted an inquiry into the case, but was unable to obtain the necessary records from Monsanto and the University to carry out its investigation, particularly with respect to suspected teratogenic and embryotoxic effects. The GAO auditors concluded that cows injected with rBGH had mastitis (udder infection) rates one-third higher than untreated cows, and recommended further research on the risk of elevated antibiotic levels in milk produced using rBGH.[32]

Monsanto's rBGH was approved by the FDA for commercial sale beginning in 1994. The following year, Mark Kastel of the Wisconsin Farmers Union released a study of Wisconsin farmers' experiences with the drug. His findings exceeded the 21 potential health problems that Monsanto was required to list on the warning label for its Posilac brand of rBGH. Kastel found widespread reports of spontaneous deaths among rBGH-treated cows, high incidences of udder infections, severe metabolic difficulties and calving problems, and in some cases an inability to successfully wean treated cows off the drug. Many experienced dairy farmers who experimented with rBGH suddenly needed to replace large portions of their herd.[33] Instead of addressing the causes of farmers' complaints about rBGH, Monsanto went on the offensive, threatening to sue small dairy companies that advertised their products as free of the artificial hormone, and participating in a lawsuit by several dairy industry trade associations against the first and only mandatory labeling law for rBGH in the United States.[34] Still, evidence for the damaging effects of rBGH on the health of both cows and people continued to mount.[35]

Efforts to prevent labeling of genetically engineered soybean and maize exports from the United States suggest a continuation of the practices that were designed to squelch complaints against Monsanto's dairy hormone. While Monsanto argues that its "Roundup Ready" soybeans will ultimately reduce herbicide use, the widespread acceptance of herbicide-tolerant crop varieties appears far more likely to increase farmers' dependence on herbicides. Weeds that emerge after the original herbicide has dispersed or broken down are often treated with further applications of herbicides.[36] "It will promote the overuse of the herbicide," Missouri soybean farmer Bill Christison told Kenny Bruno of Greenpeace International. "If there is a selling point for RRS, it's the fact that you can till an area with a lot of weeds and use surplus chemicals to combat your problem, which is not what anyone should be doing."[37] Christison refutes Monsanto's claim that herbicide-resistant seeds are necessary to reduce soil erosion from excess tillage, and reports that Midwestern farmers have developed numerous methods of their own for reducing overall use of herbicides.

Monsanto, on the other hand has stepped up its production of Roundup in recent years. With Monsanto's U.S. patent for Roundup scheduled to expire in the year 2000, and competition from generic glyphosate products already emerging worldwide, the packaging of Roundup herbicide with "Roundup Ready" seeds has become the centerpiece of Monsanto's strategy for continued growth in herbicide sales.[38] The possible health and environmental consequences of Roundup-tolerant crops have not been fully investigated, including allergenic effects, potential invasiveness or weediness, and the possibility of herbicide resistance being transferred via pollen to other soybeans or related plants.[39]

While any problems with herbicide-resistant soybeans may still be dismissed as long-range and somewhat speculative, the experience of U.S. cotton growers with Monsanto's genetically engineered seeds appears to tell a very different story. Monsanto has released two varieties of genetically engineered cotton, beginning in 1996. One is a Roundup-resistant variety and the other, named "Bollgard," secretes a bacterial toxin intended to control damage from three leading cotton pests. The toxin, derived from *Bacillus thuringiensis*, has been used by organic growers in the form of a natural bacterial spray since the early 1970s. But while *B.t.* bacteria are relatively short-lived, and secrete their toxin in a form that only becomes activated in the alkaline digestive systems of particular worms and caterpillars, genetically engineered *B.t.* crops secrete an active form of the toxin throughout the plant's life cycle.[40] Much of the genetically engineered maize currently on the market, for example, is a *B.t.* secreting variety, designed to repel the corn rootworm and other common pests.

The first widely anticipated problem with these pesticide-secreting crops is that the presence of the toxin throughout the plant's life cycle is likely to encourage the development of resistant strains of common crop pests. The U.S. EPA has determined that widespread resistance to *B.t.* may render natural applications of *B.t.* bacteria ineffective in just three to five years and requires growers to plant refuges of up to 40 percent non-*B.t.* cotton in an attempt to forestall this effect. Second, the active toxin secreted by these plants may harm beneficial insects, moths, and butterflies, in addition to those species that growers wish to eliminate.[41]

But the damaging effects of *B.t.*-secreting "Bollgard" cotton have proved to be much more immediate, enough so that Monsanto and its partners have pulled five million pounds of genetically engineered cotton seed off the market and agreed to a multimillion dollar settlement with farmers in the southern United States. Three farmers who refused to settle with Monsanto were awarded nearly $2 million by the Mississippi Seed Arbitration Council.[42] Not only were plants attacked by the cotton bollworm, which Monsanto claimed they would be resistant to, but germination was spotty, yields were low, and plants were misshapen, according to several published accounts.[43] Some farmers reported crop losses of up to 50 percent. Farmers who planted Monsanto's Roundup-resistant cotton also reported severe crop failures, including deformed and misshapen bolls that suddenly fell off the plant three-quarters of the way through the growing season.[44]

Despite these problems, Monsanto is advancing the use of genetic engineering in agriculture by taking control of many of the largest, most established seed companies in the United States. Monsanto now owns Holdens Foundation Seeds, supplier of germplasm used on 25-35 percent of U.S. maize acreage, and Asgrow Agronomics, which it describes as "the leading soybean breeder, developer and distributor in the United States."[45] This past spring, Monsanto completed its acquisition of De Kalb Genetics, the second largest seed company in the United States and the ninth largest in the world, as well as Delta and Pine Land, the largest U.S. cotton seed company.[46] With its Delta and Pine acquisition, Monsanto now controls 85 percent of the U.S. cotton seed market.[47]

The company has been aggressively pursuing corporate acquisitions and product sales in other countries as well. In 1997, Monsanto bought Sementes Agroceres S.A., described as "the leading seed corn company in Brazil," with a 30 percent market share.[48] Earlier this year, the Brazilian Federal Police investigated an alleged illegal importation of at least 200 bags of transgenic soybeans, some of which were traced to an Argentine subsidiary of Monsanto.[49] According to Brazilian law, foreign transgenic products can only be introduced after a period of quarantine and testing to prevent possible damage to native flora. In Canada, Monsanto had to recall 60,000 bags of genetically engineered rape ("canola") seed in 1997.[50] Apparently the shipment of Roundup-resistant seed contained an inserted gene different from the one that had been approved for consumption by people and livestock.

While Monsanto's herbicides and genetically engineered products have been focuses of public controversy for many years, its pharmaceutical products also have a troubling track record. The flagship product of Monsanto's G.D. Searle pharmaceuticals subsidiary is the artificial sweetener aspartame, sold under the brand names NutraSweet and Equal. In 1981, four years before Monsanto purchased Searle, a Food and Drug Administration Board of Inquiry consisting of three independent scientists confirmed reports that had been circulating for eight years that "aspartame might induce brain tumors."[51] The FDA revoked Searle's license to sell aspartame, only to have its decision reversed under a new commissioner appointed by President Ronald Reagan.

A 1996 study in the *Journal of Neuropathology and Experimental Neurology* has renewed this concern, linking aspartame to a sharp increase in brain cancers shortly after the substance was introduced. Dr. Erik Millstone of the University of Sussex Science Policy Research Unit cites a series of reports from the 1980s linking aspartame to a wide array of adverse reactions in sensitive consumers, including headaches, blurred vision, numbness, hearing loss, muscle spasms, and induced epileptic-type seizures, among numerous others.[52] In 1989, Searle again ran afoul of the FDA, which accused the company of misleading advertising in the case of its anti-ulcer drug, Cytotec. The FDA said that the ads were designed to market the drug to a much broader and younger population than the agency had advised.

Searle/Monsanto was required to take out an ad in a number of medical journals, which was headed "Published to Correct a Previous Advertisement which the Food and Drug Administration Considered Misleading."[53]

MONSANTO'S GREENWASH Given this long and troubling history, it is easy to understand why informed citizens throughout Europe and the U.S. are reluctant to trust Monsanto with the future of our food and our health. But Monsanto is doing everything it can to appear unperturbed by this opposition. Through efforts such as their £1 million advertising campaign in Britain, their sponsorship of a new high-tech Biodiversity exhibit at the American Museum of Natural History in New York, and many others, they are trying to appear greener, more righteous and more forward looking than even their opponents.

In the U.S. they are bolstering their image, and likely influencing policy, with the support of people at the highest levels of the Clinton Administration. In May of 1997, Mickey Kantor, an architect of Bill Clinton's 1992 election campaign and United States Trade Representative during Clinton's first term, was elected to a seat on Monsanto's Board of Directors. Marcia Hale, formerly a personal assistant to the president, has served as Monsanto's public affairs officer in Britain.[54] Vice President Al Gore, who is well known in the U.S. for his writings and speeches on the environment, has been a vocal supporter of biotechnology at least since his days in the U.S. Senate.[55] Gore's Chief Domestic Policy Advisor, David W. Beier, was formerly the Senior Director of Government Affairs at Genentech, Inc.[56]

Under CEO Robert Shapiro, Monsanto has pulled out all the stops to transform its image from a purveyor of dangerous chemicals to an enlightened, forward-looking institution crusading to feed the world. Shapiro, who went to work for G.D. Searle in 1979 and became the president of its NutraSweet Group in 1982, sits on the President's Advisory Committee for Trade Policy and Negotiations and served a term as a member of the White House Domestic Policy Review.[57] He describes himself as a visionary and a Renaissance Man, with a mission to use the company's resources to change the world: "The only reason for working at a large company is that you have the capability of doing things on a large scale that really are important," he told an interviewer for *Business Ethics*, a flagship journal for the "socially responsible business" movement in the United States.[58]

Shapiro harbors few illusions about Monsanto's reputation in the United States, recounting with sympathy the dilemma of many a Monsanto employee whose neighbors' children might wince when they find out where the employee works. He is anxious to demonstrate that he is in step with the widespread desire for systemic change, and is determined to redirect this desire toward his company's ends, as he demonstrated in a recent interview with the *Harvard Business Review*: "It's not a question of good guys and bad guys. There is no point in saying, 'If only those bad guys would go out of business, then the world would be fine.' The whole system has to change; there's a huge opportunity for reinvention."[59]

Of course, Shapiro's reinvented system is one where huge corporations not only continue to exist, but exercise an ever-increasing control over our lives. But Monsanto has reformed, we are told. They have successfully cast off their industrial chemical divisions and are now committed to replacing chemicals with "information," in the guise of genetically engineered seeds and other products of biotechnology. This is an ironic stance for a company whose most profitable product is an herbicide, and whose highest profile food additive appears to be making some people very sick. It is an unlikely role for a company that seeks to intimidate critics with lawsuits and suppress criticism in the media.

Monsanto's latest Annual Report, however, clearly demonstrates that it has learned all the right buzzwords. Roundup is not an herbicide, it is a tool to minimize tillage and decrease soil erosion. Genetically engineered crops are not just about profits for Monsanto, they're about solving the inexorable problem of population growth. Biotechnology is not reducing everything alive to the realm of commodities—items to be bought and sold, marketed and patented—but is in fact a harbinger of "decommoditization": the replacement of single mass-produced products with a vast array of specialized, made-to-order products.[60] This is Newspeak of the highest order.

Finally, we are to believe that Monsanto's aggressive promotion of biotechnology is not a matter of mere corporate arrogance, but rather the realization of a simple fact of nature. Readers of the Monsanto Annual Report are presented with an analogy between today's rapid growth in the number of identified DNA base pairs and the exponential trend of miniaturization in the electronics industry, a trend first identified in the 1960s.

Monsanto has dubbed the apparent exponential growth of what it terms "biological knowledge" to be nothing less than "Monsanto's Law." Like any other putative law of nature, one has little choice but to see its predictions realized and, here, the prediction is nothing less than the continued exponential growth of Monsanto's global reach.

But the growth of any technology is not merely a "law of nature." Technologies are not social forces unto themselves, nor merely neutral "tools" that can be used to satisfy any social end we desire. Rather they are products of particular social institutions and economic interests. Once a particular course of technological development is set in motion, it can have much wider consequences than its creators could have predicted: the more powerful the technology, the more profound the consequences.

For example, the so-called Green Revolution in agriculture in the 1960s and seventies temporarily increased crop yields, and also made farmers throughout the world increasingly dependent on costly chemical inputs. This spurred widespread displacements of people from the land, and in many countries has undermined the soil, groundwater, and social land base that sustained people for millennia.[61] These large scale dislocations have fueled population growth, urbanization, and social disempowerment, which have in turn led to another cycle of impoverishment and hunger.

The "second Green Revolution" promised by Monsanto and other biotechnology companies threatens even greater disruptions in traditional land tenure and social relations. In rejecting Monsanto and its biotechnology, we are not necessarily rejecting technology *per se*, but seeking to replace a life-denying technology of manipulation, control and profit with a genuinely ecological technology, designed to respect the patterns of nature, improve personal and community health, sustain land-based communities and operate at a genuinely human scale. If we believe in democracy, it is imperative that we have the right to choose which technologies are best for our communities, rather than having unaccountable institutions like Monsanto decide for us. Rather than technologies designed for the continued enrichment of a few, we can ground our technology in the hope of a greater harmony between our human communities and the natural world. Our health, our food, and the future of life on earth truly lie in the balance.

NOTES

[1]"Chemical Producers: Dow Chemical, Du Pont, Monsanto and Union Carbide have ranked among Top 10 biggest chemical makers since 1940," *Chemical and Engineering News*, January 12, 1998: 193.

[2]Marc S. Reisch, "From Coal Tar to Crafting a Wealth of Diversity," *Chemical and Engineering News*, January 12, 1998: 90.

[3]Pamela Peck, "Vermont's Polystyrene (Styrofoam) Boycott," Barre, Vermont: Vermonters Organized for Cleanup, 1989.

[4]Theo Colborn, Dianne Dumanoski and John Peterson Myers, *Our Stolen Future* (New York: Penguin Books, 1996): 90.

[5]Michelle Allsopp, Pat Costner and Paul Johnson, *Body of Evidence: The Effects of Chlorine on Human Health*, University of Exeter, Greenpeace Research Laboratories, May 1995.

[6]Colborn, *et. al*, *op. cit.*: 101-104.

[7]Jonathan Kozol, *Savage Inequalities: Children in America's Schools* (New York: Crown Publishers, 1991): 7, 20.

[8]"Death of Animals Laid to Chemical," *The New York Times*, August 28, 1974: 36.

[9]Colborn, *et. al*, *op. cit.*: 116.

[10]Times Beach Action Group, "Citizen Inquiry Uncovers Blatant Violation of Environmental Law

Surrounding the Proposed Times Beach Incinerator," St. Louis, November 1995.

[11]Philip Shabecoff, *A Fierce Green Fire: The American Environmental Movement* (New York: Hill and Wang, 1993): 210-212; Brian Tokar, *Earth for Sale: Reclaiming Ecology in the Age of Corporate Greenwash* (Boston: South End Press, 1997): 59-60; Times Beach Action Group, *ibid.*

[12]Lisa Martino-Taylor, "Legacy of Doubt," *Three River Confluence*, No. 7/8, Fall 1997: 27.

[13]Personal communication, August 5, 1998.

[14]Peter Downs, "Is the Pentagon Involved?" *St. Louis Journalism Review*, June 1998.

[15]Peter H. Schuck, *Agent Orange on Trial: Mass Toxic Disasters in the Courts* (Cambridge, Massachusetts: Harvard University Press, 1987): 86-87, 155-164. Monsanto's share of Agent Orange production was 29.5 percent, compared to Dow's market share of 28.6 percent, however some batches of Agent Orange contained more than 47 times more dioxin than Dow's. The other defendants in the case were Hercules Chemical, Diamond Shamrock, T.H. Agriculture and Nutrition, Thompson Chemicals, and Uniroyal.

[16]Cate Jenkins, "Criminal Investigation of Monsanto Corporation—Cover-up of Dioxin Contamination in Products—Falsification of Dioxin Health Studies," USEPA Regulatory Development Branch, November 1990.

[17]"Monsanto Corporation: A case study in greenwash science," in Jed Greer and Kenny Bruno, *Greenwash: The Reality Behind Corporate Environmentalism* (Penang, Malaysia: Third World Network, 1996): 141.

[18]Jock Ferguson, "Chemical company accused of hiding presence of dioxins," Toronto *Globe and Mail*, February 19, 1990: A9. The punitive damages in *Kemner vs. Monsanto* were overturned on appeal two years later.

[19]Cate Jenkins, *op. cit.*

[20]Stock analyst Dain Bosworth, quoted in Kenny Bruno, "Say it Ain't Soy, Monsanto," *Multinational Monitor*, Vol. 18, No. 1-2, January/February 1997; Mark Arax and Jeanne Brokaw, "No Way Around Roundup," *Mother Jones*, January-February 1997.

[21]Testimony of Champion Paper Company, Vermont Forest Resources Advisory Council, Island Pond, Vermont, June 26, 1996.

[22]Carolyn Cox, "Glyphosate Fact Sheet," *Journal of Pesticide Reform*, Volume 11, No. 2, Spring 1991.

[23]*ibid.*

[24]Carolyn Cox, "Glyphosate, Part 2: Human Exposure and Ecological Effects," *Journal of Pesticide Reform*, Volume 15, No. 4, Fall 1995.

[25]Sylvia Knight, "Glyphosate, Roundup and Other Herbicides—An Annotated Bibliography,"

Vermont Citizens' Forest Roundtable, January 1996.

[26]Pesticide Action Network North America, "Monsanto Agress to Change Ads and EPA Fines Northrup King," January 10, 1997.

[27]"Case of Mislabeled Herbicide Results in $25,000 Penalty," *Wall Street Journal*, March 25, 1998: B9.

[28]J. Greer and K. Bruno, *op. cit.*: 145-46.

[29]Cited in Sarah Anderson and John Cavanagh, "The Top 10 List," *The Nation*, December 8, 1997: 8.

[30]Craig Canine, "Hear No Evil," *Eating Well*, July/August 1991: 41-47; Brian Tokar, "The False Promise of Biotechnology, *Z Magazine*, February 1992: 27-32; Debbie Brighton, "Cow Safety, BGH and Burroughs," *Organic Farmer*, Spring 1990: 21.

[31]Andrew Christiansen, *Recombinant Bovine Growth Hormone: Alarming Tests, Unfounded Approval*, Rural Vermont, July 1995; also B. Tokar, *op. cit*: 28-29.

[32]A. Christiansen, *op. cit.*: 10, 17; U.S. General Accounting Office, "FDA's Review of Recombinant Bovine Growth Hormone," August 6, 1992 (GAO/PEMD -92-96).

[33]Mark Kastel, *Down on the Farm: The Real BGH Story*, Rural Vermont, Fall 1995.

[34]Brian Tokar, "Biotechnology: The debate heats up," *Z Magazine*, June 1995: 49-55; Diane Gershon, "Monsanto sues over BST," *Nature*, Vol. 368, March 31, 1994: 384. The Vermont state labeling law was defended by the state on the grounds of consumer preference, rather than public health, and was ultimately struck down by a federal judge, who ruled that mandatory rBGH labeling was a violation of the companies' constitutional right to refuse to speak.

[35]D.S. Kronfeld, "Health management of dairy herds treated with bovine somatotropin," *Journal of the American Veterinary Medical Association*, Vol. 204, No. 1, January 1994: 116-130; Samuel S. Epstein, "Unlabeled Milk from Cows Treated with Biosynthetic Growth Hormones: A Case of Regulatory Abdication," *International Journal of Health Services*, Vol. 26, No. 1, 1996: 173-185.

[36]Sonja Schmitz, "Cloning Profits: The Revolution in Agricultural Biotechnology," University of Vermont, 1998, to be published.

[37]K. Bruno, "Say it Ain't Soy, Monsanto," *op. cit.*

[38]Monsanto Company 1997 Annual Report: 16, 37.

[39]"Roundup Ready Soybean: A Critique of Monsanto's Risk Evaluation," Greenpeace (Chicago, U.S.A.) 1997.

[40]Hope Shand, "*Bacillus Thuringiensis*: Industry Frenzy and a Host of Issues," *Journal of Pesticide Reform*, Vol. 9, No. 1, Spring 1989: 18-21;

Ricarda A. Steinbrecher, "From Green to Gene Revolution: The Environmental Risks of Genetically Engineered Crops," *The Ecologist*, Vol. 26, No. 6, November/December 1996: 273-281; Brian Tokar, "Biotechnology vs. Biodiversity," *Wild Earth*, Vol. 6, No. 1, Spring 1996: 50-55.

[41] Union of Concerned Scientists, "EPA Requires Large Refuges," *The Gene Exchange*, Summer 1998: 1; Union of Concerned Scientists, "Transgenic insect-resistant crops harm beneficial insects," *The Gene Exchange*, Summer 1998: 4; Union of Concerned Scientists, "Managing Resistance to Bt," *The Gene Exchange*, Vol. 6, No. 2/3, December 1995: 4-7.

[42] Allen R. Myerson, "Monsanto Paying Delta Farmers to Settle Genetic Seed Complaints," *The New York Times*, February 24, 1998: D9; "Monsanto to Pay Cotton Farmers," *Financial Times* (U.S. Edition) February 25, 1998; Union of Concerned Scientists, "Mississippi Seed Arbitration Council Rules Against Monsanto," *The Gene Exchange*, Summer 1998: 1.

[43] Union of Concerned Scientists, "Bt Cotton Fails to Control Bollworm," *The Gene Exchange*, Vol. 7, No. 1, December 1996: 1; Susan Benson, Mark Arax and Rachel Burstein, "A Growing Concern," *Mother Jones*, January/February 1997; Anne Reifenberg and Rhonda L. Rundle, "Buggy Cotton May Cast Doubt On New Seeds," *Wall Street Journal*, July 23, 1996.

[44] Union of Concerned Scientists, "Unexpected Boll Drop in Glyphosate-Resistant Cotton," *The Gene Exchange*, Fall 1997: 1; Pesticide Action Network North America, "Problems with Herbicide Tolerant Cotton in U.S.," October 7, 1997.

[45] RAFI Communiqué, *The Life Industry 1997: The Global Enterprises that Dominate Commercial Agriculture, Food and Health*, Rural Advancement Foundation International, November/December 1997. The comment about Asgrow was quoted by Brewster Kneen in *The Ram's Horn*, No. 160, June 1998: 2.

[46] Monsanto Company 1997 Annual Report, p. 17; RAFI Communiqué, *op. cit.*; Union of Concerned Scientists, "Expanding in New Dimensions: Monsanto and the Food System," *The Gene Exchange*, December 1996: 11.

[47] Edward Hammond, Pat Mooney and Hope Shand, "Monsanto Takes Terminator," Rural Advancement Foundation International, May 14, 1998.

[48] RAFI Communiqué, *op. cit.*

[49] "Investigation: Police close circle around illegal cultivation of soybeans," *Correio Braziliense*, January 31, 1998.

[50] Peter Montague, "Genetic Engineering Error," *Rachel's Environment and Health Weekly*, June 5, 1997.

[51] Quoted in Peter Montague, "Brain Cancer Update," *Rachel's Environment and Health Weekly*, November 14, 1996.

[52] Erik Millstone, "Increasing Brain Tumor Rates: Is There a Link to Aspartame?" University of Sussex Science Policy Research Unit, October 1996.

[53] Richard Koenig, "Rich in New Products, Monsanto Must Only Get Them on the Market," *Wall Street Journal*, May 18, 1990.

[54] Beth Burrows, "Government Workers Go Biotech," Edmonds Institute, May 19, 1997.

[55] See, for example, Senator Al Gore, "Planning a New Biotechnology Policy," *Harvard Journal of Law and Technology*, Vol. 5, Fall 1991: 19-30.

[56] "Genentech Names Moore New Head of Government Affairs Office Based in Washington, D.C.," Genentech company press release, April 13, 1998.

[57] Monsanto World Wide Web page: http://www.monsanto.com/MonPub/NewMonsanto/Officers/BioShapiro.html

[58] Mary Scott, "Interview: Robert Shapiro—Can we trust the maker of Agent Orange to genetically engineer our food?" *Business Ethics*, January/February 1996: 49.

[59] Joan Magretta, "Growth Through Sustainability: An Interview with Monsanto's CEO, Robert Shapiro," *Harvard Business Review*, January-February 1997: 80-81.

[60] Monsanto Company 1997 Annual Report: 10.

[61] See, for example, Vandana Shiva, *The Violence of the Green Revolution: Third World Agriculture, Ecology, and Politics* (London: Zed Books, 1991).

BRIAN TOKAR is the author of *Earth for Sale* (South End Press, 1997) and *The Green Alternative* (Revised Edition: New Society Publishers, 1992). He teaches at the Institute for Social Ecology and Goddard College, both in Plainfield, Vermont, USA.

"TERMINATOR SEEDS THREATEN AN END TO FARMING"

By Hope Shand and Pat Mooney; *Global Pesticide Campaigner*, June 1998, Vol. 8, No. 2

One of the basic tenets of farming is being theatened by a new patent developed with U.S. taxpayers' money. Hope Shand and

Pat Mooney of the Rural Advancement Foundation International (RAFI) bring us up-to-date on this new technology.

By the year 2000 farmers may no longer be able to save seed or breed improved varieties. The 12,000 year old practice of farm families saving their best seed from one year's harvest for planting the next season may be coming to an end. In March 1998, Delta & Pine Land Co. and the United States Department of Agriculture (USDA) announced that they had received a U.S. patent on a new genetic technology designed to prevent unauthorized seed saving by farmers.[1] On May 11, 1998 Monsanto announced that it would acquire Delta & Pine Land Co. for U.S. $1.8 billion.[2] This means that the seed-sterilizing technology is now in the hands of the world's third largest seed corporation and the world's second largest agrochemical corporation.[3] Monsanto's total 1996 revenues were U.S. $9.26 billion, and the company's genetically engineered crops are expected to be used on approximately 50 million acres worldwide in 1998.[4]

The patented technology enables a seed company to genetically alter seed so that it will not germinate if replanted a second time. The patent is broad, applying to plants and seeds of all species, including both transgenic (genetically engineered) and conventionally-bred seeds. The developers of the new technology say that their technique to prohibit seed-saving is still in the product development stage, and is now being tested on cotton and tobacco. They hope to have a product on the market sometime after the year 2000.

USDA researchers stated that they have spent approximately U.S. $190,000 to support research on what RAFI is calling "Terminator" technology over the past four years. Delta & Pine Land, the seed industry collaborator, devoted U.S. $275,000 of in-house expenses and contributed an additional U.S. $255,000 to the joint research. According to USDA spokesman, Willard Phelps, Delta & Pine Land Co. (now owned by Monsanto) has the option to exclusively license the patented technology that was jointly developed by USDA researchers and Delta & Pine Land.[5]

USDA wants the technology to be "widely licensed and made expeditiously available to many seed companies," said USDA's Phelps. The goal is "to increase the value of proprietary seed owned by U.S. seed companies and to open up new markets in Second-and-Third-World countries," said Phelps.

Melvin J. Oliver, a USDA molecular biologist and primary inventor of the technology, explained why the U.S. government developed a technology that prohibits farmers from saving proprietary seed: "My main interest is protection of American technology. Our mission is to protect U.S. agriculture, and to make us competitive in the face of foreign competition. Without this, there is no way of protecting the technology [patented seed]."

USDA stands to earn royalties of about 5 percent of the net sales if a product is commercialized. The day after the patent was announced, Delta & Pine Land Company's stock rose sharply.[6] While USDA and seed industry profits may increase, these earnings come at enormous cost to farmers and to food security around the world. USDA researchers interviewed by RAFI expressed a strong allegiance to the commercial seed industry, and an appalling lack of awareness about the potential impacts of the technology, especially in the South.

IMPACT IN THE SOUTH A genetic technology designed to prevent farmers from saving seed would have enormous adverse impacts in the South—and that is precisely the market being targeted. Murray Robinson, president of Delta & Pine Land Co., stated "We expect [the new technology] to have global implications, especially in markets or countries where patent laws are weak or non-existent."[7] The company's press release claims that its new technology has "the prospect of opening significant worldwide seed markets to the sale of transgenic technology for crops in which seed currently is saved and used in subsequent plantings."[8]

Up to 1.4 billion resource-poor farmers in the South depend on farm-saved seed and seeds exchanged with farm neighbors as their primary seed source.[9] A technology that threatens to restrict farmer expertise in selecting seed and developing locally-adapted strains is a threat to food security and agricultural biodiversity, especially for the poor. The threat is real, especially considering that USDA and Delta & Pine Land (now Monsanto) have applied for patent protection in countries and regions throughout the South—from Madagascar to Mali, from Brazil to Benin, from China to Vietnam.

If the Terminator technology is widely licensed, it could mean that the commercial seed industry will enter entirely new sectors of the seed market —especially in self-pollinating seeds such as wheat, rice, cotton, soybeans, oats, and sorghum. Historically there has been little commercial interest in non-hybridized seeds such as wheat and rice because there was no way for seed companies to control reproduction. With the patent announcement, the world's two most critical food crops—rice and wheat, staple crops for three-quarters of the world's poor—potentially enter the realm of private monopoly.

If Monsanto's new technology provides a genetic mechanism to prevent farmers from germinating a second generation of seed, then seed companies will gain the biological control over seeds that they have heretofore lacked in non-hybrid crops.

Nobody knows exactly how many farmers in industrialized countries save seed from their harvest each year. By some estimates, 20 percent to 30 percent of all soybean fields in the U.S. midwest are typically planted with farmer-saved seed. Most North American wheat farmers typically rely on farm-saved seeds and return to the commercial market once every four or five years.[10] Almost all of the wheat grown on the Canadian prairies is from seed produced in the communities in which it is grown. The same is true for lentils and peas.[11]

MORE OPTIONS FOR FARMERS? Proponents of the terminator technology are quick to point out that farmers will not buy seed that does not bring them benefits. Farmers are not stupid, they make rational choices. But market choices must be examined in the context of privatization of plant breeding and rapid consolidation in the global seed industry. The top 10 seed corporations control approximately 40 percent of the commercial seed market.[12] Current trends in seed industry consolidation, coupled with rapid declines in public sector breeding, mean that farmers are increasingly vulnerable and have far fewer options in the marketplace.

A new technology that is designed to give the seed industry greater control over seeds will ultimately weaken the role of public breeders and reinforce corporate consolidation in the global seed industry.

Advocates of Terminator technology claim that it will be an incentive to plant breeding investment, and a boon to food production in the South because seed companies will have an incentive to invest in crops that have long been ignored by the commercial seed industry. RAFI rejects this claim. Private companies are not interested in developing plant varieties for poor farmers because they know the farmers can't pay. Even national public breeding programs tend to focus on high-yielding, irrigated lands leaving resource-poor farmers to fend for themselves. Proponents of the Terminator maintain that poor, seed-saving farmers will still be able to choose between Terminator seed or sticking with standard varieties and open-pollinated varieties developed by the public sector.

It is not hard, however, to envision a very different scenario. Even public breeders will be pressured by cash-starved institutes to adopt the Terminator technique in order to prevent "unauthorized" seed saving and to recoup their research investment. After all, it was a publicly-funded institution, the USDA, that developed this anti-farmer technology. It is likely that public breeders wanting access to patented genes and traits controlled by the private sector will be forced to adopt the Terminator as a licensing requirement.

Far from improving plant breeding, the Terminator could drive hundreds of millions of farmers out of plant breeding and, since no one else will breed for their needs, out of agriculture altogether. This represents an enormous threat to world food security. Half the world's farmers are poor and can't afford to buy seed every growing season, yet poor farmers grow 15 percent to 20 percent of the world's food and directly feed at least 1.4 billion people— 100 million in Latin America, 300 million in Africa, and one billion in Asia.[13] These farmers depend upon saved seed and their own breeding skills in adapting other varieties for use on their often marginal lands.

BIOSAFETY CONCERNS Molecular biologists who have studied the patent have mixed views on the potential ecological hazards of the sterility trait. The concern is that the sterility trait from first generation seed will "infect" (via pollen) neighboring fields of open-pollinated crops and/or wild relatives growing nearby. Some biologists believe that pollen will not escape, and if it does, it would not pose a threat. With certain applications of the Terminator technology, however, even if the sterility gene does not last long in the environment, it could still pose a threat to nearby crop fields or wild relatives of the plant.[14] The danger is that neighboring crops could be rendered "sterile" due to cross pollination—wreaking havoc on the surrounding ecosystem and endangering the ability of farmers to save seed from crops growing nearby. Given that the technology is new and untested on a large scale, biosafety issues remain a valid and extremely important concern.

BIOSAFETY VS. FOOD SECURITY? The seed industry is expected to defend the Terminator technology by arguing that it will increase the safety of using genetically-engineered crops. Since the seed carries the sterility trait, say proponents, it is less likely that transgenic material will escape from one crop into related species and wild crop relatives. The seed industry is expected to argue that this built-in safety feature will speed up biotech advances in agriculture and increase productivity. Based on this reasoning, it is likely that the industry will enlist government regulators and environmental organizations in backing the Terminator. Biosafety at the expense of food security is no solution. Both must be considered, but human safety through food security must be our primary concern.

THE TERMINATOR MUST BE TERMINATED At the 4th Conference of the Parties (COP) to the Convention on Biological Diversity meeting in Bratislava, Slovakia, May 4-15, 1998, the terminator technology was widely discussed and debated. The Philippines called for a resolution banning the technology, which was supported by delegates from Kenya, Zambia, Pakistan, Rwanda, and Sri Lanka. When it was announced on May 12 that the Delta & Pine Land Co. had been acquired by Monsanto, concerns were heightened about the potential dangers of this technology for farmers and food security. The COP concluded that more information is needed to assess the potential consequences of the terminator technology on conservation and sustainable use of biological diversity, and requested that the issue be considered by its Subsidiary Body on Scientific, Technical and Technological Advice (SBSTTA).

A genetic technology that aims to sterilize seed threatens to extinguish the right of farmers to save seed and breed new crop varieties, and threatens the food security of 1.4 billion people. RAFI and other nongovernmental organizations are calling for a global ban on the use of the Terminator technology. Both the patent and the technology should be rejected on the basis of common sense, food security, and agricultural biodiversity.

Rural Advancement Foundation International (RAFI), P.O. Box 640, Pittsboro, North Carolina 27312; Tel: (919) 542-1396; Fax: (919) 542-0069; e-mail rafiusa@rafi.org; Web site: www.rafi.ca.

NOTES

[1] Delta & Pine Land Company press release, March 3, 1998. The patent is benignly titled, "Control of Plant Gene Expression" (U.S. patent no. 5,723,765).

[2] Monsanto press release, May 11, 1998, "Monsanto Acquires Two Seed Companies to Broaden Availability of Ag Biotech."

[3] RAFI (Based on the combined 1997 seed revenues of DeKalb, Asgrow, Delta & Pine Land and other Monsanto seed subsidiaries, RAFI estimates that Monsanto is now the world's third largest commercial seed company, after Pioneer Hi-Bred Intl. and Novartis. Shortly before this GPC went to press, Monsanto announced a merger with American Home Products (parent company of Cyanimid). This new company is potentially the largest agrochemical company in the world.

[4] Monsanto, op. cit.

[5] Wilard Phelps, personal communication, March 10, 1998.

[6] Anonymous, "Delta & Pine stock up after patent awarded" March 4, 1998. Reuters wire story.

[7] Murray Robinson, president of Delta & Pine Land Co., personal communication.

[8] Delta & Pine Land Company, op. cit.

[9] Food and Agriculture Organization of the U.N., "The State of the World's Plant Genetic Resources for Food and Agriculture," (Background Documentation prepared for the International Technical Conference on Plant Genetic Resources, Leipzig, Germany, June 17-23, 1996), Rome, 1996.

[10] Greg Hillyer, "Saved-Seed Busters," Progressive Farmer, January, 1998. Telephone inter-

view with Murray Robinson, President, Delta & Pine Land Seed Co., March 1998.

[11]Personal communication with Ian McCreary, farmer, Saskatchewan, Canada. McCreary is also a policy manager for the Canadian Food Grains Bank, a Canadian NGO working on food security issues.

[12]RAFI Communique, "The Life Industry," November/December, 1997.

[13]FAO, op. cit.

[14]Doreen Stabinsky, California State University at Sacramento, personal communication.

REACTIONS TO THE TERMINATOR "This is a patent that is too profitable for companies to ignore," says Camila Montecinos of the Chilean-based Center for Education and Technology. "We will see pressure on national regulatory systems to marginalize saved-seed varieties and clear the way for the Terminator. One point four billion farm families are at risk."

"Governments should make use of the technology illegal," she insists. "This is an immoral technique that robs farming communities of their age-old right to save seed and their role as plant breeders. It should be banned." To this, corporate breeders argue that the new technology simply does for hard-to-hybridize crops what the hybrid technique did for maize. Hybrid seed is either sterile or fails to reproduce the same quality characteristics in the next generation. Thus, most maize farmers buy seed every year. "Poor farmers can't afford hybrids either," Montecinos points out, "but there's a key difference. The theory behind hybridization is that it allows breeders to make crosses that couldn't be made otherwise and that are supposed to give the plant higher yields and vigor. The results are often disappointing but that's the rationale. In the case of Terminator Technology, there's absolutely no agronomic benefit for farmers. The sole purpose is to facilitate monopoly control and the sole beneficiary is agribusiness."

CET (Centro de Educación y Tecnología)
Casilla 16557, Correo 9, Santiago, Chile
Tel: 011-56-2-234-1141
Fax: 011-56-2-233-7239
cettco@entelchile.net

Aside from sky-rocketing seed costs, Neth Daño of the Philippines-based civil society organization SEARICE sees a threat to the environment and to long term food security. "We work with farmers who may buy a commercial variety, but its breeder wouldn't recognize it five years later. Women select the best seeds every year and over time the rice molds itself to the farm's own ecosystem. Women also cross the commercial variety with other rice strains to breed their own locally-adapted seeds. The Terminator could put an end to all this and increase crop uniformity and vulnerability. It poses a threat to the culture of seed sharing and exchange that is led primarily by women farmers."

SEARICE
83 Madasalin Street, Sikatuna Village, 1101 Quezon City, Philippines
Tel: 63-2-433-7182
Fax: 63-2-921-7563
searice@philonline.com.ph

RURAL ADVANCEMENT FOUNDATION INTERNATIONAL RAFI is dedicated to the conservation and sustainable improvement of agricultural biodiversity, and to the socially responsible development of technologies useful to rural societies. RAFI is concerned about the loss of genetic diversity—especially in agriculture—and about the impact of intellectual property rights on agriculture and world food security. RAFI is an international non-governmental organization headquartered in Winnipeg, Manitoba (Canada) with affiliate offices in Pittsboro, North Carolina (USA).

4 CENSORED

Recycled Radioactive Metals may be in Your Home

"NUCLEAR SPOONS"

By Anne-Marie Cusac;
The Progressive; October 1998

The Department of Energy has a problem: what to do with millions of tons of radioactive metal. So the DOE has come up with an ingenious plan to dispose of its troublesome tons of nickel, copper, steel, and aluminum. It wants to let scrap companies collect the metal, try to take the radioactivity out, and sell the metal to foundries, which would in turn sell it to manufacturers who could use it for everyday household products: pots, pans, forks, spoons, even your eyeglasses.

You may not know this, but the government already permits some companies, under special licenses, to buy, reprocess, and sell radioactive metal: 7,500 tons in 1996, by one industry estimate. But the amount of this reprocessing could increase drastically if the DOE, the Nuclear Regulatory Commission (NRC), and the burgeoning radioactive metal processing industry get their way. They are pressing for a new, lax standard that would do away with the special per-

mits and allow companies to buy and resell millions of tons of low-level radioactive metal.

If the rules change, the metal companies could increase their output a hundredfold. And the standard the companies seek could cause nearly 100,000 cancer fatalities in the United States, by the NRC's own estimate.

"We're looking at an exponential increase," says Diane D'Arrigo, a staff member at the Nuclear Information and Resource Service, which is fighting the push to recycle radioactive metal. "Think about the metal you come into contact with every day. Your IUD, and your bracelets, your silverware, the zipper on your crotch, the coins in your pocket, frying pans, belt buckles, that chair you're sitting on, the batteries that are in your car and motorbike, the batteries in your computer."

A June 30 memorandum from John Hoyle, NRC Secretary, announces the Commission's decision to establish a new, legal dose of radiation for metals released from nuclear facilities.

"This level should be based on realistic scenarios of health effects from low doses that still allows quantities of materials to be released," says the letter. "The rule should be comprehensive and apply to all metals, equipment, and materials, including soil."

Metal companies want that standard to be in the vicinity of 10 millirems per year. A millirem is a unit of measure, based on the standard man, that estimates the damage radiation does to human tissue. The NRC studied the health effects of such a standard back in 1990. It found: "A radiation dose of 10 mrem per year . . . received continuously over a lifetime corresponds to a risk of about 4 chances in 10,000" of fatal cancer. That translates to 92,755 additional cancer deaths in the United States alone.

Many scientists argue that any release of hot metals into the product stream is a serious health hazard.

John Gofman is a former associate director of Livermore National Laboratory, one of the scientists who worked on the atomic bomb, and co-discoverer of uranium-233. "There is no safe dose or dose rate below which dangers disappear. No threshold-dose," said Gofman. "Serious, lethal effects from minimal radiation doses are not 'hypothetical, 'just theoretical,' or 'imaginary.' They are real."

Karl Morgan, known as the father of health physics, shudders at the idea of more and more radioactive metal entering people's homes. He is particularly worried about dental fillings. "You certainly don't want people going around with radioactive teeth," he says.

Some of the most dangerous radioactivity around the home, says Morgan, will be the metals people unintentionally ingest. "Some of these find their way directly into the human body, especially copper and iron, stainless steel [from] knives and forks," he says. "It doesn't help any cell in the human body if you send an alpha particle through it."

Richard Clapp, associate professor in the department of environmental health at the Boston University Schools of Public Health, says you may soon need to fear household products you have most contact with: "If you're sitting on it, or if it's part of your desk, or in the frame of your bed-where you have constant exposure and for several hours," you will be in most danger.

Clapp, who published a study on the increases in leukemia and thyroid cancers associated with low-level radiation exposure among people living near a Massachusetts nuclear power plant, says radioactive metal recycling will raise overall radiation levels. "Who in their right mind would want to do that?" he asks. "This is the legacy of an industry gone mad."

It's early August, and I'm attending the "Beneficial Reuse" conference of the Association of Radioactive Metal Recyclers, in Knoxville, Tennessee.

"We were not always called Beneficial Reuse," says Val Loiselle, chairman of the association, during his opening speech. "In our first year, we were called the Radioactive Scrap Metal Conference."

This is the sixth annual gathering of radioactive metal recyclers. There is a special session for those interested in recycling depleted uranium and a presentation on recycling radioactive concrete.

"I got my start in the commercial nuclear power business," says Leo Hill, the general manager and president of GTS Duratek. "Nowadays, when I go by a scrap yard or an automobile wrecking place, I think, 'This stuff is beautiful.' I'm in the garbage business, and I love it."

"I was born a Hindu, and a central feature of the Hindu religion is reincarnation," says Shankar Menon of Menon Consulting in Sweden. "And being trained as an engineer, it's just a short step to the recycling of metals. I'm actually thinking of the soul in them."

But this conference is not so much about the soul of the metal as its sale. "In the scrap business, there's probably about $3 billion in the region, if you count Ohio, Kentucky, and Indiana," says Frederick Gardner, who is in charge of business development for Decontamination and Recovery Services of Oak Ridge, Tennessee. "The cheaper we can handle this stuff, the bigger business this will be."

Still, there are a few kinks to be worked out in the plan to reprocess radioactive scrap: for instance, public opinion. "What's it going to take to get the public swung around to say, 'OK, I don't like it, but I guess you've proven it's safe'?" asks Gardner, who is making a presentation. He answers his own question with an overhead that reads, The Main Point: It All Starts With the Salesman.

"We can tackle the public on the notion that radioactivity is an effluent, not a waste," says Loiselle, comparing radioactivity to car exhaust. "This industry has a right to effluence just like any other industry. And it cannot be zero. No industry has zero effluence."

Peter Yerace, waste coordinator for the Department of Energy's Fernald project in Ohio, displays an overhead slide: Public Perception Problems: Fears of Radiation, Suspicion of DOE.

Fernald has "lots of copper," 120 tons of ingots, says Yerace. He proposed releasing copper that was slightly contaminated with uranium. "When I went in front of the public, I got the crap beat out of me," he says. People asked, "Are my kid's braces going to be made out of that copper?" Yerace told them the metal could enter consumer products. "I went as far as a copper IUD. That's what it's made of," he says. But he tried to reassure them the metal would be of such low levels of radioactivity that it wouldn't be dangerous.

I step into the hallway during a break and hear a voice from one of the display booths. "Come on over and get your CO-2 pellets," calls Chris Wetherall, president of Cryo Dynamics Inc., a company specializing in "cryogenic decontamination and waste minimization." He opens a cooler and cold steam spills onto the table. He dribbles a cup full of dry-ice pellets into my palm. They sting, so I drop them to the carpet, and they bounce away. As I rub my hand on my pants leg, Wetherall explains that the dry ice will decontaminate metals, wood, concrete, and fabrics, while causing no waste. "It sterilizes everything it touches," he says.

But while CO-2 sterilizes some surfaces, not all the "hot spots" on radioactive metal can be scrubbed off. This is particularly true for metals that are radioactive inside and out, which is one reason why companies cannot legally reprocess them. The DOE and the private firms want to be able to recycle these "volumetrically contaminated" metals, too.

Loiselle explains that the government is getting away from measuring exactly how much radiation it will allow in any given product. Instead, it is making more general target assessments based on risk and is considering setting an allowable dose standard. Many industry members advocate a standard that would allow for the release of all metal estimated to give off doses of radiation at 10 to 15 millirems per year. "The dose shouldn't be ridiculously low," Loiselle says. "We've gone too far toward making it zero. That's really not fair to the industry. Nothing is zero. Pick a number, and you'll have a lot of friends here. We'd rather be regulated at 10 millirems or thereabouts."

As Loiselle explains it, the public has no idea what doses it encounters in household products and car parts because the current release standards for those who get special permits are set so close to zero that the radiation is not measurable. "The public health is better served by something measurable," he says. "In a sense, that means a looser or a less stringent standard. Wouldn't it be better if it were something we could measure?"

Not all industry people agree with that. Steven Stansberry, business development manager for Manufacturing Sciences Corporation, doesn't buy the argument that the public needs a measurable standard. "Personally, I'm not an advocate against it because I work in the industry, and it doesn't scare me," he tells me at his plant in Oak Ridge. "But raising it just so you know it's out there in the public seems a little backwards. If you can't measure it, at the worst case it's minimal. At the best case, it's not there," he says. "If it's dose-based, you know it's there all the time."

Some scientists argue that exposure to continual low-dose radiation is potentially more dangerous than a one-time high-level dose. "The cancer curve rises more steeply at low doses than high doses," says Steve Wing, an epidemiologist at the University of North Carolina-Chapel Hill.

In the gravel lot outside U.S. Ecology in Oak Ridge, I am looking at drums labeled radioactive and sludge and metal boxes (called B-25s or Sea-Lands) identified by millirem dose rates—.4 mr/hr, .8 mr/hr, 2 mr/hr, 5 mr/hr. "This is not a glamorous industry," says Tom Gilman, the company's government accounts manager. In addition to handling low-level radioactive wastes, says Gilman,

U.S. Ecology recycles metals contaminated with low-level radioactivity. Most come from commercial sites, but he says some are from the DOE.

Companies pay U.S. Ecology to remove the radioactive metal from their property. If the metal is not highly radioactive and is contaminated only on the surface, the plant scrubs it, then sells it as clean scrap. From there, the metal travels to a steel mill and enters the consumer market. U.S. Ecology is "turning waste into assets," says Gilman.

But Gilman is careful to say the assets his company is recycling into the metal stream aren't completely clean. "'Acceptable' levels is the word to use," he explains. "There's always going to be some level of radioactivity."

We enter what Gilman calls the survey building. Here, he says, workers search bags with a Geiger counter to find hot pieces of trash.

"So the bags could have radioactive stuff in them?" I ask.

"Anything in this room could have radioactive stuff in it," says Gilman. "Except us." He laughs.

We leave the building. Nearby, sits a chirping Geiger counter. From the pine woods, comes the long drone of locusts. "This is the year for them," says Gilman.

In the next building, we pause near a large pile of bent and perforated radioactive metal beams. "This is structural steel," says Gilman. "They're going to blast this, cutting out the hot spots to make new products to keep America great." Gilman points toward my notebook, gesturing with each word. "Write that," he says. "To keep America great."

Early in the 1980s, gold jewelry in Buffalo, New York, was a hot item. When a local television station offered to survey gold jewelry, it turned up three radioactive pieces in the first two days. "As a result of this finding, the New York State Health Department began a comprehensive campaign in 1981 to find radioactive, contaminated jewelry," reported the journal *Health Physics* in 1986. "More than 160,000 pieces were surveyed, and, of these, about 170 pieces turned out to be radioactive—mostly from western New York and nearby Pennsylvania." News accounts from the early '80s reported that at least 14 people had developed finger cancer and several people had suffered amputations of their fingers and even parts of their hands as a result of the hot jewelry.

The reports alleged that the radioactive gold came from the state-owned Roswell Park Institute, a center for cancer research and treatment. The rings contained small amounts of radon that had originally been used to treat tumors. Most of the jewelry dated from the 1940s.

Two attempts to sue the state of New York over the occurrence—one by a woman whose husband died after skin cancer metastasized throughout his body, another by a woman whose finger had to be amputated—failed. According to a May 14, 1983, A.P. report, the judge in one of the cases "ruled that the clock on the statute of limitations begins running at the time of injury." The court also ruled that Roswell Park could not be held responsible because it was "merely a hypothesis" that the gold had come from there.

The hot gold rings—and the cancer associated with them—may be a sign of things to come.

While radioactive metal reprocessing may pose health threats to consumers, it's the scrap metal workers and foundry workers who are likely to receive the most exposure.

A 1987 NRC bulletin describes tiny, extremely hot particles less than one millimeter in any direction (called radioactive fleas) that can cause serious damage to people who accidentally touch them. Such minute but extremely radioactive bits of metal could easily hide away in loads of otherwise low-level metal.

Michael Wright, director of health, safety, and environment for the United Steelworkers of America, claims there is also serious danger to workers from low-level radioactivity in steel. "You can't inhale a piece of steel," says Wright. "But if you melt it, there's a substantial risk of breathing it in. That's orders of magnitude more dangerous."

Ordinary precautions like wearing respirators won't be enough to protect workers, says Wright. "There isn't anything that protects people."

In addition to cancers, "these exposures also can cause neurologicalproblems," says Jackie Kittrell, a lawyer with the American Environmental Health Studies Project, an Oak Ridge organization that represents workers who have suffered heavy metal exposure and radiation poisoning while on the job. Radioactive metal exposure can "interfere with immune system function," she says.

Even the Steel Manufacturers Association takes a dim view of radioactive metal. Christina Bechak, vice president of the association, expresses a concern that radiation will accumulate on the machines used for shredding and smelting the metal. "Scrap metal is valuable, but we don't want radioactive scrap," she says. Nor is she happy with the proposal to let companies release this metal freely. "The detectors [in the factories] are set very sensitive," says Bechak. She fears that extremely hot scrap will be able to enter the plants in loads of low-level metal, since the detectors do not distinguish between levels of radioactivity. If the detectors sound an alarm for every shipment of low-level metal, the workers may be tempted to ignore the warning or to set the detectors to a less sensitive, and potentially more dangerous, reading. "All the radioactive metal is going to set off the detectors," she says.

The DOE is so eager to get radioactive metal off its hands that it has hired an arm of British Nuclear Fuels, called BNFL, to do the job. The British-government-owned company has already started work at several large buildings on the K-25 site in Oak Ridge that were originally used to manufacture highly enriched uranium for nuclear warheads as part of the Manhattan Project. The $238 million contract stipulates that the company may recycle for profit all the metals it recovers, including a large amount of formerly classified nickel.

When British Nuclear Fuels released 7,000 metric tons of metal contaminated with low-level radioactivity for recycling into consumer goods in Britain earlier this year, it caused an uproar. A spokesman for British Nuclear Fuels explained his philosophy to the London paper *The Independent*. "It's recycling," he said. "If you have a cup of coffee, you don't throw the cup away, you reuse it."

BNFL's U.S. project has run into a roadblock. A coalition of environmental groups and unions—including the Natural Resources Defense Council, the Nuclear Information and Resource Service, and the Oil, Chemical, and Atomic Workers Union—recently won a suit that claimed the Department of Energy had neglected to consider the environmental impact of all the metal it planned to release for recycling. The court ordered the DOE to perform an Environmental Impact Statement. The Department of Energy acknowledges 100,000 pounds of metal have been shipped out already, but this metal, the DOE claims, is clean.

Meanwhile, at the K-25 site in Oak Ridge, there have been problems this summer that have nothing to do with BNFL. The DOE accidentally released two hot metal items and claimed they had been thoroughly checked for radiation contamination. In both cases, the state of Tennessee caught the hot releases and returned them to the DOE. "Unfortunately or fortunately, however you look at it, the only pieces of metal the state looked at were the ones found to be radioactive," says John Owsley, assistant director of the DOE's oversight division.

"In years past, a lot of material went out of these facilities that wouldn't meet commercial-world standards," says Michael Mobley, the director of the division of radiological health in the Tennessee Department of Energy and Conservation. And the cavalier attitude at the DOE is no help, he says. "There's been some issue about this: 'Well, if we miss one or two spots it's no big deal because the standard is so strict.' If every once in a while stuff is going out that's hotter than standard, how much is going out that's hotter than standard? Their survey processes are just going to evolve into nothing."

The amount of radioactive metal that already enters manufactured goods is difficult to pinpoint. "We just don't keep that kind of data," says Bob Nelson, chief of the low-level waste and regulation issues section in the NRC's Division of Waste Management.

Vince Adams, who heads the DOE's National Center of Excellence for Metals Recycle, a center committed to recycling as much metal as possible from decommissioned DOE facilities, says that Oak Ridge has released 2,610 tons in the past decade. All the other DOE sites together released 11,129 tons in that time.

Loiselle says that companies tend to protect their data, but he estimates the industry received 15,000 tons of metal from the DOE and commercial reactors during 1996. Approximately half that metal was recycled.

Those thousands of tons are nothing compared with the heaps of metal we could see as more and more nuclear reactors tumble to the ground in the next 20 years.

The sheer volume of available radioactive metal is astonishing. "DOE has 3,000 to 4,000 facilities that are in D and D [Decommission and Decontamination] state," says Loiselle. "There are 123 commercial nuclear power plants. Thirteen of these are entering the decommissioning pipeline. As these plants come down, we will be seeing lots of metals and equipment."

According to Adams, the DOE's database shows 1,577,000 stockpiled metric tons for both the DOE and the NRC combined.

"And that is dwarfed by what we've got coming," says Jane Powell, program manager of the DOE's metal recycling center. She points to all the metal at the gaseous diffusion plant in Oak Ridge that was used for the Manhattan Project. That plant now sits idle, awaiting demolition crews. "They have one tunnel there that is a half-mile long," says Powell. "We joke and say you can see the curvature of the earth. You can actually look down and see where the light stops. We are going to have metal coming out of our ears."

That could mean substantial profits for the radioactive metal industry. "We've got metal. We've got a need for it," says Powell. "We need to make it economically viable so that going out and getting virgin metal isn't the answer. We are going out in the real world to create a business. It is a business."

The NRC is planning on unveiling its proposed new standard in October, explains Robert Meck, who is currently conducting research on the standard for the NRC. The standard, he says, will use millirem doses. It will involve "the concept of an average member of the critical group—a group of individuals who can realistically be expected to have the highest dose," he explains. The standard will not invoke "the worst case imaginable. It's really a concept that makes it applicable to the real world."

This approach downplays risks to the sick, the elderly, the young, and those who are particularly sensitive because they are exposed to abnormal amounts of radioactive material through their work. It also fails to specify a maximum dose any member of the public would be allowed to receive.

"After age 45, there is a much more dramatic association of radiation with cancer," says David Richardson, a postdoctoral research associate at the University of North Carolina, Chapel Hill, who assisted with a recent study of Oak Ridge nuclear workers sponsored by the

Centers for Disease Control. "This is very low-level radiation. What we're looking at is cancer death."

This study adds evidence to Alice Stewart's 1950s research that discovered cancer incidence rose sharply among children whose mothers were exposed to x-rays while pregnant.

A dose-based standard would also change the way the regulators see radioactivity. No longer would they measure how much radioactivity each piece of metal gives off. Rather, the regulators would use a theoretical estimate of how much damage a piece of radioactive metal does to the human body.

"Each of the objects could meet government standards on its own, but there's no limit to the number of objects a person could be exposed to," says D'Arrigo of the Nuclear Information and Resource Service.

"You should err on the side of safety and not expose the public," says Wing, who led a DOE-funded study on nuclear workers at Oak Ridge that concluded low-level radiation exposure is four to ten times more dangerous than previously believed. He says the plan to allow more radioactive metal into the manufacturing process is "like a massive experiment."

While the DOE and the radioactive metal recyclers await a new NRC standard for releasing more hot metal in the United States, the stuff already appears to be causing trouble overseas.

"Our fear is that entrepreneurs have found a way to market it into countries that don't have our strict standards," says Kittrell of the American Environmental Health Studies Project. In June 1996, Chinese officials in Tianjin, a port city 100 miles southeast of Beijing, stopped a 78-ton shipment of radioactive scrap metal from the United States. Some of the scrap was 30 times the official Chinese safety limit for radioactivity. According to an article in *European Business Report*, the metal came from discarded equipment that had belonged to a U.S. fertilizer company.

An April 4, 1994, article in *The Advocate*, a Baton Rouge, Louisiana, paper, suggests such exports may be widespread. "Radioactive metal is being welcomed by smelters in China, where a booming economy is driving up the demand for steel," reporter Peter Shinkle wrote. Shinkle discovered that three major U.S. oil companies—Texaco, Mobil, and Phillips—were exporting large shipments of oil-field pipe and equipment "encrusted with radium, a radioactive material that is carried to the surface in oil production."

Shinkle spoke with representatives of the three companies. All shared their discovery of the large Asian market for radioactive metal.

"Since 1993, the three companies have shipped some 5.5 million pounds of radioactive steel scrap to China from Louisiana and Texas," Shinkle found.

"We have every reason to believe they handle it safely in China," Pierre DeGruy, spokesman for Texaco Exploration and Production Inc., told *The Advocate*. "The radioactive material reached a high reading of 2,000 microrems per hour, DeGruy said. That's about 400 times the background radiation levels from natural sources in Louisiana," *The Advocate* reported.

The companies all told Shinkle that they planned to keep selling radioactive scrap to China.

"They need steel, and they're looking to get it any way they can," said Larry Wall, spokesman for the Mid-Continent Oil and Gas Association. "And the oil companies can sell the metal to the Chinese rather than paying for its costly cleaning or disposal at radioactive waste facilities in the United States."

Texaco and Phillips Petroleum say they no longer send the metal overseas. They now reprocess it here in the United States. Mobil spokesman Bill Cumming says the company has not exported metal to China since 1996, but might again in the future. "It remains a legal option for us to do so," he says.

Nina Sato, a Japanese journalist and author of the book *We Are All Exposed*, gave the only talk at the Beneficial Reuse conference that strongly criticized the recycling of radioactive metal. Her reason: It is showing up in Taiwanese buildings. "In the past two days, we have heard about how recycle and reuse are good things," she began. "My stories talk about when it turns out to be a disaster."

As of January 1998, says Sato, there were 178 buildings known to be contaminated with radiation in Taiwan. The buildings contained 1,573 apartments. Residents began to find radiation contamination in steel pipes and fittings.

According to news reports on the incidents, some Taiwanese officers knew about the apartments constructed out of radioactive steel bars, but concealed that information from tenants for more than a decade. The apartments showed some background radiation levels at more than 1,000 times that of most buildings in Taiwan. The people who lived in the apartments suffered from congenital disorders, various cancers, and unusual chromosomal and cytogenetic damage, reported *The Lancet*.

"Taiwanese are still living in the buildings because it's not easy to move out," says Sato. She cites high housing prices in Taiwan and the impossibility of selling an apartment once people know it has radioactive contamination.

So the inhabitants tend to come up with practical, if questionable, solutions. "Sometimes it's only in the kitchen," says Sato. "You just close the kitchen. Sometimes it's only one bedroom. You close the bedroom."

Sato says radioactive metal is coming into Asia from former Soviet bloc countries and from the United States. "The worst thing is," she says, "Russian metal is very cheap."

Sato is afraid of accidentally buying a contaminated product. "When I go to the department store, I always bring my Geiger counter," she says. "Frying pan, tatatata," she imitates the sound of a Geiger counter going off. "I'm afraid it's made in China."

"In the future, radiation will be with you all the time," says Sato. "Because no one tried to stop it. All they talk about is money, money, money."

Sato's speech did not dampen enthusiasm at the conference. As Shankar Menon ended his talk, he displayed an overhead slide: This Is a Radioactive World. He added, "This is something we have to put up with, like traffic."

ANNE-MARIE CUSAC is Managing Editor of *The Progressive*. This article was made possible by a grant from the Fund for Investigative Journalism, Inc.

5 CENSORED

U.S. Weapons of Mass Destruction Linked to the Deaths of Half a Million Children

"MADE IN AMERICA, IT'S NO ACCIDENT THAT IRAQ HAS WEAPONS OF MASS DESTRUCTION. U.S. CORPORATIONS HELPED SUPPLY THEM."

By Dennis Bernstein;
Bay Guardian; February 25, 1998

In January 1991 Iraqi president Saddam Hussein launched a barrage of long-range Scud missiles against Israel and Saudi Arabia. Dozens of people were wounded or killed—including 28 U.S. soldiers who were asleep in their bunks when the Scuds hit. According to declassified secret nuclear, chemical, and biological logs kept by the Pentagon, Israeli police "confirmed nerve gas" at the site where the missile landed in downtown Tel Aviv. While the incident was widely reported in the press, it was rarely mentioned that the technology used to increase the range of the missile that hit Israel, and to create the nerve gas that was apparently carried inside, was supplied to Iraq by U.S. and western corporations. Likewise, when U.S.-led allied forces bombed more than 30 chemical and biological weapons facilities during the 1991 war with Iraq, much of the deadly toxins that were released into the upper atmosphere, only to fall back down on the heads of U.S. forces, were created with the generous support of U.S. firms and America's leading politicians.

At one point, just a year before Iraq invaded Kuwait, Pentagon officials invited key Iraqi military technicians to a special conference in Portland, Oregon, that amounted to a crash course in how to detonate a nuclear bomb.

Even today, the chemical, biological, and possibly even nuclear weapons U.S. troops could face in Gulf War II might as well be stamped "Made in the USA." As the United States threatens to bomb Iraq for the third time this decade, the irony is brutal: Many of the same politicians, news media outlets, and interest groups that are promoting Gulf War II either supported or ignored the policies of the Reagan and Bush Administrations that gave Iraq its deadly arsenal.

In fact, the problem goes far beyond the Middle East: If Saddam Hussein is capable of launching chemical, biological, or nuclear attacks, it will be the result of a long-standing U.S. policy of allowing defense contractors and other powerful corporations to sell the technology of death to almost anyone in the world who is willing to pay for it.

The Iraqi situation, former CIA military analyst Patrick Eddington told the *Bay Guardian*, "goes to the heart of the concept of nonproliferation and whether something like the international Chemical Weapons Convention is going to have any credibility."

"It has no chance of working if the countries who are the primary signatories, and for that matter the primary suppliers of dual-use technology," Eddington said, referring to technology that can be used for both civilian and military purposes, "are still cranking this stuff out and supplying it. It's a two-faced policy—and that definitely includes the United States."

OUR FRIEND SADDAM Documents obtained by the *Bay Guardian*—many of which have been available for years, released during Congressional investigations—shed disturbing light on the U.S. policy of arming Saddam Hussein, a policy that may again result in the exposure of hundreds of thousands of U.S. soldiers—and millions of civilians—to dangerous chemical and biological weapons.

"If tomorrow the Iraqis fired a missile with biological warheads on it," Gary Milholland of the Wisconsin Project for Nuclear Arms Control told the *Bay Guardian*, "the missile itself would have been purchased from Russia, upgraded with help from Germany, and the bacteria would be based on a strain imported from the United States."

"What we're looking at is a program made in the west," said Milholland, who testified as an expert witness before Congress in 1992 on the arming of Iraq by the west. "The west supplied the materials, the knowledge, and the people."

In fact, some critics say that Iraq's deadly arsenal is the best argument against the Clinton Administration's planned bombing campaign.

"A bombing campaign against suspected chemical and biological storage sites is literally a game of chemical and biological Russian roulette," said Eddington, who resigned last year to protest the agency's refusal to tell Gulf War vets the truth about their potential exposure to chemical weapons.

"We are looking at potential fallout that can kill a large number of people. You could be looking at anywhere from hundreds to tens of thousands of deaths."

In the early 1980s the Reagan Administration chose to support Iraq over Iran in their bloody war. Neither country was exactly an ally, but the White House considered Iran the worse of the two nations, and Cold War politics (along with a U.S. desire to maintain control of oil supplies in the Middle East) put us on the side of Iraq.

In accordance with a long and continuing tradition and policy, that meant the U.S. would arm Iraq to the teeth—without much concern for the long-term consequences.

According to a 1990 report, "The Poison Gas Connection," issued by the L.A.-based Simon Wiesenthal Center (See sidebar), more than 207 companies from 21 western countries, including at least 18 from the United States, contributed to the buildup of Saddam Hussein's arsenal. Subsequent investigations turned up more than 100 more companies participating in the Iraqi weapons buildup.

The frontline cheerleader for America's corporate contributors to Saddam, the man who paved the way for Iraq to purchase millions of dollars worth of weapons and dangerous dual-use technology from U.S. corporations, was none other than the architect of Gulf War I, former president George Bush.

In a stunning July 27, 1992, speech on the floor of the House of Representatives, House Banking Committee chair Henry Gonzalez drove the Bush connection home in no uncertain terms:

"The Bush Administration deliberately, not inadvertently, helped to arm Iraq by allowing U.S. technology to be shipped to Iraqi military and to Iraqi defense factories," Gonzalez said. "Throughout the course of the Bush Administration, U.S. and foreign firms were granted export licenses to ship U.S. technology directly to Iraqi weapons facilities despite ample evidence showing that these factories were producing weapons."

Gonzalez, who was accused by administration officials of jeopardizing national security for going public with his gritty revelations, also stated: "The president misled Congress and the public about the role U.S. firms played in arming Iraq."

Documents gathered by Gonzalez and other independent investigators show that despite U.S. intelligence reports dating back to 1983 documenting Saddam's mass gassing of the Kurds and Iranians in the ongoing Iran-Iraq war, Bush pressed for support of the Iraqis. In a damning October 21, 1989, cable from Secretary of State James Baker to then Iraqi foreign minister Tariq Aziz, only a year after the mass gassing of the Kurds, Baker assured the Iraqis that the United States was very eager for a close working relationship with Saddam Hussein. "As I said in our meeting," Baker wrote, "the U.S. seeks a broadened and deepened relationship with Iraq on the basis of mutual respect. That is the policy of our president."

According to Gonzalez, senior Bush aides successfully lobbied against the concerns of other government officials to allow Iraq to purchase the technology—technology that could be adapted for both civilian and military purposes. These high-level Bush officials, including Baker, forced this policy through despite substantial available evidence that the Iraqis were furiously working on developing nuclear weapons and other devices of mass destruction.

The CIA reported at a top-secret intelligence briefing in November 1989 that Iraq "is interested in acquiring a nuclear explosive capability" and to this end "is ordering substantial quantities of dual-use equipment." Nevertheless, Bush and other top U.S. officials continually pressured the Agriculture Department's Commodity Credit Corporation (CCC) and the U.S. Export-Import Bank to give Iraq credit for farm products and manufactured goods. From 1983 to 1990 the CCC provided Iraq with $5 billion in credits and loans to purchase U.S. exports. Between 1984 and 1990 the Eximbank insured $297 million of additional exports. As recently as seven months before the 1990 Iraqi invasion of Kuwait, Bush issued an order allowing the bank to provide even more credit to Iraq.

NUCLEAR KNOW-HOW State Department documents drafted after Bush became president in 1989 warned that Iraq would rise out of the ruins of its eight-year war with Iran as a "great military and political power, and [Iraq] is aiming higher." They also indicated that Iraq was planning to use "a big-stick approach" to the border conflict with Kuwait.

According to Gonzalez's July 27, 1992, floor speech, as late as the fall of 1989, only months before Iraq invaded Kuwait, George Bush signed a top secret National Security Decision directive, known as NSD 26, ordering closer ties with Saddam Hussein and Iraq: "Normal relations between the United States and Iraq would serve our long-term interests and support stability both in the Gulf and the Middle East," stated the top secret directive. "The United States remains committed to support the individual and collective self-defense of friendly countries in the area."

The Bush directive also encouraged U.S. firms to participate in the reconstruction of the Iraqi economy, "particularly in the energy area, where they do not conflict with our nonproliferation and other significant objectives."

And participate they did. According to House and Senate Banking Committee investigations, in the five years preceding the Gulf War, the U.S. Department of Commerce licensed more than $1.5 billion of strategically sensitive American exports to Iraq. Many were directly delivered to nuclear and chemical weapon plants as well as to Iraqi missile sites. More than 700 licenses were issued to U.S. corporations doing business in Iraq; many of these licenses were for the shipment of this dual-use technology to Iraq.

In April 1990, U.S. intelligence reported to the Bush Administration that Hussein "has strengthened his ties to terrorist groups and may use terrorism to intimidate his Arab and western opponents." But Bush Administration backchannel and international diplomatic and financial support continued unabated.

The cooperation between U.S. suppliers and Iraqi weapons planners continued up to the beginning of the war. U.S. technicians and officials moved back and forth easily between the two countries.

In one of the more stunning incidents, in September 1989, just one year before the Iraqi military stormed over the Kuwaiti border, U.S. military officials invited several Iraqi technicians to attend a "detonation conference" at the Red Lion Inn in Portland, Oregon.

The conference—the Ninth Symposium (International) on Detonation, was a crash course from the world's experts on how to detonate a nuclear weapon. Among the named sponsors of the conference were the Office of Naval Research, the Air Force Armament Laboratory, the Army Armament Research, Development and Engineering Center, the Army Ballistic Research Laboratory, Lawrence Livermore National Laboratory, Los Alamos National Laboratory, the Naval Sea Systems Command, Naval Surface Warfare Center, Office of Naval Technology, and Sandia National Laboratories, according to the conference proceedings.

The three Iraqis attending, M. Ahadd, S. Ibrhim, and H. Mahd, were all representing Al Qaqaa State Establishment in Iraq. Al Qaqaa, according to an Oct. 27, 1992, report by the Senate Committee on Banking, Housing, and Urban Affairs, "was Iraq's major explosives and rocket fuel factory." It was also a "filling station for ballistic missiles" and home for Iraq's nuclear weapons program.

Joining the Iraqis in this quaint setting on the Columbia River, learning all about nuclear bomb detonation, were 445 participants from 20 countries, including Israelis and technicians from South Korea.

The list of U.S. corporations that teamed up with Saddam reads like a who's who of America's favorite defense contractors. According to the Wiesenthal report and the Senate Banking Committee they include Hewlett-Packard, Honeywell, and Sperry/Unisys among others.

BUSH'S SECRET WEAPONS In a letter dated July 9, 1992, 20 Democratic members of the House Judiciary Committee petitioned the attorney general to appoint a special prosecutor to investigate "serious allegations of possible violations of federal criminal statutes by high-ranking officials of the Executive Branch."

Among the potential criminal violations cited in the petition were making false statements, obstruction of justice, concealment or falsification of records, perjury, mail and wire fraud, conspiracy to defraud the United States or to commit an offense against the United States, and financial conflict of interest by high executive branch officials.

The 1992 letter further cited the Bush Administration's "willful and repeated failure" to comply with requests by the House Judiciary and other committees for both documents and witnesses.

According to the 27-month Gonzalez Investigation, the Bush Administration set up an "interagency" group after the Gulf War to prevent Congress from finding out about U.S. aid to Iraq before the Kuwait invasion.

Gonzalez's concerns centered on the handling by the Justice Department of the investigation into Banka Nazionale del Lavoro (BNL) in Atlanta. Most of Iraq's purchases of sensitive technology were handled by BNL. According to Gonzalez, Iraq had set up a secret network to buy equipment for missiles and for nuclear, chemical, and germ weapons. More than $5 billion in soft loans were funneled through the bank to the Iraqis in the five years leading up to the war. According to Gonzalez's compelling investigation, almost half of the $5 billion was funneled directly into Iraq's ambitious weapons program.

The Bush Administration's task was to limit the investigation to one low-level bank official in Atlanta, resisting any attempt to connect the Iraqi loans to high administration officials or to BNL's mother bank in Italy and other shady institutions, such as the Bank of Credit and Commerce International (BCCI), the CIA's bank of choice.

To this end, at least five federal agencies apparently misled, lied to, and blatantly stonewalled prosecutors in charge of the BNL investigation. According to a strongly worded October 1992 statement by the then chair of the Senate Intelligence Committee, David Boren, in support of the appointment of a special prosecutor, the CIA "with strong advice" from the Justice Department "authored a misleading letter to the acting U.S. attorney in Atlanta" regarding the BNL investigation. "In light of this new information," Boren stated, "I call on the attorney general to meet his obligations... and appoint a special prosecutor."

To make his case, Boren cited the concerns of the federal judge in the stymied BNL case. In a sharp rebuke of the government's behavior, Judge Marvin Shoob accused Bush officials of stonewalling and deception in the BNL case and joined the call for a special prosecutor.

"High-level officials in the Justice Department and the State Department met with the Italian ambassador," stated the frustrated federal judge, and "...decisions were made at the top levels of the United States government and within the intelligence community to shape this case." Shoob also noted that "the local prosecutor in this matter received... highly unusual and inappropriate telephone calls from the White House Office of Legal Counsel."

Despite the strong words from Boren, Gonzalez, and Shoob, a special prosecutor was never appointed, and no administration officials were ever indicted or even forced to testify. Low-level bank officials ultimately took the rap for a multi-billion-dollar, illegal, secret government scheme, spearheaded by the president of the United States, to arm Iraq.

And the cover-up, thanks to Clinton officials, continues to this day. During the 1992 presidential campaign, Gore called the coverup of the secret Bush policy to arm Iraq "bigger than Watergate ever was," but in a January 16, 1995, report, the Clinton Justice Department absolved the Bush Administration and stated that it had found no evidence "that U.S. agencies or officials illegally armed Iraq."

WAR CRIMINALS London *Independent* reporter Robert Fisk has written movingly about riding back to Tehran in a train with young Iranian soldiers returning from the front during the bloody war with Iraq—a war fueled by western politicians and western arms dealers. "All of them were coughing up Saddam Hussein's poisons from their lungs into blood-red swabs and bandages," writes the veteran Middle East reporter. "And the mustard gas that was slowly killing them permeated the whole great 20-carriage train as it thundered up from the desert battlefields of the first Gulf War." Fisk points

out it was not only United States and the Europeans provided Saddam with to create nuclear, chemical, and biological weapons, but the means to efficiently deploy them.

"The Americans had sold him helicopters to spray the crops with pesticide," Fisk said, "the 'crops,' of course, being human beings." And in an astounding revelation Fisk stated, "I later met the [German] arms dealer who flew from the Pentagon to Baghdad with U.S. satellite photos of the Iranian front lines to help Saddam kill more Iranians."

Iranians weren't the only victims. Tens of thousands of U.S. soldiers and military personnel were doused with chemical and biological warfare agents in the first Gulf War. In fact, Gulf veterans have filed a billion-dollar class action lawsuit in federal court in Galveston, Texas, against companies that supplied Iraq with the dual-use technology to create its weapons of mass destruction. Among the companies named are Bechtel, M.W. Kellog, Dresser Industries, and Interchem Inc.

Vic Silvester, a plaintiff in the lawsuit, told the *National Law Journal*, "The companies that made the chemicals and biologicals should pay." Silvester said his son, a Gulf vet, suffers from a variety of serious medical conditions from exposures, including nerve damage, rashes, severe headaches, and chronic fatigue. "He can't sleep," Silvester said, "and when he goes to the store, he can't remember what he went to get."

Silvester makes a compelling point. After World War II, several German civilians were hanged for making chemical gas available to the Nazis. Employees of IG Farben were convicted in a

British court in Hamburg of crimes against humanity because it was shown they had known that Hitler's regime was using Farben's gas to slaughter civilians in Nazi concentration camps.

"Two of the principals of that firm were hanged for aiding in crimes against humanity," wrote Rabbi Marvin Hier in the introduction to "The Poison Gas Connection," put out by the Simon Wiesenthal Center. "International legal scholars should look seriously at this relative precedent."

SIDEBAR:

KILLING THE CREATOR
Famed Iraqi artist Laila al-Attar was one of the casualties of Clinton's last air strike.
By Dennis Bernstein

'It was really something I will never forget," Iraqi artist Mohammed al-Sadoun recalled in an interview from his Virginia home February 17. "I was watching CNN and suddenly I heard that a famous Iraqi artist was killed, and I tried to recognize the image as it was displayed on TV: It was Laila's house, and there was nothing left of it."

Laila al-Attar was director of the Iraqi National Art Museum and a powerful force in gaining recognition for women artists in Iraq and throughout the Middle East. She was also, her daughter Rema remembers, "very beautiful, very well respected, and very kind."

On June 27, 1993, just after 2 A.M. and two years after the end of the Gulf War, U.S. bombers reduced al-Attar's home to a bit of acceptable collateral damage. "There was no warning," Rema, who now lives in the Bay Area, quietly

told me in a recent interview. "We were sound asleep. We heard an explosion and felt the walls shake. We tried to get out but we couldn't do it. The whole house collapsed on top of us."

President and commander-in-chief Bill Clinton ordered the bombing of Baghdad to foil an alleged Iraqi plot to assassinate former president George Bush. Bush was on his way to visit Kuwait for a gala postwar victory celebration. The death plot was a ruse and was never confirmed by any named source.

The president has never apologized to the family or to the people of Iraq for snuffing out one of their most cherished artists. "I don't even think he knows about it," Rema said. "Nobody has ever called me."

"It was really tragic and a big loss for those close to the art community," Al-Sadoun said. He was in Baghdad just before the bombing doing research on Iraqi art for his Ph.D., and al-Attar's work was a part of the research. "I remember all the sweet time we spent together, visiting her every day at the museum and her house. We had meetings; we had a lot of things."

Laila al-Attar contributed to the Iraqi community in many ways, al-Sadoun said. "First as a very fine woman artist, but also as an art leader, where she was involved with art business, curating exhibitions, international exhibitions such as the 1988 exhibition.

"The exhibition brought thousands of artists to Iraq from many different countries, including the United States. To find a female leading an art establishment in a country like Iraq, with an Arab-Muslim culture, was really significant."

It was also quite significant in the Arab community that al-Attar's paintings contained naked women, mingling with trees and the natural environment. "I am trying to bring into the society of ideal faith," she wrote in introducing one of her exhibitions, "the role of women, the dignity of their existence and their humanity. My instrument to accomplish that is made of lines blended with waves of color, sincere feelings, and true wishes that arrive at a state of satisfaction."

Rema, or "little deer," was blinded in one eye by the 1993 bombing. She left Baghdad soon after and underwent extensive face surgery in Los Angeles and Canada before moving to the Bay Area. She was 24 when "the bombs changed everything," she said. "I was very deep under and no one could hear me. I was dying by the time they got through. They didn't get to my parents for another two hours. It was two hours too late."

She said she was not only terrorized by the bombing but also confused. "It had nothing to do with us. My father was a successful businessman. My mother was an artist. I used to work as a display designer in a museum. We had nothing to do with politics."

Rema said she's concerned about her brother, who miraculously escaped serious injury from the bombing that turned his parents, his home, and his entire way of life into rubble. "I'm very worried about my brother," she told me. "He is still in Iraq, and they are getting ready to bomb."

"PUNISHING SADDAM— OR THE IRAQIS"

By Bill Blum; *I.F. Magaine;* March/April 1998

"We have heard that a half million children have died," said *60 Minutes* reporter Lesley Stahl, speaking of U.S. sanctions against Iraq. "I mean, that's more children than died in Hiroshima. And—and you know, is the price worth it. Her guest, in May 1996, U.N. Ambassador Madeleine Albright, responded: "I think this is a very hard choice, but the price—we think the price is worth it."

More recently, Secretary of State Albright has been traveling around the world to gather support for yet more bombing of Iraq. The price, apparently, is still worth it. The price is, of course, being paid solely by the Iraqi people— a million or so men, women and children, dead from the previous bombings and seven years of sanctions.

The plight of the living in Iraq, plagued by malnutrition and a severe shortage of medicines, is, as well, terrible to behold. Their crime? They have a leader who refuses to let United Nations inspectors search every structure in Iraq for "weapons of mass destruction," including presidential palaces. After more than six years, those inspections have located and destroyed significant stocks of forbidden chemical, biological and nuclear weapon material. But the U.N. team, dominated by the United States and Great Britain, still refuses to certify that Iraq is clean enough. Inasmuch as Iraq is bigger than California, the inspectors might understandably find 100 percent certainty impossible to achieve. But Iraqis see another U.S. agenda—the ouster of Saddam Hussein. The seemingly endless dispute over the inspections and the maintenance of tough sanctions, many believe, are simply the means to that end.

President Clinton and his advisers have given weight to that suspicion by declaring that the sanctions will remain as long as Saddam Hussein holds power. In recent weeks, however, the administration has put a different gloss on the policy during the State of the Union address, Clinton tried to lift the Iraqi standoff from a personal confrontation to a more principled pedestal. Clinton called for a stronger Biological Weapons Convention and spoke about how the United States must "confront the new hazards of chemical and biological weapons, and the outlaw states, terrorists and organized criminals seeking to acquire them." Saddam was just the most prominent miscreant to cross the line, a dangerous example to others, Clinton suggested. Yet, Clinton's words concealed a more complex reality. For who among the president's listeners knew, and who among the media reported, that the United States had supplied Iraq many of the source biological materials which Saddam's scientist needed for a biological warfare program? According to 1994 Senate Banking Committee reports, the U.S. Commerce Department permitted private American suppliers to deliver a veritable witch's brew of biological materials to Iraq. The committee traced the shipments at least back to 1985 and followed the pattern through November 28, 1989. The exports were cleared despite reports that Iraq had used chemical warfare and possibly biological warfare against Iranians, Kurds, and Shiites since the early 1980s. "These biological materials were not attenuated or weakened and were capable of reproduction," said one Senate report dated May 25, 1994. "It was later learned," the panel wrote on October 7, 1994, "that these microorganisms exported by the United States were identical to those the United Nations inspectors found and removed from the Iraqi biological warfare program. "Among the U.S.-origin biological agents that often produce slow, agonizing deaths were: *Bacillus Anthracis*, cause of anthrax; *Clostridium Botulinum*, a source of botulinum toxin; *Histoplasma Capsulatam*, cause of a disease attacking lungs, brain, spinal cord and heart; *Brucella Melitensis*, a bacteria that can damage major organs; *Clotsridium Perfringens*, a highly toxic bacteria causing systemic illness; *Clostridium tetani*, highly toxigenic ; and *Escherichia Coli (E.Coli)*; genetic materials; and human and bacterial DNA.

Compliant Clients? The timing of the shipments corresponded with a secret Reagan Administration policy of aiding both sides in the Iran-Iraq war. That ruthless strategy contributed to a drawn-out conventional war that claimed the lives of about one million soldiers on the two sides. It also fit with an observation made by Noam Chomsky in a PBS appearance on September 11, 1990: "It's been a leading, driving doctrine of U.S. foreign policy since the 1940s that the vast and unparalleled energy resources of the Gulf region will be effectively dominated by the United States and its clients, and, crucially, that no independent, indigenous force will be permitted to have a substantial influence on the administration of oil production and price."

In line with that analysis, even after the Persian Gulf War, Washington looked to the emergence of a pro-U.S. military leader to replace Saddam, not to less manageable popular challenges. As an ABC documentary reported on

February 7, first President Bush and then President Clinton stood by while Saddam's army crushed democratic uprisings in 1991 and 1996, respectively. In an interview with Peter Jennings, former national security adviser Brent Scowcroft pithily summed up the U.S. preference. "A general with a brigade," Scowcroft explained. Iraqis may wonder about other double-standards from Washington.

As the American public and media are being prepared to accept and cheerlead the bombing of Iraq again, the stated rationale is that Iraq is an "outlaw" state which is ignoring a U.N. Security Council resolution. But the United States did not regard itself as an "outlaw" state when it continued a covert war against Nicaragua in the mid-1980s in defiance of the World Court, the U.N. organization established to enforce international law. Washington brushed aside international objections, too, when it invaded Panama in 1989 and continues to do so by maintaining a harsh trade embargo against Cuba that recently drew the condemnation of Pope John Paul II. Washington also will not tolerate overly nosy inspectors in its own backyard. Less than a year ago, the U.S. Senate established restrictive ground rules for international inspectors in the United States when they are examining chemical weapons facilities. At that time, the Senate showed concerns about U.S. sovereignty that parallel Iraq's current objections over the composition of inspection teams and demands to search presidential palaces. The Senate act implementing the so-called Chemical Weapons Convention stipulates that "the president may deny a request to inspect any facility in the United States in cases where the president determines that the inspection may pose a threat to the national security interests of the United States." Another section of the act grants the president veto power over individual inspectors, with that judgment not "reviewable in any court."

Clinton may be on shaky legal ground himself in enforcing U.S. terms on Iraq. The U.N. has not specifically authorized any of its members to use force in this case. One reporter picked up on that point at a February 6 joint news conference by Clinton and Prime Minister Tony Blair. "What gives Britain and the United States the right to go it alone on this?" the reporter asked. There was no response.

Ready for War? At press time, a new round of bombing against Iraq looked inevitable. The boys were busy moving all their toys into position; some armchair warriors safely ensconced at the Pentagon were already envisioning the decorations hanging from their chests. But there might be one hope for the Iraqi people. The *Washington Post* reported that Defense Secretary William Cohen has indicated that "U.S. officials remain wary of doing so much military damage to Iraq as to weaken its regional role as a counterweight to Iran." (February 1, 1998) So perhaps, in the not too distant future, when Iran begins to flex its muscles, Washington might see the Iraqis less as a cause of "instability" than a bulwark against "instability."

Amid the constantly shifting sands of Middle East politics—and American geo-political interests in the region's oil reserves—it might not do to have Iraq completely pulverized. Next time, Iraq might be needed to help dish out some good ol' American "diplomacy" to Iran.

"OUR CONTINUING WAR AGAINST IRAQ"

By retired President, Institute
for Space and Security Studies,
Most Rev. Dr. Robert M. Bowman,
Lt. Col., USAF;
Space and Security News; May 1998

In the March 1991 *Space and Security News*, we reported that in Desert Storm we had dropped 300 to 400 million pounds of high explosives on Iraq. This onslaught destroyed tens of thousands of buildings and essentially every bridge, power plant, and industrial facility in the country. We estimated the death toll at a quarter of a million Iraqis, including at least 100,000 civilians, of which half were children. We said, "Is this reason for euphoria? The survivors have little food, no water, no electricity, no sanitation, only pestilence and civil war." Along with many others, we predicted dire consequences if we failed to rebuild what we had so efficiently destroyed.

Some (even among our subscribers) chastised us for exaggerating the impact of the war on the Iraqi people. Now here we are seven years later, and the shocking death toll from the Gulf War has been dwarfed by that from our continuing war against Iraq. Not only have we failed to rebuild what we destroyed; we have imposed economic sanctions which have prevented the Iraqis and everyone else from doing so.

In the seven years since the end of Desert Storm, roughly one and a half million Iraqis have died as a direct result of U.S./U.N. sanctions. It is now estimated that among those who have lost their lives are three quarters of a million children under the age of five! And the dying goes on. UNICEF says that a million Iraqi children are seriously malnourished, and about 150 are dying every day.

Seven years ago, the United States condemned Saddam Hussein for torching the Kuwaiti oil fields, causing serious ecological consequences. Yet our government didn't tell us that our troops had used some 500 tons of depleted uranium (DU) weapons (bombs and artillery shells). Depleted Uranium is mostly U-238, the stuff left over when you extract from natural uranium the U-235 to make atomic bombs. It won't set off a chain reaction, but it is radioactive, with a half-life of millions of years. DU weapons are used because they penetrate armor more easily than conventional shells. But our troops who handled these radioactive weapons weren't warned about their dangers. Now, veterans groups are finding out that some 400,000 American troops were exposed to radiation from this depleted uranium. Symptoms from short-term exposure include nausea, vomiting, weakness, and diarrhea. Those receiving heavier doses could sustain damage to the liver, kidney, chromosomes, and immune system. Other effects of long-term exposure are cancer, genetic damage, birth defects, and death.

Veterans groups are rightly concerned that this radiation exposure could be at least a contributing cause to much of the "Gulf War Syndrome" afflicting tens of thousands of veterans. But what of the Iraqis who survived the million DU weapons fired at them? When a DU shell explodes, it coats the whole area with toxic radioactive dust. Cancer rates among children are up enormously. It's impossible, of course, to determine the cause of any particular cancer. So no one knows how many cancers are caused by DU exposure and how many by other carcinogens in their war-devastated environment. But with birth defects, it's another story. Not only are rates up, but the types of birth defects being seen are those known to be caused by radiation. We've seen these things before, most notably among the Pacific islanders exposed to radiation by atmospheric nuclear testing in the 1940s and '50s.

Our own veterans are just finding out what happened to them seven years ago. But neither their government nor ours is warning Iraqi children about the radiation in their soil, in their drinking water, and in the twisted bits of metal they collect as souvenirs of the war.

Thus Iraqi children are still being damaged by the leftovers of Desert Storm. And the continuing sanctions are preventing their environment from being cleaned up. The sanctions are also preventing those afflicted from receiving medical treatment. There is hardly any medical technology. Medicines, needles, sterile bandages, even safe water are almost impossible to find in the hospitals of Iraq. Used needles are boiled in water and reused, a procedure which does not prevent the transmission of crippling and deadly diseases.

Seven years after the end of Desert Storm, the war against the people of Iraq continues. There must be a better way of insuring that Iraq never uses weapons of mass destruction on its neighbors.

Index

20/20, 78, 91, 231
60 Minutes, 118-119, 123, 384
1990 Census, 240, 267
2000 Census, 240, 251, 265, 267
AARC Corp., 345-346
ABC, 78, 90-91, 155, 210, 216, 385
ABC World News Tonight, 210
abortion, 53, 64, 146, 275
Abu-Jamal, Mumia, 59, 90-91
Abzug, Bella, 340
Accelerated Strategic Computing Initiative, 48
Accuracy in Media (AIM), 40, 154, 309
acetochlor, 35, 339
ACLU *see* American Civil Liberties Union
Acteal, 54, 98
Adbusters, 272
ADM, 333, 346
Afghanistan, 212, 236
AFL-CIO, 133, 290, 338
Africa, 39, 92, 94, 108, 120, 189, 233, 235-236, 279,
    309, 315, 326, 365
Africa News, 92
Agence France Press, 194
Agent Orange, 162, 352, 361-362
agrarian reform, 33, 330
agribusiness, 343, 347, 349, 367
agricultural chemicals, 349
Agricultural Research, 346
agriculture, 38-41, 208, 282, 286, 331, 342, 344-349,
    353, 357, 360-363, 365-367, 379
AIDS, 53, 92, 103, 120, 234, 236, 299, 301, 304-305 *see*
    also HIV.
AINFO News Service, 56
Al Khayat al Jadida, 194
Albright, Madeleine, 384
Algeria, 71
Allen, Donna, 19, 94
Allied Technology Group, 43
Al-Mithaq, 193
Al-Nahar, 193
Al-Quds, 193, 195-196
Alternative Education Project, 301
Alternative Media/Acitivist Resource Guide, 271-323;
    Media Activist Organizations and News Services,
    309-323; National Alternative Publications, 271-309
Alternet, 135, 309, 318
Al-Uma, 193-194
American Bar Association, 66
American Civil Liberties Union (ACLU), 107, 278
American Environmental Health Studies Project, 372,
    375
American Federation of Teachers, 83-84
American Home Products, 40, 346, 349, 355, 366
American Indians, 85
American Judicature Society, 65-66
American Library Association (ALA), 17, 20, 239-240,
    279, 289, 296, 310
American Medical Association, 62, 114, 121, 338, 361
American Museum of Natural History, 358
American Writer, 273, 320
AmeriCares, 207-213
Ameritech, 126

ammonium nitrate, 350
Amnesty International, 63, 70, 106-107, 109, 306
Amoco, 211
anarchism, 273, 290
Angola, 70, 237
anthrax, 44, 385
anti-abortion extremists, 52
antibiotics, 49, 92, 157; resistence to, 49
antidepressants, 92
anti-nuclear groups, 48
antipsychotics, 92
antitrust laws, 127
antitrust watchdogs, 138
AP Online, 119
AP Worldstream, 107
apartheid, 94, 326
Arafat, Yasser, 193-197
Argentina, 70, 100, 115
Arias, Oscar, 100
Aristide Foundation for Democracy, 204
Barnet, Richard, 19
Bay of Pigs, 246, 258, 261
BBC, 74, 111
Bank of Credit and Commerce International (BCCI), 381
Banka Nazionale del Lavoro (BNL), 381
Beaubrun, Mondesir, 201
Bechtel Corporation, 47, 382
Belgium, 77-78, 106
Benin, 364
Bertin, Mireille Durocher, 201
BGH, *see* bovine growth hormone.
Biodevastation Network, 40
biodiversity, 38, 331, 344, 358, 362, 364, 366-367
biological weapons, 44-45, 94, 118, 377-378, 382, 385
Biological Weapons Convention, 385
biosafety, 365-366
biotechnology, 35, 40-41, 49-51, 104, 341-343, 346,
    348, 354, 358-362, 366
birth control, 51-53, 64, 110, 113
birth defects, 45, 355, 387-388
Blair, Tony, 386
Boeing, 101, 125, 212
Bolivia, 109-110
Bosnia-Herzegovina, 8, 72-73, 74, 212
Boston Globe, 68, 101-102, 104, 110, 119, 200, 260-261
botulinum toxin, 385
botulism, 44
bovine growth hormone (BGH), 154-158, 355-356, 361
Bradlee, Ben, 29
breast cancer, 34-37, 97, 335-341
Breast Cancer Action, 37
Breast Cancer Awareness Month (BCAM), 34-35, 37,
    336, 339, 341
Breast Cancer Prevention Program, 340
Brio, 78
Bristol-Meyers Squibb, 131
Britain, *see* United Kingdom
British Nuclear Fuels (BNFL), 373
British Petroleum, (BP) 70-71
British Royal Family, 227-228
Buchanan, Patrick, 200
Buffalo News, 117

Bulletin of the Atomic Scientists, 100, 276
Bundestag Press, 93
Bureau of Land Management (BLM), 85-87
Bureau of Prisons, 107
Bureau of the Census, 241, 338,240-241, 251, 265, 267
Burma, 70, 92
Bush, Barbara, 211
Bush, George, 199, 211-212, 378-379, 383
Bush Administration, 379-382
Business Ethics, 277, 359, 362
Butler Report, 45
Butler, Richard, 45
California Commission on the Courts, 65
California First Amendment Coalition, 311
California Prison Focus, 59, 277
Cambodia, 92, 159
Campaign for Food Safety, 40
Campaign for Press and Broadcasting Freedom, 150
Campus Alternative Journalism Project, 311
Canada, 12, 16, 33, 105-106, 137-144, 146-148, 150-151, 157-158, 269, 271-272, 276, 287, 290, 296-299, 302, 304, 310, 316, 320, 327, 334, 337, 357, 367-368, 384
Canadian Association of Journalists (CAJ), 138, 140
Canadian Broadcasting Corporation (CBC), 137-138, 141
Canadian Press, 140
cancer, 34-37, 41-42, 45-46, 60-63, 78, 93, 96-98, 103, 109, 123-124, 154, 157-158, 218-219, 222-223, 335-341, 352, 362, 368-369, 371-372, 374-375, 387-388
Cancer Industry Tour, 341
Cancer Prevention Coalition, 103
Cancer Research, 61
capital gains tax, 146-147
capitalism, 104, 146, 198, 200, 207, 295
CAQ, *see CovertAction Quarterly*
carcinogens, 34-36, 78, 98, 102-103, 130, 339-340, 350, 388
Carter Administration, 100
Cassini space probe, 123-125
Catholic Church, 51-53
Catholics for a Free Choice, 52
Catholic Health Care West, 52
CBC, *see* Canadian Broadcast Corporation
CBS, 103-104, 119, 131, 169, 210
CBS Evening News, 210
CBS This Morning, 103-104
Cedras, General Raoul, 200
Center for Constitutional Rights, 174, 180-181
Center for Study of Responsive Law, 126
Centers for Disease Control (CDC), 61, 120-122, 176, 180, 216, 375
Central America, 28, 281
Central Intelligence Agency (CIA), 12, 16, 28-29, 55, 70, 93, 106, 135, 162, 199-201, 204, 211-213, 246, 251, 255, 258-261, 264-266, 269-270, 377, 379, 381
Center for Education and Technology (CET; Centro de Educación y Tecnología), 348-349, 367
Challenge, 12, 192-196
Chamber of Commerce, 32, 34, 328-329
Channel One, 105
Charleston Gazette, 32
Chase Manhattan, 125
Chemical Bank, 125
chemical industry, 35-36, 266, 336, 338, 340, 350
Chemical Manufacturers Association (CMA), 36, 338
chemical sludge, 351
chemical weapons, 45, 94, 117, 118-119, 163, 352, 377-378, 382, 385-386
Chemical Weapons Convention, 377, 386
Chernobyl, 46

Chevron, 56-58, 98
Chiapas, 54-56, 183
Chicago Life, 60
Chicago Tribune, 61, 103, 108-109, 116, 328
child labor, 116, 328
Chile, 100-102, 109-111, 113, 213, 264, 367
China, 42, 47, 63-64, 98, 101-102, 115, 117, 252-253, 342, 364, 375-376; Mother and Child Health Law, 64; National People's Congress, 64
Chiquita, 28
cholera, 49, 94, 233, 235
chlorinated chemicals, 36, 337
Chlorine Chemistry Council (CCC), 36, 338, 379
Chomsky, Noam, 45, 135, 165, 385
Christian Aid, 106
Christian Science Monitor, 100, 102, 278
Chrysler, 126
CIA, *see* Central Intelligence Agency
Cincinnati Enquirer, 28
Citicorp, 126
civil rights, 66, 106, 133, 171, 181, 277
class inequality, 144
Clean Air Act, 266
clean air standards, 33, 330
Clinton Administration, 48, 54, 77, 80, 100-101, 107, 199-200, 210, 255, 257, 260, 266, 327-328, 358, 378
Clinton, Bill, 11, 45, 47-48, 54, 72, 77, 80, 95, 100-101, 107, 109, 113, 120, 129, 199-201, 210, 220, 227, 230, 242, 246, 252, 255, 257, 259-261, 263, 266-267, 269, 326-328, 358, 378, 382-383, 385-386; impeachment of, 45-46, 96, 186, 230, 269
CNN, 12, 28-30, 102, 113, 153, 158-163, 383
CNN Talkback Live, 113
CNN Worldview, 102
coal, 66, 360
Coca-Cola, 87-89
Cockburn, Alexander, 92, 162, 183
Cold War, 47, 55, 67, 69, 71, 75-76, 102, 137, 239, 258-261, 378
Colgate-Palmolive, 131
Colombia, 71, 93
Colombia Bulletin, 93
Commerce Department, *see* Department of Commerce (U.S.)
commercialism, 150, 167-168, 178, 181, 303
Commission on the Roles and Capabilities of the United States Intelligence, 270
Commodity Credit Corporation, 379
Communications Act of 1934, 156, 168, 175, 184
Communism, 55
Communist states, 42
Communities for a Better Environment, 37
Community Reinvestment Act, 326
Comprehensive Test Ban Treaty (CTBT), 47-48
Consumer Product Safety Commission (CPSC), 77-78
Consumer Reports, 20, 279
contraception, 53, 111
Convention on Biological Diversity, 366
Convention on the Elimination of All Forms of Discrimination Against Women (CEDAW), 64
copper, 117, 213, 368-370
corporate culture, 353
corporate media, 11, 59, 95, 129-132, 144, 153, 170, 172, 198, 201, 207
corporate political action committees, 65
cosmetics industry, 102-103
cotton, 38, 40, 234, 342-343, 347, 355-357, 362-364
Council of Canadians, 150
Council on Environmental Quality, 80
Council on International Business, 32, 329

CounterPunch, 92, 119, 280
CovertAction Quarterly (CAQ), 66, 69, 72, 92, 94, 104,
   106, 110, 123, 134, 213, 277
crime, 68, 96, 121-122, 130, 140, 144, 215-225, 229,
   231, 245, 279, 384
Croatia, 212
crops, 38-40, 51, 75, 93, 139, 162, 341-344, 347-349,
   355-357, 359, 362-367, 382; hybrid, 348-349, 367
Cronkite, Walter, 125
Cuba, 191, 198, 204, 246, 258, 280, 326, 386
Cuban missile crisis, 261
Cultural Environment Movement, 19, 313
CURE, 59
Czech Republic, 101
Daily News (New York), 19, 204
Daimler-Benz, 126
Dalai Lama, 63
Dalgety, PLC, 346
Dallas Morning News, 85-86, 102, 117
"Dark Alliance" series, 29
Dark Night Field Notes, 54, 280
Dateline, 208-209
D'Aubuisson, Robert, 56
DDT, 339, 350
death squads, 11, 54, 70
Defense Department, see Department of Defense (U.S.)
Defense Intelligence Agency, 252, 264
Defense Systems Limited (DSL), 70-71
DEHP, 77-78
Delta Land and Pine Company, 38, 57, 70, 288, 342-
   344, 347, 357, 362-364, 366-367, 371
Democracy Now, 56
Democratic Left, 32, 281, 332
Democratic Republic of Congo, 108, 237
Denmark, 51, 77-78
Denver Post, 32
Department of Agriculture (U.S.), 38-39, 341-348, 353,
   363-365
Department of Commerce (U.S.), 267, 380
Department of Defense (U.S.), 68-69, 241-242, 249,
   253-254, 257, 260, 262, 264, 267
Department of Energy (U.S.), 41-42, 47-48, 123, 125,
   240, 255-256, 263, 368, 370-371, 373-375
Department of Health and Human Services (U.S.), 120,
   247, 254
Department of the Interior (U.S.), 85-86
Department of Justice (U.S.), 209-210, 245, 251, 253,
   257, 381-382
Department of Labor (U.S.), 117
Department of Transportation (U.S.), 115
depleted uranium (DU), 35, 45-46, 131, 213, 341, 360,
   369, 387-388; weapons, 45, 387
Desert News, 118-119
desktop publishing, 134
Detroit Metro Times, 37, 336, 338
DINP, 78
dioxin, 117, 281, 339, 351-353, 361
Disney, 83, 116, 207, 327
DNA, 50, 62, 242, 359, 385; rDNA, 50
Doctors Without Borders/Médecins Sans Frontières, 233-
   234, 237
Diamond Works, 71
Douglass, Frederick, 188
Dollars and Sense, 104, 281
domestic violence, 52
Donaldson, Sam, 91
Doskoch, Bill, 137
Dow Chemical, 333, 346, 352, 360
downsizing, 84, 166, 247
Dresser Industries, 382
Drillbits & Tailings, 71

drinking water, 75, 388
drugs, 54-55, 67, 92-94, 119-120, 216, 218, 234-235,
   339-340, 349; dealers, 67; economy, 58; drug experi-
   ments, 120; prices, 92; war, 54, 67, 69
DU, see depleted uranium
Du Pont, 35, 131, 341, 360
Dunifer, Stephen, 171, 173, 181-182, 187-188
Earth First!, 118, 282
Earth Island Journal, 37, 87, 282
ECHELON, 105-106, 269
e-coli, 44, 355
Ecologist, The, 38, 40, 49-50, 117, 282, 349, 362
ecology, 40, 42, 149, 273, 276, 361-362, 371
Economic Policy Institute, 117
Economist, The, 119
Egypt, 115
Eisenhower, Dwight, 258
El Mozote massacre, 29
El Niño, 235
El Salvador, 30, 55-56
electric batons, 63
Electronic Data Systems, 104
electroshock devices, 108-109
Electronic Freedom of Information Act (EFOIA), 249,
   257
Electronic Public Information Newsletter, 249-250
Eli Lilly, 119
Energy Department, see Department of Energy (U.S.)
England, 40, 190, 338 see also United Kingdom
Enron, 70
environmental groups, 266, 328, 331, 373
Environmental Protection Agency (EPA), 35, 76, 78,
   121, 242, 266-267, 339, 350-354, 357, 361-362;
   Toxic Release Inventory, 354
environmental protection laws, 139
Environmental Quality Commission, 117
Equal Opportunity Employment Commission, 19
estrogens, 36, 337-338; replacement therapy (ERT), 337
Ethiopia, 212, 234
Ethyl, 33, 334
eugenics, 111
EU Product Safety Emergencies Committee, 77
EuropaBio, 50
Europe, 30, 33, 40, 42, 50, 77, 88, 106-107, 211, 213,
   222, 269, 333, 358
European Commission, 77-78
European Parliament, 47, 106, 269
European Space Agency, 123-124
European Union (EU), 77, 106-107, 325, 333
Executive Order 12958, 261, 263, 268
Executive Outcomes, 70-71
Extra!, 93-94, 117, 231, 283
Exxon, 77, 126
fascism, 30
Fairness and Accuracy in Reporting (FAIR), 132-133,
   140, 149, 268, 283, 286, 311, 314, 317, 319-320,
   326, 370
Fairness Doctrine, 168
Faludi, Susan, 19, 95
Families Against Mandatory Minimums, 59
Family Health International, 112
family planning, 52, 112
famine, 39, 208, 211-212, 233-234
Fantesk, 347
farmers; farming, 37-40, 75, 79, 139, 154, 157, 204,
   331, 341-345, 347-349, 355-357, 360, 362-367
FBI, see Federal Bureau of Investigation
FCC, see Federal Communications Commission
FDA, see Food and Drug Administration
FDB (Denmark), 78

Federal Bureau of Investigation (FBI), 215, 231, 245, 257, 259-260, 266, 269
Federal Communications Commission (FCC), 12, 20, 94, 133, 156, 165, 167-169, 171-178, 180-188, 242-243, 250
Federal Computer Week, 253, 257
Federal Election Commission (FEC), 245
Federal Emergency Management Agency (FEMA), 79-80
Federal Insecticide, Fungicide and Rodenticide Act (FIFRA), 353-354
Federal Radio Commission (FRC), 167-168
Federal Reserve, 126
Federal Technology Ttransfer Act of 1986, 345
Federal Times, 240, 247, 256, 262, 267
Federal Trade Commission (FTC), 53
Federation of American Scientists, 102, 268-270
feminism, 273, 284
fertilizer, 209, 350, 375
fetal death, 350
fetal tissue experimentation, 51
Financial Times, 71, 362
Finland, 63
First Amendment, 12, 16, 94-95, 131, 133, 184, 311, 316, 318, 329, 399
First Interstate, 125
Fisher-Price, 116
Fluffy Cellulose, 347
fluoridation; flouride, 74-76, 96; toxicity of, 74
Foetex, 78
food,
   additives, 359; crops, 93, 348, 364; production, 209, 365; safety, 40, 342; security, 39, 344, 348, 363-368; staples, 348, 364; subsidies, 33, 330; supply, 326
Food and Drug Administration (FDA), 35-36, 61, 102-103, 113, 119, 154, 157-158, 250, 260, 339, 355, 358, 361
Food Lion suit, 155
Forbes Magazine, 163
Ford, Gerald R., 269
forestry, 21, 33, 331, 354
formal agents of social control 215, 217, 222-224
Fortune 500, 127, 345
Fox Television, 12, 153-156, 158; Fox News, 155
France, 32, 46, 51, 102, 106, 190, 194, 327
FRAPH, 200-201
Fraternal Order of Police, 91
Free Radio Berkeley, 171-173, 181-183, 188
free radio movement, 166, 285
free speech movement, 12, 94, 165
Free Speech TV, 133, 314
Free Speech vs. the FCC, 174, 180-181
free trade, 116, 139, 325, 327, 330
Freedom Forum, 172
Freedom of Information Act (FOIA), 77, 106, 239, 249-250, 257, 259-260, 262, 264, 268, 270, 313, 315, 345, 352
Freeport McMoRam, 70
French Revolution, 197
Fresno Bee, 127
Front, The, 77
Fund for Investigative Journalists, 315, 376
Fund for Modern Courts, 66
Funding Exchange, 285, 321
GAFE, 54
Gannet, 116
GAO, *see* General Accounting Office
Gap, The, 93, 312
garment workers, 140
Gateway Green Alliance, 40
GATT, *see* General Agreement on Tariffs and Trade
gay and lesbian magazine, 272, 275, 285, 298

gay and lesbian writers, 291
gene transfer, 49-51
General Accounting Office (GAO), 124, 241, 253-254, 355, 361
General Agreement on Tariffs and Trade (GATT), 32-33, 93, 116, 130, 139, 325-326, 330-334, 338
General Electric (GE), 35, 58, 125, 208, 341
General Motors (GM), 92
genetic engineering, 39-40, 49-51, 285, 341, 343, 346, 357, 362-364, 366; of food, 40, 50; of plants, 39
genetic pollution, 39
genetically modified seeds, 37, 341
Gerbner, George, 19
Germany, 46, 77-78, 171, 254, 350, 366, 378
Ghana, 110
Gingrich, Newt, 263
Glenn, John, 125, 227, 229
Global biodiversity, 331
Global Pesticide Campaigner, 37, 286, 362
globalization, 329, 332, 335
Globalvision, 133, 315
Globe & Mail, 28, 68, 89, 101-102, 104, 110, 119, 141, 151, 156, 160, 200, 235, 248, 260-261, 271, 273, 318, 333, 353, 361, 381, 400
glyphosate, 353-354, 356, 361
Golden Chance Coal Company, 66
Gonzalez, Juan, 19
Gore, Al, 247-248, 250, 256-257, 358, 362, 382
Government Communications Security Bureau (GCSB), 105; declassification of government documents, 263
Government Performance and Results Act, 256
Government Printing Office (GPO), 240, 249, 251, 256, 262
Governors Island Accord, 200
Grass Roots Recycling Network (GRRN), 88-89
grassroots organizing; organizations, 59, 131, 133, 170, 209, 213, 321
Great Britain, *see* United Kingdom
Greece, 17, 51, 134, 189, 192, 197
Green Revolution, 360, 362
greenhouse gas emissions, 328
Green Guide, The, 34, 339, 341
Greenpeace, 51, 79, 106, 352, 356, 360-361
Gridcore Corp., 345
Grossman, Karl, 110, 123
Guardian (London), 74
Guatemala, 55, 235, 265
Guinea, 119, 236
Gulf War, 45, 148, 186, 210-212, 377-378, 380-383, 385, 387
Gulf War Syndrome, 387
Haäti Progras, 207
Habitat International Coalition, 332
Hague Tribunal, the, 72
Hamas, 193, 195-196
Haiti, 111, 197-207; Duvalierism, 199
Harvard Business Review, 359, 362
Hasbro, 116-117
health care, 35, 51-53, 55, 114, 129, 139, 223, 231, 234, 236, 241, 275, 339
Health Department, 42, 75, 372
health maintenance organizations (HMOs), 51-52
Health Physics, 42, 372
Helms-Burton Act, 326
Helms, Richard, 159
herbicides, 35, 93, 162, 339, 352-356, 358-359, 361-362; acetochlor, 35; Roundup, 156, 342, 353-356, 359, 361
Hernandez, Aileen C., 19
Hewlett-Packard, 44, 381
High Frequency Active Auroral Research Program, 140

Hightower, Jim, 287, 315, 338
Hightower Radio/United Broadcasting, 133, 315
Hiroshima, 48, 384
Hispanic Education and Media Group, 316
Hitler, Adolf, 171, 383
HIV, 53, 236, 299
HMOs, *see* health maintenance organizations
Hollinger Inc., 138, 147
Holocaust, 266
Honduras, 93, 212, 265
Honeywell, 44, 381
hormones, 20, 35, 153-154, 337-338, 361; in foods, 33, 330
Horn, Steve, 255, 257
House Committee on Government Reform and Oversight, 251
House International Relations Committee Subcommittee on the Western Hemisphere, 55
House Judiciary Committee, 269, 381
House of Representatives, 100, 241, 252-253, 267, 378
housing, 129, 167, 172, 190-191, 278, 330, 332, 376, 380
Housing and Land Rights Committee, 332
Houston Chronicle, 113, 211
Howard, John, 109
Human Events, 111
Humanist, The, 116
human rights, 12, 32, 55, 59, 63-64, 70-71, 85-87, 100, 108, 120, 140, 144, 189-197, 199, 209-210, 236, 251, 265, 272, 287, 303, 313, 315, 326, 329-332, 335; violations of 55, 85, 140, 191, 196, 265
Human Rights Information Act, 251
Human Rights Tribune, 287, 329
Human Rights Watch, 55, 59, 63, 194, 196
Hussein, Saddam, 44, 46, 93, 102, 210, 220, 377-380, 382, 384-385, 387
hybridization, 349, 367
Hyde, Henry, 269
hydraulic fluids, 350
IBM, 114
Iceland, 94
I.F. Magazine, 43, 287
IG Farben, 382
Illegal Immigration Reform and Responsibility Act of 1996, 113-114
IMF, *see* International Monetary Fund
immigrants; immigration, 92, 97, 144, 218; illegal, 92, 144
impeachment, 45-46, 96, 186, 230, 269
Imperial Chemical Industries, 34, 336
imperialism, 111, 201
In These Times, 32, 100, 103, 288, 325
in vitro fertilization, 51
Independent, The, 81, 309, 318, 373
Independent Television Service, 72, 316
India, 39-40, 47, 49, 61, 64, 70, 111, 255, 288, 296, 342
Indian Law Resource Center, 87
Indianapolis Star, 104
Indonesia, 70, 139, 145
industrial chemicals, 35, 248, 339, 350, 353
infant death, 350
infanticide, 64
infectious diseases, 49, 234
InfoActive Kids, 288, 312
information age, 166-167, 276
Information Industry Association, 251
Information Security Office, 268
Insight, 114, 116, 289
Institute for Alternative Journalism (IAJ), 133, 292, 309
Institute for Global Communications, 135, 321
insurance, 58, 65, 79-80, 114, 126, 200, 215, 266

Intellectual Freedom Action News, 20, 289
intelligence budget, 269-270
Interagency Security Classification Appeals Panel, 260
Interchem Inc., 382
International Action Center, 12, 192, 213, 317
International Agency for Research on Cancer, 35, 340
international arms bazaar, 140
International Atomic Energy Agency, 42, 45
International Campaign for Tibet, 65
International Center for Technology Assessment, 41
International Chamber of Commerce, 32, 34, 328-329
International Committee of Lawyers for Tibet, 63-65
International Conference on the Ownership and Control of the Media, 134, 189, 197
International Energy Agency, 42, 45, 83
International Journal of Health Services, 361
International Mesothelioma Interest Group, 61
International Monetary Fund (IMF), 130, 204, 330
International Paperworkers' Union, 298
International Television (ITN), 72, 74
International Union of Electronic, Electrical, Salaried, Machine and Furniture Workers, 290
International Workers of the World (IWW), 183, 288
Internet, 56, 88-89, 97-98, 106, 132-135, 156, 163, 171, 173, 179, 181, 186-187, 249-250, 252-253, 257, 259, 262, 265-266, 271-272, 278, 314, 400
Interprovincial Trade Agreement, 139
Intifada, 196
investigative journalism, 132, 140, 142, 144, 153, 163, 277, 287, 293-294, 312, 315, 317, 376
Iran; Iranians, 191, 198, 259, 378-379, 382, 385-387
Iran-Contra scandal, 30
Iraq; Iraqis, 12, 43-46, 93, 189, 191, 197, 207-213, 220, 252-253, 377-388
Iraq Sanctions Challenge, 208-210, 213
Israel, 102, 191-194, 196-197, 377
Italy, 78, 106, 381
Jackson, Jesse, 92
Jane's Defense Weekly, 102
Japan, 47, 107, 243, 254, 354
Jennings, Peter, 210, 386
Jensen, Carl, 15, 17, 19, 95, 98-99, 138, 143, 230
Jericho Amnesty Campaign, 59
Jhally, Sut, 20
John Paul II, Pope, 211, 386
Johnson Controls, 47
Johnson, Nicholas, 20
Jones, Paula, 227-228
Jordan, Vernon, 227
Journal of the American Medical Association (JAMA), 62, 121, 338, 361
Journal of Neuropathology and Experimental Neurology, 358
junk food news, 16-17, 95, 140, 227-232
Justice Department, *see* Department of Justice (U.S.)
Karpatkin, Rhoda H., 20
KEN-GRO Corp., 345
Kennedy, John F., 258-259, 261
Kennedy, Joseph, 56
Kennedy-Kassebaum Bill, 114
Kenya, 366
KGB, 107
Kissinger, Henry, 159-160, 200
Klotzer, Charles L., 20
K-Mart, 116, 131
Kodak, 116-117
Korean War, 35, 335
Kosovo, 73, 212, 233
Kozol, Jonathan, 350
Kranich, Nancy, 20, 96
Krug, Judith, 20

Ku Klux Klan, 190
Kurds, 379, 385
Kuwait, 212, 377, 379, 381, 383
Kyoto Protocol, 331
Kwitny, Jonathan, 30
La Prensa, 212
labor, 21-22, 33, 58, 70, 84, 116-117, 129, 133, 143-
    145, 147, 149, 188, 213, 273, 291-292, 305-306,
    320, 323, 328-330, 333-335; movement, 188, 273,
    320, 330; organizers, 133; unions, 22
laissez-faire, 32, 332
Lancet, The, 158, 376
Land and Water, 93, 197, 248, 354
land mines, 101, 192
Lappé, Frances Moore, 20
Largent, Steve, 263
Latin America, 39-40, 100-101, 235, 251, 264, 294, 365
Latin American Review, The, 199
Lavalas Political Organization (OPL), 198, 200, 204-207
Lawrence Livermore Laboratory, 44, 380
left-wing conspiracy theory, 30
*Less Access to Less Information By and About the U.S.
    Government*, 17, 239-270
Levin, Carl, 253
Lewinsky, Monica, 95-96, 98, 227, 229, 243, 252
libel laws; libel suits, 74, 132, 142
Library of Congress THOMAS system, 240
Libya, 191
Lincoln, Abraham, 189
Livingston, Robert, 263
LM Magazine, 74, 292
Lobbying Disclosure Act of 1995, 253
Lockheed Martin, 47, 101, 125
London Observer, 74
Los Angeles Times, 78, 109, 111, 113, 116-117, 120,
    130-131, 135, 183, 206, 219-220, 222, 266
Louverture, Toussaint, 198
Love Canal, 29
Low Power FM stations (LPFMs), 183
LSD, 120
Lutz, William, 20, 96
Luxembourg, 51
Lysol, 352-353
Madagascar, 235, 364
Madison, James, 129
MAI, *see* Multilateral Agreement on Investment
maize, 348-349, 356-357, 367
malaria, 49, 111, 234-235
Mali, 364
Mallinckrodt Inc., 346
Malveaux, Julianne, 20, 97
Manhattan Project, 74-76, 373-374
manganese, 121-122
Marconi, Guglielmo, 167
marijuana, 68
Mars 96 space probe, 109
Marshall Plan, 333
martial law, 68
Masala, 292
Mattel, 77-78, 116-117
McChesney, Robert W., 94, 168, 179, 184, 207
McDonald's, 346
MCI, 58
Media Alliance, 174, 180-181, 318
Media and Democracy Conventions, 131
media bias, 143, 293
media concentration, 150
media democracy, 13, 129, 131, 133, 135, 179, 318
Media Education Foundation, 20, 318
Media in the Dark Ages conference, 17
Media Report to Women, 19, 94, 292

media watchdogs, 145
Medicaid, 53, 110, 267
Medicare, 137, 241, 254
Meese, Edwin, 30
mercury, 29, 117, 258
Merger Watch, 53
mergers, 51-53, 125-127, 145, 160, 167, 170, 283
metals, 41-42, 82, 117, 122, 368-371, 373-374; radioac-
    tive, 11, 41-43, 46, 368, 376; scrap, 42, 46, 169,
    369, 372, 375
Mexican Army Airborne Special Forces Groups, 54
Mexican Drug War, 54
Mexico, 54-56, 92, 108, 116, 140, 179-180, 281
Miami Herald, 205-206
Michel, Smarck, 202
microbroadcasting, 172, 177-178
microradio, *see* radio
Microradio Empowerment Coalition, 178
Mid-Continent Oil and Gas Association, 376
Middle East, 46, 82, 100, 194, 196, 279, 281, 293, 377-
    378, 380, 382-383, 386
Middle Eastern oil resources, 46
migration, 78, 235
milk, 12, 153-154, 156-158, 355, 361
Milwaukee Journal Sentinel, 120
mining, 29, 33, 70, 86, 331
MMT, 33, 334
Mobil, 42, 126, 375-376
Mohawk First Nations, 140
Mojo Wire, 37, 341-342, 345
Monsanto, 7, 35, 37-40, 154-158, 341-343, 349-364,
    366
Mother Jones, 79, 94, 122, 134, 293, 341, 345, 361-362
Moynihan, Daniel Patrick, 246, 261, 263
Ms., 51-53, 111, 113, 228, 293
MSNBC, 172
Multilateral Agreement on Investment (MAI), 32-34,
    130, 325-335
Multinational Monitor, 40, 69, 77-78, 93, 117, 126, 294,
    361
Murdoch, Rupert, 154
mustard agents, 117
M.W. Kellog, 382
Mycogen, 346
NAB, *see* National Association of Broadcasters
Nader, Ralph, 157
NAFTA, *see* North American Free Trade Agreement
Nagasaki, 48
Napalm, 162
NARA, *see* National Archives and Records Administra-
    tion
NASA, 123-125
Nation, The, 19, 47, 65-66, 116, 134, 361
Nation's Business, 127
National Archives and Records Administration (NARA),
    243-244, 248, 250, 254, 258, 261, 263, 266, 268
National Association of Broadcasters (NAB), 166, 172,
    177, 180, 184, 186-187
National Association of Home Builders, 80
National Association of Realtors, 80
National Breast Cancer Awareness Month (NBCAM),
    336, 339, 341
National Cancer Institute (NCI), 36, 60-62, 336, 339-
    340
National Center for Agricultural Utilization Research
    (NCAUR), 346-347
National Center for Health Statistics, 216
National Flood Insurance Program, 79-80
national identification card, 113
National Institute of Environmental Sciences (NIEHS),
    103

National Institutes of Health (NIH), 61-62
National Law Journal, 242, 382
National Lawyers Guild, 12, 176, 180, 184, 188
National Partnership for Reinventing Government, 254
National Public Radio (NPR), 169, 172, 185
National Security Agency (NSA), 105-107, 259, 268-269
National Security Archive, 264
National Security Council, 109, 260
National Security Decision, 379
National Science Foundation, 250
National Toxicology Program (NTP), 103
National Treasury Employees Union, 76
National Vaccine Information Center (NVIC), 61-63
National Whistleblower Center, 245
National Writers Union, 320, 338
NationsBank, 126
NATO, 73, 101, 108, 213
Natural Fibers Corp., 345
Naval Research Laboratory, 248
Nazis, 72, 171, 213, 224, 260, 266, 382-383
Nazi concentration camps, 72, 383
Nazi War Crimes Disclosure Act, 260
Nazi War Criminal Interagency Working Group, 260
NBC, 130-131, 208
NCC Washington Update, 262-263, 268
Nelson, Jack, 97
neoliberalism, 179, 205, 335
nerve gas, 28, 117-118, 153, 158-159, 161-163, 377
Netherlands, the, 77-78
Netscape, 126
New Democratic Party (NDP), 141, 147
New England Resistance Against Genetic Engineering, 40
New World Order, 333
New Zealand, 105-106, 140, 269
News Corporation, 207
Newsday, 121, 127, 212, 264
News From Indian Country, 85-86
New World Vistas, 125
Newsletter on Intellectual Freedom, 20, 296
News Watch Canada, 12, 137, 143, 147, 150-151, 293, 313, 318, 320
New York Catholic Conference, 53
New York Free Media Alliance, 174, 180-181
New York Times, The, 19, 36-37, 71, 78, 91, 95, 101-102, 114, 118, 121, 127, 130-131, 135, 198-200, 202-204, 212, 219, 241, 251, 259, 264, 328, 360, 362
NGOs, 329-331, 333, 347, 367
Nicaragua, 29, 55, 212, 386
Niger Delta, 57, 70
Nigeria, 56-57, 70, 98, 331
Nixon, Richard, 159, 162, 258, 261, 264, 268
Nordstroms, 131
Noriega, Manuel, 56
Norplant, 110-113
North American Free Trade Agreement (NAFTA), 32-33, 93, 116-117, 130, 139-140, 145, 326-328, 331-332, 334
North Korea, 102, 252
North, Oliver, 212
Northwest Coalition for Alternatives to Pesticides, 353
Norway, 51, 106, 278
Novartis, 104, 343, 366
NPR, *see* National Public Radio
nuclear accelerators, 47
nuclear bomb, 47-48, 377, 380
nuclear power, 42-43, 124-125, 369, 374
Nuclear Information and Resources Service, 368, 373, 375

Nuclear Program of the Natural Resources Defense Council, 48
nuclear reactors, 42, 374
Nuclear Regulatory Commission (NRC), 41-43, 368, 372, 374-375
nuclear testing program, 48
Nuclear Waste News, 42
nuclear weapons, 47-48, 263, 377, 379-380
nuclear workers, 374-375
NutraSweet, 156, 358-359
Oatrim, 346
Obey, David, 256
Objective Individual Combat Weapon, 94
Office of Information Warfare, 252
Office of Management and Budget (OMB), 249-250, 257, 265, 298
oil, 33, 42, 45-46, 56-57, 70, 81-83, 93, 126, 139, 209, 211, 330, 351, 373, 375-376, 378, 385-387; companies, 42, 70, 82, 93, 211, 375-376; extraction of, 33, 57, 330
Oil, Chemical and Atomic Workers Union, 373
Okinawa, 243
OMB Watch, 249-250, 257, 265
omnibus appropriations bill, 262-263
O'Leary, Hazel, 255
On The Issues, 267, 296
OPEC *see* Organization of Petroleum Exporting Countries
Operation Desert Fox, 45
Operation Desert Storm, 45, 387-388
Operation Readi-Rock, 68
Oregonian, 119
Organization of American States (OAS), 85-87
Organization for Economic Cooperation and Development (OECD), 33-34, 325-326, 328-329, 333
Organization of News Ombudsmen, 16, 227
Organization of Petroleum Exporting Countries (OPEC), 82
organochlorines, 338, 340, 350
Orlando Sentinel, 116, 127
Oslo agreement, 192
Pacifica Radio, 20, 56
pack journalism, 142
Pakistan, 212, 342, 366
Palestinian Authority (PA), 192-194, 196, 280, 286-287, 298, 302, 304, 313, 322
Palestinian press, 192-194, 197
Palestinian National Council, 196
Palestinian Press Law, 194
Palestinian Secret Security, 193
Panama, 386
Paper Tiger Television, 133, 174, 180-181, 321
paramilitary police, 67
Parenti, Michael, 20
Parks, Rosa, 170, 173-174, 178-179
Patent and Trademark Office, 251
PBS, 45, 141, 385
PCBs, 117, 122, 350-351
Peace Action Network, 48
Pennsylvania Environmental Network, 76
Pentagon, 12, 54, 94, 100-101, 140, 148, 158, 160-162, 186, 200, 242, 251, 258, 261-262, 361, 377, 382, 386
Pentagon Papers, 261
People's Decade for Human Rights Education, 332
People's News Agency, 135, 321
People's Rights, 197
People's Video, 133, 321
Pepsi, 104
Persian Gulf, 19, 385
pesticides, 33, 35, 37, 96, 209, 286, 330, 336-337, 339-341, 353, 361-362, 382

pharmaceutical, 35-37, 40, 92, 104, 110-111, 119-120, 210, 235, 260, 336, 339, 346, 358
Pharmacia & Upjohn, 131
Philadelphia Inquirer, 266
Philippines, the, 61, 111, 115, 366-367
Phillips Petroleum, 42, 375-376
Phoenix Gazette, The, 219
phthalates, 77-78
Physicians for Social Responsibility, 109
Pinochet, Augusto, 102, 264
Pioneer Hi-Bred, 343, 366
plastic soda bottles, 87
plasticizer additives, 77
plasticizers, 77-78
plastics, 35, 76, 79, 88, 116, 122, 336-337, 350
PLO, 192
plutonium, 46, 75, 109-110, 123-125
Poland, 101, 211
police, 11, 30, 66-70, 90-91, 97, 106-107, 138, 144, 192-193, 202-203, 215, 218, 220, 222-223, 235, 357, 362, 377
polio vaccine, 60-61, 98
Political Action Committees (PACs), 65, 245
polychlorinated biphenyls, 350
polystyrene, 350, 360
polystyrene plastics, 350
polyvinyl chloride (PVC), 77-79
Popular Mechanics, 122
Popular Revolutionary Army, 55
Population Council, 111-112
Population Research Institute, 111
pornography, 186
poverty, 97, 140, 144, 147, 235, 285, 304, 307-308, 351
Powell, Colin, 160-161, 212
Preamble Center for Public Policy, 327
preservatives, 209
President's Advisory Committee for Trade Policy and Negotiations, 359
Presley, Elvis, 264
Press Democrat, 77
Preval, Rene, 201, 204-205
Princess Diana, 107, 268-269
Prison Activist Resource Center, 59
Prison Moratorium Project, 59
Prisoner's Rights Union, 277
prisons, 58-59, 64, 91, 97, 107-109, 119-120, 191, 195-196, 223, 235, 277, 285, 290, 300, 303; expansion; 58; industry, 58-59, 191; reform, 59
pro-choice movement, 146
Procter & Gamble, 131
Progressive, The, 41, 94, 102, 108, 300, 368, 376
Progressive International Media Exchange (PRIME), 134
Progressive Media Project, 123, 321
Progressive News Wire, 135
Project Censored, 11-13, 15, 17, 19, 21, 24, 31, 92, 94-99, 119, 123, 125, 130-131, 135, 137-138, 140-141, 143, 151, 170, 189, 230, 271, 321-322, 399-400; Alternative Press Links, 135; How to Nominate a Censored Story, 400; mission statement, 9, 399; national judges, 15-16, 19, 31, 94
Project Censored Canada, 12, 137, 151
Project on Government Oversight, 245
Project Paperclip, 213
Project Underground, 71
Prometheus Radio Project, 177-178, 180-181
Proquest, 11
Prozac, 119
public affairs programming, 168
Public Citizen, 34, 92, 300, 326, 328
Public Citizen's Health Research, 92

public health, 41, 49, 75, 98, 103, 122, 218, 222, 248, 259, 311, 334, 338, 354, 361, 369, 371
Public Health Reports, 122
Public Interest Research Group, 126
public relations, 18, 25, 36, 50, 72, 124, 144, 149, 161, 213, 299, 338, 349
Rachel's Environment & Health Weekly, 34, 36, 93, 121, 335, 362
racism, 68, 111, 284, 336
radiation, 41-42, 45-46, 123-124, 336, 368-376, 387-388; exposure to, 45, 123-124, 369, 375, 387
radio, 12, 18, 20, 56, 68, 94, 131-133, 137, 141, 154, 165-175, 177-188, 194, 196, 204, 213, 285, 294, 306, 315, 319, 321, 323; microradio, 8, 12-13, 94, 131-134, 165, 167-169, 171-175, 177-188; petitions for rulemaking, 175; underground stations, 174
Radio Act of 1912, 167
Radio Act of 1927, 167
Radio For All, 181
Radio Free Europe, 213
Radio Liberty Fund, 213
Radio Libre, 172
radioactive metal, *see* metals
radioactive recycling, 41, 369
radioactive scrap, 42-43, 369-370, 372, 375
radioactive waste, 96, 376
RAFI, *see* Rural Advancement Foundation International
rainforest ecosystems, 352
Ramadan, 45
Ramsey, JonBenet, 227-228
rBGH, *see* bovine growth hormone.
rDNA, *see* DNA
Reagan Administration, 211, 351, 378, 385
Reagan, Ronald, 30, 358
Reappraising AIDS, 301
Record, The, 250
recycling, 8, 41-43, 87-89, 369, 371, 373-374, 376
reductions in force (RIF), 247
Refuse and Resist, 90
Reporter's Committee for Freedom of the Press, 322
reproductive rights, 51, 111, 284
Resource Conservation and Recovery Act (RCRA) of 1976 , 242, 353
Reuters, 106-107, 195, 206, 251, 366
Revolutionary Worker, 90, 302
Risk Management Plans (RMP), 266
R.J. Reynolds, 248
Roll Call, 245, 254, 256, 263
Roman Catholic Church, 51-53
Romania, 235
Rose Sheet, The, 104
Roundup, *see* herbicides
"Roundup Ready" *see* seeds
Royal Canadian Mounted Police, 107, 138
Royal Jordanian Air Force, 210
Rural Advancement Foundation International (RAFI), 38-40, 343-344, 347-349, 362-363, 365-368
Rushdie, Salman, 74
Russia, 42, 46, 48, 101-102, 106, 109, 378
Rwanda, 235, 366
saccharin, 350
Sacramento Bee, The, 107
Salk Vaccine, 60
Salt Lake Tribune, The, 85, 231
San Diego Union-Tribune, 119, 127
San Francisco Bay Guardian, 43, 92-93, 105
San Francisco Chronicle, 32, 57, 78, 114, 127
San Jose Mercury News, 29, 258
Sandinista government, 212
sarin gas, 12, 153, 159-163
Saudi Arabia, 101, 377

Schering Plough, 346
Schiller, Herbert I., 20, 98
School of the Americas (SOA), 54-56, 302
scrap metal, *see* metals
Seaman, Barbara, 20
SEARICE, 348-349, 367
Searle, 358-359
Sears, 131
Securities and Exchange Commission (SEC), 250-251
seeds, 11, 37-40, 96, 139, 341-345, 347-349, 356-357, 359, 362-365, 367; companies, 38, 342-344, 347-348, 357, 363-366; costs, 348, 367; industry, 39, 343, 363-366; market, 38-39, 343-344, 348, 357, 364; "Roundup Ready," 342, 355-356, 361
Seinfeld, Jerry, 227, 229
Seldes, George, 30
Senate, 34, 44, 101, 110-111, 162, 249, 263, 265, 326, 358, 380-381, 385-386
Senate Banking Committee, 380-381, 385
Senate Committee on Banking, Housing, and Urban Affairs, 380
Senegal, 236
Serbs, 72-73
sexual assault, 52
sexual orientation, 183
Shell Oil, 70-71
Shiites, 385
Shoshone Nation, 85-87
Sierra Leone, 71, 234-235
Simian Virus 40 (SV40), 60-62
Sinclair, Upton, 98
sleeping sickness, 234, 237
Slingshot, 54-56
Slovakia, 366
sludge, 219, 299, 351, 371
Small Business Administration, 132, 250
Smith Barney, 58
Smith, Erna, 21
smoking, 122, 158, 248
Social Security, 113-115, 231, 262, 331
socialism, 272-273, 298
Society of Professional Journalists, 157
soda industry, 88
soil erosion, 356, 359
solar power, 82, 124-125
Solutia, 353
Somalia, 139
sorghum, 347, 364
Sout Falastin, 194
South Africa, 94, 108, 279, 315, 326
South America, 100, 109, 341-342
South Korea, 115, 380
Southeast Asia, 28, 162, 345
Southeast Asian Regional Institute for Community Education, 345
Southam, 138
Soviet Union, 51, 234, 261
soybeans, 347, 355-357, 362, 364
Space and Security News, 43, 45, 303, 387
Spain, 78, 230, 327
Special Response Teams (SRT), 67
Special Weapons and Tactics (SWAT), 66-67, 69
Sperry/Unisys, 44, 381
Spice Girls, 227
Springer, Jerry, 227, 229
Sprint, 58
Spotlight, 107
Sri Lanka, 366
St. Louis Journalism Review, 20, 352, 361
Starr, Kenneth, 228, 243, 269

State Department (U.S.), 209-210, 251, 259-260, 326, 328, 379, 381
Statistics Canada, 140
Steal This Radio (STR), 174-175, 180
steel, 42, 368-369, 371-372, 375-376; steelworkers, 304, 372
Steel Manufacturers Association, 372
sterilization, 39, 51, 55, 64, 113
Stockpile Stewardship Program (SSP), 47-48
Stone, I.F., 2, 30
Structural Adjustment Programs (SAPs), 330
stun belts; guns, 107-109
styrene, 350
Subsidiary Body on Scientific, Technical and Technological Advice (SBSTTA), 366
subsidies, 33, 80, 101-102, 199, 330, 332-333
Sudan, 92, 191, 233-234, 237
sulfur, 82
sulfuric acid, 350
Sun, The, 147-148, 345
Sun Sentinel, 117
Super Slurper, 346, 347
Supreme Court, 65, 85-86, 95, 116, 185, 248, 267
SWAT Teams, *see* Special Weapons and Tactics
sweatshop, 116-117
Sweden, 78, 86, 369
Switzerland, 94
synthetic fabrics, 350, 353
Tailwind, 28-29, 158-162
Taiwan, 42-43, 101, 376
tamoxifen, 35-37, 339-340
Tao Communications, 179, 181
TCI, 207
Telecommunications Act of 1996, 169, 184, 187
telephone, 58, 105-106, 126, 243, 269, 310, 382
television, 12, 20, 42, 46, 72-73, 130, 132-133, 137, 141, 153-155, 157-158, 160, 169, 174, 177, 180-182, 185-186, 196-197, 200, 206, 208, 216, 223-225, 230, 274, 306, 313-316, 321-323, 372, 383
terminator plants, 39
Terminator seeds, 11, 37, 39, 342, 345, 362
terrorism, 68-69, 191, 218, 380
Texaco, 42, 375-376
Thailand, 70, 115
think tanks, 104, 148, 213, 310, 317
Third World, 39, 71, 110-111, 113, 116, 140, 273, 294, 333, 361-362
Third World Resurgence, 37, 49, 347
Tibet, 63-65, 305
Time, 102, 134
Time Warner, 131, 158
Times Beach Action Group (TBAG), 351, 361
Titan IV rocket, 123-124
Titanic, 208, 227-228
tobacco, 38, 65, 248-249, 259, 338, 343, 347, 363
Toronto Star, The, 140, 148
torture, 56, 63, 65, 107-109, 190, 193, 195
Total, 70
Toward Freedom, 63, 305
toxic chemicals, 77, 247, 336, 354
toxic dumping; waste, 33, 219, 330
Toxic Links Coalition, 37, 341
toxic waste, 219
toxins, 102, 117, 121-122, 242, 281, 377
toy companies; toys, 77-79, 97, 116-117, 120, 386
trade unions, 149-150, 209
transgenic monocrops, 39
transgenic products, 357
transnational corporations, 33, 39, 70-71, 94, 325, 327-330, 332-334, 340
Traveler's Group, 126

Treasury Department (U.S.), 255
Tribune Des Droits Humains, 32
Tripp, Linda, 227
TRW, 125
Truman, Harry S, 258
tuberculosis, 49, 234
Turner, Ted, 29, 158
Tuskegee Syphilis Trials, 120
TV, *see* television
TWA, 58
Tyco, 126
Uganda, 237
U.K., *see* United Kingdom
UKUSA, 105-106
U.N., *see* United Nations
UNESCO, 183
Union of Concerned Scientists, 41, 362
Union Producers and Programmers Network, 306, 322-323
UNICEF, 44, 208, 387
UNICOR, 58-59
United Arab Emirates, 101
United Auto Workers, 303
United Broadcasting, 133, 315
United Kingdom (U.K.), 45-46, 51, 71, 74, 76, 102, 105-106, 108, 269, 349, 358, 373, 384, 386 *see also* England; MI6, 70
United Nations (U.N.), 40, 43-45, 47, 63-64, 71, 86, 112, 139, 190, 200, 202-204, 207-208, 210, 220, 208, 236, 331, 366, 384-387
United States (U.S.),
    Army, 23, 54-55, 70, 79, 94, 117-119, 134, 161, 202, 247, 352, 380, 386; biased coverage of Bosnia, 72; embargo against Cuba, 326, 386; judicial system, 65-66, 97, 108; Marines, 68; Navy, 248, 257; nuclear program, 47-48, 240; tax dollars, 54, 56, 104, 117
United States Council for International Business (USCIB), 327-328
United Steelworkers of America, 372
Universal Declaration of Human Rights, 189-190, 192, 329
Unocal, 70
UNSCOM, 45-46
UPPNET News, 306, 323
Uruguay Round of the General Agreement on Tariffs and Trade, 330
uranium, 45-46, 75-76, 213, 369-370, 373, 387
USDA, *see* Department of Agriculture (U.S.)
U.S. Agency for International Development (USAID), 111-112
U.S. Army Chemical Corps, 352
U.S. Army Corps of Engineers, 79
U.S. Army Special Forces, 54-55
U.S. Department of Agriculture, *see* Department of Agriculture (U.S.)
U.S. Ecology, 42, 371
U.S. Export-Import Bank, 379
U.S. Holocaust Assets Presidential Advisory Commission, 266
U.S. Imperial Chemical, 336
U.S. News and World Report, 104
U.S. Space Command, 109-110, 125
Utne Reader, 137, 306
vaccination; vaccine, 60-62, 98, 346
Valley Monitor, 216
Vatican, the, 211
Vegetarian Times, 104
Veteran's Administration, 120, 250
Viacom, 207
Viagra, 227, 229
Victoria's Secret, 58

Vietnam, 12, 35, 137, 153, 161, 163, 220, 241-242, 306, 335, 340, 352, 364; War, 12, 137, 153, 161, 163, 220, 335, 352
Village Voice, 106-107, 306
vinyl, 77-79, 117
violence, 52-53, 64, 67, 73, 100, 122, 190-191, 199, 203-204, 215-221, 284, 362
Virginia Fibre, 211
Voices 21, 332
Wall Street Journal, 79, 113, 119, 354, 361-362
Wal-Mart, 116, 131
War and Peace Digest, 307
War on Drugs, 54-55, 67, 93
Warner Brothers, 327
Washington Free Press, 111
Washington Post, 19, 55, 78, 107, 121-122, 127, 131, 172, 197, 199, 201-202, 212, 241-247, 249, 251-256, 258, 260, 264-266, 268-270, 328, 386
Washington Times, 32, 108, 248, 251, 267
Watergate, 29, 258, 261, 382
We Interrupt This Message, 323
Webb, Gary, 16, 27, 135
Weidenfeld, Sheila Rabb, 21, 98
welfare, 93, 97, 102, 110, 114, 170, 246-247, 307, 399; reform 93, 97, 114
Wells Fargo, 105, 125
Wellstone, Paul, 247
Western Shoshone Defense Project, 87
Western Shoshone National Council (WSNC), 85-87
wheat, 341, 343, 347-348, 364
whistle-blower law, 156
white-collar crime, 279
White House, 30, 91, 124, 211-212, 228, 241, 243, 245, 248, 252, 254-259, 261, 264, 268, 351, 359, 378, 382
White House Domestic Policy Review, 359
Willey, Kathleen, 227
Winfrey, Oprah, 229
Winnipeg Free Press, 139
Wisconsin Farmers Union, 355
Women for Mutual Security, 192, 323
Women's Community Cancer Project, 37, 340
Women's Environment and Development Organization (WEDO), 45
women's health, 20, 36-37, 51-52, 97, 112-113, 284, 295, 308
Women's Health Journal, 113
Women's Institute for Freedom of the Press, 19, 94, 323
Women's Wear Daily, 104
World Bank, 204, 330
World Conference on Breast Cancer, 340
World Court, 44, 386
World Health Organization (WHO), 35, 208, 235, 340
world hunger, 285
World Trade Organization (WTO), 33-34, 326, 330, 333
World War I, 35, 335
World War II, 33, 35, 72, 75-76, 213, 254, 260, 266, 333, 335, 382
World Wide Web, 17, 71, 125, 157, 362
Y2K; year 2000 computer breakdowns, 229, 254
yellow fever, 94
Yugoslavia, 72-73
Z Magazine, 40, 134, 180, 309, 361
Zaire, 71
Zambia, 366
Zapatistas, 54-56, 165, 170, 179-180
Zeneca, 35, 37, 336, 339-341
Zinn, Howard, 21, 98, 135
Z-Trim, 346-347

About the Author/Director

PETER PHILLIPS is an Associate Professor of Sociology at Sonoma State University and director of Project Censored. He teaches classes in Media Censorship, Power, Class Stratification, and Social Welfare. He assumed the directorship of Project Censored in the spring of 1996. His first two books were *Censored 1997* and *Censored 1998* from Seven Stories Press.

Phillips had a long career in human service administration. His experiences include two and half decades of community service and social activism, such as serving as an employment and training programs administrator, a Head Start director and the executive director of a family counseling center.

Phillips earned a B.A. degree in Social Science in 1970 from Santa Clara University, and an M.A. degree in Social Science from California State University at Sacramento in 1974. Several years of adjunct college teaching led him to the University of California, Davis, where he earned an M.A. in Sociology in 1991 and a Ph.D. in Sociology in 1994. His doctoral dissertation was entitled, *A Relative Advantage: Sociology of the San Francisco Bohemian Club*.

Phillips is a fifth generation Californian, who grew up on a family-owned farm west of the Central Valley town of Lodi. He has a 27-year old son, Jeff who is also a University of California, Davis graduate. Phillips now lives in rural Sonoma County with his three pet chickens: Millie, Silly, and Booster.

GARY WEBB, who wrote the introduction, is the author of *Dark Alliance: The CIA, the Contras, and the Crack Cocaine Explosion*. He has received more than 30 journalism awards including, in 1991, a Pulitzer Prize.

PROJECT CENSORED MISSION STATEMENT Project Censored, founded in 1976, is a non-profit project within the Sonoma State University Foundation, a 501(c)3 organization. Its principle objective is the advocacy for and protection of First Amendment rights and freedom of information in the United States. Through a faculty, student, community partnership, Project Censored serves as a national press/media ombudsman by identifying and researching important national news stories that are under-reported, ignored, misrepresented, or censored by media corporations in the United States. It also encourages and supports journalists, faculty, and student investigations into First Amendment and freedom of information issues through its Project Censored Yearbook, Censored Alert Newsletter, and nationwide advocacy.

How to Nominate a Censored Story

Some of the most interesting stories Project Censored evaluates are sent to us as nominations from people all over the world. These stories are copied from small-circulation magazines or newspapers and Internet news services. If you see a story and wonder why it hasn't been covered in the mainstream media, we encourage you to send it to us as a Project Censored nomination. To nominate a *Censored* story send us a copy of the article and include the name of the source publication, the date that the article appeared, and page number.

CRITERIA FOR PROJECT CENSORED NEWS STORIES NOMINATIONS

1. A censored news story is one which contains information that the general United States population has a right and need to know, but to which it has had limited access.

2. The news story is timely, ongoing, and has implications for a significant number of residents in the United States.

3. The story has clearly defined concepts and is backed up with solid, verifiable documentation.

4. The news story has been publicly published, either on the Internet or in print, in a circulated newspaper, journal, magazine, newsletter, or similar publication from either a foreign or domestic source.

5. The news story has direct connections to and implications for people in the United States, which can include activities that U.S. citizens are engaged in abroad.

We evaluate stories year-round and publish important stories in our *Censored Alert* newsletter. The final deadline for nominating a Most *Censored* Story of the year is October 1st. Please send regular mail nominations to the address below or e-mail nominations to: censored@sonoma.edu. Our phone number for more information on Project Censored is (707) 664-2500.

> Project Censored Nominations
> Sociology Department
> Sonoma State University
> 1801 East Cotati Avenue
> Rohnert Park, CA 94928

Thank you for your support.

8 8 8 8

> Peter Phillips
> Director, Project Censored